Preface

A period during which for most young men the world has been either a place in which to laugh, or to cry. Soldiers do not cry, though there are times when they would rather like to do so.[1]

Lieutenant Raymond Money, 12 Squadron, RFC

The pioneering aviators of the Royal Flying Corps (RFC) lived their lives amidst a strange dichotomy as they moved from safety to dire danger, and back again in a matter of hours. This created a dreadful strain that could soon shred anyone's mental health. On the ground, they were cloistered in simple but adequate accommodation several miles behind the lines. Farmhouses, barns, huts, tents and even a canal boat were used, but they were all far better than the squalor faced by the infantry scurrying in their muddy trenches. Flying personnel were blessed with beds, blankets and even sheets. They could set up a decent mess and socialise to their heart's content, with a smorgasbord of entertainments, including perhaps an old out-of-tune piano, access to drink and occasional vigorous games of mess rugby. There were visits to local towns which offered tantalising glimpses – and sometimes more – of the female of the species. A glimpse was probably never enough for most of these very young men. What more could a chap want? There was no danger here, no hidden peril, other than the off-chance of a German bombing raid. But that was nothing compared to the torrent of screaming shells endured by the soldiers at the front; indeed, it was little more than any relatives back in London had to endure from the Zeppelin and Gotha raids.

Although there was plenty to amuse them on the ground, it was no laughing matter when they were flying over the front. Both the pilots and the observers had to be good at their jobs, or they would surely die. They needed first-rate eyesight and had to develop 'air vision' to see hostile aircraft before it was too late. Pilots had to be masters of their machines, to understand their capabilities and – perhaps even more important – their limitations. They had to fly accurately, but at the same time be able to fling their aircraft about like mad things in the tumult of a dogfight. They had to be quick-thinking and capable of split-second reactions, where a wrong turn might mean death. Pilots and observers also had to be excellent shots, capable of snap-shooting accurately at a target that could be moving at more than 100mph. They had to be courageous and not panic in the face of extreme peril. A cool head in action was one that might survive. But they also had to keep up their concentration and not fall prey to mental sluggishness, even when flying at extreme altitudes, suffering agonies from the freezing cold and fighting off the effects of oxygen starvation. Yet many were fresh from only a brief training that left them as little more than tethered goats to the German aces. Death lurked in the skies, zooming in its winged chariots out of the sun or bursting from the clouds. A moment's loss of concentration, or a tactical blunder, could consign them to being shot down and falling thousands of feet until the crunching impact of *terra firma* brought a terrible relief. But better that than a punctured petrol tank, the first flickers of flame, then the roaring inferno and the agonies of incineration.

> What was the great difference between trench life and this life? In the trenches you faced death every second not knowing when it would come to you, but in the Flying Corps you could certainly say between flights that you had so many more hours to live, on the other hand, in the air, you could see death coming to you if your machine caught fire at a good height, with no parachute, you knew that it was the end, you could either stay in the machine or jump – but either way death was coming to you.[2]
>
> Sergeant Harold Taylor, 25 Squadron, RFC

No wonder some jumped. The absence of parachutes in aircraft, which were then considered too bulky and impractical for the cramped cockpits, was often mentioned.

> These men shared all the hazards of the air war. They endured the searing tensions of daily anti-aircraft fire and of almost daily combat, often in outdated aeroplanes, knowing always that each flight could be the last; that there was no escape should their plane break a wing or burst into flames. For there were then no parachutes.[3]
>
> 2nd Lieutenant Arthur Gould Lee, 46 Squadron, RFC

At least the pilot was to some extent the master of his own destiny. The observer in a two-seater was a passenger, and there could be a particular horror awaiting them if their pilot should be killed. They would often be left helpless, with nothing to look forward to but a terrible death.

> Picture the helplessness of an observer whose pilot has been killed in a fight. The weight of the dead body leaning against the control column or 'joystick' causes the machine to dive vertically. The observer has no parachute; he must just resign himself to his doom. The wires of the helpless plane scream as it dives faster and faster to the ground with the observer now, no doubt, huddled at the bottom of the cockpit waiting for the end. There is a tearing, ripping noise as pieces of the covering are torn by the winds, and slowly the craft is bereft of its fabric. Now it's a mere skeleton, but still the observer holds on. What thoughts must flash through his mind! Then, a heavy thud, a splintering

Laugh or Fly

The Air War on the Western Front, 1914–1918

Peter Hart & Gary Bain

Pen & Sword
MILITARY

First published in Great Britain in 2024 by
Pen & Sword Military
An imprint of Pen & Sword Books Limited
Yorkshire – Philadelphia

ISBN 978 1 39905 014 2

Typeset by Mac Style
Printed in the UK by CPI Group (UK) Ltd, Croydon, CR0 4YY.

Pen & Sword Books Limited incorporates the imprints of After
the Battle, Atlas, Archaeology, Aviation, Discovery, Family History,
Fiction, History, Maritime, Military, Military Classics, Politics,
Select, Transport, True Crime, Air World, Frontline Publishing, Leo
Cooper, Remember When, Seaforth Publishing, The Praetorian Press,
Wharncliffe Local History, Wharncliffe Transport, Wharncliffe True
Crime and White Owl.

For a complete list of Pen & Sword titles please contact

PEN & SWORD BOOKS LIMITED
47 Church Street, Barnsley, South Yorkshire, S70 2AS, England
E-mail: enquiries@pen-and-sword.co.uk
Website: www.pen-and-sword.co.uk
or
PEN AND SWORD BOOKS
1950 Lawrence Rd, Havertown, PA 19083, USA
E-mail: uspen-and-sword@casematepublishers.com
Website: www.penandswordbooks.com

We dedicate this book to the men of the RFC, RNAS and RAF. Their collective heroism in fighting a strange new war high up in the clouds and without parachutes is beyond praise.

Laugh or Fly

The remarkable series of airmen's reminiscences leaping from the pages of this book illuminate, by carefully chosen stepping stones, exactly what it was like to be a Great War airman. The stories and recollections are so vivid, they really seem to take you with them. One moment you are in your mess, singing with your comrades; then another reminiscence, even on the same page, can place you in the mind of a young pilot lying in his bed, trying to sleep, with his thoughts racing back to just a few hours beforehand when he was flying at 15,000 feet, watching his best friend being killed in some furious aerial combat. What we read in this book exposes the hell of air fighting; a new warfare which these men were literally inventing even as they flew above the trenches. Many survived thanks only to their skills and devoted support for one another. Many others paid with their lives.

Trevor Henshaw (2023)

Contents

noise, a huddled heap. Two dead, mangled bodies are extricated from the debris and reverently buried.[4]

Air Mechanic Ira Jones, 10 Squadron, RFC

Somehow, the aviators had to come to terms with these brutal realities of air warfare, for they too were dealing out death. Young men fresh out of school had to cope with the knowledge that they were inflicting the most agonising of deaths on their German contemporaries. A variety of mental techniques were used to blur away the horrors or any guilt.

By virtue of living on the surface, by turning away our faces and refusing to acknowledge death, by casting off that thin veneer of civilisation with the excuse that we were, after all, as it were, hired 'assassins' in the cause of patriotism, we were able to sit down and enjoy a good breakfast. How marvellously can the human mind adapt itself, how easily persuade itself that its course is right, from a nation to the individual; so that all experience, all knowledge, even religious beliefs can be laid on one side until the lust to kill is satisfied, leaving a charred and blackened earth and the sweet sickly smell of blood.[5]

Flight Lieutenant Robert Compston, 8 (Naval) Squadron, RNAS

It was all summed up best by that tremendous chronicler of a young pilot's life, Cecil Lewis.

The strain was only there for two and a half hours perhaps twice a day. The rest of your time was your own – once you were out of the air it was quiet. It was safe. You were 15 to 20 miles behind the lines, you had a comfortable bed, you had sheets, even an electric light. You didn't have this strain that could occur if you never could get out of gunfire and the possibility of being hit even when you were asleep. We lived always in the stretch or sag of nerves. We were either in deadly danger or no danger at all. This conflict between something like being at home, and being in really a quite tight position, had a great effect on us all and produced a certain strain probably because of the change.[6]

Lieutenant Cecil Lewis, 56 Squadron, RFC

They were dependent for their survival on the mechanical reliability of their aircraft; or the random minute adjustments on the dial sights some thousands of feet below them by an unseen German anti-aircraft gunner; or of a never-ending fund of good fortune in visceral combat with German aircraft day-in and day-out, high above the Western Front. There was little or nothing for them to laugh about in the air. But when back on the ground they tried to put aside their fears. To crack jokes, to see the funny side, and even commemorate their imminent demise in the following funny, but graphic song.

The Dying Airman

Oh, the bold aviator was dying,
And as 'neath the wreckage he lay, he lay,
To the sobbing mechanics about him,
These last parting words did he say:
Two valves you'll find in my stomach,
Three sparkplugs are safe in my lung, my lung,
The prop is in splinters inside me,
To my fingers the joystick has clung.
And get you six brandies and sodas
And lay them all out in a row,
And get you six other good airmen,
To drink to this pilot below.
Take the cylinders out of my kidneys,
The connecting rod out of my brain, my brain,
From the small of my back take the crankshaft,
And assemble the engine again![7]

Yes, you've likely seen this before – it has been anthologised to death! But go back and read it properly this time. It is graphic, it is morbid, but most of all it is funny, genuinely funny. It typifies the spirit of these airmen. They had a nervy courage, laced with an understanding of how tenuous a grip they had on life. As they bellowed out *The Dying Airman* in their messes, many knew that they might soon share the mangled airman's fate, or worse still be burnt to crisp. But they had to laugh. What else was there?

Chapter 1

Up, Up and Away!

In the case of a European war between two countries, both sides would be equipped with large corps of aeroplanes, each trying to obtain information of the other, and to hide its own movements. The efforts which each would exert in order to hinder, or prevent the enemy from obtaining information, would lead to the inevitable result of a war in the air, for the supremacy of the air, by armed aeroplanes against each other. This fight for the supremacy of the air in future wars will be of the first and greatest importance.[1]

Captain Bertram Dickson, Royal Field Artillery

In December 1903, in a faraway place, two brothers, Orville and Wilbur Wright, began a series of powered flights that would change the face of warfare. Gradually, short hops became proper flights of several miles as they explored the capabilities of the eponymous Wright Biplane. News began to spread, and reactions were varied. Some saw the potential early on. Lieutenant Colonel John Capper paid the Wright brothers a visit and came back more than a little impressed.

They have at least made far greater strides in the evolution of the flying machine than any of their predecessors. If carried to a successful issue, we may shortly have as accessories of warfare, scouting machines which will go at a great pace, and be independent of obstacles on the ground, whilst offering from their elevated position unrivalled opportunities of ascertaining what is occurring in the heart of the enemy's country.[2]

Lieutenant Colonel John Capper, Army School of Ballooning, Aldershot

On the other hand, the featherweight, underpowered aircraft looked impractical as a weapon of war, and even some of the greatest of pre-war theorists struggled at first to grasp what lay ahead.

Aviation is fine as sport. I even wish officers would practice the sport, as it accustoms them to risk. But, as an instrument of war, it is worthless.[3]

General Ferdinand Foch, École Supérieure de Guerre

As the pioneers of the air began to multiply around the world, some visionaries were becoming seriously worried. H.G. Wells, the famous purveyor of futuristic fiction, vigorously expressed his fears in – where else – the *Daily Mail*.

This foreigner-nvented, foreigner-built, foreigner-steered thing, puts the case dramatically. Within a year we shall have – or rather they will have – aeroplanes capable of starting from Calais, circling over London, dropping a hundredweight or so of explosive upon the printing machines of the *Daily Mail* and returning securely to Calais for another similar parcel.[4]

   H.G. Wells

Soon there was an outcry and the military scrambled to try and catch up any ground they had lost in the endless armaments race with foreign powers.

All the heads of departments are very anxious to get on with this – Lord Haldane told me so last night, Mr Churchill told me so two or three days ago, and the Chancellor of the Exchequer himself is anxious to see it done, and wisely: but what is the best method to pursue in order to do in a week what is generally done in a year? At the present time in this country we have, as far as I know, of actual flying men in the army about eleven, and of actual flying men in the Navy about eight, and France has about 263, so we are what you might call behind.[5]

   Brigadier General David Henderson, Air Committee

As well as the prospects of aircraft, there was a good deal of investment in airships, following the example of the German Zeppelins. For the British, the somewhat tortuous work of designing and constructing their own giant airship was commenced in 1909. At last, in 1911, it was completed. It was certainly huge – some 512 feet long and 48 feet in diameter, with a vast gasbag capacity of some 700,000 cubic feet. It was soon christened *Mayfly*, which proved all too appropriate – it may fly, and it may not. It did not, and broke its back while tied to its mooring mast. The *Mayfly* had to be written off as an expensive failure.

   The British Army was certainly taking an interest in aviation. The restricted load capacity of aircraft made any visions of bombs and machine guns raining death from the sky still somewhat premature, but the value of aerial reconnaissance was obvious – offering as it did the chance to see beyond the far horizon. Generals may be accused of an unnatural obsession with horseflesh, but they were not blind to the attractions of knowing what their enemies were up to. In 1911, the Air Battalion, Royal Engineers, was created, and by the autumn was being deployed in army manoeuvres. It was not really a success, as there were pitifully few pilots and most of them fell victim to breakdowns and forced landings. Of these, the most remarked upon was that experienced by Lieutenant Herbert Reynolds, who had the misfortune to run into a thunderstorm.

The tail of the machine was suddenly wrenched upwards as if it had been hit from below, and I saw the elevator go down perpendicularly below me. I was not strapped in, and I suppose I caught hold of the uprights at my side, for the next thing I realised was that I was lying in a heap on what ordinarily is the under surface of the top plane. The machine in fact was upside down. I stood up, held on and waited. The machine just floated about, gliding from side to side like a piece of paper falling. Then it over-swung itself, so to speak, and went down more or less vertically sideways until it righted itself momentarily the right way up. Then it went down tail first, turned over upside-down again, and restarted the old floating motion. We were still some way from the ground, and took what seemed like a long time reaching it. Fortunately, I hung on practically to the end, and according to those who were looking on, I did not jump till about 10 feet from the ground.[6]

Lieutenant Herbert Reynolds, No. 2 Company, Air Battalion, Royal Engineers

The people looking on turned out to be two bathers *au naturel*, but this so paled into insignificance in comparison to the drama of the crash-landing that few of the more than fifty people who gathered at the scene seemed to notice – although this nudity was considered worthy of note in the official history, *The War in the Air*, written several years later!

In 1912, there was a further reorganisation as the Air Battalion mutated into the Royal Flying Corps (RFC), which was originally intended to have military and naval wings, backed up by a Central Flying School at Upavon in Wiltshire. The 'Senior Service' was having none of it, and by July 1914 the naval wing had gained its formal independence as the Royal Naval Air Service (RNAS), which began to coalesce round the Naval Flying School at Eastchurch in Kent. A series of aeroplane trials were begun to identify those aircraft best suited to military service, while the RNAS also experimented with seaplanes capable of landing and taking off from water.

The gradual progress of military aviation would be demonstrated in the large exercises held across East Anglia in the autumn of 1912. Airships and aircraft were deployed by both sides. The invading Red Force (commanded by Lieutenant General Sir Douglas Haig) was facing the Blue Force (Lieutenant General Sir James Grierson). Both were aware of the value of aerial reconnaissance, but Haig's airmen failed to locate one of Grierson's divisions, and as a direct result he was surprised by a counter-attack and adjudged to be trounced by most impartial observers. Grierson was very impressed by what had been achieved, but more than that he foresaw that aircraft meant the development of aerial combat.

The impression left on my mind is that their use has revolutionised the art of war. So long as hostile aircraft are hovering over one's troops all movements are liable to be seen and reported, and therefore the first step in war will be to get rid of the hostile aircraft. He who does this first or who keeps the last aeroplane afloat will win, other things being approximately equal.[7]

Lieutenant General Sir James Grierson, GOC Eastern Command

But some caution was required. Not all troop movements or deployments could be discerned, as Haig had found to his cost. Bad weather could prevent flying or reduce visibility to almost nothing. The natural wastage of aircraft was also terrifyingly high, which meant that a general would soon 'burn through' his meagre aviation resources, even without the intervention of the enemy.

Senior officers also sanctioned experiments in many other avenues of deploying aviation at war. Fertile minds were desperate to convert man's newfound ability to fly into a novel means of killing the enemy. From dropping bombs to fitting machine guns to aircraft, and various methods of carrying out artillery observation by sending range corrections to the guns, all avenues were explored, but most were stymied by the limitations of the aircraft available. Nevertheless, the process had begun.

*   *   *

There was a tremendous upsurge of interest in flying in civilian life. Aviation magazines were soon being published, relaying to the avid readers the most intricate details of men and machines that took to the air. Airfields began to multiply, while a mixture of military and civilian-orientated flying schools were established. Flying displays by the most famous pilots of the day were popular and drew huge crowds. These men became household names, with their exploits blazoned across the newspapers, some of which sponsored competitions for new distance records. Many of the first pilots were fantastic characters.

> Clarence Winchester was a freelance pilot with his own aeroplane giving joyrides to people for something like a pound a time. He used to put the passenger in the aeroplane and then start frightening them to death by telling them that they mustn't touch this and whatever they do, not to lean against that wire – it was absolutely death if they got tangled up with it. By the time they took off they were jelly! When we asked him why he did this he said, 'Well they think they get their money's worth if they're really frightened!'[8]
> Eric Furlong, Hall School of Flying, Hendon

Some of these aviation pioneers went on to found huge aircraft manufacturing corporations. But at the time they were far less august personages.

> Handley Page was a wonderful lecturer because he kept our attention by having sex references in his lessons! For instance, he used to say, 'When the centre of pressure got near to the centre of attraction – then things worked!' That sort of thing. At a social event one time a rather beautiful young girl was presented to Handley Page, and she had on her dress a model aeroplane and she was proudly showing this off to him, 'Do you like my aeroplane?' 'Well, as a matter of fact I wasn't looking at the aeroplane, I was looking at the landing ground!'[9]
> Eric Furlong, Hall School of Flying, Hendon

A fortunate – wealthy – few could even follow in their heroes' footsteps. This was an expensive and dangerous undertaking, as one civilian enthusiast discovered.

> I asked Howard Wright to build me this monoplane, which we placed upon the market as proprietors. She was fitted with an Anzani engine of nominal 25 horsepower, but which really gave about 18–20 horse-power. She usually ran for about 5 minutes, and then got overheated and tired and [stopped]. I took my little Avis to Brooklands about February 1910. I partitioned off a corner of my shed, and slept in a hammock, so that I was able to take advantage of the still hours in the early morning. It is amusing to look back now and remember how I used to watch anxiously a little flag which I flew above my shed, to see what strength of wind was blowing. At first, I never used to go out until the flag was practically hanging from the mast or was only flapping very gently in the light air, which occurred usually in the very early morning.[10]
> Alan Boyle

In many cases this was the blind leading the blind. Nobody knew much about the science of aviation, most having only half-baked theories; indeed, as it was only a few years since the first flight, how could it be otherwise?

> We were all learners at Brooklands in those days: I am the possessor of a silver cup kindly presented by the Brooklands Race Club authorities for making a circular flight, which shows we were not very advanced. In fact, no one except Grahame-White and A.V. Roe knew anything about it at all, and they didn't know much![11]
> Alan Boyle

One early airman, Louis Strange, discovered that braggadocio boasting and an obsession with size were already well-established American traits.

> Of the pilots who flew at Hendon at that time the names that first occur to me are Baumann, the Swiss who taught me to fly a Caudron, Temple, a Londoner who had a school of his own there, Birchenough, an Etonian from Yorkshire, Noel and Verrier, the Frenchmen, and a couple of Americans, Brock and Beatty. I remember that the latter used to talk a lot about a very fast monoplane he had over in America. We continually asked him why he did not ship it across and win all the races, but he always said, 'Gee, I can't. If I started her up on this little patch, I'd slip over the edge and lose myself in the ditch!'[12]
> Louis Strange

Strange was himself learning to fly the Wright Box Kite at Hendon under the tender instruction of Louis Noel.

When I passed on to the Grahame-White School to learn to fly Box Kites, I came under the tuition of Louis Noel, the famous Hendon instructor and demonstration pilot. He had a forceful way of expressing himself, 'I have told you how to fly; have you understood? Yes? Well, I give you the last chance to say No! Very well, you can fly, do you hear? I, Louis Noel, say you can fly; I speak no more. I go to the bar; if you commit suicide, that is bad, but if you almost do that, it will be much, much worse for you!'[13]

Louis Strange

Young men read avidly the enthralling exploits of the magnificent men in their flying machines and flocked to watch the flying shows. There was a very real excitement in witnessing people cocking a snook at the laws of gravity, even though there were many crashes that demonstrated nature would still have its way.

I used to take in the aviation journals, '*Flight*' and '*Aeroplane*'. Then in July 1911 the Gordon Bennett Cup took place at Eastchurch. I saw all the famous pilots flying. That really inspired me to think about it myself and see if I could do anything about it. I saw not only my first flying, but my first crash! Gustav Hamel got to the first pylon, turned round, overbanked and flew straight into the ground, with the engine running full on. Hamel was thrown about 25 or 30 yards, rolling over and over. The machine was a total wreck, but he was only badly bruised and didn't even break a bone. It was as big a crash as one could ever wish to see. Yet there was this fellow being hurled out of the aircraft, rolling over and over, and over – yet he almost got up unhurt. That made me think that aviation was not quite so dangerous as I thought it might be. Everyone thought I was quite mad.[14]

Donald Clappen, Blériot School of Flying, Hendon

He remained mad keen to fly, and soon he had his wish as he took private lessons at Hendon.

The first time I flew was quite by accident! The machine was not supposed to fly – it had been detuned. I was rolling across the ground, doing a straight, as I thought, when suddenly I found the ground receding under me. Of course, this was so unexpected I pushed my stick down and landed with a bit of a crash and found myself with the undercarriage spread all around me and the prop broken. Next, my instructor, a Monsieur Salmet, rushed up to me, 'Why you fly? Why you fly?' I had no answer, I didn't know! What had happened was that a gust of wind had caught my plane and it had taken off without my expecting it to.[15]

Donald Clappen

By 1911, pilots were required to pass a simple flying test to show that they had mastered their new trade. This was somewhat farcical and demonstrated rather more the limitations in what they had learnt.

> Regarding the pilot's certificate one had to do five figures-of-eight observed by two qualified pilots who acted as observers. Then came the *piece de resistance* – one had to cut off one's engine and land within 50 metres of a defined spot – the instructors themselves. If it looked as if the pupil was about to land short, the observers would walk slowly towards the spot to make sure that the pilot landed within the specified distance. I do not recall ever a single pupil being ploughed for not landing within the specified distance.[16]
> Donald Clappen

One wealthy young man had the ultimate thrill of a flight with early aviator – and noted eccentric – Samuel Cody.

> I had a passenger flight with Cody in 1911. It was a terrific thrill: first time in the air and a good look at the surrounding fields. We didn't go up very high. I don't suppose we went up more than about 300 feet at most and did one wide circuit to have a look at the weather and have a look at some of the high hills to the south, which were nearly 500 feet high – which seemed quite high in those days. I thought the world of Cody. He was deliberately dressed like his cousin Buffalo Bill Cody – cowboy hat and little beard and moustache. We expected him to produce a lasso at any moment! He was an awfully nice chap. He had a look at my big scale model I was making of [an] Antoinette monoplane that I rather liked. Cody was looking at my ailerons – balanced ailerons – and he said, 'Oh no, my boy! Warp the wings – imitate the birds, my boy!' I didn't know that quite soon every plane would have balanced ailerons. But still I liked them because they were easier to make.[17]
> Grahame Donald

Sadly, Cody was killed in a flying accident in August 1913. Nothing could disguise it; flying was still inherently dangerous, but it did not put off young Grahame Donald. Then there was a stroke of luck, although not perhaps for his father.

> My father died in 1913 – and I'm afraid he would have stopped me if he'd been alive. Very shortly afterwards I was able to buy a Blériot-type monoplane. I forget the exact price, but I think it cost me one new Rudge motor cycle and sixty pounds. It was delivered near my mother's home in Renfrewshire towards the end of October 1913. I made one or two straight hops – managed to get up and make a landing of sorts in the next field. There were very few people who could train you; you either taught yourself or you broke your neck. Flying is quite a simple process if you do it carefully. I didn't fly very far, but the fact

remains I flew the thing. I thought I was pretty good, but I can assure you I was kidding myself! It really takes an appreciable number of hours in the air to learn to fly a plane properly. At that time, I was capable of taking a plane off the ground and putting it back into the field without crashing. We used to say that any landing you could walk away from was a good one![18]
   Grahame Donald

This was the spirit that filled these early aviators.

* * *

Aircraft could not fly without the tender administrations of a variety of specialist riggers and mechanics. The RFC and RNAS both began to train up ground crew to maintain the aircraft. An engine failure or structural collapse could have fatal consequences for the pilot. The not so well-off aviation enthusiasts were drawn to this method of getting close to the aeroplanes, often in the hope of getting a flight or even being accepted for air crew training.

On parade, civilian enlistments were in the RFC clothes with the wrap-over tunic. But those who had just come from a different service, they didn't have the RFC uniform. They were all in their different uniforms – Royal Marines in their uniform and sailors in their bell-bottom trousers. All the calls were sounded by a bell and then we used to go down to the workshops and be trained in rigging. Every day was spent on the aircraft in the sheds and in the workshops. We learnt to make simple parts. In case of a vulnerable break, say a skid or something like that, we were able to make it out of any wood that was available. We learned to splice a wire cable, because the wires which formed the framework of a biplane were of seven-stranded cable. We had the plane spread out on trestles and we learned to put the covering on – sometimes linen, sometimes cotton covering. You laid this stuff on the plane, sewed it together in what they called a balloon seam and then you doped it, which used to shrink it up so that although you put it on quite slack it was drum-tight. And [we learned] how to fill up an aircraft, for instance, you must always pour the petrol through a chamois leather, small details like that.[19]
   Air Mechanic Cecil King, Central Flying School, RFC

It had been realised that starting an aircraft could not be a haphazard process. Everything had to be done in sequence, to ensure that everything and everybody was ready. Take-off was second only in peril to landing – and everyone involved in the process had to get it as right as possible.

The technique for starting the aircraft was very precise. The officer would get into the aircraft, and you would see that chocks were put in front of the wheels. Then you'd go to the propeller, and you would say, 'Petrol on! Switch off!' He would repeat after you. Then you'd turn the propeller a few times to get a sufficient charge into the cylinders of the engine. When you thought you'd got it ready to fire, you would say, 'Contact, Sir!' He would answer, 'Contact!' He would switch the thing into contact. Then you would be very careful how you approached the propeller; you'd hold it with two hands and give it a tremendous swing. If it fired it would start to run – you'd get clear and stand by the chocks. When he waved his hand, you would pull the chocks away and you knew that he was ready to take off. You couldn't say anything else, only those particular words, which were repeated afterwards by the officer, so there could be no mistake.[20]

Air Mechanic Cecil King, Central Flying School, RFC

The ground crew were an essential part of flying; without them, aircraft would never have got off the ground – well, not more than once!

Meanwhile, at the Central Flying School, a certain grizzled Scots Fusiliers officer was already making a name for himself: Major Hugh Trenchard. Born in 1873, Trenchard had an undistinguished education, hampered by accusations that he was 'clever but lazy'. In September 1893, he was commissioned into the 2nd Royal Scots Fusiliers, with whom he served in India. It soon became apparent that his unfortunate combination of taciturnity and an abrasive character did not fit into the officers' mess. Indeed, he was granted the sobriquet of 'The Camel' due to a combination of his unprepossessing appearance and habit of grunting inarticulately in any conversation. Trenchard gained active service experience commanding a mounted infantry section formed from his battalion in the Boer War. He was badly wounded in October 1900, being shot through the left lung, with spinal complications which severely restricted his ability to walk. He then showed the kind of man he really was. Whilst recuperating in St Moritz, Switzerland, he became obsessed with mastering the Cresta Toboggan Run – a truly unorthodox route to health and efficiency for a severely wounded man. Strangely, it worked, and the jolting of a toboggan crash seemed to alleviate his spinal discomfort, while the clear cold air refreshed his damaged lungs.

After a further stint of service in South Africa, he again showed his non-conformist nature by volunteering for secondment to command the Southern Nigeria Regiment, part of the West African Frontier Force, in late 1903. It proved an exciting period, leading small columns against huge numbers of African natives. Fortunately for Trenchard, his opponents lacked modern weapons, and sometimes he secured victory merely by setting off fireworks to scare them off. For six long years, Trenchard played a key role in the mapping and 'pacification' of great tracts of Nigeria, until his health finally broke under the strain and he returned to England. Seeking new challenges, he took to the air, learning to fly at the oldest permitted age. He was never a good pilot, but a flying certificate opened a new world of opportunity, and he was soon made adjutant of the Central Flying School. Here, his combination of a domineering character and administrative skills soon made a reputation.

> The second in command, Major Trenchard, used to do a lot of flying and give instruction to the officers. We called him 'Harry Lauder', because he came out of the Scots Fusiliers, and he still wore his old uniform. He had this red and white cap band the same as Harry Lauder (the comedian) used to wear. We all respected him very much, and we feared him quite a lot but there's no doubt he was very, very efficient. We were all a little bit scared of him because he was very, very severe, and his manner was quite frightening. If you were his orderly – and I was often picked to be his orderly – he used to call you to him and tell you what you had to do. He'd say, 'Now you'll follow twenty paces behind me wherever I go. If I go in a doorway and I want you to come, I'll beckon you. If not, you'll wait at the doorway till I come out!' And if he growled, 'Orderly!' you jumped to attention, stood stiffly to hear what he had to say, then you went off at the double to obey.[21]
> Air Mechanic Cecil King, Central Flying School, RFC

He was certainly a fearsome figure to the young officers detached from their parent units to learn to fly, and was not seen as a tolerant man.

> Trenchard gave the impression of being a bit of an ogre! If he went down on to the aerodrome, I used to follow him just at the prescribed distance behind; and he'd be there and watch the flying. One day he said to me, 'There's an aeroplane over there just landed. You will go over and tell the pilot to come over and report to me immediately!' I went over to him, and I said, 'Major Trenchard wants, to see you, Sir!' The pilot looked very anxious. 'Do you know what he wants orderly?' I said, 'No, I'm afraid I don't!' I followed him respectfully at the back and he went up to Major Trenchard. Trenchard said, 'You will catch the train back to your unit and I shall send your report afterwards!' The officer said, 'But Sir…' Trenchard said, 'That'll do! I'll send your report in!' No wonder they were frightened of him – evidently this man had done something wrong in the flying.[22]
> Air Mechanic Cecil King, Central Flying School, RFC

However, one young officer has left an account which shows a different, more sympathetic side of Trenchard.

> One afternoon, soon after my arrival on the [Salisbury] Plain, when I was an exceedingly shy young 2nd lieutenant, I had occasion to take into the major a special sum of money – eight pounds and some odd shillings. I did not have the exact amount and innocently took in two five-pound notes. He looked up from his papers, stared at the notes, then at me. 'I'm not a clerk! Get out and

get change!' he said in a tone which made me vanish again as quickly as ever I have done in my life. Later I returned with the exact amount and apologised rather nervously for my error. Major Trenchard put a friendly hand on my shoulder. 'That's all right, my boy, I happened to be very busy!' Something in the tone, and the fact that the man who was so busy was able to find time to take away all the sting from a well-deserved rebuke delivered to a young subaltern, sent me out of the room glowing. If he had asked me then to fly straight into a brick wall, I would have done it with a singing heart.[23]

2nd Lieutenant Henri Biard, Central Flying School, Upavon

The war was coming. and soon Trenchard would be asking thousands of young men to do the equivalent of flying into a brick wall – time and time again.

Chapter 2

At the Front, 1914

We looked on our aircraft like the cavalryman looked on his horse and we expected the pilot to bring back the aircraft to us and he expected us to send the aircraft up to him. We worked so closely together that the pilot of the machine you were working on very often took you up for a flight to bind the friendship, because he knew he was dependent on you. As a reward for our work, he would take us up and let us be observer![1]

Air Mechanic Samuel Saunders, 1 Squadron, RFC

War came like a hurricane for the Royal Flying Corps. Just a few years after the first powered flight, the RFC had been grafted onto the long-standing plans for the deployment of the British Expeditionary Force (BEF) to what would become known as the Western Front. The RFC was by no means ready for action, and considerable rapid improvisation was required to get ready in time. As deployed to France in August 1914, the RFC consisted of a headquarters commanded by Brigadier General David Henderson, two squadrons (Nos 2 and 4) equipped with the BE2 and BE2a, and two more squadrons (Nos 3 and 5) equipped with a variety of types. In all they would assemble some 105 officers and 755 other ranks. The squadrons mobilised first to the Dover area, but even this brought tragedy as the aircraft flown by 2nd Lieutenant Robert Skene, with Air Mechanic Keith Barlow acting as his observer, suffered an engine failure and tumbled from the sky, killing both men. Ever since its formation in 1912, the RFC had had to get used to a drip, drip of casualties, but these were the first in wartime. On 13 August, the assembled squadrons began to 'hop' across the Channel, which had only been crossed for the first time by Blériot five years beforehand in 1909. The headquarters, ground crews and their transport followed with the rest of the BEF over the next few days. Once across, they moved forward to concentrate at an airfield at Maubeuge. The haste with which they had been embarked was evident in the strange collection of supporting lorries.

It was a miscellaneous and unsoldierly collection of vehicles, most of which had been requisitioned from various commercial organisations. The headquarters stores lorry was a huge, covered, red van, with 'BOVRIL' painted in black letters all over it; we may have laughed when we saw it go off, but later we blessed it because it was so easy to spot from the air on the frequent occasions when we lost our transport. Our bomb lorry was originally destined for the peaceful pursuit of propagating the sale of Lazenby's Sauce (The World's Appetiser), while Peek Frean's Biscuits, Stephens' Blue-Black Ink, and the ubiquitous Carter Paterson were also represented.[2]

2nd Lieutenant Louis Strange, 5 Squadron, RFC

In common with the rest of the BEF, they had a tremendous reception from the French civilians, who were generous to a fault as they pressed bottles of wine onto the soldiers. They were never likely to refuse, but it did have consequences for young men who had never drunk anything stronger than beer before.

The French people were absolutely marvellous. They assembled along the road and gave us terrific cheers! We were loaded up with wine; bottles of wine were everywhere. The lorries had more wine than they had equipment in some cases! As a result of that, I have never drunk wine since![3]

Air Mechanic James Gascoyne, 3 Squadron, RFC

The RFC had attracted a strange collection of officers, who were not always physically impressive.

I don't know what the French people thought of this lot as the British Army. We had two officers, one Captain Carden, who had one arm, and the other Captain Brabazon, who had to walk with the help of a stick because he was partially lame![4]

Air Mechanic Edward Bolt, No. 1 Aircraft Park, RFC

One of these great characters serving in the RFC was Robert Lorraine, a much-acclaimed actor on the London stage, who had also been a keen pre-war aviator and was now serving as a lieutenant. He certainly made his presence felt to poor James Gascoyne, who seems to have led a generally sheltered life.

Robert Lorraine was quite a character. He had the most vivid flow of language I have ever heard. Prior to that I had never heard an officer swear. We were travelling up – it was the first night I think – when the station workshop, which was heavily loaded, got stuck in the mud at the side of the road. Everybody had to turn out to push this thing and dig it out. We were all covered in mud. Lorraine? Well, he was helping us on with language, if nothing else.[5]

Air Mechanic James Gascoyne, 3 Squadron, RFC

The squadrons gathered at Maubeuge, and on 19 August began their first reconnaissance flights to try to determine what the Germans were up to. They soon became aware that it was not only the Germans who provided a danger to British aircraft – as they flew over French troops, they were often shot at from the ground. This got worse when the BEF columns began to approach Mons, where they would take up their first defensive positions in the face of the German thrust through Belgium in what has become known as the Schlieffen Plan. Troops were not prepared to take a chance and tended to fire at any aircraft they spotted above them.

> We were rather sorry they had come because up till that moment we had only been fired on by the French whenever we flew. Now we were fired on by French and English. To this day I can remember the roar of musketry that greeted two of our machines as they left the aerodrome and crossed the main Maubeuge–Mons Road, along which a British column was proceeding.[6]
>
> Captain Philip Joubert de la Ferté, 3 Squadron, RFC

In an attempt to prevent such incidents, the ground crews painted Union Jacks on the lower wings of all aircraft. As we shall see, it did not work!

On 22 August, the RFC undertook some twelve reconnaissance flights. They could not miss the German columns pressing forward and threatening to outflank the British at Mons.

> We were very, very excited as we looked for them. You were very limited in your facilities; you had a map strapped on one knee and a pad with a pencil on the other – and it was rather wobbling about! As soon as we got over our area, instead of seeing a few odd German troops I saw the whole area covered with hordes of field grey uniforms – advancing infantry, cavalry, transport, and guns – the place was alive with the Germans. My pilot and I were completely astounded because it was not a little more than we'd been looking for – it was infinitely more.[7]
>
> Lieutenant Cuthbert Rabagliati, 5 Squadron, RFC

They came speeding back, and after landing were rushed by car to the General Headquarters of the BEF.

> We were ushered in, and we went into a room with a lot of elderly gentlemen covered in gold lace and all the rest of it. All these senior generals, it was Sir John French's own personal conference that was going on. Somebody announced us and he said, 'Well here's a boy from the Flying Corps, come here and sit down!' I was put to sit next to him then he said, 'Now, where have you been? Have you been flying? What have you been doing?' He called up to some man, 'Come here and just look at this!' I showed him a map all marked out. He said, 'Have you been over that area?' and I said, 'Yes, Sir!' I explained what I had seen, and they were enormously interested. Then they began reading the figures that I had estimated, whereupon I feel that their interest faded – they seemed to look at each other and shrug their shoulders. He said, 'Our information – which of course is correct – proves that I don't think you could

have seen as much as you think! Well, of course I quite understand that you may imagine that you have, but it's not the case!'[8]

Lieutenant Cuthbert Rabagliati, 5 Squadron, RFC

It certainly was the case! Yet Sir John French, C-in-C of the BEF, despite all the evidence pressed upon him from various sources, still thought it might be possible to continue the advance from Mons on 23 August.

On the morning of 22 August, the RFC also suffered its first casualty from German fire. A BE2a of 2 Squadron, flown by 2nd Lieutenant Maurice Noel, with Sergeant Major David Jillings acting as his observer, came under heavy ground fire as they carried out a reconnaissance over Ath. Their engine was running badly, but they persevered until the imposing 6-foot figure of Jillings was struck a painful blow by a rifle bullet in the lower back. He carried on for a while, but loss of blood forced him to ask Noel to return to Maubeuge. After landing, he was visited in the first aid tent, and the blood flowing down over his backside promoted the never-to-be-dispelled rumour that he had been shot in the bottom. He would return to 2 Squadron by October – so whatever the exact location of the wound, it was not too serious.

That same day, a German two-seater Albatros had the cheek to fly over Maubeuge and thus became the first airborne German aircraft sighted by the RFC. Two BE2a from 2 Squadron took off to try to catch it, and a Henri Farman from 5 Squadron also took off. The latter was piloted by Louis Strange, an imaginative officer who had had the temerity to mount an unauthorised Lewis gun on his aircraft. The urge to smite their enemies from the sky was already strong within the RFC. Unfortunately, the Henri Farman was less strong and was severely handicapped by the weight of the Lewis gun, as Strange related.

I set off in my Henri Farman, with Lieutenant Penn Gaskell to work the Lewis gun. The enemy machine made off while we were still climbing up over our aerodrome, and I imagine its occupants must have enjoyed a good laugh at our futile efforts. But my disappointment was increased when I landed, because our C.O. came to the conclusion that I should have a better chance of coming to grips with any aerial invaders if I lightened my machine by dispensing with my Lewis gun. He therefore promptly ordered me to unship both it and the mounting I had been at some pains to devise for it, telling my observer he would have to manage with a rifle in future.[9]

2nd Lieutenant Louis Strange, 5 Squadron, RFC

Next day, 23 August, came the crushing defeat of the BEF at the Battle of Mons. Later successfully rebranded as a heroic victory against overwhelming odds, it nevertheless triggered a retreat, which in turn, rather than being humiliating, or desperate, was instead reported as 'The Great Retreat'. The RFC conformed with a series of rapid moves back. Maurice Baring, a well-known literary figure who had been attached to the RFC headquarters, recalled the chaos.

> News also came that the Germans were preparing a raid on the Flying Corps in armed motor-cars. We packed up and left hastily and went to Melun. The population of the village were extremely alarmed at our departure. We tried to reassure them, but they said the Germans would be there and the place would be destroyed. We slept in a field near the aerodrome, just outside the town. In the middle of the night, it poured with rain. My valise proved to be quite rainproof, but B.K. and Salmond were soaked. We established our headquarters in a little house at the end of the aerodrome. When I say house, I am grossly exaggerating. It was a passage open to the four winds with a yard behind it and a road in front of it. It was full of flies, and dirty linen was being washed in the yard, making a terrible smell. There was no door. A small child in a field [close] by kept on playing a tin trumpet until Murat could stand it no longer and went and took his trumpet away. He then started to scream – and continued to scream for the rest of the day.[10]
>
> Captain Maurice Baring, HQ, RFC

During the retreat, the RFC continued to carry out their reconnaissance function, tracking the advancing Germans and warning of the risk of envelopment if the withdrawal was not continued. The cavalry squadrons were exhausted from their role in harassing the German vanguard, but it was apparent that aircraft could reach further, flying deep over the German columns, before returning far quicker than any man on a horse could manage. It took a toll on men and machines as many of the landing fields were rather more fields than landing strips. One who came to grief in amusing circumstances was a well-known pre-war pilot, 2nd Lieutenant Charles Gordon-Bell, a man who had a great sense of humour coupled with a bad stammer when either emotional or angry.

> Gordon-Bell landed in a cabbage field, as a result of which the Bristol Bullet turned up on its nose with its tail sticking up in the air. He was coming along the road, making for Brooke-Popham who was quartermaster general. Popham saw Bell and said, 'Oh, Bell, where's your machine?' To my surprise Bell turned round and said, 'Over in that b-b-b-blasted field of f-f-f-fucking cabbages!'[11]
>
> Air Mechanic James Gascoyne, 3 Squadron, RFC

The damage caused in these rough landings could cause hours of work for the ground crews, and inevitably some aircraft had to be abandoned and burnt-out when they ran out of time. Gordon-Bell's first stint at the front did not last long, as he was wounded on 25 August.

He got a shot in his engine which forced him to come down where he could, with the result that he landed in a tree but was thrown out of the machine and escaped with a few bruises. When he picked himself up, however, he discovered that he had been wounded slightly in the knee, and from subsequent investigations it seems likely that he was fired on by our own, or French troops. Some infantrymen could never resist the temptation to take a pot shot at an aeroplane without bothering to ascertain its nationality, and more than one airman got his baptism of fire from his own side. It was a case of 'save me from my friends' with a vengeance.[12]

   2nd Lieutenant Louis Strange, 5 Squadron, RFC

One wonders at what streams of invective must then have poured from the mouth of the irascible pilot.

It is to the credit of the RFC that during this pell-mell retreat, its pilots and observers were able to supply a stream of reconnaissance reports which proved of immense value – not to Sir John French, who was all but useless in this phase of the campaign, but to General Joseph Joffre, the French commander-in-chief. Joffre used this intelligence in planning his masterstroke counter-attack in the Battle of the Marne, which began on 6 September and would turn the course of the war. That night, the RFC headquarters fought its own stirring battle against overwhelming odds.

The squadrons were billeted in an empty girls' school in the town. There I found a comfortable and quiet bedroom. The next morning was the day the Battle of the Marne began. General Henderson said that the tune of a 'Te Deum' kept on ringing in his head. Although the battle had begun, to us it was a day of waiting. I slept again in the girls' school where some of the squadrons were billeted. A pillow fight on a gigantic scale took place. The pilots dressed themselves up in the girls' night gowns, and one of the dormitories was invaded from the outside by a herd of pilots and, though valiantly defended, was finally taken.[13]

   Captain Maurice Baring, HQ, RFC

The retreat finally ended and the RFC squadrons began to move forwards behind the rest of the BEF, joining the French Army in pursuing the Germans back towards the Aisne River.

The extraordinary part about the retreat was the contrasts that one experienced from day to day; one night sleeping under a hedge in a thunderstorm; the next in a comfortable private house; the third in the most modern type of hotel with every luxury and convenience, the whole forming a picture the impression of which has lasted throughout the war. One curious thing was, unless one was brought down or left behind near the firing line one never came up against the actual unpleasantnesses of war, and it was not until the advance to the Aisne started that those of us who had not been on ground duty, or unlucky, saw any signs of fighting other than from the air. What we saw during the advance confirmed our impressions from the air as to the unspeakableness of the Hun.[14]

Captain Philip Joubert de la Ferté, 3 Squadron, RFC

The pilots continued to carry out their role of tracking the movements of the now-retreating Germans. During this period, Louis Strange was flying with Cuthbert Rabagliati. Units on all sides were moving rapidly, which caused considerable confusion and triggered the following farcical incident.

I landed to report to the corps headquarters. Unfortunately, this had been shifted from the locality where I had received overnight instructions to make my report. Before I realised what the trouble was, we found ourselves surrounded at a respectable distance by a regiment of Zouaves. The next 5 minutes might have been amusing to an onlooker, but I cannot say I found them so. I was not at all sure of the nationality of these troops, and evidently they had decided to take no risks about mine. Half a dozen rifle bullets whizzed round our ears. Then a little old French officer on a white pony galloped up to our field and stopped the shooting. I had not put my engine off, but kept it going with the switches, and every time I switched on to keep it running, rifles all round the field went up to the 'present'. The French officer remained about 200 yards away from us, where he did his best to keep his restive pony quiet; whenever the animal gave him a moment's leisure, he waved a white handkerchief frantically up and down. Whether this was a token of surrender or an incitement to us to give ourselves up quietly, or merely the anticipation of a fond farewell, I could not gather, but we thought it best to humour him by returning the compliment. I had, however, decided that I could not afford to waste the time involved in giving him a satisfactory explanation of our identity! I therefore opened up the engine and headed the machine in the direction of the ancient sportsman, thinking that if the soldiers started to shoot at me again while I was taking off, the nearer to their officer I was the fewer risks I should run. The pony took fright at what it very naturally thought to be an uncouth monster. It bolted, and the officer fell off. The foremost Zouaves rushed forward to pick up and save their officer; those behind them thought discretion the better part of valour and rushed away to save themselves. Consequently my Henri Farman took off between the flustered old gentleman on the ground and his bolting pony – amid much excitement and a few odd rifle shots we waved a last farewell.[15]

2nd Lieutenant Louis Strange, 5 Squadron, RFC

Flying was impeded to some extent by a deterioration in the weather which culminated in a terrible storm on the night of 13 September. Robert Lorraine had just arrived at the front, but due to his reputation for poor flying and smashing up aircraft, he had been initially posted as an observer with 3 Squadron, which was based at Fère-en-Tardenois.

> Goss called us at 4am because of a tremendous gale. On arriving at camp, found eight machines had been blown over during the night and smashed. But for the action of sentries, who wrenched down tent-hangars, which were acting as balloons, bellying up and taking the machines with them, every plane would have been destroyed, and [the] British Air Force temporarily out of action. When we arrived, machines were standing exposed, closely packed in a field. Officers and men were working frantically to peg planes down and cover the engines with tarpaulin, in slashing rain and squalls. Every gust would lift some machine into the air, [and] falling, it fouled its neighbour and that one the next, so that the whole line was continually in confusion and in danger of being wrecked. Charlton's Blériot was blown straight up on its tail, where it stayed poised for several seconds, and then fell backwards, smashing both wings. Salmond dashed out from between two haystacks where he had been working on maps and shoved and pushed with the rest of us.[16]
>
> 2nd Lieutenant Robert Lorraine, 3 Squadron, RFC

It was the first of many such storms that autumn and winter. One of the uncomplaining ground crew pressed into desperate service was a young fitter by the name of James McCudden, who observed the following.

> Rain pouring in torrents, wind howling like mad, and all the hangars level with the ground flapping about the machines. To make things more cheerful, there were deep ditches around the hangars to catch the water, and every minute or so one heard a loud splash, to the accompaniment of curses and oaths, as some unfortunate mechanic fell into one of these drainage pools.[17]
>
> Air Mechanic James McCudden, 3 Squadron, RFC

We may well hear more of McCudden.

The German retreat stopped on the ridge line behind the Aisne River as the Battle of the Aisne commenced on 13 September. The Germans had dug trenches which stemmed the British and French advance and would ultimately trigger the 'Race to the Sea' as the two sides desperately tried to outflank each other. With the advent of trench warfare and a fixed line on the ground, the men of the RFC began to experience new and challenging dangers in what was already a risky business. Robert Lorraine recalled his first flight over the new trench lines in a BE2a piloted by Captain Lewis.

Went through heavy rifle fire at Filain Wood. Found fourteen bullet holes in the machine after landing, two of them within a foot of my head. 'Archie' greeted us on east of the enemy's position. Soissons in flames. Heavy artillery fire on both sides. Could scarcely recover from my excitement. Most spectacular, although troops looked like ants and white puffs from shells bursting in a line made it seem like a toy battle. Even rifle-fire that spattered against [the] wings of our plane was unreal, and the anti-aircraft shells that burst with a dull flash and cough, rocking the plane, were the most completely unreal of all.[18]
2nd Lieutenant Robert Lorraine, 3 Squadron, RFC

As September wore on, so the number of German anti-aircraft guns seemed to increase. The bursting shells and a realisation of what could happen at any moment began to gnaw away at their nerves.

The Germans are getting awfully energetic with their anti-aircraft guns. Their zeal is worthy of much praise, and it is not for want of trying that they have been unsuccessful in bringing any of us down with shell fire so far. They will get somebody soon with 'Archibald' as their shooting is improving every day. We ought to have some anti-aircraft guns also. All we have is a miserable pom-pom which is no use for putting the fear of God into one, in the way that 'Archibald' does. 'Archibald' can reach you at 10,000 feet, and belches forth dirty yellow and black smoke and chain shot – and the noise of the shell bursting is almost enough to make one stall the machine with fright. The pom-pom shell on the other hand only bursts on percussion and its maximum height of smoke trail is only 4,500 feet.[19]
Lieutenant William Read, 3 Squadron, RFC

In typical RFC fashion, this new threat had been given the harmless nickname of 'Archibald', or 'Archie'. It came from the habit of one young pilot, Lieutenant Amyas Borton of 5 Squadron, RFC, who used to bellow out, 'Archibald, certainly not!' whenever an anti-aircraft shell burst near his machine. This was from a ribald monologue performed by the renowned comedian and music hall artiste George Robey, which charted in a number of verses a frustrating relationship with a young lady who was unwilling to engage in fornication, before or after the sanctity of marriage.

> Archibald, certainly not!
> Get back to work at once, sir, like a shot.
> When single you could waste time spooning
> But lose work now for honeymooning!
> Archibald, certainly not![20]

Such an insightful exploration of the married condition must strike a chord in the minds of many.

The RFC was already expanding, with new squadrons and aircraft being despatched to the front. It had proved its worth with simple reconnaissance flights, but now it was busy carving out new methods of operating to maximise the discomfiture of the Germans. The first advance was the replacement of the notebook to record their observations on a reconnaissance flight with a camera to provide a photographic record that could later be blown up to reveal details that were impossible to see from the aircraft in flight. On 15 September 1914, the first photographic reconnaissance was carried out by Lieutenant George Pretyman and Sergeant Frederick Laws of 3 Squadron, RFC. The images that resulted were so blurred as to be almost useless, but then the scientists and practical men stepped in, sorting out the right type of camera and lens, working out how to fit the camera for best results. By early 1915, the RFC would be able to produce thousands of glass plate photos that when taken from directly above, could be pieced together to form a mosaic map which greatly assisted in the planning of operations. A new science of photographic interpretation was also born, to reveal the locations of gun batteries, machine guns, new trench lines, barbed wire and headquarters. It would render the Germans naked before the guns of the Royal Artillery – if only they could hit them in the absence of any lines of direct observation from the ground.

Artillery observation was the next step – but how? Experiments using different coloured Very lights to indicate errors in the fall of shot had been unsatisfactory. What next? To us, the answer seems obvious, but wireless transmitter and receiver sets in 1914 were heavy and the aircraft low-powered. Eventually, it was decided to take up just a transmitter to allow a one-way communication with the artillery batteries on the ground. On 18 September, the first wireless artillery observation flight took place, conducted by Lieutenant Donald Lewis and Lieutenant Baron James of 4 Squadron, RFC. It was soon found that simple wireless messages could guide the shells down onto the target. Once this principle was established, then the relentless development work could commence. The result was that the aircraft of the RFC could not only pinpoint worthwhile targets behind the German lines, but also range the shells down upon them – so long as the officers of the Royal Field Artillery were willing to accept 'orders' from junior officers up in the clouds. Together, these roles would be the defining functions of the RFC in the Great War.

For the British, the 'Race to the Sea' culminated in the First Battle of Ypres, which began on 19 October. The weather was foul, which limited the effectiveness of the RFC contribution. But there was another irritating problem. Pilots expected the Germans to shoot at them, but the continued trickle of casualties from 'friendly fire' was a severe annoyance over their own lines. The Union Jack markings on the lower wings were proving little more than an amorphous smudge, with only the red cross of the Union Jack being visible. As a result, this was often mistaken for the German Maltese cross. On 26 October, there was another tragic case that illustrated the necessity for a more visible marking for RFC aircraft.

Hosking and Crean did a tactical reconnaissance early but were unable to locate batteries owing to clouds. They went up later and did it. The clouds were low, so it was arranged that they should fly over one of our batteries to observe for ranging. The machine came down in flames and was completely demolished. Pilot and passenger had both been wounded by our own infantry fire when at a height of about 1,000 feet with the large Union Jack plainly visible.[21]

Major G.H. Raleigh, 4 Squadron, RFC

As a result, the RFC adopted the French circular 'target' (or roundel) marking, exchanging blue for red and red for blue, to preserve national distinctions.

By this time, 6 Squadron, RFC, had arrived and was immediately deployed in the skies above Ypres. With the squadron was Lanoe Hawker, who recalled an early flight on 28 October.

I was out again today – dodging 'Archie' with some success, tho' this time we could hear and see them bursting behind us. When they get the range, a horrid metallic sort of noise like a short burst of a powerful klaxon [is] followed by a metallic bang, leaving a yellow puff from high explosive, the more usual, or white, from shrapnel. Some of them are very good and put shells all-round the machines, [which is] most alarming when the concussion shakes the whole machine. It is quite an unusual thing for a machine to come in without a bullet or two – I got five today – the planes cover such a large area, but it is very rare that the vitals are injured, and it takes quite a lot to damage the planes. We feed in luxury here; it is really very extraordinary. As long as we are here, we might not be at war, while in under an hour we are in the thick of it, and then back again in calm and peace before another two hours are up.[22]

Lieutenant Lanoe Hawker, 6 Squadron, RFC

The unique nature of aerial warfare, where periods of intense danger were interspersed with intervals of complete safety, was already evident. In the air it was bloody murder! On the ground? Well, some at least lived in the lap of luxury.

A fine lot of good things arrived from Fortnum and Mason, *pâté de foie gras* much appreciated. The smaller fry in tins we are putting by for a rainy day – as there are several of us, and we get lots of fresh meat, so we don't need them yet. The potted meats are always acceptable to do as a savoury or for tea – and cakes. Will you send me some more cigarettes from same place? We are living on the fat of the land, everyone has parcels of good things, if I get a chance I'll try and take some tins up to the trenches, as those things like duck and peas would be acceptable I've no doubt, but for us fellows who get good fresh meat, well-cooked, we don't really need them.[23]

Lieutenant Denys Corbett Wilson, 3 Squadron, RFC

One wonders what the 'fellows' in the trenches thought of this largesse?

The RFC had another role, in the wish to rain death upon the Germans by means of bombing. Once again, they knew what they wanted to do – the question was how? How did they fit the bombs to the aircraft? How did they release them? Samuel Saunders was one of the ground crew pioneers, solving such problems to the best of their abilities. It was all a bit makeshift.

> We'd made some light racks up that we could fit on the fuselage bottom of the Moranes just by fitting four pins in position. We had a wire going round each bomb so that when the wire was pulled the bomb dropped down. We had to fuse these bombs with fulminate of mercury detonators. They came in a box, half a dozen at a time wrapped in cotton wool. We had no instructions, so we got the bombs, unscrewed the top and when we wanted one of these detonators I'd just say, 'Chuck us a detonator, Charlie!'[24]
>
> Air Mechanic Samuel Saunders, 1 Squadron, RFC

There was a cheerful attitude to the dangers posed by the various types of bombs.

> They took the bombs without detonators and gave them to the smith. He had a little portable forge, and he actually welded a piece of metal on to the live bomb. He was careful to keep it cool all the while with water! When that job was on, we gave him a very wide berth and he would say, 'Well what are you chaps walking right over there for? What's the matter?' So, he merrily did a great pile of these bombs![25]
>
> Air Mechanic Cecil King, 5 Squadron, RFC

Many of the pilots and observers devised their own means of carrying and releasing bombs. Amongst them was Cuthbert Rabagliati.

> We were served out with various kinds of bombs which we used to carry in our machines and drop on likely targets whenever we found any. I and my co-pilot were using a French shrapnel bomb, it was a contraption about 4 inches wide and about 8 or 10 inches long. We used to dump it over the side hoping that you wouldn't hit one of your own wires or your wheels as it went. I thought we could improve on that, and I made, in the squadron workshops, a metal tube which I put through the floor of my seat right down and fastened it on to the central skid of my Avro machine. We could drop bombs right through it without entangling ourselves with anything.[26]
>
> Lieutenant Cuthbert Rabagliati, 5 Squadron, RFC

So far so good – what could go wrong? Plenty!

I dropped two, and all went well. I dropped the third – but it wasn't apparently the same size as the others and to my horror it stuck in the tube. Not only did it stick in the tube, but it stuck with the detonator of the bomb lower than the level of my wheels – which was a bit exciting. We tried everything, I even tried to climb out over the side, but I couldn't get it out. I passed a note back to my pilot telling him what had happened – and I watched him read it – his face it was a sight![27]

Lieutenant Cuthbert Rabagliati, 5 Squadron, RFC

They were in a terrible predicament. If they landed, it seemed certain that the bomb would go off, with fatal consequences. They flew round for a long time, doubtless pondering their fate.

We came back to the squadron, came in very low and I wrote a message. I put it in a message bag and dropped it down in front of the hangars, telling them what had happened and saying that when we landed to keep well away, because obviously the whole thing was going to blow up. We landed right away at the far end of the aerodrome – as far away as we could possibly get! We were for it, but we didn't want to blow up the whole squadron as well! I suppose my pilot was a bit scared and he landed much faster than usual. We skimmed along at practically ground level and the edge of the aerodrome was covered in uncut corn that was quite high. The stalks of corn wrapped themselves round the detonator of the bomb and had wrenched it right out of the bomb so that when we finally landed, we had no detonator, and it did nothing! You can imagine the feeling of touching the ground, drawing your feet and knees up – knowing perfectly well that that was the end – and suddenly there was a bounce, then another bounce, then you began running along. Your reaction? All I know is I leapt out of the machine when it was still running, and I gather my pilot did too! When it finally came to a stop there we were lying with complete silence. I got up to try and go to it – whereupon my pilot called out, 'For God's sake stay still, you've done enough damage for one day!'[28]

Lieutenant Cuthbert Rabagliati, 5 Squadron, RFC

On 11 November, Lanoe Hawker even attempted a little regicide with some of his colleagues in 6 Squadron.

We heard that the Kaiser was expected in a little town today so four of us called on him and left cards, I left three, one weighing 16 lbs and two about 8 lbs each. I dodged one 'Archie' that had given us a bad time yesterday but ran into another instead and got a piece thro' my wing. Again, this afternoon five of us went out on a little raid and I got rid of four more and some smaller grenades.[29]

Lieutenant Lanoe Hawker, 6 Squadron, RFC

The problem with using such small bombs was that anything other than a direct hit was unlikely to do much damage to its target. Furthermore, the aircraft then in use could carry such a small bomb load that any idea of mass bombing was impossible. To make matters worse, there was no bombsight worthy of the name – bombing was a matter of guess work. Maurice Baring summed up the dilemma neatly in recalling a German 'raid'.

> A German left a card on us, *pour prendre congé*, from the air. He dropped a bomb on the aerodrome. It fell in the field, on the opposite side of the road to where No. 5 Squadron were established. Theoretically, it was a beautiful shot, practically it hit a turnip. And this was the case with many bombing efforts in the future.[30]
>
> Captain Maurice Baring, HQ, RFC

By this time there were some elements of the RNAS joining the fray, with what would soon be named 3 Squadron being deployed to France to operate against German Zeppelins and assist in reconnaissance. Initially, they had mainly been occupied in beetling about in improvised armoured cars. Once they started flying, their commanding officer, Commander Charles Samson, left a perfect picture of the horrors of winter flying in an open cockpit.

> It was a cold-blooded business seeing the snow being scraped off the aeroplane before you started; this frequently had to be done owing to the aeroplanes having to be kept in the open all the time. The cold was really awful, and whatever clothing you put on you began to get frozen after half an hour or so. I used to put on so many clothes that I could hardly walk, and then get into the aeroplane feeling warm; but after half an hour one's feet and hands used to start to get numb and gradually you got frozen all over. Once we got so cold that I told Wilson I was going to land outside our house at Malo, as I couldn't stand it any longer, so down we came. By the time we had landed [I] could hardly feel the controls and had lost practically all power of movement. Whilst the blood was returning to my feet I was suffering agonies, and I am afraid I was rather brusque to two pretty nurses that arrived and asked me when I was going up again.[31]
>
> Commander Charles Samson, 3 Squadron, RNAS

But then again, it was pretty chilly on the ground too, with snow falling on to men in a water-, ice- and mud-filled trench. And there were no pretty nurses in the trenches!

Chapter 3

Learning to Fly, 1914–16

A pilot whose muscles are rigid when flying should do one of two things: (a) unstiffen (b) give up flying![32]
  Major Charles Burke, 2 Squadron, RFC

With the RFC having proved its value in 1914, a massive programme of expansion was embarked upon. This was hampered in the early stages, as most of the available aircraft and best pilots had already been despatched to the front. This left a dearth of flying instructors capable of training the new generation of aviators, which mirrored the situation the army faced when most of the trained army staff officers had clamoured to be posted to their regiments – where many were promptly killed – leaving the army denuded of experienced staff. This shortage of instructors and aircraft would dog the RFC until pilots had completed their first tour of duty and could then be redeployed back home to train the hundreds, later thousands, of pilots and observers who would be needed at the front. The men left behind to sort out this mess were the Director of Military Aeronautics, Major Sefton Brancker, and the new commander of the Military Wing in the UK, Lieutenant Colonel Hugh Trenchard.

Trenchard was magnificent. Although thirsting to go and fight with his own regiment, the Scots Fusiliers, he was in his element in those first months of the war. He conjured a new squadron into existence out of practically nothing in a way that took my breath away. He combined tremendous power of getting through work with the ability to apply his energy to none but the essential factors. His dominating personality swept aside difficulties and tore red tape into shreds. Woe betide the shirker and the faint-hearted – they withered under the blast of his searching vehemence and were lost.[33]
  Major Sefton Brancker, Directorate of Military Aeronautics, RFC

And where did the recruits come from? That seemed to be the least of the problems. The popularity of flying in the pre-war years had created a large number of young men who were desperate to take to the skies. At this time, it was still a somewhat clichéd view that a pilot needed a light touch, such as would be gained by horse riding and hunting with hounds. As a result, many of the early recruits were from a similar background.

We were late in beginning, but once we had begun, we were not slow. We were rich in engineering skill and in material for the struggle. Best of all, we had a body of youth fitted by temperament for the work of the air, and educated, as if by design, to take risks with a light heart – the boys of the public schools of England. As soon as the opportunity came, they offered themselves in thousands for a work which can never be done well when it is done without zest, and which calls for some of the highest qualities of character – fearlessness, self-dependence, and swift decision.[34]

Walter Raleigh, Official Historian of the Great War's air war

There was sometimes a rather strange approach taken in the tests to determine whether a subject was suitable for recruitment, as Geoffrey Hall experienced.

The nerve man was rather decent, though he had drastic methods. He put me in a revolving chair, told me to shut my eyes, and spun the thing round till my head reeled. Following this you had to walk along a red line in the carpet, and balance on one leg for a minute. You've no idea how difficult they both are. The last test was the most difficult of the lot. He balanced a tuning fork on a flat box and told me to lift it till it was at right angles to my body. I raised the thing very cautiously and, just as I got it into position, the doctor, who was standing behind me, let off a big clapper with a noise like a gun. It seemed such an unnecessary thing to do that I put the box down and asked him what he did that for. He laughed for quite a while, and finally said he thought I would do, but I wasn't to smoke while I was in the RFC. The heart man wanted to know if there had ever been any lunacy in the family. I said not so far. Then he wanted details of the whole family and enquired affectionately after your health. Then he started to worry about my father's people, and I pointed out that I didn't carry the family tree about with me, which seemed to satisfy him. The eyesight test consists principally of matching different coloured wools.[35]

Geoffrey Hall

But many of the recruits had already enlisted in the conventional army. Here, many of them found themselves bored senseless by the endless grind of basic training. They wanted to be at the front, to be in action, before the war was over. Little did they know that years of war still stretched out before them, which would afford them all too plentiful opportunities to die for King and Country. But patience is not a common trait amongst the young.

I was in a young officers' camp in East Yorkshire, spending the days in wearisome routine work and awaiting impatiently my turn to go out to France. I was convinced that the War would be over before I could get out and put all this theoretical war-making into practice. Some one – I believe it was dear old Major Lock of my regiment – said to me one day, 'If you're in such a hurry to be killed, why don't you apply for the Flying Corps? They are asking for lightweights who can ride, and ski, and know Morse and Semaphore, and all that kind of thing. They give them 3 weeks' training, and then send them out to France as observers.' I began to make inquiries, and soon discovered that people were tumbling over each other trying to join the Corps. To some, the idea of emptying bombs into Germans in bulk made more appeal than trying to stick them up individually with a heavy rifle and bayonet. I realised that I, too, was of this opinion, so decided to have a shot at it.[36]

2nd Lieutenant Raymond Money, 3rd East Yorkshire Regiment

Even if they got to the front, there were many military duties that offered little chance of excitement. William Sholto Douglas was serving with the Royal Artillery, where he had the misfortune to fall foul of his commanding officer.

My work in the ammunition column could never have been described as a tournament. It had settled down into a dull routine of hauling our meagre supplies of shells in to the batteries and then returning to the back areas; and even if a few shells were flung at us now and again as we were not returning it was not a particularly exciting business. Apart from that my day was occupied with looking after the horses, and too many of them, poor brutes, were dying from exposure. I was finding that the life of a gunner subaltern was becoming a pretty depressing business. The possibility of being able to fly had in it the greatest fascination, and as I watched those who were lucky enough to be doing it that fascination soon became something akin to a passion. What with the tyranny of my commanding officer and the mud and the misery of the animals and the discomfort of being literally stuck on the ground I came to feel that aviation, even if only as an observer, was the life for me. I put in an application for a transfer to the Royal Flying Corps, and since the only good feature about my relationship with my C.O. was his readiness to see the back of me, I doubt if any such application was ever approved quicker than that one. The only adverse criticism that I received from anybody on the step I had taken came from my mother. In a letter she wrote, 'You must be mad!'[37]

Lieutenant William Sholto Douglas, 14 Squadron, RFC

Others chafed, literally and figuratively, under the hard physical labour experienced by the infantry. One such was Arthur Harris, who was serving with the 1st Rhodesia Regiment in South Africa.

We marched from one end of that country to the other, carrying everything we possessed – a generally empty water bottle, a nearly empty haversack, 250 rounds of ammunition and a rifle. We out-marched the Boer commandos who were with us on horseback and one realised the truth of the saying that a man can always, given equal conditions, out-walk a horse. The result was I have never walked a yard since if I could avoid it. I knew it was no good trying to get on to a horse because horses were out – I thought I might try to be a gunner and get a seat on a limber, but they seemed to be full up. I went round to the War Office where I was interviewed by a rather supercilious young man. When I said I would like to fly, which I realised was something I could do sitting down not walking, he said, 'So would 6,000 other people! Would you like to be 6,001 on the waiting list?'[38]

Arthur Harris

Albert Kingsford was in Egypt when he and his pal 'Rooty' saw their first aircraft, which had just returned from a bombing mission. They were both entranced.

The bamboo affair was a Maurice Farman Shorthorn, so the airman told us. 'Rooty' showed his ignorance by inquiring if it really did fly. Of course, it would fly: it had been known to reach a height of 5,000 feet, could carry two men at once, and bombs, which were thrown overboard in the hopes of hitting the enemy or something belonging to him. 'What about the armoury?' says 'Rooty', pointing to his belt. 'You mean the pistol?' queried the airman. 'Yep!' 'Ah! to pot the enemy airman with!' he replied. Lor! Some shooter this feller, thought I, this must be some sport, potting at one another in the air! This sport, as I considered it, impressed me; I would certainly have to give it a pop at once. Yes, an airman I would be, some big game hunting this, great fun dropping bombs overboard and potting at some other bird in the air with a pistol. Next morning, I appeared at the orderly room with the request for an army form 'X.Y.Z'. Duly filled, I handed it to the adjutant, who, with an inquiring look, asked, 'Tired of life?' I assured him, 'No!' 'Well, what the hell do you want to transfer to the Flying Corps for?'[39]

Lance Corporal Alfred Kingsford, New Zealand Medical Corps, NZEF

Kingsford was peremptorily turned down, but he had got the 'bug' and would soon secure the transfer he craved. As the war went on, it was evident that not only public schoolboys were attracted to the RFC. One young man transferring in was of distinctly working-class origins.

When the adjutant sent for me to-day and informed me of my transfer to the RFC, I could have kissed him, although he has the most repulsive 'mug' of any man that I have ever met. Yes! I could have kissed it; such was my unbounded delight. Now for the Boche! I am going to strive to become a scout pilot like Ball. Watch me! I wonder what Fate has in store?[40]

2nd Lieutenant Edward Mannock, 40 Squadron, RFC

Fate had indeed got great things in store for Mannock; but it might also be said he had signed his own death warrant. Yet that was the future.

* * *

Over the first two years of the war, a detailed programme of training was constructed from almost nothing. It would prove flawed, but it was still a considerable achievement and provided the groundwork from which improvements could be made. Before the war, pilots had received their *ab initio* flying training and qualified for a flying certificate from private schools. As the war moved into 1915, this function was gradually overtaken by events and the RFC began to take over the flying instruction from start to finish. It was also realised that pilots needed to have a solid grounding in the science and engineering of flying. As a result, schools of instruction were established at Wantage Hall, University of Reading, and another in the august surrounds of Christ Church College, Oxford. The cadets were taught and examined in a wide variety of technical subjects before they got anywhere near a cockpit.

> In a few days I received orders to report to the school of ground instruction at Reading, and with these orders a list of kit and uniform which I would need as a temporary 2nd lieutenant on probation (Special Reserve) in training, and an allowance with which to buy this equipment. Since I already knew a good deal about the requirements of a junior officer in the Army, I did not get caught by the attempts of enthusiastic salesmen to sell me, 'Everything that a young officer needed!' Had I bought everything suggested to me I would have needed a special Crossley tender to take my gear around in. The regulation uniform of the time was khaki. A rather smart forage cap, and a tunic done up to a high collar and folding across the chest to button up invisibly at the side. It was known in the service as a 'maternity jacket', possibly because it made any superfluous weight around the middle extremely visible. The uniform was completed by riding breeches, and either puttees or field boots. The latter of course gave tremendous scope, since nowhere could the field boot be so exclusive, so polished, so superb as in London.[41]
>
> 2nd Lieutenant Gordon Taylor, No. 1 School of Military Aeronautics, Reading

They studied the inner mysteries of aero engines, the complexities of air frames and rigging, and the workings of flying instruments. They also had to master simple navigation and meteorology; wireless signalling and Morse code; the basics of aerial photography and artillery observation; and finally, an introduction to armaments including the Vickers machine gun, the Lewis gun and bombs. This was a heavy workload for any young man, and some faltered.

> Our programme is roughly: up at about 6am (!) parade at 6.30 for half hour physical and other drill, then exercise of any sort, breakfast at 8.00. Parade 8.45, marched up to museum for workshops and instruction from NCO instructors – obviously very good men – from 9.00 till 11.45. Lecture 11.45–12.30. Lunch 1.00. Parade at 2.00 for workshops same as morning till 3.30 with lecture, then free till mess at 7.30 – must attend – then nothing till bed. Place locked up at 1.00am. In the workshops we do all sorts of things

on rigging, bombs, artillery observation, or reconnaissance, photography, a little wireless signalling (Morse) besides engines, doing them in squads with various instructors. This morning we had a very good introductory lecture on rigging and the theory of flight, followed by afternoon of signalling. After the four weeks we have an exam and then go home and wait for wire summoning to flight squadron for actual flying – or repetition of course if failed![42]

2nd Lieutenant Arthur Rhys Davids, No. 2 School of Aeronautics, Oxford

William Fry was exceptionally lucky in that the exigencies of the service meant he dodged the exams altogether.

We were all suddenly ordered off to various aerodromes for initial flying training. We could not believe our luck at escaping that examination although there was a half-hearted attempt to bluff us into believing we should have to take it at our new units. It was lucky that I escaped the usual examination as I could never have passed one, however simple. The internal combustion engine was a closed book to me and the sergeant instructors who tried to teach us about them might just as well [have] been talking Russian. I can say that when I went on the course, I was ignorant of the relative uses of petrol and oil in an engine.[43]

2nd Lieutenant William Fry, No. 1 School of Aeronautics, Reading

Once the cadets finally started their flying instruction, they were introduced to the flying miracle known as the Maurice Farman Longhorn.

With much pushing and pulling it was carefully arranged so as to face into the wind, although to us laymen the manoeuvre was a little obscure, since the bows of the aeroplane were almost identical with its stern. It had an elevator stuck out in front upon curving outriggers of wood, and a double set of elevators fixed to wooden spars at the stern. But for the propeller which drove the machine inexorably forward and the arrangement of the pilot's seat and controls, it might have been designed to travel in either direction.

Officially it was called after its inventor, a Maurice Farman Biplane, but it was better known as a Longhorn, because of the outriggers to the forward elevator. A slightly more modern sistership was called the Shorthorn, because the inventor had, rather rashly we thought, done away with the outriggers and elevator. The allusion was, of course, to different breeds of cattle, and taking them all round the aeroplanes of Monsieur Farman's breeding were pleasant beasts. But except for slowness and docility the resemblance to cows ended with the horns. To the uninitiated eye the Longhorn presented such a forest of struts and spars, with floppy white fabric drooped overall, as inevitably brought to mind a prosperous seaport in the heyday of sailing ships, whilst piano wire was festooned everywhere to such an extent that the wrecking of a few of these machines before the lines in Flanders would have provided our troops with an impenetrable entanglement. At the sight of the craft before us, we put our heads on one side like puzzled terriers.[44]

2nd Lieutenant Duncan Grinnell-Milne, RFC Shoreham

Cecil Lewis summed up the attractions of the Maurice Farman in a grossly sexist manner.

Maurice Longhorns were not, judged by contemporary standards, remarkable for their streamlined beauty; but they were waiting for us, and we were wild to get at them – which is, after all, a fair basis for any romance.[45]

Lieutenant Cecil Lewis, RFC

At last, the eager pupils made their first flight with their instructor at the controls. This was intended to get them used to being in the air.

The pilot and his passenger settled down into their elevated seats, adjusted goggles, helmets, etcetera, and took a long look round as though it might be their last. After listening a while to the engine, the pilot waved [his] hands, attendant mechanics removed wooden blocks from beneath the wheels, and the machine moved forward slowly, lurching slightly over the uneven ground like a cow going out to pasture. The alarm clocks ticked much louder; the mass of shipping, the network of piano wire, the nacelle with its occupants, all hanging rather mysteriously together, moved away at increasing speed. The draught from the propeller rippled the grass, rushing back to make us duck and clutch at our caps. When I looked again the Longhorn was scurrying across the aerodrome at the most alarming speed. It seemed impossible that the various parts should still be holding together. The machine hugged the ground; the curving horns, the wheels and skids, the tail-booms were all buried in the uncut grass through which the propeller seemed to be blazing a trail, and that and the noise of the receding engine made me think of nothing so much as a lawnmower running amok. I watched, holding my breath. And – lo! – it began to unstick from the earth. It rose a few inches; higher; it flew! O wondrous contrivance, 'Hail to thee, blithe spirit, bird thou never wert!' Shelley should have been a pilot. Nowadays I suppose that such a machine in flight would seem ridiculous even to a child, but to us it was impressive enough. It was flying – that alone was sufficient![46]

2nd Lieutenant Duncan Grinnell-Milne, RFC Shoreham

Sometimes, things could go wrong, as the harassed instructors were not always aware of what stage their respective pupils had reached. This could lead to a lot of bad language and hurt feelings all round. Jack Wilkinson had not had his familiarisation flight, or indeed ever touched the aircraft controls, before he was unknowingly thrust in at the deep end.

Captain Tabernacle, the flight commander, spotted me late one afternoon as I mooned about outside the hangars. 'Here!' he called. 'Put a helmet on and climb in! Hurry up!' he rapped out. 'It'll be dark soon!' I fastened on a helmet and climbed in. Slowly the clumsy machine trundled across the aerodrome and bounced leisurely into the air. When the altimeter showed 200 feet we made a left turn, swung wide over the mess, turned left again and came charging in over the sheds. I felt a tap on my helmet. 'All right, take her down!' shouted Tabernacle. Take her down? My hat! But how? I pushed the joystick forward. 'That must be right!' I thought. The engine somehow ran faster than even I thought necessary, and the ground rushed upward. 'Close the throttle, you idiot!' yelled my instructor, suiting the action to the word and closing it for me. It was just as well he did, for I had only the haziest notion where the throttle was. With the engine ticking over and the wind whistling through the wires we dived straight for a patch of the aerodrome where I had decided to descend. 'No! No! Glide, dammit, not dive!' I yanked the joystick back. The nose rose steadily. 'Oh hell! Haven't you any sense of proportion? Leave her to me!' I released the controls, and we made another circuit. 'Now,' said Tabernacle as we approached the aerodrome again. 'Listen! Throttle slowly back, stick slowly forward – a glide you see? You were trying to ram the ground, your way! Now I'm holding her just off the ground – take hold and let her settle – no!' The nose of the machine cocked up ever so slightly, and we sat down with an almighty crash. 'Oh, God!' We bounced once more; but this time the wheels ran along the ground. 'What the devil do you think you're playing at? How long "dual" have you had?' 'None!' I answered meekly. 'Eh, what's that?' 'This is my first time up!' I explained. 'Oh, is it!' Tabernacle was somewhat mollified and smiled. 'I quite thought you'd had an hour or two's dual with Pearman. Well, that's how not to do it!'[47]
Lieutenant Jack Wilkinson, Northolt Airfield

Having survived his unconventional introduction to flying, Wilkinson began dual flying instruction with his instructor, with a series of 10–20-minute flights totalling about 150 minutes in total. There was a lot of abuse of the hapless ingénue pilot.

Here we go again after about 2½ hours 'dual' instruction made up of 10 and 20 minute flips. Pearman, 'For God's sake see that your nose is down – down! You bloody fool! When you make a turn! If you start spinning a 'Rumpety' you'll never be quite the same again. Now take her in and land her – hell's delight! You can't glide horizontally! Not for long anyway. Now you're going to scoop the roof off the 'B' Flight's shed – I never did see such a fool! Glide, you idiot, glide! Now hold her, hold her!' Crump! We bounce into the air again with the agility of a lobster. 'Oh my God!' Crump! We bounce again – harder this time, but not so high. 'Oh, you bloody cow!' Me or the 'Rumpety'? Rumble-rumble-rumble. We have landed. 'Well, that's what I call a damned fine three-piece landing – you, me and this blasted kite! How you get away with it I don't know! Take her off again!'[48]

Lieutenant Jack Wilkinson, Northolt Airfield

On the other hand, Frederick Powell's instructor preferred to communicate in a more traditional sign language.

The instructor sat behind me in this dual control Maurice, and he flew the machine while I lightly put my hands on the controls. He talked, so the conversation was shouting over the noise of a rattling engine. It was very difficult to hear. Sign language was very useful – in fact, I think the most useful sign was the two fingers![49]

2nd Lieutenant Frederick Powell, Farnborough, RFC

Flying was like walking a tightrope. If the pupil was ham-fisted, then he invited a sudden and unpleasant demise. The margins for error were almost non-existent.

A pilot must learn to steer a steady course between the Charybdis of spinning, the remedy for which was not yet known, and the Scylla of diving into the hard ground. Stalling – that was a word I heard on everyone's lips: to lose flying speed and, in consequence, all control of the machine. There were other minor difficulties to be reckoned with: mainly those connected with the strength, or rather the weakness, of the aeroplanes of those days. At all points one encountered either the unknown, or else more or less certain structural dangers. It was, they told me, courting death to dive the majority of machines at any appreciable angle, [as] the speed and increased strain would pull the wings off. To bank too steeply might involve a sideslip or loss of flying speed, either of which might quickly develop into the irremediable spin.[50]

2nd Lieutenant Duncan Grinnell-Milne, RFC Shoreham

Edward Mannock impressed one instructor during his first training flights – mainly because of his insouciant attitude.

Mannock, unlike many pupils, instead of jamming the rudder and seizing the joystick in a herculean grip, looked over the side of the aeroplane at the earth, which was dropping rapidly away from him, with an expression which betrayed the mildest interest. I liked him immensely from that moment. He made his first solo flight with but a few hours' instruction, for he seemed to master the rudiments of flying with his first hour in the air and from then on threw the machine about as he pleased.[51]

Captain F. Chapman, RFC Hendon

However, Mannock had an impulsive and impatient nature, which he demonstrated when training at Hendon. This might have cut his career short before it had started, as he might well have been returned to the Royal Engineers.

> Mannock was of a most tempestuous nature; even then nothing daunted him, and indeed, he had been at Hendon only a very short time – some two weeks or so - when being impatient and wanting to fly solo on his own, he went onto the tarmac early one morning – there was no-one about, just two mechanics – jumped into a Caudron and flew around the aerodrome for 10 minutes or so. On landing he was severely reprimanded by the C.O., who ordered him to remain grounded until further orders.[52]
> 2nd Lieutenant Arthur Graves, RFC Hendon

Overall, the flying instructors had a lot to put up with. They were often driven to distraction.

> Sergeant Saunders was good. He throttled down and shouted when he had to and sometimes, he hit me over the crash helmet to emphasise a point, but he respected my (probationary) commission. I remember once when I nearly stalled the machine, the bang on the helmet and his furious, 'What the bloody hell do you think you are doing, Sir?'[53]
> 2nd Lieutenant Thomas Traill, RFC

However, not all the instructors were paragons of common-sense and virtue. Frederick Powell had returned from his first stint as a scout pilot on the Western Front. He had been posted as an instructor at RFC Cambridge, but he was a livewire character who was soon itching to get back on active service.

> It suddenly dawned on me that I was wasting the war, because here I was in the Home Establishment and my ambition was to get out to France. Knowing my wing commander, I rang him up and asked if I could be posted overseas. And he, to my annoyance, said, 'No, Powell, it's about time you came home and did a job of work!' That annoyed me, and that night lying in my bed, I thought, 'Now, I'll do something nobody else has ever done – tomorrow morning I will loop off the ground.' My Bristol Bullet had a maximum speed level of about 70 miles an hour but I thought that if I held it down just over the top of the grass until I was going flat out then I could go up in a very big loop, when I got to the top, pull the joystick into my tummy, whip the tail over and then gravity plus the engine would pull me round. Next morning, I went off and tried this – I pulled up in the loop, flipped it – and realised I hadn't enough room! I think my life was saved by some sheep grazing at the far end of the grass airfield. They all started to run out star fashion away from me and I was so interested in the sheep that I didn't stiffen myself up. There

was a bean field at that corner – the beans were about 2 feet high. When the crash came, I went straight into the deck at about 150 miles an hour straight into the earth in the bean field. I shot through the front of the aircraft, my belt broke, I hit my head on the instrument board and was knocked out. My legs had shot through the rotary engine and another quarter of a turn and I would have lost both my legs. As it was, I finished with the engine in my crutch. The only thing I could see of the aircraft above the bean field was the very tip of the rudder. The ground was hard and not one bit had sunk more than a few inches into the earth – it was flattened like a pancake. My C.O., seeing this, stopped everyone from running out because he knew it was going to be a nasty mess. So he strolled slowly across to the crash and when he got there he found me singing the latest song of the time which was:

> 'Sprinkle me with kisses
> A lot of loving kisses
> If you want my love to grow.'[54]
>
> Captain Frederick Powell, RFC Cambridge

He would survive to return to the fray, and indeed to be interviewed by the Imperial War Museum some sixty years later. What a character!

Another instructor guilty of a different kind of offence featured in a story told by Harold Balfour of his time at RFC Shoreham.

> I fear that one of our flight commanders had gone astray with a young lady in Brighton, to the intense anger and indignation of the mother when she discovered the condition of her daughter. She did not know the culprit's name, but only that he used to loop a Martinsyde Scout off the Brighton front, in full view of the windows of her house. Bursting with determination, she sailed up to the aerodrome and demanded from the commanding officer to see the 'looper'. The C.O., having a shrewd idea as to the identity of the culprit, replied perfectly truthfully – as he did loop the Martinsyde – that he was the 'looper'. The good lady knew that the individual she wanted was not the commanding officer, but beyond this, in view of the C.O.'s words she was unable to penetrate and at last retired beaten from the field. The flight commander discreetly left for France within the next few days.[55]
>
> 2nd Lieutenant Harold Balfour, RFC Shoreham

When the instructor judged the moment right, the pupil would be sent up for his first solo flight. This was a nerve-wracking business, for if they made a mistake there was no helping hand to guide them or correct the error. They would have to live or die with the consequences.

Adjusting the throttle to slowest running, I stared round fearfully at the ghastly collection of struts, tail-booms and spars that had once again resolved itself into a dense forest in which I should presently be as lost as any 'Babe in the Wood'. Through wire entanglements I caught sight of two mechanics grinning at me. Horrible ghouls, gloating over my forthcoming demise! Was there no way out? I turned my face to the morning sky where the light was still growing. Like the tenor in *Tosca* I had never loved life so much. Not a breath of wind anywhere, save the slight draught of the slowly revolving propeller. I sniffed the air, and inspiration came to me. Perhaps if I got out of the nacelle and strolled nonchalantly over to the sheds murmuring, 'No lift in the air!' I should be granted a reprieve! I looked hastily over the side. Below stood the instructor. 'Get well out across the aerodrome before you take off!' he said, 'and don't taxi too fast!' I nodded speechless and buckled up the safety-belt. In those days the newspapers still occasionally referred to an aeroplane pilot as 'the intrepid rider' and upon the instant when Longhorn and I rose gently into the air I came to know that the expression referred to me. I was intrepid whether I liked it or not. And I was certainly a rider. I squatted rigidly upright upon the edge of my elevated seat, holding the handlebars delicately between forefinger and thumb, treading the rudder pedals as though I were walking upon unbroken eggs. I was remembering my lessons, anxiety was diminishing. I looked quickly about me. Everything seemed to be all right. But it would not last unless I continued to be very, very careful. I glued my eyes to the front elevator. I was indeed off the ground: nearly 400 feet! It was exhilarating at this altitude. But only momentarily so; I had to get back. My wristwatch showed that I had been in the air for no less than 3 minutes. Worthing Pier was beginning to come close.[56]

2nd Lieutenant Duncan Grinnell-Milne, RFC Shoreham

After a couple of gentle turns, he passed over Brighton and headed back to Shoreham.

The aerodrome came towards me again, passed by directly underneath. I risked a glance over the side. There was quite a crowd of pupils on the tarmac. They were staring up, watching me; I was on my first solo and it was proving to be successful. But I was not home yet, and pride comes before a fall! Hurriedly I touched wood, there was a lot of it around me. The speed indicator showed 38mph. Too slow! Down with the nose – but gently. Unless I was gentle as a nursing mother something dreadful would happen. I would spin into the ground and wake up to find, at the best, wings very different from those I coveted sprouting from between my shoulder blades. Over Shoreham town I pushed the nose firmly down and pulled back the throttle. The Longhorn commenced to glide towards the aerodrome. The air speed settled down to a steady 42mph. What was going to happen when these two met, the aeroplane and the aerodrome? I was sure I could never bring myself – alone, unaided – to 'flatten out' at just the right moment. There would not be much noise, I thought, a heavy crunch and then struts, spars, wires, white fabric would all collapse and fold themselves about me. I would remain sitting in the crushed nacelle until they sent a party from the sheds to liberate me; and their laughter would be restrained only if I were seriously hurt. Meanwhile the ground seemed to be coming up in normal fashion. I could see the daisies in the grass beneath me. Time to flatten out. With the utmost gentleness I pulled back the handlebars, treading nervously on the harmonium pedals to bring the nose dead into wind. The front elevator rose, the noise of wind in the wires died away. I stared ahead like a hypnotised rabbit. From directly underneath there came a hollow rumble, from further astern a scraping sound; the machine shook, gave a gentle lurch. My heart rose to my throat with alarm. What was happening? Still keeping my head rigidly to the front, I squinted down at the speed indicator. Nothing! At the altimeter – zero. I looked boldly over the side. The grass was very near, almost motionless, I could see each blade. Fuzz from a dandelion blew slowly past the lower plane. I had landed. As I taxied back to the sheds two mechanics came out to guide the machine in. 'How did you get on?' a fellow pupil asked. 'Oh, all right!' I answered carelessly.[57]

2nd Lieutenant Duncan Grinnell-Milne, RFC Shoreham

Things did not always pass so smoothly. There were so many things that could go wrong; and go wrong they often did.

Another youth was having his first flight by himself. He suddenly arrived from the air over the sheds and, contrary to all rules, across the wind, but made a fair landing. Instead of slowing up on the ground, for some unknown reason the throttle opened, and he sailed gaily along and through a fence with a great crash. What the fence overlooked in the machine, a telegraph post took in hand and reduced the aeroplane to matchwood. We all tore across to pick [him] out and found him swinging his helmet and walking about the wreck remarking 'I say, what devilish luck!'[58]

2nd Lieutenant John Brophy, RFC Castle Bromwich

There were just so many different errors of omission or commission that they could make. A moment's thoughtlessness could lead to disaster, or a write off.

One afternoon a group of pilots standing on the tarmac saw a stationary Longhorn in the centre of the aerodrome. A pupil had just landed and accidentally stopped his engine. Sooner than wait for the mechanics to run out to him, he got down from the nacelle and attempted to start the engine himself. He succeeded better than he had expected. One swing of the propeller and the alarm clocks went off with a bang. He had unwisely left the throttle half open and before he could skip out of the way he was knocked down by the tailplane as the machine moved briskly off. Picking himself up he then ran after her, shouting 'Hi!' But that only seemed to increase Mrs Longhorn's hurry, and presently she took off quite on her own, landing after a free flight of a few hundred feet in the upper branches of a stout elm. 'Birds nesting at your age? You ought to know better!' said a waggish mechanic waving a forefinger at her.[59]

2nd Lieutenant Duncan Grinnell-Milne, RFC Fort Grange

At some stations, watching young pilots career about the sky became quite a spectator sport for the more ghoulish locals.

At Doncaster there was usually a number of spectators outside the railings along the edge of the aerodrome watching the flying. We pupils always insisted they were there in the hope of witnessing a crash, so sometimes at weekends when there were more spectators than usual, we would make a life-size dummy and drop it out of a machine on to the aerodrome. The motor ambulance rushed out as arranged, made much fuss of placing the body on a stretcher and driving off with it as if to the mortuary. We were sure that the spectators went home the happier for having seen what they hoped for.[60]

2nd Lieutenant William Fry, 5 Reserve Squadron

Having managed their first solo flight, the pupil would receive additional dual flight lessons with his instructor to polish his skills, but he would also be sent up for numerous solo flights. They would also be despatched on cross-county flights to improve their basic navigation skills.

It was an extension of what we'd done before. Learning how to find your way about really, across country. Offshore, along the coastline and getting up [to] some reasonable heights. I remember being frightfully proud to find myself at 4,000 feet. In fact, I remember writing home to my mother to tell her I'd been up to 4,000 feet. Got a letter back saying it was most interesting, then a note of horror in her letter, 'You don't mean to tell me you were up there all alone!'[61]

Sub Lieutenant Grahame Donald, RNAS Eastchurch

Some pilots still made mistakes which betrayed their staggering ignorance of the basics of flying.

One day a pupil took up a machine, and when he came in to land instead of flattening out, he flew straight into the ground, completely wrecking the aeroplane, although he himself crawled out unhurt. His commanding officer came up to tell him exactly what he thought of his exhibition, and to ask him why he had made no apparent effort to land the machine properly. Before he could say anything, the pupil burst out in indignation: 'Sir, the carelessness of your mechanics is disgraceful. When I hit the ground, my altimeter was still registering several feet!' As an altimeter registers thousands of feet with no finer gradation than 100 feet and is probably never nearer than 100 feet in accuracy, it is not a suitable instrument with which to judge one's landing. Apparently, this pupil thought it was as accurate as the second hand of a watch, so he put his head inside the cockpit and just glided down, intending to watch till the needle registered '0', and then pull the stick back and expect to find the ground just touching his wheels![62]

2nd Lieutenant Harold Balfour, RFC Shoreham

The pupils still had much to learn before they passed their flying certificate. Even after they were posted to a home base or squadron for continuation training, they still had to practice their flying, racking up the number of hours spent in the air. Most navigated by following rivers or railways, which were both clearly visible from the air. And there was one invaluable piece of advice to remember.

Well, there was one piece of gospel which was preached to all Flying Corps pilots in those days, 'If you've got to have a forced landing, pick out a big house and land beside that because you're sure to get good entertainment!'[63]

Lieutenant John Hopkins, RFC Retford

Given the unreliable nature of aircraft engines, forced landings were not uncommon. Pilots gained the ability to look ahead and always have a feasible landing ground in mind in case the engine cut out without much warning. But sometimes there was nothing to it but to crash-land wherever gravity took them.

I took off one day from Hounslow for a practice flight in a Maurice Farman, [and] I was only about 100 feet off the ground when the engine started cutting. Losing power, I found myself heading for some trees, and to avoid smashing into them I made a quick and very rough landing in an orchard, carefully steering my aircraft between two of the fruit trees. But there was not enough room! Both pairs of wings were neatly chopped off, and I went gently rolling on in the cockpit with the undercarriage and centre section intact. My logbook states, 'Smashed machine, engine intact!' Of far more importance to me – I was also intact![64]

Lieutenant William Sholto Douglas, RFC

Seeking an emergency landing ground was also much more difficult if there was no land beneath them, as Charles Chabot discovered when his engine failed while he was on a solo flight over the Channel while based at Dover.

I was making my way to Dover when, 'Bbumf!' Out went the engine – complete engine cut. Well, there's only one thing to do when you're sitting over the Channel and you have an engine cut and that is to come down and sit *on* the Channel. So, that is what I did. It was quite an interesting experience. She floated on her bottom planes for a little while and the bottom planes gradually filled, the bottom planes went down, and she was resting on her top planes. I saw that I'd got to swim for it – or do something. Here a most awkward thing happened. In town overnight I had bought myself a new pair of boots. Now the thing to do was to wear knee-length boots, very tightly fitting, and mine were marvellous ones! This sort of boots was all right when you'd got an orderly to help you off with them at home, but when you're sitting in an aircraft in the middle of the Channel, getting them off is not funny at all! Even by wedging the heel of the boot in against the rudder bar and that sort of thing, I couldn't get the darn things off and swimming in the Channel with these boots on didn't sound at all funny – I wondered whether I was going to see myself drowning as a result of my conceit in these very, very smart knee-length boots. Then there was a 'Choof! Choof!' noise and a Navy steam pinnace came out from Dover. Somebody had seen this aircraft come down in the Channel and before the top plane got completely waterlogged the pinnace had thrown me a rope and that was that![65]
  Lieutenant Charles Chabot, 15 Squadron, RFC

* * *

Overall, human nature is such that there is no doubt that many of these brash young men did become overconfident far too early in their career as pilots. They moved from tremulous caution to a wild enthusiasm and totally unjustified confidence in their own abilities. This had been noticed even in the pre-war days.

Everyone who takes up flying becomes converted from disbelief into enthusiasm. Shortly after his conversion he may, or may not, kill himself.[66]
  Major Charles Burke, 2 Squadron, RFC

One example of the perils of over-confidence was witnessed by Christopher Bilney, who was undergoing flying training with the RNAS.

A chap named Wimbush was always shooting a hell of a line in the mess about this, that, and the other. He got onto the subject of spinning Avros. He couldn't understand how these clots spun Avros into the ground, and so on and so forth! The very next day he bit the dust good and hard with a spin in an Avro from about 800 feet. And he got away with it. He started off in the front seat and somehow or other, when they picked up the pieces, he was in the back seat with the gun ring around his waist and how he managed that, I don't know. But we didn't hear any more about spinning Avros from him![67]
  Sub Lieutenant Christopher Bilney, RNAS Cranwell

Accidents were frequent and most pilots had at the back of their mind that this was a dangerous business. After all, there was plenty of evidence laid out in the most brutal fashion right in front of them.

> Well, my flying is going on fine, but I am very sorry to say that a great many of our men have been killed in the last few weeks. It is rotten to see the smashes. Yesterday, a ripping boy had a smash, and when we got up to him, he was nearly dead, he had got a 2-inch piece of wood right through his head and died this morning. If you would like a flight, I should be pleased to take you anytime you wish.[68]
>
> 2nd Lieutenant Albert Ball, RFC

The insouciance with which he describes this gruesome death and then in the next line invites his correspondent up for a joyride demonstrates a true devil-may-care spirit. There were many examples of pupils getting carried away with what they were doing and making potentially fatal mistakes, despite the very best efforts of those around them. A future observer was watching one pilot's adventures.

> The pilot of a Caudron had been up a long time, and his flight commander became concerned about the petrol supply. He tried all means of getting the fellow down, including firing rockets, and having every other machine put away, and eventually the Caudron did land – only to take off again immediately. The pilot then proceeded to practise landings in different parts of the aerodrome, while a furious flight commander raged up and down the tarmac – and sent men out in all directions to stop him. When taking off for the last time, the Caudron's petrol supply gave out, and the machine went straight into the moat. It was a lovely crash, and of course everyone was there to see it. 'I hope, oh, I do hope, the [fucker's] dead' exclaimed the flight commander. Of course, the pilot wasn't dead, but he did have to go to hospital for a week or two.[69]
>
> 2nd Lieutenant Raymond Money, RFC Fort Grange

By their very nature, the young pilots were somewhat brash. But not all of them. Arthur Rhys Davids was a sensitive young man, who found the boisterous nature of RFC mess life a little too *outré* for his more refined tastes.

> You can't imagine how I long to discuss Buddhism and other things with you, but it can't be done through letters. Then when I start discussing religion or something interesting at mess I find (a) it is against mess rules! (b) it is hard to find anyone with any ideas on the subject. You also can't imagine how much I loathe the army and how much my thoughts are always in Cotterstock or Eton. I just drift on quite mechanically. Nobody except the little few I have collected around me understands me in the least: above all nearly everybody is

so common and so sordid – especially after Eton, where one did make friends: here one merely makes acquaintances by the score. I have found one really admirable person called Wilcox who has just been married: he is really artistic, but even he is saturated with a veneer of Cockney common-sense which just mars the perfect friend. There are so few individuals here: nearly all are animal creatures; some have manners, very few sympathy – which is everything, in fact only another word for love. My thoughts are very wild, and it's so hard to put them into numbers, it's like putting a square peg into a round hole. Someday when I get time, I shall shape the peg to fit![70]

2nd Lieutenant Arthur Rhys Davids, Central Flying School, Upavon

Amongst the more bumptious element were the likes of Duncan Grinnell-Milne. With his flying training all but done, he allowed himself to dream of what might be when at last he reached the Western Front.

An improvement upon older models of the same type, it was believed to attain no less than 76 miles an hour at full speed. It was known as the BE2c; its engine was the 90 horse-power 'RAF' the letters standing for Royal Aircraft Factory, the home of those expert minds whose latest and most immaculate conception this aeroplane was. I gazed at the pilot with envy while my imagination soared faster than the swiftest biplane. I too would steer a wonderful BE2c and learn to manoeuvre it with graceful ease. I would fly such a machine in France; my wings would darken the skies above the expectant battlefront, the enemy's secrets would be disclosed to me. At my approach Zeppelins would hurry home, their huge sheds leap up in flames beneath my deadly rain of bombs, Berlin would pass sleepless nights. So much for the colourful imagination of extreme youth![71]

2nd Lieutenant Duncan Grinnell-Milne, RFC Shoreham

Unrealistic? Yes! But a sign of the spirit that filled most of these young pilots.

*   *   *

Pilots were not the only ones being trained. The two-seaters needed trained observers able to fire the Lewis guns, map read, operate the wireless and learn Morse Code, ready to guide the guns of the Royal Artillery batteries.

There were about eight of us on the course, and for the next fortnight we practised signalling, and attended lectures, and went up on practice reconnaissances on which we had to write reports. We also practised artillery observation both from the air and in a hangar, where a model village and trench system had been built, enabling the would-be observer, mounted in the roof, to spot and locate the flashes of tiny bulbs concealed variously over the ground.

Locations and corrections were signalled down by the observer by means of a Morse buzzer. This was in June 1915, and I do not believe that the training of observers was, or could have been, any better carried out throughout the years that followed. I do not know to whom the chief credit was due, but probably to Captain Wyllie who was our chief instructor. He set a high standard, too! I'm afraid I must have a very low sense of honour, for, in order to make sure that my final reconnaissance report should be satisfactory, I borrowed a car and did a ground reconnaissance of the rolling stock in Eastleigh Junction, and various other local features, before handing in my report. The Authorities had just instituted a badge for observers. It took the form of a wing, elevated, and ending in a large 'O'. I would like to tell you what this was promptly nicknamed, but it would not be convenable![72]

2nd Lieutenant Raymond Money, Fort Grange

Jack Wilkinson had a cynical view of the value of the lectures delivered by veteran observers.

Work consisted of listening to lectures from observers who had been in France and now recounted their experiences to us with becoming modesty. These were very informal talks and we gathered that: (a) 'It was damned cold up there!' (b) The pilot's method of attracting his observer's attention was to hit him on the head, and (c) 'It was damned cold up there!' It was only when someone started the ball rolling by asking questions that we got our 'instructor' (who had most likely bought his first razor yesterday) to open up and tell us how to recognise Hun machines? In which case he obligingly drew silhouettes on the blackboard, how many machines went out at a time, how long an observer's course in England could be made to last (very important this), how long a patrol lasted, and so on. But even when our curiosity had been satisfied, the lecturer usually rounded off his remarks by reminding us that, 'It was damned cold up there!'[73]

Lieutenant Jack Wilkinson, No. 1 School of Military Aeronautics, Reading

Some pilots were reassigned for observer training if they failed their flying training. Algernon Insall had lost all confidence in his ability to land an aircraft after a bad flying accident.

I soon found that the main function of an observer, during the training period of an RFC pusher aircraft squadron in this country, was to act as ballast. His other duties included the very simple one of starting the rotary monster, bearing the illogical name Gnome, imprisoned in its cage behind the pilot, plus that of accepting full responsibility for any error in navigation on the part of the helmsman. It was, I suppose, only natural that the newly fledged pilot, conscious of the stature conferred upon him by the embroidered wings he now wore upon his breast, should regard himself as far more infallible, when it came to pinpointing his whereabouts over strange country, than the shivering half-wit crouching in his cramped cockpit in front of him, who always appeared to be having the greatest difficulty in the handling of his ordnance survey map.[74]

2nd Lieutenant Algernon Insall, 11 Squadron, RFC

There were also air mechanics and fitters who wanted to become air crew, preferably pilots, for whom an observer status was a step further on the journey to control of the joystick. Ira Jones had managed to get himself posted for observer training when he had a potentially disastrous meeting with Charles Gordon-Bell, who had been assigned to a training role after his service in France.

I marched into [Captain Gordon-Bell's] office, saluted smartly, and announced, 'Air Mechanic Jones reporting, sir.' 'Oh, y-yes,' he said. 'Y-y-you are c-coming to be t-t-trained as an o-observer?' Having re-developed a childhood stammer under the strain of working with the howitzer batteries, I replied, 'Y-y-yes, sir.' Bell shot out of his chair, took the monocle out of his eye, grabbed his cane threateningly, and in an awful voice said: 'Y-y-you are not b-b-bloody w-well m-m-mimicking me, are you, J-Jones?' Now the more a stammerer hears another man stutter, the worse his own affliction becomes. Completely unnerved by this time, I could only gasp out: 'N-n-no, sir.' Bell glared at me suspiciously for what seemed a couple of minutes. Then he said: 'Y-y-you can g-go, now. I'll s-s-see you again.'[75]

Air Mechanic Ira Jones, 10 Squadron, RFC

By this time, Gordon-Bell's fame had spread right across the RFC and numerous stories were told of his stammer, his sense of humour and his foul language!

Gordon-Bell suffered from terrible stammering. He crashed in the country one day, and a policeman came up and said, 'Have you had an accident, sir?' Gordon-Bell said, 'N-n-n-n-no, you b-b-b-bloody f-f-f-fool, I a-a-a-always land like th-this'. He was responsible for a very famous RFC word, which is supposed to illustrate a very sharp turn. He used to call a sharp turn a 'split arse turn'! If one did anything suddenly or quickly, you did a split arse turn![76]

2nd Lieutenant Frederick Powell, Farnborough, RFC

With men such as these, the future of the RFC was in good hands.

At the Central Flying School, I remember one morning Gordon-Bell walking down the tarmac. All the pupils sitting by the shed doors in their overalls sprang to attention. As always, Gordon-Bell was followed by his two little dogs, and as he passed the pupils he stammered out in a quiet voice, 'G-g-good-morning!' The pupils saluted and said in chorus, 'Good-morning, Sir!'

Gordon-Bell stopped, screwed his eyeglass tighter into his eye, and looking at the group said, 'I w-wasn't saying g-good-morning to you, I was saying g-good-morning to the dogs, but g-good-morning all the same!'[77]

Lieutenant Harold Balfour, Central Flying School

Chapter 4

The Fokker Scourge, 1915

After the rigid discipline that I had known in the Royal Horse Artillery the free and easy way in which things were done in the RFC was very much to my liking. Although most of the pilots were regular army officers, they were all men of a different breed from what I had become accustomed to since joining the artillery. I was now in the company of individualists, some of whom, I was soon to find, could even be regarded as at least eccentrics – if not downright crazy.[1]

2nd Lieutenant William Sholto Douglas, 2 Squadron, RFC

The RFC was blossoming under the stress of war. It still performed a strategic reconnaissance role, its aircraft penetrating deep into German territory to monitor railway stations and military centres, watching for the kind of large-scale troop movements which might allow General Headquarters staff to discern the plans of their opposite numbers. But the development of photographic reconnaissance had a tremendous tactical value as it charted the minutiae of the German defences, allowing brigade, corps and divisional commanders to understand exactly what was facing them on their specific battlefront on a day-to-day basis.

Photographs were taken with a hand camera through a hole in the floor. I became rather the star photographer being very small and able to bend down, and adjust the camera, which one had to hold in one's hands. One only took about six plates, which one had to change by hand. On landing after taking photographs of things like supposed battery positions or railway junctions – one took them straight to Moore-Brabazon's office where they were developed. One waited there while they were developed to have a look at them because Brabazon might wish to make comments on the fact that one had been inaccurate in one's pointing of the camera. I always remember one day when the photographs were developed, they were the right place, but unfortunately Brabazon had superimposed on all my pictures a beautiful white horse of somebody who'd come to lunch.[2]

Lieutenant Archibald James, 16 Squadron RFC

At the heart of such developments was 1st Wing, which was commanded by Hugh Trenchard, who had at last escaped from his duties back in England to join the battle at the front. Trenchard monitored closely the progress made by his pilots. William Sholto Douglas gives us an indication of the cunning nature of Trenchard's methods.

The photographic officer in No. 3 Squadron, the one next in the line to the south of us, was another observer by the name of C.C. Darley. He was a great enthusiast in his work, and he had been able to get some good photographs. Whenever Trenchard visited our squadron, he would pull out of his pocket a bunch of Darley's photographs which he would show to me with encomiums, apparently believing that he was inciting me to better efforts. But as Darley and I had discovered in talking with each other that Trenchard used to do the same thing the other way around on his visits to No. 3 Squadron, showing Darley my best efforts, we soon agreed that the old boy was wasting his time.[3]

2nd Lieutenant William Sholto Douglas, 2 Squadron, RFC

This exponential advance in the quality of intelligence available went hand in hand with steady improvements in the capacity for effective aerial artillery observation. The wireless sets had no need for long range on the Western Front, and soon the priority for a relatively light and compact set was satisfied with the advent of the Sterling wireless. Squared, lettered and numbered maps were also issued to the artillery and RFC army cooperation squadrons to allow both gunners and aerial observers to pinpoint a target to within a few yards. But how to improve the correction of the fall of shot? Step forward Donald Lewis.

I have evolved a more elaborate system of ranging applicable chiefly to heavy siege howitzers where economy of ammunition is most important. I have a celluloid disc with circles inserted at 25, 100, 200, 300, 400 yards radius according to the scale of the map. Outside are painted the figures of a clock. The circles are lettered A to E. The disc is pinned with its centre on the target and its XII–VI diameter towards the battery firing. Shots are then signalled down according to their position on the map, C9, B2, etc. This will eliminate all error except that of map reading and I think it well worth trying. I intend to try it the next time I range the 9.2".[4]

Captain Donald Lewis, 9 Squadron, RFC

A further simplification meant the centre line between six o'clock and twelve o'clock was always to be towards true north, and there was some tinkering with the circles. But the basic principle of the 'Clock Code' was established as early as January 1915.

These notable advances by the RFC made planning of an infantry assault and the supporting artillery bombardment much easier. General Douglas Haig, commander of the British First Army, was a collegiate planner and thus called in Trenchard for a meeting at an early stage of the plotting for the Battle of Neuve Chapelle. Haig was intent on demonstrating his full acknowledgement of the importance of the RFC role – indeed, there is little doubt he was trying his best to get Trenchard 'on side'.

I tried to explain what I thought they would do in future besides reconnaissance work, how our machines would have to fight in the air against German machines and how we should have to develop machine guns and bombs. He was interested. Then he said he was going to tell me something that only three or four people in the world yet knew; in March, somewhere in the vicinity of Merville and Neuve Chapelle, we were to launch an attack on the Germans. I was not to tell anybody. He asked: 'What will you be able to do?' I explained rather badly about artillery observation, reporting to gun batteries by Morse and signal lamps, and of our early efforts to get wireless going. On the map I showed him the position of my squadrons and said what their several tasks could be. When I'd finished, he said: 'Well, Trenchard, I shall expect you to tell me before the attack whether you can fly, because on your being able to observe for the artillery, and carry out reconnaissance, the battle will partly depend. If you can't fly because of the weather, I shall probably put off the attack.'[5]

Lieutenant Colonel Hugh Trenchard, RFC

Despite everyone's best efforts, the Neuve Chapelle offensive, which commenced on 10 March 1915, was a failure. Although the salient around the village was pinched out as the assaulting infantry broke through, the attack then broke down in circumstances of total confusion. The Germans reacted swiftly and any brief opportunities for exploitation were closed down before the battle petered out after a couple more days of hard fighting.

In the spring of 1915, there were further developments in aviation. As the importance of aerial reconnaissance and artillery observation grew ever more obvious, so there was a great desire to destroy the German aircraft carrying out the same role. In truth, there was never an amicable relationship between opposing aviators: both sides had always sought to inflict pain, suffering and death on their opposite numbers – the question was how? Most aircraft were still unarmed or had only small-arms weapons.

The first time I ever encountered a German machine in the air both the pilot (Harvey-Kelly) and myself were completely unarmed. Our machine had not been climbing well, and as I was considered somewhat heavy for an observer, Harvey-Kelly told me to leave behind all unnecessary gear. I therefore left behind my carbine and ammunition. We were taking photographs of the trench system to the north of Neuve Chapelle when I suddenly espied a German two-seater about 100 yards away and just below us. The German observer did not appear to be shooting at us. There was nothing to be done. We waved a hand to the enemy and proceeded with our task. The enemy did likewise. At the time this did not appear to me in any way ridiculous – there is a bond of sympathy between all who fly, even between enemies. But afterwards just for safety's sake I always carried a carbine with me in the air. In the ensuing two or three months I had an occasional shot at a German machine. But these encounters can hardly be dignified with the name of 'fights'. If we saw an enemy machine nearby, we would fly over towards it, and fire at it some half-a-dozen rounds. We scarcely expected to shoot the enemy down; but it was a pleasant break in the monotony of reconnaissance and artillery observation. I remember being surprised one day to hear that an observer of another squadron (his name, Lascelles, sticks in my memory to this day, though I never met him), had shot down a German machine in our lines with a rifle.[6]

2nd Lieutenant William Sholto Douglas, 2 Squadron, RFC

Douglas is referring to the incident when Captain Ralph Vaughan and 2nd Lieutenant John Lascelles, in their BE2c 1669 of 4 Squadron, shot down an Aviatik on 17 April. Lascelles had fired some twenty-four rounds before fatally wounding the German pilot, causing his aircraft to plunge to the ground.

There were many wild schemes to try and secure a 'kill' – such as attempts to dangle a weight on a long cable with which to entangle an opponent's propeller. Not surprisingly, the latter failed. Some tried to drop steel darts or small incendiary bombs onto an enemy! No successes were reported. Another idea was to lower a bomb fitted with hooks to 'cling' to an opponent's aircraft before the bomb was remotely detonated. It never stood a chance of success. The real answer was to mount machine guns, and that awaited firstly improvements in aircraft lifting power, but also a realisation that the weight of the Lewis gun would be considerably reduced if they removed the radiator cooling casing which was not needed in the cold temperatures found at altitude. Everything began to change with the advent of the Vickers Fighter (FB5). This was a powerful pusher aircraft with a Lewis gun fitted for the observer in the front seat. They trickled out to the front and initially were flown by some of the 5 Squadron pilots from April 1915.

As the RFC struggled to carry out its various new tasks, there were several campaigns launched by the press and politicians back home. It was the considered opinion in some quarters that the RFC was not equipped with the 'right' aircraft and this had left them vulnerable to superior German machines. Apparently, the RFC high command should 'magic up' some new types of aircraft. Even the normally benign figure of Maurice Baring was irritated at such posturing.

About this time one of the periodical air agitations was going on in London. The worst of these agitations was that they were too late to be of any use. It is no use making an agitation for obtaining in a few days' time what it takes a year or more to make. The net result as far as we were concerned, I tabulated as follows in my diary on April 8th:

Results of air agitation:
A) Positive. Not the hastening of one bolt, turn-buckle, or split-pin.
B) Negative.
  1) General hindering of operations in France.
  2) Danger of spread of alarm and despondency among the younger personnel of the RFC.

This last factor was one which never seemed to occur to anyone in England.[7]

Captain Maurice Baring, HQ, RFC

Whatever the press might think, the real war went on in France and Flanders.

The German gas offensive launched the Second Battle of Ypres on 22 April 1915. As the Germans surged forwards into the gaping holes gas created in the Allied lines, a new role was discovered for the RFC – that of the tactical contact patrol. This was not something that anyone was really prepared for, and initial attempts were somewhat crude. On 25 April, Lanoe Hawker took off alone in his BE2c 1780 to try to determine the limits of the German advance.

We still clung on to that part of St Julien south-east of the stream which seemed to be forming our line of resistance at the moment. From here the line went north-east again and I had a very careful look at that bit of ground, circling and going over it again and again till I could make sure of the exact positions we held. It was while flying low over a big farm to the north of this bit that I received a bullet just above my left ankle that solved the problem as to who held the farm! It was remarkably painful at first and I headed for home but as I could use my foot, I turned back to deny the Germans the satisfaction of having driven me off, placed the farm carefully on the map and then turned and went home.[8]

Captain Lanoe Hawker, 6 Squadron, RFC

The RFC also attempted what became known as interdiction bombing, trying to prevent German reinforcements arriving at the front by cutting rail links – bombing stations, bridges and sidings. With just a few aircraft available, each only capable of carrying one 112lb bomb and further hampered by the lack of an effective bombsight, they were unlikely to hit or damage the targets – even without the close attentions of German anti-aircraft defences concentrated around such vital logistical centres. Bombing was not yet an effective weapon.

The French were still doing nearly all the 'heavy lifting' when it came to fighting on the Western Front. However, the British were required to launch a couple of spoiling attacks to try to support the gigantic French offensive raging like fury in the Vimy Ridge–Artois area. The first of these was the Battle of Aubers Ridge, which began on 9 May 1915. To the British pilots, the preparatory barrage seemed a stupendous affair.

Well, the great attack is proceeding; it started at 5 in the morning, and I never thought to see such a sight. I was out from 5 to 7 observing for effect for a group of batteries and had a wonderful view of the bombardment that was to commence operations. Our targets were just south-west of the Bois de Biez, and the shooting along the whole line was simply wonderful – if you can imagine the whole German line of trenches getting an absolutely continuous shower of high explosive and shrapnel, you have it! It never ceased for 2 hours, the big howitzer was in one group, and to see its shots was extraordinary. They call it 'Granny' and the 9.2 'Mother'. Well, I saw Granny hit various things, one the distillery, just on the Estaire La Bassée road between Bois de Biez and Violaines, a huge cloud of yellow smoke enveloped the whole thing after the shot and there is no more distillery! I saw it hitting Aubers, all over the place. Also, Fromelles, but what impressed me most was the continuous and never ceasing hail of shrapnel and high explosives that kept bursting right in the German trenches and on such a lovely morning, too; it was really terrible. La Bassée has been well shelled and the old church tower is no more. Everything is burning, every house, farm and cottage – the country is so pockmarked with shells that it is literally altering the whole face of the landscape! If the Germans continue to stick this bombardment, they are stout fellows. I've never dreamt of such an inferno, in my worst nightmares. It is rather wonderful come to think of it, that this is the greatest battle I suppose the world has ever seen, and surely the greatest bombardment, and I saw it from the front of the stalls, high above it all in my little old aeroplane![9]

Lieutenant Denys Corbett Wilson, 3 Squadron, RFC

The bombardment had flattered to deceive, and the attack was a dreadful failure. On the very next day, poor Denys Corbett Wilson was dead, his Morane 1872 shot down in flames by 'Archie' whilst out on another artillery observation patrol. His observer, 2nd Lieutenant Isaac Woodiwiss, was also killed.

On 10 May 1915, an amazing incident happened that can still cause chills to run down the spine of even the calmest. It occurred when Louis Strange was in combat with an Aviatik in his Martinsyde Scout 2449.

We were somewhere over Menin, and the Hun was still gaining height, though we were both near the tops of our respective ceilings. Not all the enemy aircraft were equipped with machine guns in those early days, but the German observer potted at me from the rear cockpit with a parabellum pistol, and as some of his bullets came unpleasantly close, I thought it high time to retaliate, and gave him a drum from my Lewis gun without much effect. But when I wanted to take off the empty drum and replace it with a full one, it seemed to jam, and as I was unable to remove it with one hand, I wedged the stick between my knees and tugged at the obstinate thing with both hands. After one or two fruitless efforts, I raised myself up out of my seat in order to get a better grip, and I suppose that my safety belt must have slipped down at the critical moment. Anyhow, my knees loosened their grip on the stick just as the Martinsyde, which was already climbing at its maximum angle, stalled and flicked over into a spin. As I was more than half out of the cockpit at the time, the spin threw me clear of the machine, but I still kept both my hands on the drum of the Lewis gun. Only a few seconds previously I had been cursing because I could not get that drum off, but now I prayed fervently that it would stay on for ever. I knew it might come off any moment, however, and as its edge was cutting my fingers badly, I had to get a firmer hold of something more reliable. The first thing I thought of was the top of the centre section strut, which at that time was behind and below the Lewis gun, but as the machine was now flying upside down, I had sufficient wits left to realise that it was behind and above me, though where it was exactly, I could not tell. Dare I let go the drum with one hand and make a grab for it? Well, there was nothing else for it but to take the risk; I let go and found the strut all right, and then I released my other hand and gripped the strut on the other side. I was then in a more comfortable position, and at least I felt rather more part of my machine than I had done in my original attitude. My chin was rammed against the top plane, beside the gun, while my legs were waving about in empty air. The Martinsyde was upside down in a flat spin, and from my precarious position the only thing I could see was the propeller – which seemed unpleasantly close to my face – the town of Menin, and the adjacent countryside. Menin and its environs were revolving at an impossible angle – apparently above me and getting larger with every turn. I began to wonder what sort of a spot I was going to crash on. Then I got angry and cursed myself for a fool for wasting time on such idle speculations, while at the same time it dawned on me that my only chance of righting the machine lay in getting my feet into the cockpit. If I could manage it, I knew that I was bound to fall automatically into the cockpit when the machine came over. I kept on kicking upwards behind me until at last I got first one foot and then the other hooked inside the cockpit. Somehow, I got the stick between my legs again and jammed on full aileron and elevator; I do not know exactly what happened then, but somehow the trick was done. The machine came over the right way up, and I fell off the top plane into my seat with a bump. I grabbed at the stick with both hands and thanked my lucky stars. I had only a very hazy idea myself as to what had really happened, but I felt happy to be alive, and thought it simply marvellous that I was still able to control the machine.[10]

Captain Louis Strange, 6 Squadron, RFC

It had truly been the most incredible escape.

The RFC performed valuable work during the Aubers Ridge fighting, but there was a continued problem in attempts to carry out contact patrols, designed to see what was happening and report back to headquarters to allow the appropriate tactical interventions and artillery support bombardments. The pilots and observers were still stymied by their inability to see what was really happening on the ground, or indeed to get messages back to the right place at the right time. This failure would be repeated in the equally disastrous Battle of Festubert launched on 15 May, as was glumly recorded by Archibald James.

I was sent out to observe the progress of the battle, so far as I could from 5,000 feet. It had been arranged that, in order to let those in the air see how far they'd got, the most advanced troops would from time to time put out white strips of cloth about eight foot long and a foot wide. To my astonishment when I arrived at almost first light the whole of the battlefront was covered with white strips. What in fact had happened was that the methodical Germans had lined their trenches with wooden boards. Our bombardment when it hit a trench blew out a number of planks which scattered round and were quite indistinguishable from the white strips the troops were supposed to put out.[11]

Lieutenant Archibald James, 16 Squadron, RFC

Contact patrols would remain a problem throughout the war.

In the summer of 1915, Brigadier General Sir David Henderson was posted back to the War Office, and in his place Hugh Trenchard was promoted to brigadier in command of the RFC on the Western Front. This was the man who would guide the RFC through most of the rest of the war. His assistant was Captain Maurice Baring. It seemed an unnatural partnership – the bluff, inarticulate Scot and the cultured, amusing literary gentleman – but somehow it worked perfectly.

When General Trenchard took over, the RFC consisted of three wings and a headquarters. The first thing he wanted me to do was to make notes for him. The general's system of note-making was like this. He visited squadrons or depots or aircraft parks as the case might be and took someone with him who made notes – for the next four years the someone was myself – of anything they wanted. In the evening the notes used to be put on his table typed, and then he would send for the various staff officers who dealt with the matters referred to in the notes and discuss them. The first thing he would ascertain was if the matter mentioned in the note had a real foundation; for instance, whether a squadron which complained that they were short of propellers had not in fact received a double dose the day before. If the need or the complaint or the request was found to be justified and reasonable, he would proceed to hasten its execution and see that the necessary steps were taken. If the requests were found to be idle or baseless, the squadron or the petitioner in question would be informed at once. But where the general differed from many capable men was in this: he was never satisfied with investigating a request, or a grievance, or a need or a suggestion. After having dealt with it he never let the matter rest, but in a day or two's time he would insist on hearing the sequel. He would find out whether Squadron 'B' had received its split pin, or what Mr. 'A.' had answered from England when asked for it. This did not conduce to our repose, but it did further the efficiency of the RFC.[12]

Captain Maurice Baring, HQ, RFC

Trenchard was often incapable of expressing himself clearly – and the following illustrates that perhaps it was as well he did not try too often.

I'm not asking you to do anything I wouldn't do myself. Just because I'm condemned to ride about in a big Rolls-Royce and sit out the fighting in a chair, you mustn't think I don't understand.[13]

    Brigadier General Hugh Trenchard, Headquarters, RFC

But, by the end, Baring almost worshipped his cantankerous master.

At least you cannot overestimate the pedestal I put him on! He was and is one of the few *big men of the world* and incomparably finer and bigger than anyone I have met in my life in any one of the services, army, navy, air, or politics, in any country; and a big brain, lightning intuition as well as his obstreperous overwhelming character, personality, and drive.[14]

    Captain Maurice Baring, HQ, RFC

Trenchard had already formed a close working relationship with General Douglas Haig, commanding the First Army, something that would prove invaluable for both men throughout the war.

New squadrons and new aircraft were continuing to arrive at the front. On 25 July 1915, 11 Squadron, the first proper scout squadron, which was entirely equipped with Vickers Fighters, arrived at the front. The machine's slow speed and limited armament meant it was already approaching obsolescence, a process that was accelerated by the near-simultaneous arrival of the first few examples of the famous Fokker E.1 Monoplane. As an aircraft, the Fokker was not particularly impressive, being similar to the Morane Parasol, but it had a machine gun with an interrupter gear to allow it to fire through the arc of the propeller, so that to aim the gun you aimed the whole aircraft at the target. At first, the potential of the Fokker was rather lost as it was originally used to escort German reconnaissance aircraft. Indeed, on 11 August, one hapless Fokker was unfortunate to encounter the redoubtable Captain Lanoe Hawker and his trusty observer, Lieutenant N. Clifton, flying in a FE2a 4227, a new two-seater pusher that as the FE2b would ultimately replace the Vickers Fighter.

We had not seen any Hun monoplanes, and when [the Fokker] appeared about 1,000 feet above us, we both thought it was one of No. 1 [Squadron]'s Moranes from Bailleul, until he started shooting, [when] Lanoe kept us in as steep a turn as the F.E. could manage with the other going round on the outside. He got fed up and straightened out, by luck right in front of us and even I couldn't miss him. The earlier one that day I think must have been very close to getting us, as it was the only time I have actually heard the bullets go past, they sounded just in front of my face. I well remember the abuse we had to stomach following the confirmation of the Fokker we got over Lille, when it transpired that this came from [his brother] Tyrell [Hawker]![15]

    Lieutenant N. Clifton, 6 Squadron, RFC

The Fokker was not yet the scourge it would become. Like every new weapon of war, it had to be assessed and the best tactics devised to maximise its potential.

* * *

One of the new squadrons arriving was 12 Squadron, which was mainly equipped with the BE2c – a marginal improvement on the BE2a. One of their young observers, Raymond Money, left an excellent account which encapsulates the spirit of a squadron getting ready for war in September 1915. As an observer, he did not fly out to France but accompanied the squadron transport by sea.

> After two or three days in Le Havre we started on the long journey across Northern France to St. Omer. The motor transport of a squadron was very considerable, consisting of touring car, six Crossley tenders and six Leyland lorries, if I remember rightly, and our three-day journey in the heat and dust of late August was a tremendous affair. Of course, the lorries limited the pace to not more than 20 miles an hour, and the cloud of dust which the column raised could be seen behind us for miles. The French had not yet become blasé about English forces, and we met with quite a warm welcome at every stoppage. We paid for everything, probably fairly dearly, and I don't think I've ever eaten so many grapes. I'm afraid we five younger observers were a bit of a nuisance to the C.O. Windsor and Whitehead were the ringleaders, and at each stopping place from Le Havre onwards we investigated the towns, hotels, shops and cafés like a pack of terriers. We treated the war, and particularly our manner of going to it, as a kind of glorified Cook's Tour.[16]
> 2nd Lieutenant Raymond Money, 12 Squadron, RFC

Once safely *in situ* at St Omer, they began to prepare their BE2cs for action. Even this was an excuse for merry banter, or bullying, depending on perspective.

> Every stone made a difference, and whether we should carry a Lewis gun or not, and, if so, how few drums of ammunition, was considered on every occasion. Heavy observers were anathema, and I remember seeing Lees send Windsor back one day to take off some of his heavy flying clothing. This was sheer bullying, of course; but people got a lot of fun out of bullying Windsor, who was one of the most engaging, amusing buffoons I've ever met.[17]
> 2nd Lieutenant Raymond Money, 12 Squadron, RFC

The officers' mess was soon established and a vigorous social life ensued.

> A middle-aged captain who had spent several years in the West African Frontier Force lived with us – and was the means of our free drinks system coming to an end. Until his arrival all our wines and spirits were common property, and

appeared on our mess bills as a general charge just like messing, breakages, etc. We were all fairly young and had not cultivated a taste for heavy drinking. In spite of this, we were very cheerful – rather noisily so as far as I can remember. The only times we broke out were on the comparatively rare occasions of a guest night. We found that our West African friend had altogether different ideas concerning alcohol. In addition to doing himself quite well on sherry, port, and liqueurs, he consumed about a bottle and a half of whisky each day. So we had to start the chit system. 'West Africa' was quite an amusing companion from 6pm to 10pm, and told us many tall stories of natives, to repeat which here I am told would lower the tone, but after about 10pm he would relapse into speechlessness – a condition in which he remained until luncheon the following day.[18]

2nd Lieutenant Raymond Money, 12 Squadron, RFC

Apparently, being an observer on a dawn mission with this august gentleman was a miserable affair.

First up, the squadron carried out a series of familiarisation flights to enable the pilots and observers to get their bearings. Money was not that impressed by what he saw as he flew over the front at about, 1,000 feet, low enough to come under some ground fire.

At last, I could see the lines, and even distinguish those of the Germans from our own, because Spratt flew along them for a minute or two. They looked ridiculously close together and at the same time ridiculously inadequate. Was that all that was reducing the war to static impotence? Yet when one noticed the two, or sometimes three, lines of support trenches, one thought again. We were being fired at pretty heavily by rifles and machine-guns, and one or two bullets came through the planes. I happened to see one. It looked as though some invisible person had just stuck a big finger through the fabric. Spratt sheered off to our own side of the lines, and I thought it was quite time, too. I had not come to this war to get shot![19]

2nd Lieutenant Raymond Money, 12 Squadron, RFC

Later, their first long-distance reconnaissance missions began. Here, Money was introduced to the pleasure of 'Archie'.

I did a reconnaissance to Valenciennes with Lees a few days later. It was an unpleasant trip. 'Archie' fairly smothered us, and as we couldn't get higher than four thousand feet for some reason or other, even the field guns and machine guns had a go at us. The war seemed to have ceased in every direction except ours, and it seemed grossly unfair because we couldn't hit back. I felt like a huge pheasant flying frightfully slowly over all the game shots in the country.[20]

2nd Lieutenant Raymond Money, 12 Squadron, RFC

Perhaps more terrifying, after one long-range mission, Money had the doubtful pleasure of a censorious interview with an irate Trenchard.

I did a long reconnaissance to Brussels with one of the 'B' Flight pilots. He worked out a compass course, allowing for the wind as far as we could judge it, and said he would take me there over a layer of clouds disposed at about 5,000 feet. I thought this was a splendid idea. It saved me trouble and meant a comfortable 'Archie-less' journey. At about the time when we should have been over Brussels, the clouds began to break up most conveniently, leaving large gaps, and through one of these we saw a large city which the pilot took for Brussels. Unfortunately, a very unusual physical feature was prominent; one canal crossing another one at right angles. I looked at the map. Did one canal cross another at right angles immediately west of the city? It did not. But a hasty search discovered that exactly such a feature found itself at Liege! I had great difficulty in convincing the pilot that we were so far off our course, but eventually we got back to Brussels, and I counted rolling-stock on the railways, and endeavoured to find signs of military interest, a search in which I was very unsuccessful. We arrived home intact with only 5 minutes' petrol left. I had to go down to headquarters with my report and met with a very chilly reception. It was my first interview with Trenchard, and I understood why his nickname was 'BOOM'! He was expressing his disapproval of someone in no uncertain terms, and his voice did 'BOOM' – throughout the chateau! All he said to me was, 'H'm, you don't seem to have seen much!' but I came away cursing myself for a fool for not having given my imagination a certain amount of play.[21]

2nd Lieutenant Raymond Money, 12 Squadron, RFC

Being in such close quarters with the irascible Trenchard could be awkward, as one of their pilots, the irrepressible Louis Strange, recalled somewhat glumly.

Unfortunately, General Trenchard's memory was a bit too accurate for my liking, for as soon as he set eyes on me, he asked what I was doing out there again when he imagined that he had sent me home for a squadron. He told me I must go home and made a note of the matter; I did not think he was serious at the time but was soon destined to find him a man of his word. My first reconnaissance in No. 12 Squadron, with Lieutenant Garrod as my observer, took me all round the old hunting ground I knew so well. I was delighted to fly over Fives Aerodrome and drop my visiting cards – in the shape of some twenty small bombs – on my former opposite numbers. Just as we were making for home, however, something went wrong with the engine; I thought that my first flight in this squadron was going to be my last, as that silly old engine kicked up an infernal row, while the vibration was positively appalling every time I was tempted to open the throttle. Somehow, I managed to nurse the machine to within 3 or 4 miles of our lines, and then, realising that at our low flying height it was neck or nothing, I pushed the throttle wide open. We thumped and banged our way along and got home all right.[22]

Captain Louis Strange, 12 Squadron, RFC

Strange developed an amusing perspective of the trials and tribulations of these long-range reconnaissance flights.

In war it is entirely your own fault if you run out of petrol when coming home against a head wind after a 4 or 5 hours' reconnaissance, or if you fail to come down on the right spot after a couple of hours cloud flying. It is your own fault if enemy aircraft spot you first, and it is likewise your own fault if after spotting a hostile machine you get shot up by another formation streaking down from out of the sun just when you have your opposite number nicely sighted. It is, furthermore, your fault if you allow your squadron to drift too far down wind in a dogfight and leave its machines with no margin of petrol for emergencies when they have to fight their way home again. It is your fault if you have nowhere to make a landing when the engine fails just after you have taken off; in the event of a forced landing your machine is a glider that should take you down safely on any possible landing place. It is your fault – well, it is a golden rule to assume that whatever goes wrong, is your fault. You may save yourself a lot of trouble if you act accordingly.[23]

Captain Louis Strange, 12 Squadron, RFC

It was not long before Strange became 'unstuck' when Trenchard spotted him on the airfield.

A few days later the squadron was allotted a Bristol Scout, much to my delight, as I imagined I was going to fly it instead of crawling about the air in a BE2c. I was just fitting it up with a Lewis gun when General Trenchard came along, with Maurice Baring, his A.D.C. 'I thought I told you, Baring, to remind me to send Strange home?' he began; and then, turning to me, he boomed out, 'Go home at once, Strange!' 'Yes, Sir!' I replied, saluting smartly. 'Go home at once, Strange,' he repeated; 'In that machine, now!' His visit occurred about three in the afternoon. The wind was 35 miles per hour on the ground, while the machine to which he pointed was a dilapidated Maurice Farman. All the same I could do nothing but salute again and take him at his word. I therefore gave orders for the machine to be started up, and, without bothering to look for a helmet or goggles, got up into the nacelle and staggered off towards the west. I had, of course, no intention of flying to England that night, as it would have been an absolute impossibility. When I had climbed up to 1,000 feet, I found the wind far too strong to make any headway at all, so I just throttled back and drifted slowly across the aerodrome. When I thought I was safely out of sight down east, I turned down wind and landed on No. 6's aerodrome at Abeele.[24]

Captain Louis Strange, 12 Squadron, RFC

The presence of the RFC headquarters at St Omer was also a temptation to the Germans, who launched several bombing missions on the airfield. The BE2c then proved sadly inadequate in an interception role.

They came over at heights varying from 10–14,000 feet, and as it was as much as a B.E. with observer and Lewis gun could do to get to 10,000 feet in about an hour and a half, we were remarkably unsuccessful in bringing them to combat. More than once, one of our machines landed at the end of its three-hour patrol, and a bored, cold, and hungry observer was eagerly asked, 'Did you see the Hun?' or 'Did you have a scrap?' When the disgusted reply was given, 'What Hun?', he would learn that a German had been over and dropped bombs. On one occasion we were very unpopular with a certain general on headquarters staff, whose early morning effort at the bottom of the G.H.Q. chateau garden had been suddenly interrupted by a salvo of machine gun fire from the air. We preferred to take his caustic comments on our failure to see the German machine in silence, rather than admit that a numb-fingered observer, firing a few rounds through his Lewis gun to prevent the oil from freezing, had let the gun muzzle describe an arc like that of a garden hose.[25]

2nd Lieutenant Raymond Money, 12 Squadron, RFC

One can but admire the tactful nature of the obfuscation of the exact nature of the nameless general's 'early morning effort' at the bottom of the garden.

* * *

The RFC was governed by the necessity of supporting in every possible way the operations of the BEF on the ground. That was its function. In turn, the BEF under Sir John French was harnessed to the overall plans of the French Army, the dominant partner on the Western Front. Joffre was planning a gargantuan offensive on the Artois and Champagne fronts, while the British were required to attack at Loos, a small part of a much bigger plan, but still the 'Big Push' as far as the BEF was concerned. As they prepared, incremental advances continued to be made in both aerial photography and artillery observation. One example of this was the advent of a system of engaging important – yet fleeting – targets of opportunity. This was an early form of the 'Zone Call' whereby through the signal 'JJ', coupled with a target square location on the map, the massed batteries on a corps front would be allowed to smother that location with shells. As was already becoming routine, the whole of the Loos area was photographed, and prospective targets identified. One new pilot who had just joined 16 Squadron was thoroughly briefed.

The duties of the Royal Flying Corps were announced in a secret document accompanied by a very secret map. The map was handed round to be seen and initialled by each officer. It showed the general scheme of the forthcoming campaign, the points to be attacked after the success of the first great blow at Loos. The time and date of each further advance were marked, the distances of the objectives growing once the trench lines had been passed. And after the trenches – open warfare! Red lines and arrows showed the roads by which our transport would advance. The red lines ran eastward for miles before meeting a vertical black stroke south of Lille, representing the first position at which the enemy might hope to make a stand against our terrific onslaught. Thence dotted red lines with smaller arrows, dates with question marks in brackets showed that the great advance was to be pressed still farther. The roads to Brussels were shown. 'Brussels by Christmas!' it was said. My impatience grew tremendously. I must hurry or the war would be over before I could win my spurs in the air. I need not have worried.[26]

Lieutenant Duncan Grinnell-Milne, 16 Squadron, RFC

However, the bumptious Duncan Grinnell-Milne did not fit well into 16 Squadron, which was run by the somewhat staid figure of Major Hugh Dowding and manned by a coterie of pilots who seemed old and stuck in their ways.

The real trouble with me in this squadron was that I did not in the least understand the others. If I did anything good, they seemed to regard it as impudence; if I did nothing, they did not speak to me, or so much as acknowledge my existence. It would, I think, have pleased them most had I been sent away in disgrace. That would have given them something to talk about. One of the pilots had developed piles. He was very shy and ashamed about it himself. But it became the standing joke of the squadron. Everyone sniggered whenever he came near, and coarse innuendoes were continually made in his hearing. My own troubles seemed much smaller by comparison. I was glad that I had not got piles![27]

Lieutenant Duncan Grinnell-Milne, 16 Squadron, RFC

The RFC performed well during the Battle of Loos, which commenced on 25 September 1915, but some of its functions were hampered by poor visibility, which rendered useless efforts to monitor the infantry progress by contact patrols. As the battle raged on, the weather worsened, with both fog and rain dogging the aviators' efforts. Soon it was apparent that the offensive had – in the broadest sense – failed on both the British and French fronts. The next phase of fighting at Loos was largely concerned with resisting the inevitable German counter-attacks.

October saw the real advent of the much-vaunted 'Fokker scourge' as the Fokker EI was augmented at the front by the EII and EIII variants. They were still not overly numerous, but the Germans were blessed with a few influential pilots who, over the coming months, would develop a whole new language of aerial warfare, perfecting the role of the scout. Max Immelmann and Oswald Boelcke were the best known, twin aces who unleashed the Fokker scourge: diving down out of the sun or clouds to secure surprise, attacking from behind to get a quick victory before their opponents could react. Boelcke was also at the forefront of developing the first formation attacks, with one Fokker acting as 'point', engaging an enemy, whilst two more Fokkers protected his 'tail'. The 'Immelmann Turn' allowed a Fokker pilot to go into a half loop, before rolling out while inverted, to leave him still able to fire at his victim, whilst having gained a small height advantage.

One account by Immelmann of his success in shooting down a Vickers Fighter 5462 flown by Captain Charles Darley of 11 Squadron, with his observer Lieutenant Reginald Slade, over Cambrai on 26 October, gives us an idea of what the RFC was facing.

I had just climbed to 3,500 when I saw an enemy airman fly over the lines by Arras and make for Cambrai. I let him fly on eastward for a while. Then I took up the pursuit, hiding behind his tail all the time. I followed him for about a quarter of an hour in this fashion. My fingers were itching to shoot, but I controlled myself and withheld my fire until I was within 60 metres of him. I could plainly see the observer in the front seat peering out downward. 'Knack-knack-knack!' went my gun. Fifty rounds, and then a long flame shot out of his engine. Another fifty rounds at the pilot. Now his fate was sealed. He went down in long spirals to land. Almost every bullet of my first series went home. Elevator, rudder, wings, engine, tank and control wires were shot up. The pilot (Darley) had a bullet in the right upper arm. I also shot his right thumb away. The machine had received forty hits. The observer (Slade) was unwounded. His machine gun was in perfect working order, but he had not fired a single shot. So complete was the surprise I sprung on him.[28]

Leutnant Max Immelmann, 62 Section, German Air Service

The Fokker threat made the shortcomings of the BE2c even more apparent. Ira Jones recalled one aerial fight that exemplified the difficulties of the British trying to fight an agile opponent with seemingly everything against them.

Now, there were four socket mountings on the B.E., intended to cover a wide field of fire. To get a shot at the enemy when his pilot was outmanoeuvred, the observer had to keep changing the Lewis gun from one socket to another. If a plane got under your belly, none of the sockets was any good. You just couldn't get at him. Seeing this blighter, and being unable to do anything about it, was more than I could stand. I yanked the gun out of the rear socket, leaned over the right side of the cockpit and, holding the Lewis like a rifle, let go with a burst. I had reckoned, however, without the recoil of the gun and the effect of the slipstream on an insecurely held weapon. Before I had let off twenty rounds, the gun slipped out of my gloved hands. I shall never forget the look of horrified surprise on O'Hara Wood's face when he saw our only gun sailing down past the Fokker. My own feelings were beyond description. To say I felt naked is understating the fact. The Hun must have seen the gun whizz past him. I shall never know whether he was one of the rare enemy sportsmen or merely stunned by surprise. To our astonishment, he broke off the action. We never saw him again. All the way home, as my pilot slithered the aircraft from side to side to prevent a surprise attack, my thoughts were of the direst. Instead of the coveted observer's wing, I was much more likely to get a court-martial. To my relief, when O'Hara Wood got out of the plane, he took one look at my woebegone face and burst out laughing.[29]

Air Mechanic Ira Jones, 10 Squadron, RFC

*   *   *

Over on the Ypres front, one young pilot had begun to make a reputation for himself while flying a Vickers Fighter with 5 Squadron in a series of combats, accompanied by his trusty observer, Aircraftman J. Shaw. One such scrap had occurred on 19 September in their Vickers Fighter 1651.

I was flying one day on one of these patrols, a little bit to the east of Ypres. I saw an Aviatik. I was higher than he was, which was quite unusual in those days, so I dived down towards him. I shouted to my gunner, and he, being a very good shot, got him. It started to swerve down, and down, and down, and down! I was naturally anxious to see whether it crashed. I was fighting with the Vickers Fighter to try and keep my wing out of the way so that I could watch the German, see whether he had fallen on the ground or not, but I could not. In desperation, I said, 'All right, you brute, you want to go to the right! Come round!' I swung round on a bank and just coming up on my tail was this enormous great aeroplane – two tails. I told the gunner to stick his gun pointing upwards and just keep his finger on the trigger so that I aimed the machine underneath the nacelle. To my intense delight we must have hit him, because two tails went down in a slow spiral and crashed at a racecourse just behind the German lines.[30]

Lieutenant Frederick Powell, 5 Squadron, RFC

Not long afterwards, Powell had a very lucky escape when he became obsessed with shooting down a German two-seater until he realised, somewhat belatedly, that he had gone too far over the German lines and would have to break off the action before he ran out of fuel. This was easier said than done.

I thought, 'I'm going to have a breakfast of sauerkraut unless I break away!' I waited until I thought the gunner was not paying attention, and immediately stuck my nose down, came onto a vertical bank – and at that moment he fired. He hit nearly everything on the aeroplane except me. He burst the petrol tank and all my lovely streamlined wires went – I had to come back. I was then at about 5,000 feet and quite a long way over the lines. I had to fly in a straight line on a glide with no engine. I prayed to God that the Boche would not turn round and have a go at me, because I was completely powerless. I got back just over the lines and landed in a small field by a battery of the Royal Artillery. I was met by the battery commander who said, 'You bastard!' 'Why?' He said, 'We've been two days digging in! Now the Boche have seen you land they'll put their guns on this spot and we'll have to dig out and move away again! Thank you!'[31]

Lieutenant Frederick Powell, 5 Squadron, RFC

Shortly before, in September 1915, Robert Lorraine had been posted as a flight commander to 5 Squadron. He would now once again be a pilot. On 26 October, he and his observer, Lieutenant Eric Lubbock, were flying in their Vickers Fighter 5459 when they sighted a German aircraft about 4 miles away. They were soon engaged in a spirited duel.

I had asked Lubbock to hold his fire till I gave him the order, for I meant to engage at the closest possible quarters. As we drew near to the German, approaching each other nose to nose, I pretended to outclimb him. He opened fire at about 400 yards, and I stood my machine nearly on its tail to mislead him into thinking I was trying to gain the uppermost position, and so lure him on.[32]

Captain Robert Lorraine, 5 Squadron, RFC

At last, they were in the right position.

We both opened fire at about 50 yards. I fired again at about 25 yards, firing twenty-six rounds, and then my machine [gun] jammed. I heard Lorraine give a great shout but felt neither fear nor triumph. Then our machine turned downwards. As I fired my last shot, I had seen the German turn down. I knew that if he got below us my machine gun was the only one that could fire at him, so I worked away trying to unjam it. We were diving, I [was] standing almost on the front of the body.[33]

Lieutenant Eric Lubbock, 5 Squadron, RFC

Lorraine seems to have handled the Vickers Fighter well in the combat that ensued.

I quickly dived, passing just below him with about 5 feet between my upper plane and his wheels, firing from both guns meanwhile, continuous fire with the enemy pilot as target. Directly I had passed under him, I turned and found him diving steeply. I dived after him, re-opening fire from both guns, which jammed. At one moment my dive became so vertical that Lubbock, who had released himself from the strap that bound him to the seat, so as to have freer movement to work his gun, was almost thrown out of the machine. I continued to dive, hoping to fire, when I saw the enemy crash behind our front lines. By this time, I was about 60 feet above the ground, and had to redress the machine from the dive into horizontal flight – an operation which is not without considerable danger, as the strain thrown on the wings under these conditions is very severe.[34]

Captain Robert Lorraine, 5 Squadron, RFC

The mad dive brought them under fire from German machine guns on the ground. It had been a close-run thing, for in the freezing cold, both their Lewis guns had failed them. Then a new German aircraft appeared at about 9,000 feet. Having wrenched the Vickers Fighter out of the dive, Lorraine did not hesitate but began to climb up to engage this new adversary. Lubbock realised that somehow, he had to get the Lewis guns working again.

Both our guns – Lorraine's and mine – had jammed at the same moment, I spent another 5 minutes unjamming Lorraine's gun, and finally got both guns working. We saw another enemy coming in the distance, and Lorraine went all out to climb and attack, while I put my stiff and aching hands in my mouth, praying for sufficient life to come back to them – they were frozen. Then our engine stopped and we were helpless, so we turned and glided homewards. Unable to reach the aerodrome, we landed in a ploughed field, a beautiful landing.[35]

Lieutenant Eric Lubbock, 5 Squadron, RFC

The strain of the near-vertical dive, followed by the sudden climb, had been too much for their engine. Sceptics at the squadron might have speculated that this was the only good landing Lorraine ever managed – he was still a renowned ham-fisted pilot. Lorraine and Lubbock then went to visit the crashed German aircraft that they had shot down.

The luckless Boche had fallen 20 yards behind our front-line trench. The pilot was shot through the stomach; the observer, a boy of seventeen, only had his head grazed. In spite of his fall, he will be all right, but yesterday he was crying and absolutely nerve-broken. No wonder, poor thing. The pilot was dead before they could get him away. The German observer says he was given to understand that we tortured all our prisoners and wondered when it was going to be over. He was also much surprised to hear that he was going to be taken to England, as the German Navy has control of all the seas, and England is completely cut off! Now one can understand why they go on fighting.[36]

Lieutenant Eric Lubbock, 5 Squadron, RFC

The two men had very different reactions to the scene.

> I was very elated at the result of the combat and somewhat shocked to find Lubbock in tears. 'Just think of his mother,' he said. 'I hate this killing business!' 'Think of your mother,' I said. 'You can't win wars by weeping over the enemy's dead!'[37]
>
> Captain Robert Lorraine, 5 Squadron, RFC

Archibald James, previously an observer, had been sent back to England to learn how to fly. He had then been posted to 5 Squadron, where it is fair to say that he and Lorraine were as chalk and cheese. James was somewhat pompous, reacting badly to Lorraine's larger-than-life character.

> By the time I got to No. 5 Squadron Robert Lorraine had completely lost his nerve. Many of the pre-war fliers regarded the aeroplane as such a delicate instrument that they didn't like combat use. Robert had one success for which he'd been given the Military Cross when – with a brilliant observer called Eric Lubbock – they met a German and shot him down. It was on this achievement that Robert had lived ever after. He used to spend hours sitting in his aeroplane running the engine, no doubt imagining himself engaged in successful combats. He was such an actor that there was no such thing as Lorraine – there was only the man acting the part, which he happened to be cast in at that moment. When he was a flying officer he was just a jolly flying officer. When he became a flight commander he immediately dressed as he thought a flight commander would dress and became much more pompous. When the mistake was made of promoting him to a squadron he became quite intolerable because he didn't know how a major in real life would behave. So he acted as he supposed a major would behave, which was quite intolerable. He drove people to distraction and nearly to mutiny. He had to be sacked.[38]
>
> Captain Archibald James, 5 Squadron, RFC

Far less censorious was Frederick Powell, who by this time had been allotted to fly the FE8 scout – his pride and joy – which had been assigned to 5 Squadron. It was a single-seater pusher armed with a single Lewis gun, and capable of some 94mph with a service ceiling of about 14,500 feet. Powell did not doubt Lorraine's courage, but he certainly seems to have endorsed doubts over his piloting skills – accusing him of holding the joystick 'like a barmaid pulls a pint'.

> When it came my turn to go on leave, I went and asked the C.O. that no one should fly the FE8 while I was away. 'I can't promise you that,' he said. 'But no one will fly it except Lorraine!' That was enough for me. I did not go on leave. The C.O. thought I was extraordinarily keen. Nothing of the kind, I couldn't bear the machine – the pride of my life – to be mishandled by Lorraine.[39]
>
> Lieutenant Frederick Powell, 5 Squadron, RFC

Time passed and he once again reached the top of the leave roster. Clearly, Powell had gained in experience, and this time he came up with a clever ruse.

> I stayed out until I was due to go on leave again. We had more casualties then, so it didn't take quite so long before I was due again. The second time, I went to my rigger, and I said, 'Look Shaw, this machine is now "soggy" with castor oil. Take it all down straight away tomorrow morning first thing, strip all the fabric off, put the new fabric on, re-dope it. Don't hurry! Take ten days!' I went on my leave and when I came back it was ready for tests![40]
> Lieutenant Frederick Powell, 5 Squadron, RFC

In his interview recorded with the Imperial War Museum (IWM) years later, Frederick Powell explains his decision.

> At that time of the war an aeroplane and its pilot were indivisible. They weren't swapped about. No pilot went and flew another pilot's aircraft. They were guarded as jealously as one's girl-friend! They weren't shared at all![41]
> Lieutenant Frederick Powell, 5 Squadron, RFC

It is chastening to realise that many RFC pilots were too young to have had real girlfriends.

*   *   *

Whilst admiring the deeds of the men in the air, we must not forget the hard graft of the ground crews. As the demands grew on the RFC, so more strain was put on the limited number of aircraft, which, after all, were hardly the sturdiest of machines in the first place.

> My main job was engine-fitter, to look after the engine, see that the fuel and everything was in working order and properly adjusted. When I thought that that engine had done sufficiently long-running I'd just say to the pilot, 'I'll change this engine when you come down!' We took this engine out and we put it at the back of the hangar – took one from there and put it in the aircraft. As soon as that was installed properly and tried, then we all got together, any engine-fitters – sometimes a rigger if they weren't busy – we'd pull the engine [in the hangar] to pieces, check it up, examine it, and any part that we thought wanted renewing, we'd renew it, because we had the spares. There'd be a different engine in the same aircraft – four or five different engines in it during its lifetime. Then the fabric might be badly patched or badly damaged with the oil and petrol – perhaps that had been re-covered three or four times. Then a longeron might have been shot away – that would have been replaced. You couldn't really say how long an aircraft lasted, but we still painted the same

number on the aircraft after we'd done a big job on it! Very often we had an aircraft which was officially credited with about 120 hours' flying time, but the only thing that had actually done that 120 hours would be the number on the rudder, and that had been renewed several times.[42]

Air Mechanic Samuel Saunders, 1 Squadron, RFC

To the slightly more modern mind, this has much in common with Trigger's everlasting broom,[43] unchanging except for several new broom heads and a few new broom handles!

Another air mechanic, James McCudden, was pressed into action more and more often as a makeshift observer, all this in addition to his duties as part of the ground crew. He certainly showed a somewhat ruthless side to his character when his billets were invaded at night.

One thing that annoyed us intensely was the battalions of mice who nightly executed manoeuvres on the floor of our room. I therefore applied my inventive genius and constructed a wonderfully effective mouse-trap. We three took it in turns to inspect the trap every five minutes or so, and if there was a mouse in it, splash it went in an oil-drum half full of water, and for the next few minutes we would listen to the mice doing breast and overarm strokes in the oil-drum until the splashing finally subsided.[44]

Air Mechanic James McCudden, 3 Squadron, RFC

He would soon turn his attentions to the Germans.

* * *

The urge to drop bombs on the Germans was still strong within the RFC. Thus, after minimal training on the rudimentary bombsights, bomb racks were fitted to the BE2c which would just about carry two 112lb bombs. The men of 16 Squadron were to launch a raid on the Don Junction railway station behind German lines on the morning of 27 November 1915. As they flew over their target, Duncan Grinnell-Milne noticed that the bombs dropped from 9,000–10,000 feet were missing their target by large margins and pelting the fields on either side of the railway tracks. He decided to attack from a much lower altitude and thus dived down. However, the disadvantage of attacking at a lower altitude soon became all too apparent.

It did not seem worthwhile going to below 3,000 feet, since 'Archie' was becoming very excited and ground machine gunners were adding to the racket. Approaching the junction with the engine still throttled down I could also hear the uneven popping and crackling of rifle fire – heavier than usual, it seemed. Peering over the side, I could at first see nothing to warrant so much noise. The railway station was a bit knocked about and appeared to be deserted. A short distance out of it, on a curve well away from the junction a train was standing motionless, the engine blowing off steam. Beside it there were many agitated black dots. A troop train! The men had disembarked, and it was from them that the rifle fire was coming, machine-gun fire now as well. The cracking of bullets was getting louder and more frequent; staring down I had forgotten that I was gliding steadily lower, but all at once the bumpiness of the air, the hot fire from the ground, 'Archie' and the thought of bombs falling from above, combined to bring on something approaching panic. To use the sight was out of the question; my one idea was to get rid of the two bombs without delay. Before I knew it, I was over the station. No time to waste; I pulled both release handles. The bombs dropped off. Watching closely, I followed them down to the ground with anxious eyes. Both missed the station – of course! The first one fell in a roadway not far from a level-crossing, but far enough to be quite harmless. A flash and a big puff of smoke from the second bomb appeared in the courtyard of a house twenty yards from the railway line and about two hundred yards from the station. My aim – from which I had expected such wonderful results – had proved to be quite hopeless. Bomb-dropping under fire was not as easy as I had thought![45]

Lieutenant Duncan Grinnell-Milne, 16 Squadron, RFC

Indeed not.

*　*　*

As 1915 drew to a close, despite a certain amount of concern within the RFC and a frenzied clamour amongst the political classes back home in the UK, the Fokker scourge was never a really serious threat to the vital work of the RFC. The number of casualties did increase, but so too did the amount and variety of the work that was successfully carried out, with the number of missions flown rising and the number of hours in the air increasing exponentially to match the number of RFC squadrons deployed at the front. The Fokkers may have been deadly, but there were still only around forty in service by December. Trenchard knew that whatever casualties the RFC suffered would be as nothing compared to the numbers at risk on the ground, and he did not hesitate to press his men forward. However, until a British scout that could match the Fokker arrived on the Western Front, they would just have to fly in close formations of three or four machines, which would allow a concentrated fire of their machine guns on any attacking Fokker. This meant a slight reduction in the missions flown, as it would take three aircraft to achieve what one might have done; but the point was the work was still being undertaken.

Chapter 5

Success on the Somme, 1916

In the heat of a fight, one was too busy to go on being frightened. When an enemy fighter attacked me and tried to get on my tail, I found that, more often than not, I got extremely annoyed, particularly when I knew that he had actually opened fire at me. My first reaction would be to think to myself, 'The bastard – what the devil does he think he's doing!' And then, when a fuller realisation of what was going on had roused my ire, my thought would become, 'My God – he's trying to kill me! I'd better bloody well kill him first!'[1]

Lieutenant William Sholto Douglas, 8 Squadron, RFC

January 1916 saw new leadership for the BEF, with General Sir Douglas Haig having replaced Field Marshal Sir John French after it had become evident that his old chief was simply not up to the job. For Brigadier General Hugh Trenchard, it meant that he had the full and certain backing from Haig, who had grasped the importance of aviation, but in turn Trenchard was determined to strain every sinew to help the BEF in the coming summer offensive. With invaluable assistance from Paul de Peuty of the French Air Service, Trenchard would hammer out a relentless offensive strategy to secure the maximum advantages from air power. Trenchard believed in pushing the Germans back to keep them well away from the vital air space above the trench lines. This would allow free range for the British aerial reconnaissance, artillery observation and contact patrols. However, it was hard to achieve, as it demanded his pilots fly deep into German territory to harass and break up any German flying activity. All in all, it was no laughing matter. But it had to be done.

Artillery observation was still the key; the way that the mighty power of the vastly augmented Royal Artillery could be unlocked. Although much progress had been made, there were still problems. One was the existence amongst the artillery officers of wholly negative reactions to being told what to do with their precious guns by relatively junior personnel.

The real crux of the matter is that the artillery have a profound distrust and contempt for the Flying Corps and have a terror of 'allowing their guns to be run by the Flying Corps'. This is the phrase which is always produced in such controversies. As a matter of fact, there are many cases when the Flying Corps are the only people who can run the artillery. The artillery are apt to exaggerate their accuracy when firing without aerial observation, I think. Both sides lost their tempers.[2]

Lieutenant Thomas Hughes, 1 Squadron, RFC

Notwithstanding this somewhat pessimistic viewpoint, there had been some movement amongst the more enlightened gunners.

Battery commanders went through stages of opinion concerning co-operation with aircraft. At first, they thought it an unnecessary and unhelpful nuisance, an opinion in which they were confirmed if they had the misfortune to meet a stupid or lazy observer in the first practice. Then they began to think there might be something in it. Then they wanted us all the time. When a particular pilot or observer (sometimes one, sometimes the other, did the actual spotting) got to know a battery well, they did excellent work together. The good feeling and patience and knowledge of each other's difficulties, which only came from personal contact, did more to make the work a success than anything else. The procedure was simple. We would arrange to be over the battery at a Zero hour, ready to engage a target or targets which had been previously decided upon. Then we would call up the battery on our wireless set and look for their reply, which was given by means of strips of white cloth laid out on the ground in certain patterns according to a code. As soon as we saw their message, 'Signals clear! Carry on!' we would put ourselves in position to see the target. When a shell burst near it, we would signal the position of the burst with regard to the target by means of the clock code. This went on either until the shots became O.K.'s, or until the battery signified, by changing its ground strip signal, that it had had enough. We could, of course, at any time communicate our own change of plans, or turn the battery on to a fresh target.[3]

2nd Lieutenant Raymond Money, 12 Squadron, RFC

Meanwhile, the poor bloody infantry only looked for some relief from the torture inflicted by German artillery, mortars and machine guns. If the RFC and Royal Artillery could achieve this by working in harness, then they were all for it.

What the infantry was mostly interested in was the artillery batteries behind them being able to hit some gun or some machine gun post that was worrying them in the trenches that they would like knocked. Aeroplanes used to come up on artillery spotting, to guide these batteries on to their target. Everybody in the trenches was more interested in that aspect of flying than they were in the actual fighting in the air. Artillery observation was looked upon by the Army as a whole as the be-all and end-all of the Flying Corps.[4]

Lieutenant Archibald Yuille, East Lancashire Regiment

The infantry knew what they wanted: the question was, could the RFC deliver it?

Trenchard's concept of an aerial offensive was greatly assisted by the arrival of a stream of new aircraft, which offered hope in the battle against the Fokker. In November 1915, the first of the FE2bs began to trickle out to the Western Front to 16 Squadron. By the spring of 1916, four squadrons were fully equipped with them – 20, 22, 23 and 25 Squadrons. The FE2b was a tough two-seater pusher aircraft, capable of up to 72mph, with an effective ceiling of 9,000 feet and armed with two Lewis guns operated by the observer from his front nacelle seat. It could be considered a major step forward from the Vickers Fighter, but it was not superior in itself to the German Fokker. Nevertheless, it offered a decent chance of survival, particularly when flown in formation, flying round in circles, with each aircraft protecting the others' 'tails' when under Fokker attack. On 18 June, there was a symbol of this 'passing of the baton'. An FE2b 6346 crewed by 2nd Lieutenant George McCubbin and Corporal James Waller of 25 Squadron was in combat with the Fokker flown by Oberleutnant Max Immelmann, when suddenly damage to the Fokker's propeller caused the engine to break up the aircraft – Immelmann was killed in the resulting crash. It marked the end of the brief heyday of the Fokker, and Oswald Boelcke was despatched on an intelligence-gathering mission to the Balkan fronts. He would return. Equipped with gradually improving engines, the FE2b went through a wide variety of roles during its long career with the RFC – moving from scout patrols, to escort and photographic missions, then long-range reconnaissance and finally as a night bomber.

The DH2, an agile single-seater pusher scout, also reached the front early in 1916. Capable of up to 85mph, with a ceiling of 14,000 feet, it was armed with a single fixed Lewis gun operated by the pilot. It was not easy to fly, requiring a light touch on the joystick if it was not to go into the still-dreaded spin. Rumours soon spread that it was a death-trap, and it was known to some pessimists as 'The Spinning Incinerator'. This was soon dealt with by Major Lanoe Hawker, the first commander of 24 Squadron, which was equipped with the DH2 on their arrival at the front in February 1916. After a couple of fatal accidents, he took up his DH2 and threw it about in a display of stunt-flying, spinning every which way he could imagine, demonstrating how easy it was to recover if by accident or design a pilot put the DH2 into a spin. He followed up this practical demonstration with a lecture of exactly what his pilots must do to get out of a spin. Hawker, who was already a VC, proved an innovative squadron commander, making minor practical improvements to the DH2 and teaching his men the rudiments of deflection shooting – the necessity of shooting ahead of a fast moving target to actually hit it. Above all, he encouraged an aggressive philosophy amongst his plots, summarised neatly in the now-famous tactical orders.

Tactical Orders by officer commanding No. 24 Squadron, Royal Flying Corps:
'ATTACK EVERYTHING!'[5]
Major Lanoe Hawker, 24 Squadron, RFC

This, however, was not a unique aggressive attitude, as can be seen by the guide intended for scout pilots, 'Fighting in the Air', written by Major Lionel Rees, who would command 32 Squadron when they came out to the Western Front with the DH2 in May 1916. Some of his musings seem somewhat jingoistic, but they were of their time.

> The British pilot always likes the idea of fighting and is self-reliant. He is a quick thinker compared with the enemy, so that he has the advantage in manoeuvre. He fights for the sport of the affair, if for no other reason. The enemy pilot on the other hand, is of a gregarious nature from long national training, and often seems bound by strict rules, which cramp his style to a great extent. The enemy pilots are often uneducated men, being looked upon simply as drivers of the machine, while the gunner or observer is considered a grade higher than the pilot. This last gives a great advantage to us, as, whereas our pilots act from a sense of Noblesse Oblige, the enemy, when in a tight corner, often fails to seize and press an advantage.[6]
>
> Major Lionel Rees, 32 Squadron, RFC

The DH2 may have been very slightly slower than the Fokker, but it was able to out-turn it in combat, a vital ability when trying to get on an opponent's tail. It was also far superior to any of the German reconnaissance aircraft it encountered, whose activities were soon curtailed – something that was crucial in the run-up to the Battle of the Somme.

Another new British aircraft, that reached the front with 70 Squadron, was the Sopwith 1½ Strutter, a two-seater tractor biplane, which could reach speeds of 99mph and had a decent rate of climb, although it was somewhat restricted in manoeuvrability. Best of all, apart from its fabulously evocative name, it was the first British aircraft fitted with a synchronised Vickers machine gun firing through the arc of the propeller. The observer sat behind the pilot and had a ring-mounted Lewis gun, so overall it was a big step forward in firepower. It would be employed mainly on long-range reconnaissance missions.

The French also contributed to the strength of the RFC by making available several of the Nieuport 16 Scouts. This was a superb single-seater tractor biplane, which could reach 110mph and had a ceiling of some 15,000 feet. Both fast and manoeuvrable, it too was more than a match for the Fokker, although its firepower was limited to a single Lewis gun fitted above the centre upper wing section – so the bullets went above the propeller – and it was fired by the pilot using a Bowden wire grip fitted to the joystick.

Collectively, these four aircraft – the FE2b, DH2, Sopwith 1½ Strutter and Nieuport 16 Scout – would bring an end to the Fokker scourge, challenging the German aircraft whenever they poked their noses anywhere near the lines. It was fortunate they did, as the vulnerable BE2c was not replaced. There had also been delays in the RE8, which was designated as the next 'corps aircraft'. The BE2c, and the subsequent variants, would have to struggle on deep into 1917, wherein lay the roots of the tragedy of 'Bloody April' during the Battle of Arras.

* * *

Almost everything the RFC did in early 1916 was connected to the plans being produced by General Sir Douglas Haig for the Battle of the Somme in July. Trenchard knew what was required from the men of the RFC. They had to clear back German aircraft from the front areas to prevent them probing over the lines and revealing the British deployments and preparations. They must photograph and re-photograph every inch of the Somme front and hinterland, checking for new trenches, defences and batteries, and for signs of the arrival of German reinforcements. They must also use aerial artillery observation to enable the guns to register onto unseen targets, ready for '*Der Tag*'. When the long main preparatory bombardment started on 24 June, it was meant to clear the German barbed wire and destroy the German trenches, dugouts, headquarters, machine-gun posts and artillery batteries; all this on behalf of the infantry who would go over the top on 1 July. Bombing raids were intensified to try and damage German transport infrastructure and airfields. Problems were still anticipated in discerning where the troops had got to in the confusion of the attack, so several new methods were devised to allow for more effective aerial contact patrols. Metal triangles were carried to reflect the sun on the men's backs, and flares were carried to be lit when an aircraft klaxon sounded the signal. Whatever their part in the great offensive, the young pilots and observers had the importance of their work rammed home by visits from Trenchard himself.

> On the eve of the offensive the General Officer Commanding, 'Boom' Trenchard, with his A.D.C., visited the squadron. Sitting on his shooting-stick, he called us all up round him, gave us a bird's-eye view of the whole attack, and in his pleasant masterful way congratulated us all on our work. It had contributed, he said, more than we knew to the success of the preliminary bombardment. Artillery observation, photography, reconnaissance, all received their commendation. 'Boom' infused men's enthusiasm without effort by a certain greatness of heart that made him not so much our superior in rank as in personality. When he left, we were all sure that victory was certain, that the line would be broken, the cavalry put through, and the Allies sweep on to Berlin.[7]
> 2nd Lieutenant Cecil Lewis, 3 Squadron, RFC

When the troops went over the top at 7.30 am on 1 July, they were watched from high above by Cecil Lewis in his Morane Parasol as massive mines were set off.

> We were over Thiepval and turned south to watch the mines. As we sailed down above it all, came the final moment. Zero! At Boisselle the earth heaved and

flashed, a tremendous and magnificent column rose up into the sky. There was an ear-splitting roar, drowning all the guns, flinging the machine sideways in the repercussing air. The earthy column rose, higher and higher to almost four thousand feet. There it hung, or seemed to hang, for a moment in the air, like the silhouette of some great cypress tree, then fell away in a widening cone of dust and debris. A moment later came the second mine. Again, the roar, the upflung machine, the strange gaunt silhouette invading the sky. Then the dust cleared, and we saw the two white eyes of the craters. The barrage had lifted to the second-line trenches, the infantry were over the top, the attack had begun.[8]

2nd Lieutenant Cecil Lewis, 3 Squadron, RFC

But the barrage had in many cases not succeeded. It seemed impressive – it was impressive compared to most previous British barrages; but it did not achieve the results required. There were simply not enough guns – certainly not enough heavy guns – to smash the German defences. The length of the front attacked, and the depth of the objectives aimed at, meant that the barrage was less intensive in terms of shells per yard of trench than that fired at the Battle of Neuve Chapelle back in March 1915. Worst of all, there were not enough guns assigned to counter-battery duties, so that when the infantry emerged into no man's land, the German 5.9-inch guns could still deal death and destruction to augment the chattering machine guns. In the frenzy that ensued, all the carefully worked out methods of contact patrol were rendered almost redundant as troops under heavy fire were unlikely – or unable – to light flares.

The bombing raids also proved to be ineffective, something that might well have been predicted, given the paucity of the bomb loads delivered and difficulty in hitting the targets.

In the afternoon I went on a bomb raid to Bapaume. We crossed our lines at Albert and went up to Bapaume, about 12 miles. We got 'Archied' as soon as we got to Bapaume. We dropped our bombs, trying for the railway and some stores. Then we lit out for Arras, being heavily shelled. I dodged all over the place, and managed to avoid any direct clouts, although they managed to sift a few odds and ends of shells through my machine. I found one shrapnel bullet stuck in the wood. They were going off on all sides, and above and underneath, near Arras, and I was quite pleased to cross our lines and get out of reach. They must have put up one hundred shells at me in 15 minutes![9]

2nd Lieutenant John Brophy, 21 Squadron, RFC

The DH2s of 32 Squadron had been assigned to escort the bombing raids on the German communications. Their C.O, Major Lionel Rees, took off in DH2 6015 at 6.30 am, accompanied by another pilot, and was patrolling well to the north of the Somme when he was bounced and became involved in a dramatic dogfight.

Orders had been issued banning squadron commanders from crossing the lines, but Rees, like many others, often ignored them.

> Yesterday I had quite a good scrap. I met ten Huns altogether. The first I sent home. The second I wrecked completely. The third put a bullet through my leg so that I could not manoeuvre quickly, but he was sorry he met me before I finished with him! All the others went back across the lines and, as I am not allowed to go across, I helped them home at long range.[10]
> Major Lionel Rees, 32 Squadron, RFC

His laconic manner does not betray the seriousness of his leg wound. Rees flew back to his airfield, where his landing was watched by Gwilym Lewis.

> He landed in the usual manner – taxied in. They got the steps for him to get out of his machine. He got out and sat on the grass, and calmly told the fellows to bring him a tender to take him to hospital. I am afraid he has got a very bad wound, though he is lucky not to have had an artery in his leg shot, as I understand he would never have got back if he had. Of course, everyone knows the Major is mad. I don't think he was ever more happy in his life than attacking those Huns. He said he would have brought them all down one after the other if he could have used his leg. He swears they were youngsters on their first bombing lesson!! I don't know how he does it![11]
> 2nd Lieutenant Gwilym Lewis, 32 Squadron, RFC

This was one of relatively few aerial battles on 1 July, for the RFC had established control over the battlefield. Yet the true advantages of that situation were not yet being harvested. The aims of the bombardment were not being achieved: it was not heavy enough, it was not accurate enough, and the Royal Artillery failed to allot the correct resources to the tasks required. The result was painful indeed.

*   *   *

The RFC had been worked to distraction in the preparations for 1 July, but there was no relaxation of the pressure in the weeks that followed. On the ground, a series of attacks would follow, attempting to gain positional advantages before the next great lunge forward in the Battle of Bazentin Wood on 14 July, and then again in the Battle of Flers-Courcelette on 15 September. If anything, the demand for aerial photographs increased as the generals and their staff officers were desperate to chart the exact location and nature of the German trenches which they were about to assault. One witty witness of this whole procedure was Lieutenant Alan Bott, who had arrived at the front with 70 Squadron in mid-July. Bott was an observer flying in a Sopwith 1½ Strutter with his pilot, 2nd Lieutenant Awdry Vaucour, engaged in a series of photographic reconnaissance missions throughout the operations.

The business of taking accurately-sited photographs to compose a mosaic map, or to reveal the details of a specific location, demanded great concentration from both pilot and observer; a matter made far more difficult by the attentions of the German anti-aircraft guns. Sometimes things went wrong.

'Wouff! Wouff! Wouff! Wouff!' Pull the string, press forward the loading-handle, bring it back; 'One, two, three, four!' 'Wouff! Wouff! Wouff! Wouff!' Just as the final plate-number showed on the indicator a mighty report from underneath startled us, and the machine was pressed upward, left wing down. This was terrifying enough but not harmful, for not one of the fragments from the near burst touched us, strange to say. The pilot righted the bus, and I made the last exposure, without, I am afraid, caring what patch of earth was shuttered on to the plate. Nose down and engine full out, we hared over the trenches. 'Archie's' hate followed for some distance, but to no purpose; and at last we were at liberty to fly home, at peace with the wind and the world. 'Good boys,' said the squadron commander. The camera was rushed to the photographic lorry, the plates were unloaded in the dark hut, the negatives were developed. Half an hour later I received the first proofs, and, with them, some degree of disappointment. Those covering the first outward and return journey between Pozières and Le Sars were good, as were the next three, at the beginning of the second journey. Then came a confused blur of superimposed ground patterns, and at the last five results blank as the brain of a flapper. A jam in the upper changing-box had led to five exposures on the one plate. As you know, I am a fool. But I do not like to be reminded of the self-evident fact. The photographic officer said I must have made some silly mistake with the loading handle, and he remarked sadly that the camera was supposed to be fool proof. I said he must have made some silly mistake when inspecting the camera before it left his workshop, and I remarked viciously that the camera was fool proof against a careless operator, but by no means fool proof against the careless expert. There we left the subject and the spoiled plates, as the evening was too far advanced for the trip to be repeated.[12]

Lieutenant Alan Bott, 70 Squadron, RFC

When they were over or near to the German lines, which after all was their usual theatre of RFC operations, 'Archie' was a constant threat, although many tried to believe that it was ineffective.

'Wouff! Wouff! Wouff! Wouff! Wouff!' said 'Archie'. The ugly puffs encircled us, and it seemed unlikely that an aeroplane could get away without being caught in a patch of hurtling high explosive. Yet nobody was hit. The only redeeming feature of the villain 'Archibald' is that his deeds are less terrible than his noise, and even this is too flat to be truly frightful. Although I was uncomfortable as we raced away, the chorused, 'Wouffs!' reminded me of an epidemic of coughing I heard in church one winter's Sunday, while a fatuous sermon was read by a dull-voiced vicar.[13]

Lieutenant Alan Bott, 70 Squadron, RFC

The pilots and observers may have understood their role, but there was still total confusion amongst some elements of the great British public back home in the UK as to the nature of the air war.

As an extreme case of this haziness over matters aeronautic I will quote the lay question, asked often and in all seriousness, 'Can an aeroplane stand still in the air?' Another surprising point of view is illustrated by the home-on-leave experience of a pilot. His lunch companion – a charming lady – said she supposed he lived mostly on cold food while in France. 'Oh no,' replied the pilot, 'It's much the same as yours, only plainer and tougher!' 'Then you do come down for meals!' deduced the lady. Only those who have flown on active service can fully relish the comic savour of a surmise that the Flying Corps in France remain in the air all day amid all weathers, presumably picnicking, between flights, off sandwiches, cold chicken, pork pies, and mineral waters![14]

Lieutenant Alan Bott, 70 Squadron, RFC

There was very little picnicking during the missions flown over the Somme.

As for the bombing operations, there had been some progress in devising a bombsight to try and indicate the point when the bombs should be dropped to have a chance of hitting a target from a specific height. However, William Fry found them of little use in action.

A bomb sight had by this time been designed for use in aeroplanes and our machines were fitted with them. They were fixed on the outside of the fuselage on the pilot's right-hand so that he could look over the side and adjust and line up the sight on the target. With a view to future raids, we put in an hour or so every day practising with them over the 'camera obscura' on the aerodrome, a device which enabled the pilot's accuracy in the use of the sight to be plotted on a chart and measured. It was all very well in theory but when it came to actual bombing it took an optimist to believe that half-trained and inexperienced pilots, unable to defend themselves, harassed by anti-aircraft shell bursts all round them, and in the constant expectation of attack by German scouts could be expected to pin-point and then concentrate sufficiently to fly the right course to line up the sight on target after first adjusting it for wind speed and direction. I am sure that many, like myself, on occasion dropped their bombs hurriedly when approximately over the target, then made for home – especially if their flight leader had already done so.[15]

2nd Lieutenant William Fry, 12 Squadron, RFC

On 11 July, Lieutenant Colonel Hugh Dowding, who was commanding the 9th Wing, RFC, decided that he was unhappy with the reported results of the bombing raids carried out by his squadrons. He thus decided to show them how it was done – as John Brophy somewhat gleefully reports.

> The chief kicks about our bomb-raids have been the poor formation, leaving us in danger of being separated, and 'done in' by Huns. The colonel decided he'd lead us to show us how. He was to lead, and Captain Carr and I were next, and four others in pairs behind, and nine scouts [from 60 Squadron]. At 6,000 feet we met thick clouds, and when I came through, I couldn't see anyone anywhere, so I just flew around and finally sighted three machines. I went over and found Carr and the colonel, and two scouts, so I got into place and the colonel went over to the lines – and kept circling to get higher for half an hour – right over the lines. I thought this was a foolish stunt, as I knew the Huns could see us, and would be waiting for us. I was very surprised that they didn't shell us, but there was a battle on, and they were probably too busy. We were right over Albert, as I recognised two huge mine craters that had been sprung July 1st. When we did cross over with only two scouts, we hadn't been over more than a couple of minutes, before I saw three Fokkers coming towards us, and a couple of L.V.G.'s climbing up to us. Another Fokker was up above me, and behind, between our two scouts. I knew he was going to dive at one of us but expected the scouts to see him and attack him, so I didn't bother about him, but began to get the stop-watch time of my bomb sight to set it for dropping. While I was doing this, I suddenly heard the 'Pop-Pop-Pops!' of machine guns and knew the Huns had arrived. I looked and saw them diving in amongst us – and firing. There were seven L.V.G.'s and three Fokkers as far as I could make out, but they went so fast I could hardly watch them. Our scouts went for them, and I saw the colonel turnabout. My gun being behind me I couldn't get in a shot and turned around after Carr and the colonel. They fired some more as we went back but didn't hit me. The colonel was hit and so the show was over. He had about a dozen bullets in his machine and was hit in the hand. His gun was shot through, and his observer hit in the face. He probably won't try to lead us again![16]
>
> 2nd Lieutenant John Brophy, 21 Squadron, RFC

Of course, the RFC scouts were here, there and everywhere, forcing the Germans back, keeping them away from the crucial area above the trenches. Gradually, they developed a system of 'scrambling' when German aircraft were approaching – in the following case with DH2s.

> For a long period, we did three patrols a day – two of the flights were down for three shows a day, and the third was on standby for headquarters. I think we were the first squadron to do this as a squadron. A system of alarms was

arranged. A bell ringing both at the squadron office and the mess – and how vividly we all remember those bells – which generally seemed to ring about 2 minutes before one's relief came – for we stood by ready to leave the ground immediately the alarm rang. With the Monosoupape engine, no time was wasted in starting or warming up and quite frequently, machines were in the air well within 1 minute of the alarm bell ringing. I well remember the general alarm sounding on one occasion, on a rather dud day, when most people were in the mess. On this occasion, in 1 minute, machines were streaming out of the hangar and twelve machines were off the ground in under 2 minutes. We never found anything at all, and we all supposed afterwards that 'Archie' had been seeing things. It was probably six machines which passed four times over a gap in the clouds. To save time a large board was placed outside the squadron office with the area and number of Hostile Aircraft on it, and as one took off, one glanced at the board to see what one's task was. This was, like most of our other gadgets, Major Hawker's idea. Three and sometimes even four shows a day and throughout it all a great spirit of responsibility and unselfishness ran right through the squadron. The work done by some of the mechanics was at times tremendous – again and again work having to be continued all night to enable us to keep machines serviceable. Speaking of my own flight – which was representative – the men at that time were really wonderful. No holidays, no leave and all work, but never a grumble. I had on more than one occasion to order men to bed in the daytime, or otherwise I knew they would collapse and break down.[17]

Lieutenant Alan Wilkinson, 24 Squadron, RFC

It was an exhausting regime which brought many to the very edge.

Amongst the scout pilots making a name for himself during the Somme air fighting was Lieutenant Albert Ball flying his Nieuport Scout. It was certainly hard, unrelenting, work.

I am feeling a 'poo-poo' crock today. I went up this morning after three Huns and managed to get underneath them, but could not get nearer than 3,000 feet owing to my engine. Am spending remainder of the day trying to get it right. You ask me to let the devils have it when I fight. Yes, I always let them have all I can, but really, I don't think them devils. I only scrap because it is my duty, but I do not think anything bad about the Hun. He is just a good chap with very little guts, trying to do his best. Nothing makes me feel more rotten than to see them go down, but you see it is either them or me, so I must do my best to make it a case of them.[18]

2nd Lieutenant Albert Ball, 11 Squadron, RFC

The tension ratcheted up. These young men were flying into danger two or three times a day, and almost every day there seemed to be another casualty that swiftly eroded away the ranks, requiring a constant stream of replacements.

Really one has only just time to button up one's tunic. I am having a 'poo-poo' time, but most interesting. On the 6th, three topping chaps went off and never returned. Yesterday, four of my best pals went off and today one of our new chaps has gone over, so you can guess we are always having to get used to new faces. Yesterday I was up at 5am and during the day had twelve flights, but at last nature is asking to have its own way. However, I am not done yet. I shall get at them again soon.[19]

2nd Lieutenant Albert Ball, 11 Squadron, RFC

Anyone would find this a strain. Although Ball was successful and rapidly gaining victories, he began to feel the draining effects of exhaustion. The response was in the finest traditions of the army – sensitive, understanding and above all compassionate!

The day before yesterday we had a big day. At night I was feeling very rotten, and my nerves were 'poo-poo'. Naturally, I cannot keep on for ever, so at night I went to see the C.O., and asked him if I could have a short rest, and not fly for a few days. He said he would do his best. What has taken place has been that I have been sent to No. 8 Squadron, back on to BE2cs. Oh, I am feeling in the dumps.[20]

2nd Lieutenant Albert Ball, 11 Squadron, RFC

It could have been the end of him, but Albert Ball survived his punishment for the temerity of asking for a rest and would continue his career as a top ace.

* * *

When the pilots and observers weren't up in the air, working, they were down on the ground and living the life of 'Old Riley' in comparison to the infantry. The officers found that they could evade almost all the usual responsibilities of commissioned rank.

It was a wonderful life. We weren't bothered with parades nor with rules about uniform, nor were we expected to look after the welfare of the men in the flight – they could look after themselves better than we could. We were burdened with no responsibilities whatsoever. No senior officers in the mess were bent on keeping junior officers in their place. Those of us who had come from the regiments could hardly believe our luck.[21]

2nd Lieutenant William Fry, 12 Squadron, RFC

They had a proper mess, with walls and a ceiling, they had seats, they had tables and they had a gramophone, perhaps even a piano. They also had the opportunity for peace and quiet, something much prized on the Western Front.

We are under canvas and have our mess in the open in a small wood. It is very nice when the weather is as hot as it has been lately. Although we are within range of the shellfire from big guns at present you would not know there was a war. I am sitting in a wood out of the sun. The wind is blowing the wrong way to hear the guns and the only things to be heard are a machine gun shooting away in the distance and the mess gramophone.[22]

Lieutenant Leslie Horridge, 7 Squadron, RFC

True, their food was often basic, but it was better than the trench diet – and best of all they had access to drink.

We enjoyed a 'Battle of Waterloo' sort of life, active flying being interspersed with riding, tennis, visits to Bethune for teas, dinners, drinking etc. Our mess life was at this period also of a Waterloo flavour, with meals, correct wines, including port circulated in a correct and proper manner. Liqueurs with coffee were de rigueur. This 'officer and gentleman' kind of life did not last long, and before many weeks had passed war conditions set in and life became much less pleasant with a growing fear of death seldom far off.[23]

Lieutenant Ewart Garland, 10 Squadron, RFC

This, of course, was the dreadful trade-off these airmen faced. They may well live off the 'fat of the land', but the next morning they might well be dead.

Dinner over, the usual crowd settle around the card-table, and the gramophone churns out the same old tunes. There is some dissension between a man who likes music and another who prefers rag-time. 'Number One' leads off with the *Peer Gynt Suite*, and 'Number Two' counters with the record that choruses: 'Hello, how are you?' From the babble of yarning emerges the voice of our licensed liar, 'So I told the general he was the sort of bloke who ate tripe and gargled with his beer!' 'Flush,' calls a poker player. 'Give us a kiss, give us a kiss, by wireless,' pleads the gramophone. 'Good-night, chaps. See you over Cambrai.' This from a departing guest. Chorus, 'Good-night, old bean!' A somewhat wild evening ends with a singsong![24]

Lieutenant Alan Bott, 70 Squadron, RFC

The level of drinking can be over-exaggerated. Many of them were not used to alcohol, and most were aware that they needed a clear head at the crack of dawn the next morning.

I don't want to convey the impression that we drank excessively, or regularly. No doubt there were a few who drank a good deal, but they were not, as a rule, to be found in the squadrons along the front. Most of us were young, cheerful, and excessively high-spirited, and the changes and chances of our eventful days maintained our spirits at an easily excited level. After one glass of beer one felt exhilarated; after two, one felt inclined to break something; after three, one felt a burning desire to go and tweak the nose of the Pope before all his cardinals. The idea of a Flying Corps drinking themselves silly in order to keep their nerves in order seems incredible to me; and most certainly that kind of thing was not done in 1915 and 1916, nor was it necessary. Our life off duty, and particularly our mess life, which was all of it except for infrequent excursions into Amiens, may be imagined best by a song born of the war and the Royal Flying Corps:

> *And when I die,*
> *Don't bury me at all;*
> *Just pickle my bones*
> *In alcohol.*
> *Put a bottle of booze*
> *At my head and my feet,*
> *And then I know,*
> *My bones will keep.*[25]
>
> 2nd Lieutenant Raymond Money,
> 12 Squadron, RFC

However, when the time was right, there is no doubt that they could really let rip. Cecil Lewis lovingly recounts the story of a night that got rather out of hand after the C.O of 3 Squadron returned from Amiens with cases of whisky and champagne. After dinner they set to with a will.

> The long trestle table, covered with smeared American cloth, stood diagonally across the room: a low room, ill lit, with a rough, red-tiled floor. The gramophone was wheezing, 'I'm going back to the shack where the black-eyed' – 'Bastards go!' chipped in the adjutant. 'For Crissake put another tune on the blasted box!' 'Shampoos!' shouted the Major. 'Who's for shampoos?' 'Shampoos! Shampoos!' Shrieked the mess. Ah, ha! This was the life! This was fine! This was a drunk. A row of young men bent their heads over the long table. The Major was mixing neat whisky with champagne in a tin basin.[26]
>
> 2nd Lieutenant Cecil Lewis, 3 Squadron, RFC

Then things began to get out of order as soda siphons were pressed into action as weapons.

> Over went the table. Siphons appeared by magic. The offensive was launched. Squirt! Scream! Scream! Squirt! 'Oh you … Got him! Right in the …! More! More!' 'Give me another! Orderly! More siphons! God, I'm wet! God, what a

life!' They collapsed, chairs dripping, tunics soaking, walls running, laughing, shouting, swearing, on to the puddled floor.[27]

2nd Lieutenant Cecil Lewis, 3 Squadron, RFC

By this time, to use the vernacular, they were all paralytic, and at last Lewis stumbled off to his billet.

The drunken chorus faded down the street. In his billet our hero found his pillow black, his bed black, his chairs, table, ceiling, all covered with a film of soot. For hours and hours, the oil lamp had been smoking. 'Can't shleep here. Goddam batman. Everything shooty!' A bright idea struck into his reeling mind, 'Shleep with Mam'sel!' She was a heavy peasant girl, clogged and shawled, fruity with the rank odours of the farmyard. Her room lay through his. He lurched over and opened it. 'Mam'sel,' he announced, 'I—je ... dor-mez ... vous ... Savey?' 'Oui, oui, venez!' said a stupid voice in the darkness. He groped in the darkness, in the stuffy, feather-bedded darkness, found her in the darkness. God, what a drunk! What a bloody wonderful drunk![28]

2nd Lieutenant Cecil Lewis, 3 Squadron, RFC

One can object to his sneering tone, but surely one can also understand the pressures these very young men were undergoing. For there was an underlying air of ongoing tragedy. The casualties may not have been numerically large in comparison to the infantry, but a squadron was a very small unit and just a couple of losses made a hell of a difference. This was most apparent when returning from leave – as Lewis would discover soon enough.

'Had a good leave?' 'Fine, thanks.' I ordered some coffee. The place smelled of stale smoke. The chairs wobbled. The tablecloth was stained and dingy. The wire that held the lamp was thick with dead flies. 'Orderly!' 'Sir?' 'Whisky!' 'Sir.' 'Where's Rudd?' I asked. Only four chaps here. Where were the others? 'Killed.' 'Archie'. This morning. 'Orderly!' 'Sir?' 'Cigarettes.' 'Sir.' 'Both of them?' I couldn't believe it somehow. 'Suppose so. Machine took fire. Couldn't recover the bodies.' The boy who spoke was only eighteen too. A good pilot. Brave. Rudd had been his room-mate. God, how quiet the Mess was! 'And Hoppy?' 'Wounded: gone home.' 'And Pip and Kidd?' I was almost frightened to ask. 'Done in last night. Direct hit. One of our own shells. Battery rang up to apologise. New pilots coming.' Kidd, with the funny quirky laugh! Pip, who had seen the poppies with me. I turned instinctively to the piano. After dinner he was always there. Never again those yellow keys under those gentle hands. ... It was so still. Surely, they were near. The door would open. 'By the way, congrats on your Military Cross!' Echoes. Congrats! Congratulations. Five ghosts in the room. Five friends. Congrats! 'Thanks!' I said.[29]

Lieutenant Cecil Lewis, 3 Squadron, RFC

In the early summer of 1916, Frederick Powell had been invited by Major Robert Lorraine to command a flight in the newly formed 40 Squadron. Lorraine had always been a character, and his new rank allowed him the scope to strut a new stage.

Lorraine had just been promoted major. The major on the stage always had an eyeglass – and who should acquire an eyeglass, but of course, Robert Lorraine. When I was on one of my London leaves, I bought from Harrods a whole box of plain glass eyeglasses, with broad black ribbons. When I returned to Lorraine's squadron, I issued each one of the ribbons and eyeglasses to the officers. That night at dinner everybody wore an eyeglass. I must say that Lorraine was quite good. He took it in good part. He didn't comment at all. He didn't even try to say that he had a defective eye![30]
   Captain Frederick Powell, 40 Squadron, RFC

Powell was aware of the value of alcohol in helping young men cope with the pressure.

The centre of the squadron seemed to be in the bar. That may offend a lot of people, but it is perfectly true. When you think of these boys, with the tensions they lived through! They came in, in the evening, and asked about their best friend, 'Where is he, old George?' 'Oh, he bought it this afternoon!' 'Oh, heavens!' Now the gloom would come into a mess; the morale would die, and the reaction was immediately, 'Well, come on chaps, what're you going to have?' Although people are against alcohol, I still think that it played a magnificent part in keeping up the morale of our troops generally.[31]
   Lieutenant Frederick Powell, 40 Squadron, RFC

Powell may have taken this a little too far.

I used to have a little flask which I filled with rum. And I kept it in my tunic pocket. It got so bitterly cold, in these open aircraft in the winter, that one's moustache got frozen – a great block of ice appeared there. I used to open this little flask and just take a nip – and when you are up very, very high one little drop of alcohol and you feel as though you've been out on a bender – absolutely glorious! The effect was immediate, and when you came down a few thousand feet you were sober as a judge![32]
   Lieutenant Frederick Powell, 40 Squadron, RFC

Lorraine tried to keep his men busy, to occupy their minds with something other than the death that might await them on the next dawn patrol. The old actor could not resist putting on a theatrical show.

Lorraine found a Red Cross hut, which he saw and noted that no one seemed to own it. All the officers went off in their cars, we dismantled the hut and brought it back to our aerodrome and built it again. We then had a wonderful theatre; it had a stage and would hold about 250 and we used to do plays. We acted two unpublished plays of Bernard Shaw's and to our intense delight who should arrive to stay with us as a V.I.P. for a week but Bernard Shaw himself. In *John Bull*, I had seen an article from Bernard Shaw urging young men not to enlist. I said to Lorraine, 'You know, there is a job for a public assassin, a fellow trained by the government to kill people like this!' One week afterwards who should arrive but Bernard Shaw himself! Lorraine introduced me, 'Oh, Shaw,' he said. 'This is Powell the boy who wants to shoot you!' Shaw said, 'How do you do? I am very pleased to meet you – and you know you might have chosen somebody worse!' Lorraine at dinner excused himself. He said, 'We're doing a dress rehearsal for the men, *The Inca of Jerusalem*, one of your plays, Shaw! Powell, will you bring Shaw down as soon as he's finished his meal?' I took Bernard Shaw down to the theatre and sat on a seat just behind him. I was worried to see that all the way through this play he roared with laughter. He roared so much he actually cried and brought out a handkerchief to wipe his eyes. In those days he had a ginger beard and I remember this beard wobbling up and down. It struck me at the time that it was extremely bad form for a playwright to laugh until he cried at his own comedy. When it was finished, I leant forward and said, 'I am so glad, Sir, that you appreciate our poor efforts at your play'. He turned round, still wiping his eyes and he said, 'Do you know, if I had thought it was going to be anything like that, I wouldn't have written it!'[33]

Lieutenant Frederick Powell, 40 Squadron, RFC

There is no doubt that casualties could drain the spirit and the courage from a young man like a punctured balloon. This was particularly the case if they felt in any way personally responsible for the loss. For Harold Balfour, this was triggered early in the battle when the C.O of 60 Squadron, Major Francis 'Ferdy' Waldron, led a patrol of Morane Bullets on a dawn patrol back on 3 July.

Suddenly saw a large formation of machines about our height coming from the sun towards us. There must have been at least twelve. They were two-seaters led by one Fokker and followed by two others. I am sure they were not contemplating 'war' at all, but 'Ferdy' pointed us towards them and led us straight in. My next impressions were rather mixed. I seemed to be surrounded by Huns in two-seaters. I remember diving on one, pulling out of the dive, and then swerving as another came for me. I can recollect also looking down and seeing a Morane about 800 feet below me going down in a slow spiral, with a Fokker hovering above it following every turn. I dived on the Fokker, who swallowed the bait and came after me, but unsuccessfully, as I had taken care to pull out of my dive while still above him. The Morane I watched gliding down under control, doing perfect turns, to about 2,000 feet, when I lost sight of it. I thought he must have been hit in the engine. After an indecisive combat with the Fokker I turned home. Smith-Barry I never saw from start to finish of the fight. I landed at Vert Galand and reported that 'Ferdy' had 'gone down under control'.[34]

2nd Lieutenant Harold Balfour, 60 Squadron, RFC

Waldron was dead, and Balfour's ineffective role in the fight really bothered him; he was a thoughtful and somewhat sensitive young man. Later in July, there was another incident that further undermined his resolve.

I kept worrying and questioning myself as to what I should have done other than that which I did. So much did this disturb my mental balance that I found myself hesitating on entering a fight, which hesitation rapidly developed into nothing short of a dislike to standing up to the enemy, and a strong inclination to turn tail with a dive homewards. One day I did this when out on patrol with another Morane. We were attacked by two Fokkers and my opponent could obviously out-manoeuvre me in every way. So I acted the complete funk, and turned my nose downwards and in the direction of our lines. My companion was fighting about two miles south of me. I told myself that it was up to me to look after myself, and up to him to look after himself, and with those temporarily comforting sentiments I regained safety. My companion never returned, and when I looked back from the sanctuary of our lines, I saw a small streak of flame falling earthwards, which I knew must have been his Morane on fire, defeated by the attacking Fokker.[35]

Lieutenant Harold Balfour, 60 Squadron, RFC

This second failure triggered what might now be seen as a fully fledged nervous breakdown. Stressed, unable to sleep, Balfour was haunted by night terrors triggered by the knowledge of what dawn might bring – more life-or-death decisions, more casualties, perhaps even his own death or maiming.

The heat of the long summer days was terrific, and our flying hours were many. All these facts assisted to play upon the temperaments of those who were flying in France for the first time, and who had not got confidence either in their ability or in their aeroplanes. I can remember my bedroom companion in the farmhouse in which we were billeted, felt as I did, and how each of us lay awake in the darkness, not telling the other that sleep would not come, listening to the incessant roar of the guns, and thinking of the dawn patrol next morning. At last, we could bear it no longer, and calling out to each other admitted a mutual feeling of terror and foreboding. We lit the candles to hide the dark, and after that felt a bit better, and somehow got through that night as we had to get through the next day.[36]

Lieutenant Harold Balfour, 60 Squadron, RFC

His comrades in the squadron as a whole were obviously aware of his problem, but what could they do? Being told to 'Pull yourself together!' would hardly help. When the crunch came in the most unlikely of fashions, they were mostly sympathetic to his plight. After all, he had tried his best.

> I took a deckchair on the aerodrome, sat down, moved it to a more comfortable position and again put my weight upon it. The chair collapsed and crushed the tips of the middle fingers of both my hands. This sent me to hospital and kept me off flying for some days. Smith-Barry took advantage of the opportunity, and without any fuss or bother arranged that I should go back to England. Everybody in the squadron was very charming, and nobody said anything about the brief and inglorious part which I had played. There was no question of being sent home in official disgrace, but purely that at that time I was of no real use to the unit and therefore was better out of the way.[37]
>
> 2nd Lieutenant Harold Balfour, 60 Squadron, RFC

Balfour was no quitter; he would return to the fray with 43 Squadron in 1917.

Most of the aviators tried to use humour as a shield, to bolster their own confidence and hide their fears. One such was John Brophy, who adopted a biblical tone in his diary entry describing a typical day's work. As such, he made a joke of the whole thing.

> And there came to my hut a man, and he spake and bade me rise and hasten on foot to the lair of him who commanded the squadron. And I yawned and cursed, and yawned again, and glanced towards where one Watkins reposed, and he yawned and cursed, and we rose and drew on our garments, and wrapped ourselves warmly, for it was bitter cold, and the orb of day had not come up. We betook ourselves to where the major lurked, and were despatched to drop missiles of death on billets, wherein slept those who made war on our race. And we arose and made our way to Albert, a city of much dispute, and we carried on, and were perceived and shells arose and burst and fear dwelt in our hearts, but we carried on. And shells arose and burst, and came close, and fragments whistled, and we carried on, and when we had come to that village which is known as Gueudecourt, we pulled levers and watched. Bombs descended and seconds passed, and there appeared a burst of great size followed by others, and bricks flew and we turned. And shells arose thickly, and burst, and we trembled, and it came to pass that in the fullness of time we crossed over the battles at Mametz and Contalmaison, and were within our lines, and shells ceased, and we were even relieved, and zoomed and waved, and imitated the antics of our neighbour.[38]
>
> 2nd Lieutenant John Brophy, 21 Squadron, RFC

Of course, some episodes were genuinely funny. It would take a heart of stone not to cherish the account by Alan Bott of the series of mishaps that befell him and his pilot, Awdry Vaucour, on a mission undertaken on 24 August 1916. They had been flying in their Sopwith 1½ Strutter A890 to the south-west of Cambrai when they were hit by 'Archie'.

> Next instant the fuselage shivered. I looked along the inside of it and found that a burning shell fragment was lodged on a longeron, half-way between my cockpit and the tail-plane. A little flame zigzagged the fabric, all but died away, but, being fanned by the wind as we lost height, recovered and licked its way toward the tail. I was too far away to reach the flame with my hands, and the fire extinguisher was by the pilot's seat. I called for it into the speaking-tube. The pilot made no move. Once more I shouted. Again, no answer. His ear-piece had slipped from under his cap. A thrill of acute fear passed through me as I stood up, forced my arm through the rush of wind, and grabbed his shoulder. 'Fuselage burning! Pass the fire extinguisher!' I yelled.[39]
>
> Lieutenant Alan Bott, 70 Squadron, RFC

Perhaps Vaucour's attention was fixed on two German aircraft that had now appeared. This triggered a series of amusing misunderstandings between the two, as each appeared unable to comprehend why the other was ignoring a desperate situation.

> My words were drowned in the engine's roar; and the pilot, intent on getting near the Boches, thought I had asked which one we were to attack. 'Look out for those two Huns on the left!' he called over his shoulder. 'Pass the fire extinguisher!' 'Get ready to shoot, blast you!' 'Fire extinguisher, you ruddy fool!' A backward glance told me that the fire was nearing the tail-plane at the one end and my box of ammunition at the other – and was too serious for treatment by the extinguisher unless I could get it at once. Desperately I tried to force myself through the bracing-struts and cross-wires behind my seat. To my surprise, head and shoulders and one arm got to the other side – there I stuck, for it was impossible to wriggle farther. However, I could now reach part of the fire, and at it I beat with gloved hands. Within half a minute most of the fire was crushed to death. But a thin streak of flame, outside the radius of my arm, still flickered towards the tail. I tore off one of my gauntlets and swung it furiously on to the burning strip. The flame lessened, rose again when I raised the glove, but died out altogether after I had hit it twice more. The load of fear left me, and I discovered an intense discomfort, wedged in as I was between the two crossed bracing-struts. Five minutes passed before I was able, with many a heave and gasp, to withdraw back to my seat.[40]
>
> Lieutenant Alan Bott, 70 Squadron, RFC

They had come close to a terrible fiery death, but Vaucour still had no idea what had happened. He had other problems!

> By now we were at close grips with the enemy, and our machine and another converged on a Hun. Vaucour was firing industriously. As we turned, he glared at me, and knowing nothing of the fire, shouted, 'Why the hell haven't you fired yet?' I caught sight of a Boche bus below us, aimed at it, and emptied a drum in short bursts. It swept away, but not before two of the German observer's bullets had plugged our petrol tank from underneath. The pressure went, and with it the petrol supply. The needle on the rev-counter quivered to the left as the revolutions dropped, and the engine missed on first one, then two cylinders. Vaucour turned us round, and, with nose down, headed the machine for the trenches. Just then the engine ceased work altogether, and we began to glide down. All this happened so quickly that I had scarcely realised our plight.[41]
>
> Lieutenant Alan Bott, 70 Squadron, RFC

All that was in Bott's mind now was the chance of gliding long enough – and far enough – to get back to safety the other side of the British or French front lines. Failure could mean years in a German prisoner of war camp.

> I began to calculate our chances of reaching the lines before we would have to land. Our height was 9,000 feet, and we were just over 9½ miles from friendly territory. Reckoning the gliding possibilities of our type of bus as a mile to 1,000 feet, the odds seemed unfavourable. On the other hand, a useful wind had arisen from the east, and Vaucour, a very skilful pilot, would certainly cover all the distance that could be covered. I located our exact position and searched the map for the nearest spot in the lines. The village of Bouchavesnes was a fraction south of due west, and I remembered that the French had stormed it two days previously. From the shape of the line before this advance, there was evidently a small salient, with Bouchavesnes in the middle of the curve. I scribbled this observation on a scrap of paper, which I handed to Vaucour with the compass direction. Vaucour checked my statements on the map, nodded over his shoulder, and set a course for Bouchavesnes. Could we do it? I prayed to the gods and trusted to the pilot.[42]
>
> Lieutenant Alan Bott, 70 Squadron, RFC

Then the Germans – as was their wont – intervened to try to thwart their escape.

> Wouff! Wouff! 'Archie' was complicating the odds. Further broodings were checked by the sudden appearance of a German scout. Taking advantage of our plight, its pilot dived steeply from a point slightly behind us. We could not afford to lose any distance by dodging, so Vaucour did the only thing possible – he kept straight on. I raised my gun, aimed at the wicked-looking nose of the attacking craft, and met it with a barrage of bullets. These must

have worried the Boche, for he swerved aside when 150 yards distant, and did not flatten out until he was beneath the tail of our machine. Afterwards he climbed away from us, turned, and dived once more. For a second time we escaped, owing either to some lucky shots from my gun or to the lack of judgment by the Hun pilot. The scout pulled up and passed ahead of us. It rose and manoeuvred as if to dive from the front and bar the way.[43]

Lieutenant Alan Bott, 70 Squadron, RFC

Then, at last, there was a change in fortune as Bott and Vaucour sighted four FE2bs approaching from the west.

The Boche saw them and hesitated as they bore down on him. Finding himself in the position of a lion attacked by hunters when about to pounce on a tethered goat, he decided not to destroy, for in so doing he would have laid himself open to destruction. When I last saw him, he was racing north-east. There was now no obstacle to the long glide. As we went lower, the torn ground showed up plainly. From 2,000 feet I could almost count the shell-holes. Two battery positions came into view, and near one of them I saw tracks and could distinguish movements by a few tiny dots. It became evident that, barring accident, we should reach the French zone.[44]

Lieutenant Alan Bott, 70 Squadron, RFC

There was still the threat of fire from the German trenches as they were now very low – and well within range.

When slightly behind the trenches a confused chatter from below told us that machine guns were trained on the machine. By way of retaliation, I leaned over and shot at what looked like an emplacement. Then came the Boche front line, ragged and unkempt. I fired along an open trench. Although far from fearless as a rule, I was not in the least afraid during the eventful glide. My state of intense 'wind up' while the fuselage was burning had apparently exhausted my stock of nervousness. I seemed detached from all idea of danger, and the desolated German trench area might have been a side-show at a fair. We swept by No Man's Land at a height of 600 feet, crossed the French first and second line trenches, and, after passing a small ridge, prepared to settle on an uneven plateau covered by high bracken. To avoid landing down-wind and down-hill, the pilot banked to the right before he flattened out. The bus pancaked gently to earth, ran over the bracken, and stopped two yards from a group of shell-holes. Not a wire was broken. The propeller had been scored by the bracken, but the landing was responsible for no other damage. Taking into consideration the broken ground, the short space at our disposal, and the fact that we landed cross-wind, Vaucour had exhibited wonderful skill.[45]

Lieutenant Alan Bott, 70 Squadron, RFC

Against all the odds, they had made it. Nevertheless, the mutual recriminations that had been bubbling away during the flight now boiled over.

> We climbed out, relieved but cantankerous. Vaucour still ignorant of the fire, wanted to know why my gun was silent during our first fight; and I wanted to know why he hadn't shut off the engine and listened when I shouted for the fire extinguisher. Some French gunners ran to meet us. The sight that met them must have seemed novel, even to a poilu of two and a half years' understanding. Supposing that the aeroplane had crashed, they came to see if we were dead or injured. What they found was one almost complete aeroplane and two leather-coated figures, who cursed each other heartily as they stood side by side, and performed a certain natural function which is publicly represented in Brussels by a famous little statue. '*Quels types!*' said the first Frenchman to arrive.[46]
>   Lieutenant Alan Bott, 70 Squadron, RFC

It had been a funny business, right enough. Less amusingly, the next day, Awdry Vaucour returned to the Sopwith which had landed south of Carnoy, with Air Mechanic Hugh Warminger, whose role was to repair the aircraft, after which Vaucour could fly them back. This was duly achieved, and the two were on the way to the airfield when they were 'bounced' near Albert by three German aircraft. To make matters worse, the aircraft was hit by an anti-aircraft shell and Warminger was fatally wounded before they made another forced landing. Once again, Vaucour survived, but in far more melancholy circumstances.

Alan Bott could see a dark humour when tragic mishaps befell German opponents, although here too he was at odds with his long-suffering pilot.

> The three Germans, classed by my pilot as Halberstadts, had a great deal more speed than ours. They did not attack at close quarters immediately, but flew 200 to 300 yards behind, ready to pounce at their own moment. Two of them got between my gun and our tail-plane, so that they were safe from my fire. The third was slightly above our height, and for his benefit I stood up and rattled through a whole ammunition drum. Here let me say I do not think I hit him, for he was not in difficulties. He dived below us to join his companions, possibly because he did not like being under fire when they were not. To my surprise and joy, he fell slick on one of the other two Hun machines. This latter broke into two pieces, which fell like stones. The machine responsible for my luck side-slipped, spun a little, recovered, and went down to land. The third made off east. In plain print and at a normal time, this episode shows little that is comic. But when it happened, I was in a state of high tension, and this, combined with the startling realisation that a Hun pilot had saved me and destroyed his friend, seemed irresistibly comic. I cackled with laughter and was annoyed because my pilot did not see the joke.[47]
>   Lieutenant Alan Bott, 70 Squadron, RFC

* * *

The fighting on the Somme reached a crescendo on 15 September 1916 with the launch of the Battle of Flers-Courcelette. British tactics had advanced, their barrage and counter-battery fire had improved, and they made use of the new tanks – and of course the RFC supported them in everything they did. But the Germans had moved on too. Their tactics on the ground were mutating to try to thwart the British and French advances, but in the air – to mix one's metaphors – there was a real sea change. There were two developments that threatened the aerial supremacy established over the summer by the RFC. Firstly, the Germans had developed the next real technological advance in scout aircraft with the advent of the Albatros D.I. This fearsome brute could reach a top speed of 109mph and had a ceiling of 17,000 feet; all this with an armament of two belt-fed Spandau machine guns capable of pouring a stream of deadly bullets through the arc of the propeller. The second advance was the return of Oswald Boelcke, now appointed to command Jasta 2 – the first German all-scout Jagdstaffel. He had been on a tour of the eastern fronts and had by this time developed his famous 'Dicta', a series of simple tactical principles that he inculcated in the pilots of Jasta 2 to create a new and deadly force.

On 17 September, Boelcke led six of his Albatros scouts on their first collective patrol and intercepted a formation of eight BE2cs from 12 Squadron, who were being escorted by six FE2bs from 11 Squadron while they carried out a bombing raid on Marcoing railway junction. This was not a fair contest. The FE2bs were no match as escorts against the Albatros. No less than four were shot down with relative ease · and one of these had fallen victim to a young German pilot, Manfred von Richthofen. It was his first 'kill'; it would not be his last. To make matters worse, BE2cs on bombing raids carried no observer, just the pilot, to save weight. Two of these 12 Squadron BE2cs were also shot down. One of them, BE2c 2741, piloted by Raymond Money had a direct hit inflicted by an anti-aircraft shell.

I dropped my bombs and watched them go down, disregardful of 'Archie' which was bursting very close all round me. I knew that I should be very lucky to get back across the lines. While I was still watching for the burst of my last bomb, I heard a terrific burst, and the machine was borne suddenly upwards. In the same moment my engine ceased, and I became the centre of black smoke and flying fragments. A few seconds later I realised that I was only keeping the machine on an even keel by pushing the stick as far forward as it would go, and that most of my engine was no longer there. Apart from a gaping hole in the right bottom plane and an inside strut dangling, the machine seemed all right. I was descending gently, like a lift, almost stalled; and with the noise of my engine and propeller silenced. I looked down to see where I was going to hit the ground, and saw a train derailed and smoking, and the remaining B.E., almost on the ground, turning and twisting to get away from a Hun on his tail. It looked hopeless, and even as I watched, the B.E. hit the ground and turned right up on its nose. I would have given my life for 10 minutes and a DH2. I threw my ammunition drums overboard and the breechblock of my

Lewis gun. I had a week's supplies of subversive propaganda in the machine which I had, day after day, forgotten to drop. 'Well, they'll get it all at once!' I thought grimly. Another half minute had elapsed, and I was no more than 1,000 feet up. I speculated over what kind of a crash I should have, for I had not sufficient control to land properly, and realised that if it had not been such a perfect day, I should probably be spinning. As it was, there was not a bump in the sky. The trees of the Bois d'Havrincourt came nearer and I saw a field telegraph line. 'May as well dish that!' thought I, and in a last flicker of rage I let the stick go right back. The poor old machine reared up and then crashed heavily, and things went black. The next thing I knew I was sitting in the back of a touring car, and a voice was saying in English. 'Well, the war is over for you!'[48]

2nd Lieutenant Raymond Money, 12 Squadron, RFC

From this time on, the Germans were able to begin the process of countering Trenchard's relentless air offensive. They had in the Albatros the perfect tool for the job.

The Albatros outclassed in every way the DH2, FE2b, Sopwith 1½ Strutter and most of all the faithful BE2c. Yet the requirements of the army on the ground meant that the RFC could not wait for new aircraft to arrive. They had to press on. Edmund Lewis summed it up well as far as the DH2 pilots were concerned.

Very many thanks for the parcels and papers that have come this week. I am now living like a duke, with bedroom slippers, pillowcases and my fine new stockings. They are just what I wanted, and I now stroll about as if I owned the place. We have had quite a busy time in the last few days. It rather feeds you up to see all this newspaper talk about our supremacy in the air. We certainly had it last June, July and August, but we haven't got it now. The Huns still keep to their side of the line, while we venture over their lines, but if they wished they could sit over our aerodrome (with their fast machines) and we could do nothing against them. Perhaps this is a bit of an exaggeration, as we would certainly fight them and not run away as they do, but I don't think the Hun is good enough to face equal numbers over our side even if they have got better machines. What I mean is that a DH2 is no longer attacking but is fighting for its life against these fast Huns, and that at present we have only about half-a-dozen machines able to cope with them. Thank the Lord they haven't many of these fast ones and that given equal numbers our machines would still put up a good – very good in fact – fight against them on account of superior guts! But I suppose war in the air will always be like that. First one side has the best machines and then the other, and the side which shows most guts all through will be the winners. During this war, first we had a lead with BE2cs and Vickers; then Germans got it with the Fokkers. After that we got it with the DH2s and now the Huns are a bit superior with their fast scouts. But whereas formerly one side or the other had the mastery for many months, now it is only a few weeks, as the rate of production is much faster and new machines come out daily. At any rate I hope new machines are coming out from our side – we can't rest as we are! Please don't think I feel 'dud' from the above, as this week I have enjoyed flying and have no intention of being done in by a Hun or two.[49]

2nd Lieutenant Edmund Lewis, 24 Squadron, RFC

The RFC scouts had to cover the operations of the BE2cs and other aircraft carrying out all the 'humble' corps functions that were so essential as the fighting raged on the ground. Battle followed battle, even when the weather worsened. There was a roll call of pain and suffering, with the Battle of Morval, the Battle of Thiepval Ridge and the Battle of Le Transloy, before finishing formally – but not on the ground – with the Battle of the Ancre on 13 November. The only compensation for the British was the death in action of the redoubtable Hauptmann Oswald Boelcke. On 28 October, Boelcke and Jasta 2 were in action with some of the DH2s of 24 Squadron. In the swirling dogfight that ensued, Boelcke and his good friend Leutnant Erwin Böhme were both aiming for the same target, when their wingtips touched. Böhme's aircraft was fine, but Boelcke's wings fell apart and he plunged to his death. One of the great scourges of the RFC was now dead.

The Battle of the Somme had taken its toll, but Albert Ball had survived in the ranks of 60 Squadron. By this time, he was flying the Nieuport 17, which although not as fast as the Albatros had a tighter turning circle, which rendered it a formidable opponent in combat. Its peashooter Lewis gun was no match for the mighty twin Spandaus of the Albatros, but Ball, approaching his zenith as a deadly ace, somehow survived and prospered.

To bring down a lot of Huns you have to be patient and practically live in the air. There are not many of them about and you have to be quick and seize your chance or the bird will have flown away. Sometimes you make ten flights a day and never get a fight. Often it is in the early hours of the morning, when it is cold and you don't feel very keen on going up, that you get your chance. On a few occasions I haven't had time to put my clothes on and I have gone up in my pyjamas. It was jolly cold, I can tell you, and unfortunately, I have never brought down a Hun when clad like this! Altogether I have been brought down six times myself, generally with my engine smashed up. Always I have been lucky enough to land in my own lines; once quite close to the Sherwood Foresters, my old regiment, in which I enlisted as a private.[50]

Captain Albert Ball, 60 Squadron, RFC

It was a murderous business as an ace, but nevertheless one 'duel' he found amusing.

We kept on firing until we had used up all our ammunition. There was nothing more to be done after that, so we both burst out laughing. We couldn't help it – it was so ridiculous. We flew side-by-side laughing at each other for a few seconds, and then we waved adieu to each other and went off. He was a real sport that Hun.[51]

Captain Albert Ball, 60 Squadron, RFC

Ball was looked at in some awe by the other pilots in 60 Squadron. He did not really participate in the more boisterous aspects of mess life and was by nature a somewhat introverted type.

He was a quiet introspective little chap, and not exactly 'friendly' with anyone in particular. We were all billeted in the local village but not Ball who had a small hut on the aerodrome near his Nieuport. There he lived in solitary state with his violin and little garden – so much so that we called him the 'Lonely Testicle', or 'Pill'. He had a red spinner on his propeller and was the only one of us so 'decorated', but the Huns obviously soon got to know it! When he went on leave at this time I flew his aeroplane while mine was being patched up, or having an engine change, and during that week I couldn't get near a Hun! As soon as they saw the red spinner they dived away east. I felt very brave but had no success at all.[52]

2nd Lieutenant Stanley Vincent, 60 Squadron, RFC

One other great character was the C.O of 60 Squadron, the redoubtable Major Robert Smith-Barry. He was rebuked in the gentlest of fashions by Maurice Baring, doubtless at the instigation of the less-gentle Trenchard, when one of the 60 Squadron pilots was accused of having attacked a Martinsyde G100 of 27 Squadron in a case of mistaken identity. This was to some extent understandable, as the Martinsyde single-seater was a rare bird, a large cumbersome beast of an aircraft, nicknamed in consequence the 'Elephant' and only ever issued to 27 Squadron. As a scout it was an utter failure, hence it was being pressed into service on bombing raids – at which it was also a failure. Baring chose to express himself in verse.

Rather Bullets there be that can't abide
The fighting bombing Martinsyde.
Without the slightest rhyme or reason
They strafe him in and out of season.
This elephant is not the Hun
It must not be attacked for fun.
It isn't very hard to see
The crosses on an LVG.
On Martinsydes the British rings
Are clearly painted on the wings.

An elephant (not very large)
Is painted on the fuselage.
The G.O.C. complains this act
Displays a grievous want of tact
And recommends that you should shoot
Your bullets at a hostile brute.
Please warn your pilots, every one
We're out to fight, the bloody Hun.[53]

Captain Maurice Baring, Headquarters, RFC

William Fry recalled one of Smith-Barry's (alleged) more unorthodox and more dubious methods of dealing with a build-up of pesky routine paperwork.

Smith-Barry was being pressed by wing and brigade for reports and returns which were long overdue. One night, the squadron office, a canvas and wood hut on the edge of the aerodrome near our flight mess was burnt down and all the squadron files and papers destroyed in a few minutes. We in the squadron all took it for granted that this had been Smith-Barry's way of dealing with the backlog.[54]

2nd Lieutenant William Fry, 60 Squadron, RFC

Fry had his own problems, as early on in his career at the squadron he managed to damage his Nieuport when distracted by local scenery upon take-off.

The Nieuport had a tendency to swing when taking off unless one was quick on the rudder and on the 21st, I crashed on the aerodrome through swinging, the machine going over quickly on its back. I was unhurt but the plane had to have new top wings and rudder. We pilots were all interested in a good-looking girl, reputed to be the local miller's daughter, who stood at the end of a track on the edge of the aerodrome nearly every afternoon to watch the flying. My crash may have been due to looking at her and taking my mind off the job.[55]

2nd Lieutenant William Fry, 60 Squadron, RFC

Fry also had the privilege of meeting Major Lanoe Hawker while drinking with other young officers at a bar in the local town.

Major Hawker, VC, was then commanding No. 24 Squadron with DH2s. On looking for our tender to go home we found our driver had had too much to drink and was quite incapable of driving us. None of us could drive and we were at a loss as to what to do, especially as some of us were on the early dawn patrol. Major Hawker was standing alone on the steps of the restaurant waiting for his car. I can see him now, the image of the correct pre-war regular Royal Engineer officer, rather aloof. I was pushed forward by the others to ask him what we should do and went up to him rather like a schoolboy and said, 'Our driver is drunk, sir. What shall we do to get home?' His reply was, 'One of you had better drive!' When I admitted that none of us could he said we had better learn on the way. And that's what we did, one of us driving most of the way in third gear because he couldn't get into top. It was nearly dawn and almost time to start off on patrol when we got back.[56]

2nd Lieutenant William Fry, 12 Squadron, RFC

Just a few days later, Lanoe Hawker was killed in a duel between his DH2 and an Albatros flown by Manfred von Richthofen, whose score of victories was already climbing rapidly. Richthofen would take on the mantle of Boelcke and go on to prove even more of a thorn in the side of the British.

*   *   *

As the Somme offensive ground on, the RFC continued to carry out all its designated roles to the satisfaction of Haig and his generals. But the cost was rising. More and more aircraft were being shot down by the Albatros and other new German scouts, while for some the mental strain was just becoming too much. Some snapped, but others saw a funny side even to these personal tragedies.

Another new month and the push still going strong and no very bright outlooks for leave so far. Another youth is being put in for 'special leave' ahead of Watkins and me as his nerves are reported second class type. He has only been out four months and has not done nearly so much work as either of us. We are considering the advisability of returning, after a trip over the lines, trembling in every limb and weeping copiously and mayhap, I say mayhap, we'll get some leave.[57]

2nd Lieutenant John Brophy, 21 Squadron, RFC

When he was at last posted back for a spell of home service, Cecil Lewis felt not only a wonderful feeling of relief, but also the realisation that he was fortunate indeed to have survived the Battle of the Somme.

While I had been on the job, screwed up to the pitch of nervous control it demanded, all had been well. In fact, the only effect of a long spell at the front seemed to be to make me more reckless and contemptuous of the danger. But now that tension had been relaxed, I realised how shaky and good-for-nothing I was. Eight months overseas, four months of the Somme battle, 350 hours in the air, and still alive! Pilots in 1916 were lasting on an average for three weeks. Today it seems incredible that I came through; but at that time, I did not calculate the odds. I had an absolute and unshakable belief in my invulnerability.[58]

2nd Lieutenant Cecil Lewis, 3 Squadron, RFC

The Somme finally dribbled to a close, although bitter outbreaks of fighting flared up on the ground throughout the depths of winter. The RFC was suffering, and while the prospects for the New Year of 1917 were bleak, at least they could get drunk at Christmas. And many of them did.

> Spent the day quietly, until the evening: 7 pm saw the commencement of 'some' dinner, to which eleven of us sat down. Nothing was left of a 21lb turkey, plum pudding flaming with brandy (for which occasion the lights were put out), a dozen [bottles] of champagne and heaps of other little dainties. A highly successful dinner for which we have to thank Madam (the landlady) who did the cooking. We then went round to the men's concert, found them making awful fools of themselves, disgustingly drunk. It was an excellent concert. An exceedingly drunk 'poilu', who came in from no one knows where, caused great amusement by trying to embrace and kiss all the officers, one of whom more inebriated than the remainder of this flight, embraced the 'Frenchie' on the stage; we retired at 11.30 pm, to let the men go as they liked.[59]
>
> 2nd Lieutenant William Lidsey, 16 Squadron, RFC

Perhaps 1917 would be easier; or perhaps not.

Chapter 6

At Last! Training Improves, 1917–18

A general said some very cheerful things. The funny part was that the more he tried to mitigate the outlook he gave us, the worse he made it. At first, he suggested that we might get killed. Then, as though that were more cheering, he hazarded the suggestion that a few of us might survive.[1]

2nd Lieutenant Frederick Ortweiler, RFC

Flying training did not prepare young pilots for the experience of flying combat missions over the Western Front, or anywhere else for that matter. They had been taught to fly, but they had not been taught to fight. As such, they were easy prey for the established German aces, who had the advantage of more experience and better machines. Constant streams of new pilots were churned out by the RFC flying schools, but they had been taught to fly safely, something to be devoutly wished for in peacetime, but of little use with an Albatros perched behind them, with its twin Spandaus chattering death and destruction. They needed to be able to fling their aircraft about the sky to the very limits that the wings would stand, if they were to escape; to prosper, they needed to have a certain grasp of aerial combat techniques and be excellent marksmen.

One problem was the shortage of competent instructors. It might be thought that the situation would ease from late 1915 onwards as pilots experienced on the Western Front came home for a 'rest' period of home service at one of the flying training establishments. However, many of them were exhausted and suffering to a greater or lesser degree from combat stress. They were wary of being killed by their hapless – or is that hopeless – pupils, whom they often described as 'Huns', or in other words 'the enemy'. The training aircraft had dual controls, but there was a great scope for confusion here between nervous instructors and petrified pupils, as Gordon Taylor discovered early on when trying to land a Maurice Farman Shorthorn. It was a fraught business.

I tried to hold the controls steady so that the machine continued on down in the glide he had set as he handed over to me. I daren't in fact move them much because I had no idea of the effect of movement of controls. Somehow, I managed to keep the old 'Rumpety' going on down. There wasn't much height to lose anyway: only about 200 feet. Very soon the earth was visibly rushing up to meet us, and I realised that something would have to be done before we dived into the ground. I drew back on the control column, much over-controlling of course, and the aeroplane began to swoop up again. The engine came on, the controls were snatched out of my hands and a savage shout came back to me from the instructor, 'Bloody awful!' Again, we climbed away, went sweeping round the circuit and in for another landing. I tried to anticipate the next command, but none came, and I just sat there, feeling utterly confused and ineffectual. The grass was coming up again and another landing was upon us. The machine began to flatten out, swept low over the surface and the now familiar clatter of the wheels told me we were on the ground once more. Visibly acknowledging my existence for the first time, the instructor turned slightly and announced in a more conciliatory tone, 'That's better.' 'What's better?' I thought. Then his meaning hit me, and with it a surge of fear about the whole mad act. I hadn't touched the controls. To this day I still have no idea how the aeroplane was landed.[2]

2nd Lieutenant Gordon Taylor, 7 (Reserve) Squadron, RFC

As a result, the instructors often rather dominated the dual controls, meaning that they were doing most of the flying themselves, thereby minimising the risk to their survival from yet another ham-fisted pupil.

On my last flight I was handling the controls and was presumably making the landings. However, I felt that my instructor was actually putting the machine down himself and on the last landing I decided to find out by taking my hands off the controls altogether. The resultant landing was a poor one and Turner ticked me off properly for being a bloody fool and making a bad landing. I said, 'As a matter of fact you made the landing yourself. I did not have my hands on the controls.' He yelled, 'I suppose you think you could do better yourself!' Rather nettled, I said, 'Yes!' With that he undid his seat belt, jumped out and said, 'Well, take her off yourself!' That staggered me for a moment, as I realised I had not received more than a bare 2 hours dual instruction altogether. Not admitting that I was frightened out of my life, however, I decided to have a go at it and attempt my first solo. I took off very carefully and took a long time to climb up to 1,000 feet before daring to make my first turn. Then it took me just on an hour to pluck up enough courage to come down and make my first landing. I bumped rather solidly but had enough sense to put my engine on and go round again. I repeated this performance twice more and finally decided as it was getting dark that, whatever happened, I would not put my engine on again on coming down the third time. The last landing I made was a very good one and I taxied in quite pleased with myself, though the comments from Lieutenant Turner were anything but complimentary. But I did not mind as I had completed my first solo and had not broken anything, no doubt more by good luck than good management![3]

Raymond Brownell, Elementary Training School, Netheravon

Pilots were often asked to go solo too early – almost as if the instructor wanted rid of them once and for all. Gordon Taylor recalled a confrontation when he was suddenly ordered by his instructor to fly solo. Many would have just taken off and flown off to likely destruction, but Taylor was made of sterner stuff.

> To my utter astonishment he got out of his seat, climbed over the side and down, to stand on the grass of the aerodrome. Then he looked up and shouted to me, 'You can bloody well go solo now.' For a moment I couldn't believe he was serious. Then he started to walk away. A decision was forced on me, for better or worse. I put my hand over the side of the nacelle, felt for the switch, and stopped the engine. The instructor turned and came back, shouting at me. His voice was almost hysterical. 'What's the matter with you? Why did you stop the engine?' I shouted back at him. 'I'm not going solo!' I couldn't fly the aeroplane and I wouldn't attempt to. I had never done a take-off, nor a landing without interference, and during the total hour and a half of this nightmare experience I had only briefly flown the machine straight and level even. I hadn't come all the way from my home in Australia to kill myself at an instructor's orders. Shaken and worried, I waited for the inevitable blast. I expected to be placed under arrest. But my instructor was completely unpredictable. He called up to me in an almost friendly voice, 'What do you want to do, then?' What did I want to do? A thought shot out of my mind as a quick, innocent statement of fact. 'I want to fly with another instructor!' 'Very well then. We'll taxi in and I'll see if I can arrange it for you!' Was there a note of relief in his voice? Was I as bad as all that? At the hangar I was handed over to a tall, genial instructor, Lieutenant Prallé. I can see his name now, signed in my logbook. 'I believe you're having some trouble with your flying, Taylor.' 'Well, not exactly, sir. I just don't know how to fly the aeroplane, that's all!' 'All right. Come on out and we'll start from scratch.'[4]
>
> 2nd Lieutenant Gordon Taylor, 7 (Reserve) Squadron, RFC

Taylor's refusal had almost certainly saved him from death, injury or utter humiliation. Not all instructors were bad, but they could also have extreme methods of hammering their point home. Alfred Kingsford had only had an hour and forty minutes of dual control flying when he was taught a valuable lesson.

> 'You're heavy on controls,' Captain Archer said. He was the instructor and not a bad sort. 'Got to get out of it, understand?' He impressed that upon me, but my only reply was a grunt. Then he took me up for an hour to practise landing, but I only annoyed him by sticking her nose down too much. 'Keep her nose up!' he yelled, so I pulled the stick back a bit and along we sailed, good-o as I thought, when he suddenly bawled again, 'Keep her nose up!' I pulled the stick back a good bit. 'Don't stall her!' he shouted and pushed the stick forward. Then I must have let her get her nose down again, for he got

very excited and pushed the stick right forward, with the engine full on, until the old rattle-trap, nose pointing to earth and me in front, was doing about 90. He bawled again, 'That's right, go on, you bloody fool, now stick her nose down and kill the two of us!' So, I reversed her position and stuck her nose up once again. 'Inky' told me that from the ground it looked like a steeplechase: at any rate, it cured me. The impression on my mind of that spot of earth I was going to hit, was indelible; I'd no desire to make acquaintance with that.[5]

2nd Lieutenant Alfred Kingsford, 4 (Reserve) Squadron, RFC

Other instructors were less gruff, less bad tempered and more understanding of the difficulties of the novice and tolerant of their inevitable mistakes. Samuel Saunders explains his philosophy.

I impressed on them that flying wasn't at all difficult – and that they weren't to think that I, or any other instructors, were supermen. Because we weren't! We were only ordinary fellows. I made myself come down to their level of flying and gradually worked them up. I found that, that was a much better way of doing it. I always explained that I didn't mind how many mistakes they made, if they eventually got it correct. I found this was a very fine way of putting it over.[6]

Sergeant Samuel Saunders, 24 (Training) Squadron, RFC

However, novice pilots could be a menace even when their feet were planted firmly on the ground. William Johns certainly excelled himself.

I had not been flying very long at the time, and having done a short flip, I finished up with a nice landing on the far side of the aerodrome. Unfortunately, I lost my prop. This doesn't mean that it fell off. To 'lose your prop' in flying parlance, means that it stops. If the engine timing is correct it shouldn't stop, nevertheless it does sometimes. Well, I didn't want to drag mechanics all the way across the aerodrome to start it for me, so I decided to swing it myself. It didn't seem to be a very difficult thing to do, so, with this object in view, I got out to turn the propeller round a few times to get some gas in the cylinders of the engine. So far so good. I put the switch on 'contact' and went back to the prop and swung. I swung until I was blue in the face but couldn't get so much as a buzz out of it. Panting from the exertion and the heat – I was all wrapped up in my flying kit –I did about the craziest thing I could have done. I opened the throttle a little way. Nothing doing![7]

2nd Lieutenant William Johns, No. 1 School of Aeronautics, RFC

Now what? Johns was stumped, and after ten minutes wrestling with the recalcitrant propeller, he decided to have a little rest to get his breath back. He lay under one of the wings, considering his next options. Sadly, his next move was a blunder of epic proportions, as he decided to open the throttle just a little more. Surely it would start now? It did!

> Bang! My hand hardly seemed to touch that prop before I was flat on my back. I was soon on my feet again staring in horrified dismay at a rapidly retreating aeroplane, already half-way to the sheds, leaping and prancing like an old crow with rheumatism in his wing joints. I set off after it like a stag, yelling like fury, not that there was any need for me to strain my vocal cords. A bunch of air mechanics had already seen the old bird and were racing out to meet her. At a distance of 20 yards or so most of them changed their minds about grabbing her and flung themselves flat to get out of the way of the churning prop. One fellow grabbed a wing tip and hung on long enough to point her nose in my direction, sending up a cloud of dust from her skidding wheels. Then he fell off.[8]
>
> 2nd Lieutenant William Johns, No. 1 School of Aeronautics, RFC

With the aircraft now heading straight towards him, Johns turned round and began to try to evade the attentions of his errant steed.

> I'm no bullfighter! Just when I had abandoned all hope of escape, the brute evidently got the breeze on her tail, for she swung round again and made for the sheds, while I, panting and gasping for breath, watched her in impotent fury. To think that she should turn on me like that! At this moment what should happen but a poor unlucky hoot of a pupil, no doubt breathing a sigh of relief at having done ten minutes flying without busting anything, decided to land. He sat down right in the path of the fiendish machine running amok. My heart went out to him at that moment, but that didn't help him. He scarcely had time to realise what was happening before there was a splintering crash and he sat gazing in stupefied surprise – as if he couldn't believe his eyes – at the place where, a moment before, his lower port plane had been.[9]
>
> 2nd Lieutenant William Johns, No. 1 School of Aeronautics, RFC

Surely things could get no worse. They could!

> But my late aerial conveyance was by no means out of action. Oh no, sir! She just swung her nose round towards the C.O.'s office and off she went again as if she was thoroughly enjoying herself. There must have been a crowd of close on two hundred people chasing her by this time. Airmen, officers, cooks, mess orderlies and goodness knows who else, all in full cry after the culprit. The din sounded like the baying of a pack of hounds. I am not going into all the sad details of what the machine did but among other things she 'wrote off' a Tinside (Martinsyde Scout), an RE8 and a little 'Ack.W.' (Armstrong-Whitworth) before she tried to climb over the C.O.'s office. The place looked

as though it had been bombed by a squadron of enemy bombers and casualties came limping in from all sides of the aerodrome. I brought up the rear, the cynosure of all eyes. The C.O. was waiting for me. His expression was not that of a father welcoming a long-lost son. 'Did you do that?' he asked, breathing heavily, and pointing at the tangled remains of what, 10 minutes earlier, had been a perfectly good aeroplane. The mangled remains piled up against the squadron office were not pretty to look at. 'Yes, sir,' I replied, sadly bracing myself for the worst. The C.O. gulped, swallowed once or twice, shook his head like a man who finds it difficult to express his thoughts in mere words, turned on his heel and strode away.[10]

2nd Lieutenant William Johns, No. 1 School of Aeronautics, RFC

His CO's inarticulacy under such extreme provocation was a blessing indeed.

The young pilots were a lively bunch. Harold Price remembered a social jaunt when the weather was too windy for flying, so he and his friend attended the local church, in Price's case mainly to show off a fetching new outfit of pink trousers and his RFC 'maternity' jacket.

We arrived at about 10.40, so strolled out on Avenue Road to while away the time and admire the Easter bonnets. When we entered [the church] we were following up a very passable pretty daughter with a congenial looking mother. Smith made some remark about the pews and she invited us into hers, second to front, right-hand side of centre aisle. Of course, she put her daughter in first, and then blocked her in by her own pleasant personage, which under the circumstances made a better door than a window. When [the service] was finally over, and we went out, I had a chance to strike up a conversation with the daughter, who was delightfully interesting. A fellow gets horribly bored when he has no chance to chat with a nice girl for a month or two – and is rather inclined to appreciate a little opportunity like this. Smith seemed to find the mother also entertaining.[11]

2nd Lieutenant Harold Price, 15 Reserve Squadron, RFC

Even while training at home, RFC pilots lived their lives coping with a mixture of total safety and extreme danger. Flying accidents were common and the victim could not always walk away unscathed. Funerals were conducted with due solemnity.

At 2.00pm, we gathered at the infirmary. The artillery provided a gun carriage and cortege; the Manchester Regiment the firing party. And practically all of 41 and 15 Squadrons turned out. Eight of us were picked for bearers. The gun carriage drew up on the right of the gateway leading to the mortuary, and the firing party opposite. Opposite to these the officers had fallen in. Up the street the NCOs and men had lined up on each side. The coffin was draped in Union Jacks and covered with wreaths. As we brought it out, on the shoulder, the

firing party came to the present. Then as we made it fast on the gun carriage
the firing party took up its position in front, the officers moving in behind,
and the NCOs and men in rear. In that way we moved in a slow march toward
the cemetery, the firing party with reversed arms, and all with bowed heads. It
is one of the most impressive ceremonies I have ever experienced.[12]

2nd Lieutenant Harold Price, 15 Reserve Squadron, RFC

Whatever the actual level of their flying skills, the pupils soon became imbued with
plenty of confidence that they had mastered their trade. They knew it all; nothing
could go wrong!

Within the next two days I had completed 5½ hours solo flying and had carried
out the necessary wireless aerial test. I shudder now to think of my super
confidence and bravado at this period. While on my last solo flight I landed
in a field a few miles away from the Netheravon aerodrome and took for a
flight a very nice girl I had met at a local dance the night before. Little did she
realise the risk she was running in flying with such an inexperienced novice.[13]

Raymond Brownell, Elementary Training School, Netheravon

They would learn soon enough how little they really knew.

*   *   *

Change had begun in 1916, but it was a faltering process. The requirements for
a pilot to gain his wings had been stiffened, so that they now had to climb much
higher, switch off their engine, glide down and land within a circular area just 50
yards in diameter. Flare-assisted night landings were practiced, and they had to
complete a 60-mile cross-country flight interrupted by landings at two airfields on
the way. It was intended that no pilot should be sent to the Western Front without
at least fifteen hours' solo flying time, which was raised in December 1916 to twenty
hours. However, when this was not feasible, such as under the strains and losses
experienced in the spring of 1917, it dropped back to about seventeen hours. This
was the low point, as later that year the number of training hours again began to
increase. Indeed, they were soon required to have completed a minimum of twenty
hours' solo flying *before* they qualified for their wings. This would continue to rise
in 1918.

There was a change from a concentration on 'safe flying' to the encouragement of
aerobatics that might increase a pilot's ability to handle his machine in dangerous
circumstances. Stunt flying was no longer abhorred, but positively encouraged.
This reached its apogee at the School of Special Flying that was established at Fort
Grange Gosport by the redoubtable Lieutenant Colonel Robert Smith-Barry. He
had developed an intensive system of flying using the two-seater Avro 504 equipped
with the 'Gosport Tube', a simple invention which allowed the instructor to talk

to his pupil. Hitherto, they had to momentarily stall the engine to allow them to converse. Smith-Barry believed that aerial accidents were almost all caused by sheer ignorance; if pupils knew what they were doing and what the result of every touch on the controls would be by dint of experience, then they would be equipped to survive almost anything. Instead of frightening a beginner with dread warnings of the consequences of spinning or stalling, an instructor should teach them how to trigger the supposed disaster – and then how to get out of it alive. His methods would spread across the RFC, assisted by other like-minded instructors up and down the country. Harold Balfour witnessed an example of Smith-Barry's methods.

Captain Billy Williams took up an Avro to practice completely stalled landings. At 500 feet he stalled until the engine and propeller ceased revolving, then glided down slowly at a steep angle, rather like the descent of an autogyro, holding his machine balanced by sheer skill as a pilot. In attempting to land from the stalled glide he misjudged the final movement of the elevators and fell heavily the last few feet, crashing the undercarriage. Colonel Smith-Barry stood on the tarmac, and, without a word, watched Williams jump out of the wrecked Avro and order another. The second Avro, too, stalled heavily near the ground and crashed. Still the colonel watched unspeaking. Williams, determined to succeed, went up in a third machine, and this time achieved his purpose, making an almost stationary landing in front of his own hangar with his engine stopped. 'Good show, Williams,' he said, 'but it's a good thing for you that you didn't stop at number two!' That was Smith-Barry, who believed that the result of successful achievement justified the cost. Failure he would not brook at any cost. His actions were always direct and unequivocal.[14]

Lieutenant Harold Balfour, School of Special Flying, Gosport

Even at Gosport, it wasn't all hard work and no play.

One day, Williams, when flying off Stokes Bay, crossed a large bathing tank with canvas screen sides which was moored some 200 yards from the shore. Around the inside of the screens was a wooden walk for the bathers who used the structure as a great swimming bath. Williams found that on this particular afternoon it was given up for the use of all the young ladies from the neighbouring schools. He circled round it to the intense embarrassment of the bathers. On this day, the following week, at the same time, no less than twelve machines appeared above the tank and proceeded to disorganise the bathing party. After this, orders were issued prescribing the district a prohibited area.[15]

Lieutenant Harold Balfour, School of Special Flying, Gosport

In addition, newly qualified pilots were from this time sent to reserve training squadrons, where they would be given an opportunity to fly and gain at least five hours' familiarity with the type of aircraft to which they would be posted to serve in on the Western Front. This seems obvious, but it had not been possible previously.

There were increasing efforts to train the new pilots in the skills of aerial fighting. There was firstly a renewed emphasis in gunnery for both pilots and observers. This stretched not only to stripping and firing both the Vickers and Lewis machine guns on the ground ranges, but also using a camera gun to check their accuracy in combat simulations. Observer Jack Wilkinson found that bored pilots often threw their aircraft about in a spirited attempt to upset their passenger during such sessions.

> Fighting with a camera gun was good fun. In appearance very like a Lewis gun we found that pulling back the cocking handle moved on the film and pressing the trigger made the exposure. When the negatives were developed the prints, by means of superimposed faint circles, showed the range at which the 'burst' had been fired, whether a hit had been scored, or how much error had been made. The film allowed for sixteen exposures but owing to lag in winding it on and off, we were lucky if as many as a dozen prints showed up. On one occasion, having taken five 'shots' I became violently airsick. Both we and the 'enemy' were stunting in order to make it more difficult for the opposing observer to take steady aim and I suppose something inside me decided that it could not, or would not, stay put. Wearily I swung the camera gun round in its Scarff mounting, tried to draw a bead on the opposing aeroplane, and then a further attack of nausea seized me and I lay gasping over the side of the cockpit, gazing hopelessly at the swaying earth, the cock-eyed horizon, and the pale sun that matched my condition so damnably. 'How many more have you got to take?' the pilot called back. 'Oh, God, I dunno!' I croaked 'What?' he shouted. Then he looked round. A broad grin appeared below his goggles. 'Let's see – shepherd's pie for lunch, wasn't it?' he taunted me. But the worst was over, and I somehow managed to make the remainder of the exposures without the further loss of – shall we say – dignity![16]
>
> Lieutenant Jack Wilkinson, School of Aerial Gunnery, Hythe

Howard Andrews was another observer who ran into trouble on camera gun practice.

> It was an ordinary machine-gun with a camera strapped on the front and every time you pressed the trigger you took a photograph. We were taken up in the air, flown round and every time we saw an aeroplane on the ground or in the air, we took photographs of it. The first time I went up with this gun of course I didn't know anything – I didn't know which was ground and which was sky! The Canadian pilot was a bit of a devil, and the aeroplane went round like a drunken caterpillar. I looked round and I couldn't see aeroplanes anywhere. The pilot swore at me and pointed at the ground – I saw one on the ground, so I took a photograph and gave it up! He screamed at me, 'Where do you want to go?' I said, 'I'd like to go to Hastings!' He said, 'All right!' We got to

Hastings, and he went right round the pier – I thought it looked nice, so I took a photograph of it! I thought to myself, 'I've done myself now – I can't get this off.' We came back and landed. The squadron leader came racing over to the pilot ticking him off as apparently, he wasn't allowed to go anywhere near Hastings and not thinking I'd pressed the trigger. The next day they read out that somebody got six aeroplanes, somebody got five and he said, 'Stand up, Cadet Andrews!' I stood up and he said, 'You've got one photograph of an aeroplane, very nice, one of Hastings Pier and one of the squadron leader – and he doesn't like it!'[17]

2nd Lieutenant Howard Andrews, RFC

The single-seaters also practiced firing at ground targets, which allowed them to fire real bullets and to check their accuracy subsequently. Many were shocked to find they had scored few or even no hits. It was a very difficult business. William Johns remembered a senior instructor tearing him off a strip.

He had rather an unpleasant way of talking to pupils, making you feel as if you were about as much use as a bad headache. 'Now,' he said, after his red-hot speech, preparing to get into the cockpit I had just vacated. 'I'll show you the way to do it. Dive at the target, not glide at it. Hold your fire until the last second – say 20 or 30 feet – then zoom up over the target. Watch me!' I watched. He took off, climbed to a thousand feet, put his nose down nearly vertically and streaked like a shooting star at the target, guns spitting tracer bullets. That part of it was pretty to watch but what followed was not so pleasant. It seemed to me that he pulled out of his dive just about a tenth of a second too late. There was a crash of splintered wood, a cloud of dust rose in the air and then silence. 'Well,' I said to a pal who was standing watching the performance. 'That's that. It may be his idea of how to shoot up a target, but it isn't mine.'[18]

2nd Lieutenant William Johns, No. 1 School of Aeronautics, RFC

The RFC high command, aware of the problems of poor gunnery, began a series of courses for those pilots already serving at the front. As a sign of increasing inter-service cooperation, RNAS pilots were also invited to attend. Leonard Rochford took advantage of this, but was shocked at what the practical tests revealed. Indeed, it would change his aerial tactics.

I flew with my flight to Berck-sur-Mer where the RFC had organised a series of weekly courses in gunnery in the air and on the ground. The tests in the air were of two types and consisted of diving and firing on a floating target in a pond and firing at a canvas drogue towed by a BE2c. At my first attempt on the pond target I had seventeen hits out of two hundred possible and at a second attempt fifteen hits out of one hundred and twenty possible.

On the towed target my one and only attempt produced eighteen outers and seven inners out of a possible four hundred. These were not very good results! Considering the vital importance to us of air-gunnery at the time, it is surprising – in retrospect – that neither we nor the authorities made much effort to improve the standard which was obviously inadequate, especially amongst the newly trained pilots. Clearly, pilots were expected to develop their own skills and methods in this most important facet of war flying so, realising my low standard of marksmanship, I resorted to surprising the enemy and only firing at point-blank range.[19]

Flight Sub Lieutenant Leonard Rochford, 3 Naval Squadron, RNAS

Eventually, Schools of Aerial Fighting were established, where the very best aces would impart their acquired 'tricks of the trade' to pupils. Frederick Powell was posted as chief fighting instructor based at RFC Upavon in February 1917. He had to some extent matured after his two years of experience at the front.

My responsibility was to see that fighting instructors were actually instructing the pupils in the art of fighting: the method of attack; keeping the sun behind you where possible; always attacking from underneath and behind an aircraft. It struck me as being so ridiculous to ask a man to instruct a pupil – who is standing on the aerodrome – in the art of flying. Just to go up and fly about oneself and do a few acrobatics wasn't teaching the pupil on the ground anything at all. One might as well expect anybody who paid half a crown at Hendon to watch a flying display to come away from the aerodrome a fully qualified pilot![20]

Chief Fighting Instructor Frederick Powell, RFC Upavon

There was also a new emphasis on flying in formation. This was crucial in action for defensive purposes, especially when flying a two-seater, where the massed machine guns flying in concert had at least a chance of beating off a German scout attack. But the scout pilots also had to learn it – they too would fly in a tight formation – and had to keep to it as long as possible to maximise the 'punch' they could give to any German aircraft or formation they surprised.

When a pilot had completed all this training, he was posted on active service. On 25 July 1917, Guy Knocker thought he was ready for anything as he flew over London in his Sopwith Pup.

I have completed my tests for France. I had a topping flip yesterday. I flew over the 'Shop' at Woolwich and did a few spins, loops, rolls etc. I then went to Thames Reservoir where they have a floating target and I came down to about 100 feet over the water and fired at it with my machine gun, great fun! Then I flew off again, I was right down low over the water and I felt like a hydroplane! Then I went to Brooklands and 'fought' an RE8 – I fancy he got me with his back gun – not firing really of course! Then I flew back at 85mph. Suddenly whizz-boom and a very fast scout – a Sopwith Camel – shot past me and whipped round onto my tail! I was rather bamboozled, but eventually I did an Immelmann turn and got him off. Then we circled round, and I was in the centre and turning very fast – and he was on the outside of the circle. Eventually I got on his tail [and] then he buzzed off! I went up again later and did some beautiful stunts over the aerodrome and then – [a] crashed landing. What a blow! I flattened out too soon and pancaked – my undercarriage conked with a sickening crunch and the bus stood up gently on its nose! I wasn't in the least hurt, but I was sick at crashing![21]

2nd Lieutenant Guy Knocker, 40th Training Squadron, RFC

Knocker was confident he was ready for France, but read the quote again: he was shot down by an RE8; he was bounced all unknowing by a Sopwith Camel; and he misjudged his approach and crash-landed. Two fatal mistakes and one embarrassment – there would be no leeway for such young pilots on the Western Front.

Chapter 7

Up the Arras, 1917

People have often asked me whether it was not better to be in the infantry than the Flying Corps and vice versa – always a stupid question because it depends on individual temperament. The difference and the advantage of life in the Flying Corps was that we had three or four hours each day of intense fear, but that the rest of the time we lived in the utmost comfort.[1]

 Lieutenant Harold Balfour, 43 Squadron, RFC

O h! Oh! Oh! What a lovely war. The life of RFC airmen may have seemed like a dream to the embattled 'Tommies' in the trenches, but in the lead-up to the Battle of Arras, the pilots and observers found that life was anything but 'lovely'. The changeover in the French High Command, with the removal of General Joseph Joffre in December 1916, brought to the fore General Robert Nivelle, who had gained a dangerous degree of confidence that he had 'cracked' all the problems of modern warfare during his period in control of the successful closing phases of the Battle of Verdun. Nivelle now conceived of a massive onslaught by three French armies in the Champagne area in mid-April 1917. It was not long before French and British politicians were attracted by the promises of glittering success that he weaved around their fuzzy heads. One who was entranced by this vision of an easier, quicker, victory was the new British Prime Minister, David Lloyd George. From a position of ignorance, he had long been sceptical of the efficacy of British offensives on the Western Front, a negative position that had hardened with the dreadful losses suffered during the Battle of the Somme. He favoured an 'Easterner' policy, preferring the prospects offered by the British campaigns in Palestine and Salonika. But Nivelle offered another way: certain victory, and the British were only required to launch a major diversion earlier in April, the operations which would become known as the Battle of Arras. Lloyd George may have been a very poor general or strategist, but he was a brilliant politician. Conspiring with the French against his own generals, there was a quick 'flash of knives' at the Anglo-French Conference at Calais in February. Before he knew what was happening, a very aggrieved by-now Field Marshal Sir Douglas Haig found himself effectively placed under the overall command of Nivelle.

 Before they were so rudely interrupted, Haig and Joffre had intended to launch a vast joint Anglo-French offensive in the Somme area, followed by Haig's own pet scheme of a major attack in the Ypres area. With the advent of Nivelle, Haig and his generals buckled in to planning the Arras offensive. The new tactics so painfully acquired over the previous two years were to be deployed: crunching bombardments, the methodical targeting of German batteries with heavy fire and the layers of creeping barrages passing across the ground. But in the air, this meant much the same duties for the RFC that they had carried out so successfully during the Battle of the Somme: more photographs, more artillery observation and more long-range reconnaissance to check on German moves. So far so good, but the problem was that they would have to do all these tasks in the same aircraft that had been so comprehensively outclassed by the German scouts, particularly the Albatros DI and DII, in the closing months of 1916. Trouble was brewing.

One unit that soon found itself right in the thick of it was 43 Squadron, equipped with Sopwith 1½ Strutters and under the command of Major William Sholto Douglas. The squadron arrived at Treizennes airfield on the Western Front at the end of 1916. One of his young flight commanders was someone we have encountered before.

Harold Balfour, then a captain, came to join me in No. 43 Squadron as one of my flight commanders. He was then only twenty years of age, tall, slim, and very alert. Well above the average in intelligence, he was a highly-strung youngster who was clearly feeling the strain of the great amount of active service and operational flying that he had done. Because of that his courage and what he achieved are all the more admirable.[2]

Major William Sholto Douglas, 43 Squadron, RFC

Another 'old friend' based at Treizennes was the redoubtable Major Robert Lorraine, who was commanding 40 Squadron, flying the now equally obsolescent FE8s. Lorraine, the actor, was now playing the part of squadron commander with consummate ease, as Balfour recalled.

The whole of his organisation was stage-managed with a masterly touch. The officers' mess was filled with patent bells and alarm gongs which might go off at any moment, each one indicating some different event such as the start of a patrol, or the sighting of an enemy aeroplane. Always, when one of these went off it was the custom that not an eyelid should quiver – scarcely altering his tone of conversation he would turn to whomever was concerned: 'Gregory – I think there is an enemy around. I think you had better go,' and then on with the game of bridge. On the other hand, I have seen him on the floor, allowing himself to be rolled about by his junior officers, for always a commanding officer must be able to be 'a boy among boys' if he is to play his part to the uttermost.[3]

Lieutenant Harold Balfour, 43 Squadron, RFC

Perhaps Lorraine's greatest moment came when the Germans carried out a bombing raid over Treizennes on the night of 21 January 1917. Cometh the hour, cometh the man. It was the perfect opportunity for theatrical histrionics, and one that Lorraine would not miss.

> One night all the alarms all over the camp started ringing simultaneously. Fire had broken out in one of his sheds which housed four F.E.s. His fire-picket and our fire-picket doubled to the spot, but there was nothing to be done except to form a semicircle around the blazing hangar and let the fire burn itself out. The petrol tanks had gone up, the doped wings were burning furiously, the dried wood of the hangar likewise, while machine-gun ammunition went off with continuous pops. Adjoining the hangar was a lean-to shed which held various mechanics' tools. One little sergeant thought that he was being of help by going into the lean-to, which was not yet in flames, and starting to throw out spanners, vices, screw-drivers and other implements. Hardly had he started this somewhat futile task when with a bound Robert Lorraine entered within the ring, darted in front of the assembled squadrons, through the glare and into the shed. Seizing the little sergeant by the coat collar he pulled him away and hurled him towards the fire-picket, 'Away! If this is anybody's place it is mine!' he shouted in a voice of ringing tones which carried right across the aerodrome, and then, in order to show, and quite rightly so, that the destruction of the four burning machines was not irreparable, and that he, as the one responsible, could divert his mind to other matters more mundane, he strode to the middle of the arena and there, in the full glare of the light, performed a perfectly natural function in front of the admiring eyes of the assembled officers and mechanics.[4]
>
> Lieutenant Harold Balfour, 43 Squadron, RFC

The stream of urine did not put out the flames, but his actions appeared as a point of interest in several post-war memoirs.

> Suddenly, reflected in the light from the fire, there appeared in front of us the arresting figure of Lorraine and it was as if he had stepped out from the wings to take up his position in front of the footlights. This was the occasion for the star to play his part – and play it he did! Unbuttoning his trousers and aiming in the direction of the fire, he performed almost with contempt, and certainly with defiance.[5]
>
> Major William Sholto Douglas, 43 Squadron, RFC

What a performance!

* * *

The agony of airmen sent off, day-after-day, in by-then obsolescent aircraft was the background to the spring of 1917 as the RFC strove to carry out its responsibilities to the army. They had to get the photographs and they had to guide the shells down onto their myriad targets. If they failed, thousands of men might die when they went over the top. At this time, the FE2b was still used in a photographic reconnaissance role and even in an escort role, for which it was no longer adequate. On 4 April, 2nd Lieutenant Geoffrey Hopkins and Air Mechanic H. Friend were on a mission over the German lines in their FE2b A5486.

> I was one of the rear aircraft in a flight formation when a Hun dived on me and started shooting at very long range. Just as my observer stood up to open fire at the Hun over the top plane, there was a loud thud or clank under my seat. A bullet had penetrated the main petrol tank, on which I was sitting, and made a large, ragged hole in it – as I discovered later! The result was that air pressure in the tank immediately dropped, [and] my engine ran out of petrol and stopped. This might perhaps have been avoided if I had had the wit and time to switch over to my reserve gravity supply tank. However, one is perhaps liable to forget to do the right thing when one is being shot at and there was a very strong smell of petrol as it spurted out over my feet. When my engine stopped, we were somewhere just about above the Hindenburg Line, but the situation on the ground was so muddled and uncertain that nobody knew just which part of the area was held by evacuating enemy troops and which by ours. It was thus advisable to glide back as far as possible towards our own side of the lines. This I did. My observer took the guns off their mountings and stored them in the bottom of the nacelle, as we prepared for a crash landing. The whole locality was a mass of shell holes, old trenches, barbed wire and so on; so, I was lucky to be able to land without crashing or turning the aircraft over. We landed with a bit of a bump with the wheels either side of a shell hole and came to rest tilted up on one wing but otherwise undamaged. The place appeared to be deserted when we landed, but very shortly several khaki clad figures appeared and advised us in lurid terms to, 'Get out of that [fucking] plane before the [fucking] Jerries start to shell it!' So, we scrambled out and went down a trench for some distance, eventually reaching a dugout where some infantry officers entertained us.[6]
>
> 2nd Lieutenant Geoffrey Hopkins, 22 Squadron, RFC

They had landed near Moislains – they had indeed been fortunate to have glided that far.

Perhaps worse situated were the men still flying the BE2c and its later variants. The intended replacement, the RE8, was still delayed, so the BE2c had to carry on as the workhorse of the RFC, flying above the line dutifully photographing and artillery observing – all the while praying that they would not be intercepted by one of the dreaded new German scouts. Experienced air crews had learnt how to defend themselves as best they could.

The first precaution we took was to see that the observer knelt on his seat, facing the pilot, and ready to bring the rear Lewis gun into action. It soon became apparent that those who, when attacked, dived steeply away from the aggressor, became casualties. For this reason, the following tactics were adopted:- if far over the line: fly towards the line, doing gentle turns to right and left, and at the same time altering the height – switchbackwise. If near the line: fly towards the line, diving and doing gentle turns to the right and left. Both these methods had the advantage of keeping the best field of fire towards the enemy – rear field – whilst it made it difficult for the enemy to use his sights and to follow. If suddenly attacked: should the attack have come as a complete surprise, we thought that to do nothing, or to slightly dive, was to court disaster. For this reason, when a tracer bullet passed the machine, or guns were heard at close range, one of the following movements were made – a 'flat turn' or a 'stall'. Both these movements were sufficient to spoil the shooting of the single-seater, whilst giving one time to see it, and to make up one's mind.[7]

Lieutenant Donald Stevenson, 12 Squadron, RFC

This was all well and good; but what about the raw young pilots fresh from training in England? They were often easy meat when flying the BE2c faced by the likes of Manfred von Richthofen and the rising aces of his new squadron, Jasta 11.

Terrible problems were also experienced by the pilots and observers of 45 Squadron. They flew the Sopwith 1½ Strutter, the same aircraft that had seemed a wonderful and noble steed scant months before, but which had been rendered obsolescent by the advent of the Albatros. The lack of manoeuvrability made it almost helpless if intercepted on a long-range reconnaissance mission when a long way home. Under these circumstances, morale began to falter as men railed against the impossible circumstances they faced.

The situation became so chaotic that it was almost funny. As casualties whittled down our normal airman resources, we were reduced to calling for volunteers from line regiments. Soon even those were hard to come by, because rumours about the 'Suicide Club' were filtering down to the infantry, who became sarcastically curious to know why we couldn't supply our own gunners. Almost none of those who did volunteer had ever been up in the air; no qualifications were required of them beyond the ability to load and fire a Lewis gun. Too often those unsung heroes were airsick in the whirling's of a dogfight, or else they used the gun installation as something to hang onto instead of to shoot with. Then again, we occasionally got specimens such as my completely fearless Scottish infantry lieutenant: full of guts and ignorance, highly belligerent and trigger-happy; he itched to shoot at anything, everything, or nothing, regardless of range. In one dogfight in which our Sopwiths received unexpected reinforcements from some F.E.s from No. 20 Squadron, he opened fire on one of the F.E.s merely because it looked different, and I had to kick the rudder

Hugh Trenchard appointed Officer Commanding the RFC's units in France in Summer 1915. (*Internet Source*)

Robert Lorraine had a notable pre-war stage career in both London and on Broadway, before learning to fly. (*Internet Source*)

Louis Strange, pioneer of aerial fighting armament and tactics, and involved right through the war. (*Internet Source*)

The great early RFC air fighter and C.O. of 24 Squadron, Lanoe Hawker. He was killed in combat with Manfred von Richthofen. (*Internet Source*)

Albert Ball British ace with 44 victories, lost in air fighting over enemy territory on 7 May 1917 in his 56 Squadron RFC SE5 A4850. (*Internet Source*)

Edward Mannock who would claim 61 confirmed victories with three Squadrons. (*Internet Source*)

Cecil Lewis claimed 8 victories with 56 Squadron RFC in the summer of 1917. (*Internet Source*)

Arthur Gould Lee standing in front of his 46 Squadron RFC Sopwith Camel, probably in late 1917. (*Internet Source*)

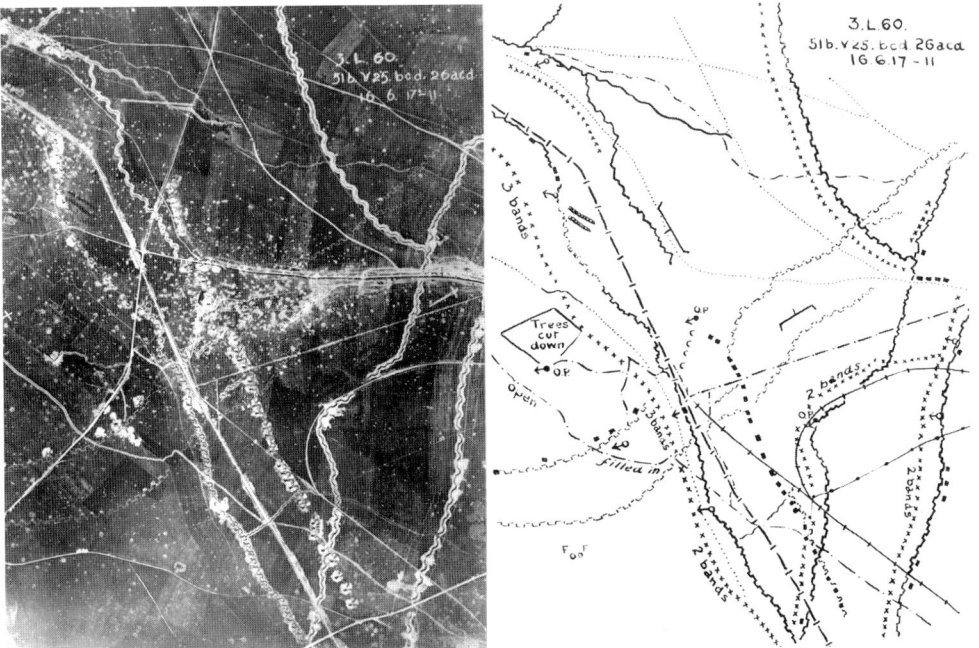

An aerial photograph with its corresponding annotated tracing – the first detailed step in the vital task of interpreting images taken, so often, at cost of lives, by Allied airmen.

The bodies of Lieutenant D. Corbett Wilson and 2nd Lieutenant I. N. Woodiwiss are grimly evident in the burnt-out remains of Morane L 1872 of 3 Squadron RFC, hit by AA on 10 May 1915. (See page 52)

Freshly dug graves somewhere in France, The aviators' graves are marked by cut down propellers for crosses.

The pilot of BE2c 4116 of 15 Squadron RFC, 2nd Lieutenant G. J. L. Welsford, was killed in the air and Lieutenant W. J. Joyce wounded and taken prisoner, after combat with Immelmann on 30 March 1916.

A Fokker Eindekker Mark III roams the sky above a patchwork of fields in late 1915.

2nd Lieutenant O. Lerwill's 24 Squadron DH2 5930, after strong winds and engine failure had caused him to descend, to be taken prisoner, on 25 March 1916.

Lieutenants H. H. Balfour and D. V. Armstrong share a joke while at 60 Squadron RFC in late 1916. Armstrong was considered by many as the most talented Camel pilot of the war.

The highly honoured and talented James McCudden pictured with his Sopwith Pup A7311 whilst back in the UK helping with training and home defence mid 1917 at Joyce RFC Green.

An air-to-air photograph of a German Albatros DV fighter, serial D717417.

A group of 40 Squadron RAF officers at Bruay in April 1918.

An SE5a of 32 Squadron. The serial number has been removed for security.

Sopwith Camel fighters around April 1918.

A German DFW CIV passes over Fromeréville, near Verdun, in March 1918.

A 58 Squadron FE2b Night Bomber being bombed up one evening.

A Handley Page O400 pilot strikes a stoical pose in front of his unit's heavy night bombers. The unit is unknown.

hard to throw his aim off. The only things I ever knew him to hit for certain were our own tail, rudder and wing tips.[8]

Captain Frank Courtney, 45 Squadron, RFC

There is no doubt that under the strain, some pilots and observers became heavily dependent on the healing powers of alcohol. Lieutenant Norman Macmillan remembered one flight with a drunk observer.

We left the ground at 6.15am. My observer was not my usual flying comrade but flew with me because his own pilot was on leave. He was still feeling the effects of the bottles he had helped to consume the night before and was very morose. We climbed in formation to 10,000 feet. At 8,000 feet the cold sobered my observer completely, and he began to talk to me through the speaking tube. For an hour he told me stories, his head buried inside his cockpit to keep out of the air blast in which it was impossible to make oneself heard down the speaking tube. Outside the cockpit the wind rush whipped one's words away instantly. Great clouds formed rapidly below us, making it impossible for us to achieve our object. Our leader fired the washout signal Very light, and we returned downward and westward towards the aerodrome. At 6,000 feet my flying companion's voice ceased. I looked back but could not see him. When we landed, he had again become alcoholically quiet, and was in a worse state than when we first left the ground. Yet all the time above 8,000 feet he had been most amazingly energised.[9]

2nd Lieutenant Norman Macmillan, 45 Squadron, RFC

Another day, another long-distance patrol. On 6 April, 2nd Lieutenant George Truscott was acting as the observer for the Sopwith 1½ Strutter A1093 flown by 2nd Lieutenant John Marshall. Truscott, something of a humourist, had come up with a 'cunning plan' to help beat the odds against him.

Truscott was mess president of 'B' Flight and kept the mess funds in assorted bunches of French currency. One morning a reconnaissance was announced which promised to be sticky (it was) and Truscott was going as observer with Marshall. As we got ready, Truscott made a big show of putting a fat envelope of paper francs into the pocket of his flying coat and informed us, 'This is my special system of self-preservation! When you observe my machine being attacked, you will all say, "Look, there go our Mess Funds!" and you will all rally round to protect me!' I suppose, at the age we were then, the idea of being shot down was always somewhat academic, so nobody took any more notice. During the show, Campbell was shot down first. Marshall, with Truscott, was flying a little high to the left and slightly behind me, and another machine was between us. Six or eight Huns were coming up, apparently too far behind to start shooting. We never knew what actually happened, but possibly a long-range fluke shot from the Huns hit Marshall's rigging, for I saw his right wing fold up and, as he twisted round, he crashed into the next machine. Both wrecks, with bits flying in all directions, missed my tail by a few feet and, of course, there was no hope for the four fellows inside. With the inevitable lack of any sense of proportion which goes with such affairs, I thought, 'Goodbye, Truscott, but what about our mess money?' And then another dogfight started and there was no time to think of anything else. When Austin, my observer, and I finally walked into the mess hut, a corporal came up to me, with a fat envelope, 'Mr Truscott told me to give you this if he didn't come back this evening!'[10]

2nd Lieutenant Frank Courtney, 45 Squadron, RFC

Not long afterwards, Frank Courtney was sent home when his fraying patience snapped.

One of the four pilots, full of anguish at the thought of the men who had been lost, in the hearing of the Brigadier General, made the classic remark which caused him to be transferred to the Home Establishment, 'Some people say that Sopwith two-seaters are bloody fine machines, but I think they're more bloody than fine!'[11]

2nd Lieutenant Norman Macmillan, 45 Squadron RFC

If only Frank Courtney had known the long-term replacement for the Sopwith 1½ Strutter had actually made its debut the day before the loss of Truscott. The Bristol Fighter was a two-seater-scout, the pilot with a forward-firing synchronised Vickers machine gun, whilst the rear gunner had a Lewis gun. So much the same, but it also had a fantastic new engine, the Rolls Royce Falcon, which powered it to a top speed of just over 110 miles per hour at 10,000 feet, with a superb rate of climb. Trenchard had held back its deployment, hoping to fling them into action at the pivotal moment, just before the battle started. That was fair enough, but instead of assigning them to an experienced unit used to flying on the Western Front, the first to be equipped with the Bristol Fighter was the inexperienced 48 Squadron. To make matters worse, on 5 April, the first patrol of six Bristol Fighters was led over the lines by the heroic figure of Captain William Leefe Robinson VC, the Zeppelin conqueror, who sadly had no experience of the latest scout tactics. Was this a patrol over a quiet area of the front, designed to let them 'bed down' in relative safety? No, of course not! It was conducted over Douai, the lair of Richthofen and Jasta 11. What happened? Guess who survived to tell the tale?

It was foggy and altogether very bad weather when I attacked an enemy squadron while it was flying between Douai and Valenciennes. Up to this point, it had managed to advance without being fired upon. I attacked with four planes of my Staffel. I personally singled out the last machine, which I forced to land near Lewards after a short fight. The occupants burnt their machine. It was a new type of plane, which we had not known before, and it appears to be quick and rather handy, with a powerful motor, V-shaped and 12 cylindered. Its name could not be recognised. The DIII Albatros was, both in speed and ability to climb, undoubtedly superior.[12]

Oberleutnant Manfred von Richthofen, Jasta 11, Imperial German Air Service

All six Bristol Fighters were shot down, with Richthofen shooting down two, taking his victory total to thirty-six. This was a disaster, but it was also understandable, perhaps even predictable. The newcomers had had no chance to realise that the Bristol Fighter was not to be flown staidly in formation, placidly reacting to events, but was itself a scout that could be thrown about the sky like any single-seater, with the bonus of a rear-gunner to defend its tail.

*   *   *

Despite the losses, the RFC carried out all its duties as required by the army, and when the Battle of Arras began on 9 April 1917, the initial stages were a resounding success. The German bastion of Vimy Ridge was overwhelmed by the Canadian Corps, while there was a dramatic advance by Third Army of some 4 miles, pressing towards Monchy-le-Preux. It was a notable achievement, but there was no breakthrough, for the Germans had switch-line defences and the heavy fortifications of the Hindenburg Line to fall back on. The wintry weather was appalling, with snow falling and gales blowing. Nevertheless, Charles Smart struggled up aloft to do what he could to help the men on the ground.

Terrific wind blowing and as bumpy as Satan. First passenger soon got fed up with things and passed me a note saying he felt sick and wanted to go home. I passed a note back reminding him that there was a war on and telling him to think of the poor devils down below. He said he couldn't stand it any longer, so I brought him in after an hour and 35 minutes and he cleared off. I got another observer (Lt Boyle) at once and went up again, this chap was the real thing, he felt very sick in the bumps but did not say anything about it. We had a great time and sent down a number of 'Zone Calls' and had the satisfaction of seeing several active enemy batteries strafed and silenced, thus making things easier for our infantry. Our shell fire today was worth seeing, the enemy lines were simply seething with bursting shells, and it looked impossible for anything to live there.[13]

2nd Lieutenant Charles Smart, 16 Squadron, RFC

The sacrifices of the RFC seemed to have been all worthwhile. Indeed, they *were* worthwhile. They had harnessed the power of the guns to fantastic effect. If this had been the end of it, then all might have been well. After all, the great 'war-winning' French offensive was planned to commence on 16 April. But as Manfred von Richthofen and the other Germans scouts plied their murderous trade, the RFC air crews found themselves caught up in what later became known as 'Bloody April', with losses multiplying at a terrifying rate. Pilots began to reach the end of their personal resources of courage. One such was Harold Balfour, who was again cracking up under the severe strain.

> This period was the one in which I first realised the full terror of aerial combat, but, at the same time, learnt in some way to cultivate a detachment of mind which enabled one, not to overcome fear but to separate oneself from it. Going into a fight, after some mental practice of attaining this state of mind, was something like going into a cold bath; but once in the fight one became impersonal: some secondary person did the right thing at the right moment; this secondary being took the initiative and would do some brave act or some clever manoeuvre; it was not oneself, for one's own real mind could watch this secondary being in operation. The trying and exhausting time was when at the end of the fight, one's personality displaced once more this secondary being and took charge of one's body; then would be realised the full terror, then would hands and feet shake, and mouth go dry with fear and the full reaction set in. This secondary being detachment was the only means that kept one going.[14]
>
> Lieutenant Harold Balfour, 43 Squadron, RFC

In the mess, they tried to maintain their morale, drinking, socialising and engaging in practical jokes and banter, like most men of their age.

> Thank goodness for Tom Purdey who, every night, used to keep us cheerful by songs at the piano and alternatively, when we got bored with that, allowed us to hold him by his feet and shake him upside down in his kilt! It may sound childish these years past, but it was only such stupid and light-hearted behaviour as this that kept us going.[15]
>
> Lieutenant Harold Balfour, 43 Squadron, RFC

But even when he was in the mess, the thoughts of the next day's trials intruded.

> Every night, in the middle of dinner, the orderly from the wing headquarters used to bring a sealed envelope to our squadron commander. [William Sholto Douglas] would open the envelope, read the squadron's operation orders from the wing, then detail out to us our jobs for the next day. Somehow food lost its attraction and spirits sank for an appreciable time after we knew the contents of that envelope.[16]
>
> Lieutenant Harold Balfour, 43 Squadron, RFC

Balfour's tour of duty ended when he lost concentration while he and his observer, 2nd Lieutenant E.H. Jones, were flying their Sopwith 1½ Strutter A8235 over the German lines in the Vimy Ridge sector on the morning of 27 April. It was easily done, but it could have had fatal consequences.

The wind had drifted me gradually eastwards while the line of the ridge itself turned rather west, tending to make my straight course one which would take me farther and farther over the enemy side. I swung for home and, putting the nose down, opened the throttle wide. The wind was against me and almost as I carried out this change of course the infantry machine-guns and rifles started at me. I swung the machine about from side to side, flying a zigzag course and managing to avoid most of the bullets, with only an occasional hole appearing in one or other of the wings. But before I had reached the front lines there was a harsh metallic clang, and the engine and propeller stopped. One of the cylinders must have been shot through and the motor, suffering internal damage, had packed up. There was nothing for it except to glide dead straight, nursing every bit of height that I had left me, if I wished to reach our sector. This was one of the most unpleasant moments that I have ever experienced, because on every other occasion when I have been fighting, I have had command of my machine, the ability to manoeuvre, and the power to retaliate. Now, my front machine-gun pointed only to the British lines. I did not dare to divert from the straight path and could only hope and trust that I should have sufficient height to land somewhere where I should not be made a prisoner or shot down by rifle fire. As I glided down the last two or three hundred feet, I said to myself, 'Well, if they say it is better to be unstrapped, I will go with the majority!' I flicked up the safety catch of my belt, and this release probably saved my life for the whole of the front part of the aeroplane was stoved in and the engine came back to where my legs would have been, both of which must have been crushed to pulp by its weight and mass. We just tipped the Ridge, with a few feet to spare, and then stalled the last 20 feet to the ground on the further side of the slope. We touched the edge of a mine crater as we dropped. I was thrown through the centre section struts directly in front of the pilot's seat, a narrow triangle which would certainly have taken a good deal of effort and skill to have wriggled through normally. I was not grazed by either of the struts or the top of the wings, which, on looking back, seems nothing short of a miracle. I was pitched headfirst on to the mud, where my body lay unconscious on the lip of a crater. My observer was less lucky for he did a long shooting dive forwards through the air from the rear cockpit at the moment of impact.[17]

Lieutenant Harold Balfour, 43 Squadron, RFC

When Balfour came to, he was in a terrible state, doubtless from the effects of concussion.

As I was put into a field ambulance I was being very sick and as the ambulance started rattling down the road some of our howitzers let off from one of the battery positions nearby. I suppose that this was too much for me, and that, with the crash, my nerves had for the moment gone. I can remember crying to myself with fright and self-pity as these appalling crashes and discharges continued.[18]
    Lieutenant Harold Balfour, 43 Squadron, RFC

One of his squadron comrades was less than generous in his assessment of Balfour's state when he was first hospitalised and then sent back to 'Blighty'.

Balfour, flight commander of 'B' Flight, is on the way home having concussion from landing in a shell hole behind Vimy. He is said to be temporarily 'loony'.[19]
    Lieutenant Alan Dore, 43 Squadron, RFC

*   *   *

There was hope for the future. It may not have seemed like that in the depths of 'Bloody April', but even at that darkest dawn, there was hope. The RE8 was beginning to arrive on stream to gradually replace the pensionable survivors amongst the BE2 veterans. Although its long gestation period meant that it was already somewhat outdated, the RE8 was nevertheless a great improvement on its predecessor, having a more orthodox seating arrangement, with the observer behind the pilot, being capable of 105mph, and armed with a forward-firing Vickers and a Lewis gun for the observer. But it was not a universal panacea, sweeping away problems. When used over-confidently, it was still vulnerable. On 13 April, 59 Squadron unwisely sent out six RE8s on a photographic reconnaissance of the crucial Drocourt–Queant switch line. Although there were six, only two were carrying cameras, the rest acting as close escorts – a function for which the RE8 was totally unsuited. There should have been a 'real' scout escort, as they would be dangerously close to Douai. Unfortunately, the escort failed to arrive, but Richthofen and Jasta 11 did. All six RE8s were soon shot down, but the RFC at least scored one victory in the reception for the survivors held in the Jasta 11 mess.

One of the Englishmen whom we had shot down and whom we had made prisoner was talking to us. Of course, he enquired after the 'red aeroplane'. It is not unknown even among the troops in the trenches and is called by them '*Le diable rouge*'. In the squadron to which he belonged there was a rumour that the red machine was occupied by a girl – a kind of Joan of Arc. He was intensely surprised when I assured him that the supposed girl was standing in front of him. He did not intend to make a joke.[20]
    Oberleutnant Manfred von Richthofen, Jasta 11, Imperial German Air Service

Oh? Yes, he surely did! Richthofen had fallen victim to a classic 'wind up', to be told and retold in the long months languishing in prisoner of war camp. Small compensation for the loss of liberty, but perhaps some muted recompense.

Strait-laced he may have appeared on the ground, but Richthofen was at the height of his considerable powers. Risible attempts were often made amongst the British pilots he culled with seeming ease to picture him as nothing more than a bully, a coward, little more than a murderer.

> This Count Richthofen you mention, Dad, is nothing to worry about. He will soon be brought down. Believe me, every machine of ours he has brought down has been a slow old artillery observation machine, practically incapable of defending itself.[21]
> 2nd Lieutenant Walter Wood, 29 Squadron, RFC

Yet Richthofen was shooting down the reconnaissance and artillery machines that did most damage to the German war effort. This was not a game; this was war.

Of all the new aircraft that debuted in 'Bloody April', the most significant was the SE5 (Scout Experimental 5), which arrived at the front with 56 Squadron at Vert Galand airfield in early April. This was a handpicked squadron, popularly rumoured to be the 'Anti-Richthofen' squadron, with amongst their ranks Captain Albert Ball. He did not take to the new aircraft, as he valued the manoeuvrability of the Nieuport 17 rather than the diving and zooming capability of the SE5, which would prove to be a great 'gun platform'. Ultimately capable of 115mph and with a ceiling of around 17,000 feet, it was armed with a Vickers firing through the propeller arc and a Lewis gun mounted on the top wing. But the SE5 was also riddled with teething problems, which reduced its considerable potential.

> They have put me on a [shit] machine, but I should like to get back to my old machine as soon as possible. Oh, I shall never be able to do my job. I must fly another machine and then I shall get along with the job.[22]
> Captain Albert Ball, 56 Squadron, RFC

Ball worked together with the squadron engineer officer, Lieutenant Hubert Charles, to tidy up the aircraft, removing unnecessary weight, sorting out the sights and thereby creating the SE5a. Ball still flew his 'personal' Nieuport granted him due to his status as the foremost RFC ace, but he also began to fly the SE5a, especially when leading his flight into action.

One young lad who joined 56 Squadron that April was 2nd Lieutenant Arthur Rhys Davids. Initially, he was spare personnel and was not given an aircraft. His response shows he was not like many other pilots in that he had been thoroughly entranced by his classical studies at Eton School.

The dear old C.O. very sportingly said I could take a day in bed, which I did, and finished off the little pamphlet on the 'Poetic View of the World', which is good reading. But then as Blake said in a curious moment 'to generalise is to be an idiot' – almost as bad as the Irishman who said it was very unlucky to be superstitious. I think one can't distinguish philosophical religious and poetic world views, though each have their points, but it was absorbing reading and taught me a lot. Then I read some 400 lines of Euripides and wrote three or four letters, altogether very delightful, though my little garret was a bit dingy. I share it now with the equipment officer of the squadron, a very amiable, extremely business-like and commonplace young man, very like the others.[23]

    2nd Lieutenant Arthur Rhys Davids, 56 Squadron, RFC

That 'commonplace young man' was none other than Hubert Charles, the man responsible for tuning up and improving the SE5a. Rhys Davids had a lot to learn.

    The French also came to the aid of the RFC by supplying the Nieuport Scout, which allowed 40 Squadron to replace their FE8s. This was a great improvement and allowed them to have a little more chance against the German scouts. They also had a livewire young pilot join their ranks – Edward Mannock. He might not have lasted long, for he was almost immediately involved in an incident while engaged in practice firing at ground targets. This could well have had fatal consequences.

Did some gun practice and in one dive from 2,000 [feet] my right bottom plane broke and fell clean away. Managed to right the machine after desperate efforts with the joystick and landed slowly and safely about half a mile away from aerodrome. Such a thing has never happened before where the pilot has not been killed or injured by the fall.[24]

    2nd Lieutenant Edward Mannock, 40 Squadron, RFC

He was being watched by William Sholto Douglas, who confirmed the unique nature, not of the accident but of the pilot's survival. Mannock was surely living on borrowed time.

I was standing watching one of the Nieuports of No. 40 Squadron swooping down on a ground target used for practice firing on the range near the aerodrome. I noticed that the pilot – who was Mannock although I did not know that at the time – appeared to be diving the Nieuport rather more steeply and fiercely than was usual. As he started to pull out of the dive the lower plane of his aircraft, which was narrower and shorter than the top plane, buckled and fell away. By all the laws that govern such events, that Nieuport should have gone plummeting into the ground; but Mannock, fully aware of what had happened, coolly throttled back his engine and managed, by first-rate flying and supported only by his top plane, to glide gently down into a field alongside our own airfield. He turned over on his back in landing, but he was unhurt.[25]

Major William Sholto Douglas, 43 Squadron, RFC

It is typical of the man that, instead of thanking his lucky stars, Mannock used his close escape as an opportunity to mess with the mind of his panicking airframe fitter, who had raced to the scene expecting to find a corpse.

By skilful piloting he managed to get the machine down safely but crashed it in a ploughed field without being hurt. It was a splendid effort. When his rigger reached the crash, Mannock scared the life out of him by asking what he meant by it! But seeing the rigger's face drop to 40 degrees below zero, he burst out laughing and cheered him up by showing him the defective strut socket that had broken.[26]

Sergeant W. Bovett, 40 Squadron, RFC

Mannock was not everyone's 'cup of tea', but he soon made a couple of good friends in the officers' mess; men who could tolerate his fiery mixture of boisterousness, left-wing socialism and the vehement manner in which he expressed any, and indeed all, of his opinions.

Mannock was an extraordinary character, and a very forceful one. We had two things in common, he and I, we were both Irishmen, and we both dearly loved an argument. He was the only man in the mess who would talk beneath the surface. Many was the time when we would argue fiercely on some highly controversial subject such as politics, socialism or religion – he usually won the argument, though heavens knows what his views really were. As a curious contrast to the warfare of the tongue, Mannock was very keen on boxing, and as I had done a good deal, we often used to blow off steam by having a set to in the mess. In fact, it used to be a stock event, if the evening was livening up, for Mannock and me to have a round or two – and he nearly always said, 'Let's hit out!' and we used to have a good slog at one another. I think, on the whole, that I used to get more than I gave, as he had the height of me, and a slightly longer reach; but I had him at footwork![27]

Lieutenant Desmond de Burgh, 40 Squadron, RFC

Mannock certainly did take some punishment from de Burgh, as he ruefully recalled.

Boxed with de Burgh. Crocked my knee and arm. Old McKechnie's farewell night as he's proceeding home tomorrow morning. Great doings. Returned to bed at 2am and to be called at 5.30. Went to St Omer by side-car to fetch a new machine, feeling like a wet rag. Mouth felt like the bottom of a parrot cage.[28]

2nd Lieutenant Edward Mannock, 40 Squadron, RFC

In his early days with 40 Squadron, Mannock had some severe problems with his nerves. He may have been loud, but it hid a sensitive nature that struggled with the manifold pressures of aerial combat.

> Mannock was not actually called yellow, but many secret murmurings of an unsavoury nature reached my ears. He showed signs of being over careful during engagements. He was further accused of being continually in the air practising aerial gunnery as a pretence of keenness – in other words, the innuendo was that he was suffering from cold feet.[29]
>   Lieutenant George Lloyd, 40 Squadron, RFC

Mannock managed to overcome these early fears – at least in the short term – and emerged with a positive attitude to the whole business of scout warfare.

> Of course, I have been very frightened against my will – nervous reaction. I have now conquered this physical defect and want to master the tactics first. The present bald-headed ones should be replaced by well-thought-out ones. I cannot see any reason why we should not sweep the Hun right out of the sky.[30]
>   Lieutenant Edward Mannock, 40 Squadron, RFC

He would certainly try his best over the next year.

*   *   *

The officers' mess was not the centre of the universe, but for many young airmen it seemed to be something very similar. In an existence torn between deadly danger and almost complete safety, it was a safety valve, a refuge, a haven; it was everything. The actual living accommodation varied across the squadrons, from farmhouses and outbuildings to huts and tents. Rhys Davids describes his hut, although here again he cannot resist a touch of snobbishness. Sadly, it was a trait he never really had the chance to grow out of.

> I have changed my quarters to one portion of what is known as a 'Nissen Hut'. We have four of them side by side, and they are made of wood with circular corrugated iron roofs. Each is divided into compartments, usually one half from the other and across the middle and one half bisected again by a partition up the centre. All the partitions are a kind of brown canvas, floors just boards, but I have bought a straw mat and also a very nice quite ordinary little flooring of carpetlet. My little den is about 4 or 5 yards long and 3 across at the bottom, and I have got the sunny side of the hut looking out on the aerodrome, with a quaint little suburban garden in front consisting of a circular bed with some bedraggled daisies and violets in, and two outer beds with nothing in them

at all except Mother Earth and some choice weeds. The man next door did it before I came in – appalling effort![31]

2nd Lieutenant Arthur Rhys Davids, 56 Squadron, RFC

The officers usually had servants, and Harold Balfour remembered his, a man called Dariers, rather fondly.

Our servant was a unique character, being a man from the Midlands, of about fifty, with a wife and several children. Every morning we used to throw boots at him when he came to waken us up. He never minded but gave us a sort of pathetic bleat. However, one morning he nearly got his own back. By my bedside was a stove which we always kept red-hot in order to warm the hut, as the snow still lay thick on the ground outside. On top of this stove the hot water for washing and shaving used to be heated in a two-gallon petrol tin. This morning, sleepily, I rolled over and there, on top of the stove as should be, was the can for the hot water, and within a few minutes the water should be boiling. But I did not give two looks before I was quite awake, out of my bed and had that tin off the stove. [My servant] had made an error and put on top of the red-hot stove a brand new sealed up full two-gallon tin of petrol! In another moment we, and the hut, would have gone up with one bang. Quite unperturbed, he explained that he had made this little slip just through forgetfulness. The nearest I ever came to murder was when he cackled at me one dawn, as I walked to my machine: 'Oh, Sir! When I see you go out in the morning, I often wonder whether you will ever come back!'[32]

Lieutenant Harold Balfour, 43 Squadron, RFC

Arthur Gould Lee recalled his first encounter with his somewhat tactless servant upon joining 46 Squadron at La Gorgue.

I went to the hut to unpack, but discovered that the batman, called Watt, had done it already. He told me that the hut, which was wooden and roomy, not a curved-roof Nissen, was quite nice except for the frogs and mosquitoes from the pond nearby, and the stench from the farmyard midden opposite. Then he said he'd been batman to Mr Gunnery, and what a nice gentleman he was, and how he was the second gentleman he, Watt, had had killed, and how very depressing it was the way they went off in the morning, bright and hearty, and just never came back. I sympathised and said I hoped I wouldn't ever give him cause for further depression.[33]

2nd Lieutenant Arthur Gould Lee, 46 Squadron, RFC

The bar, drink and companionship were important to young pilots.

Perhaps I should be able to tell stories of broken, disillusioned pilots drinking desperately in the bar, of emotional outbursts, fear, triumph, hatred, dramatic re-creations in the mess of the day's fighting. But none of that sort of thing happened. There was drama all right, but it was kept carefully out of our life on the ground. A few of the pilots got tight, mostly individuals who were inclined to get on the grog in almost any circumstances. Some of us were a little edgy, a little over-excited after a show perhaps. But on the whole life on the ground was more or less that of a country club. The bar was a place to lean quietly with a drink, a centre where we met, and chatted, and enjoyed relaxing much as we might have done in any English pub. Catterall, the bar steward, was a happy sort of chap. There was something entirely personal in his relationship with us officers. He must have seen many people who really needed a stiff drink, but he never gave any sign that he recognised this need. He just mixed the drink and passed it over the bar with perfect manners, and yet a touch of understanding and humanity. Sometimes the gaiety at the bar might have been slightly forced, when a well-established or particularly popular pilot was killed or thought to have been. But never was there any cheap drama.[34]

2nd Lieutenant Gordon Taylor, 66 Squadron, RFC

Drinking remained an important part of mess life, depending on the individuals concerned. During a 'binge' session, they often played drinking games, which once invented or adopted, were passed on to the neighbouring squadrons.

It was No. 32 RFC who at one of our parties at Bertangles taught us the game of 'Cardinal Puff'. When we played this game, everyone was expected to take part in turn. The first in the queue had his glass filled up and raising it once said, 'Here's to Cardinal Puff'. He then carried out a series of movements with his hands, each movement being done once only. Again, he raised his glass, but this time twice saying, 'Here's to Cardinal Puff Puff'. The hand movements were then repeated each time twice. Finally, the glass was raised three times saying, 'Here's to Cardinal Puff Puff Puff' and after repeating the former movements three times he drank the contents of the glass. More often than not a mistake would be made in carrying out the correct procedure and in that case the contents of the glass had to be drunk by the offender, the glass was refilled, and he had to start all over again. Very few people got through the ordeal successfully and the game usually broke up and turned into a rough-house after only a few had had a turn.[35]

Sub Lieutenant Leonard Rochford, 3 Naval Squadron, RNAS

One common feature of the mess was an old piano. Sometimes music of an improving, perhaps classical nature would be played, but more often the pianist was a ham-fisted chap, battering the hell out of an out-of-tune instrument, with oft-painful consequences. Lieutenant Oliver Stewart, who had been a student at the Royal College of Music, found one pianist to be remarkable in the sheer volume he could produce.

> He was of immense size, and he took all the front of the piano out, 'So as not to hinder the notes in coming out!' he explained. The result was that, when he was performing, one could watch all the hammers working, and a prodigious and awe-inspiring sight it was. Strictly speaking, I suppose, it was not so much piano playing as furniture removing! Incredible numbers of hammers worked at the same time, the strings became blurred with their frantic vibrations while this remarkable artist rocked on his seat and emitted a loud buzzing sound. This I will say, that although I have listened with interest to pianists from Paderewski and Pachmann to Schnabel and Cortot, not one of them – no, not one – has ever succeeded in producing the net volume of sound that this officer used to produce.[36]
>
> Lieutenant Oliver Stewart, 54 Squadron, RFC

But this was horses for courses. What was wanted was a background to the voices of tipsy pilots bellowing out the latest popular songs. All the old favourites would be performed, but also new parodies, such as one popular in the 40 Squadron mess – a bowdlerised version of poor old Lewis Carroll's *Jabberwocky* poem which in this version celebrated the success of a BE2 – or 'Quirk', as they had become known – in shooting down a fearsome Albatros.

> Twas brillig and the Slithy Quirk
> Did drone and burble in the blue,
> All floppy were his wing controls
> (And his observer too).
> 'Beware the wicked Albatros',
> The 'OC quirks' had told him flat,
> 'Beware the Hun-Hun bird and shun
> The frumious Halberstadt'.
> But while through uflish bumps he ploughed,
> The Albatros, with tail on high,
> Came diving out the tulgey cloud
> And let his bullets fly.
> One, two; one, two, and through and through,
> The Lewis gun went tick-a-tack,
> The Hun was floored, the Quirk had scored,
> And came galumphing back.
> Oh, hast thou slain the Albatros?
> Split one, with me, my beamish boy,
> Our 'RAF-ish scout has found them out',
> The C.O. wept for joy.[37]
>
> Captain William Bond, 40 Squadron, RFC

Many of the songs made little or no sense. But that was surely the point.

The binge went on until after midnight, though I can't think why. It was one of those full-out parties that start for no particular reason and go on until the drink runs out. We had some sing-songs – one fellow produced a baby concertina – and sang things like 'When this ruddy war is over, Oh how happy we shall be' and 'The green grass grew all round' and some less delicate ones such as:

> Two German officers crossed the Rhine,
> Skiboo, skiboo.
> To love the women and taste the wine,
> Skiboo, skiboo.
> Oh, landlord, you've a daughter fair,
> With lily-white arms and golden hair.
> Skiboo, skiboo, skiboolby boo, skidam, dam, dam.

And so on, for lots of verses, which become more and more blue. As for skiboo, I've no idea what it means, but it's very good for yelling out at the top of your voice when you're ginned. I went to bed with my head buzzing with all the evening's talk and songs, a mix-up of our heavy casualties and dud machines with green grass and skiboos and Albatros Scouts, all flashing confusedly in a dizzy alcoholic world. The hangover this morning lasted until lunchtime.[38]
2nd Lieutenant Arthur Gould Lee, No. 1 Aircraft Depot, St Omer, RFC

On guest night binges, mess games were also popular, although some seemed lethally dangerous.

The game started with the tossing of a coin to decide who should go 'down' first. Each side probably numbered between ten and fifteen. The side to go 'down' selects a position at one end of the room, preferably with a sofa or soft chair to be the head post. When all are down in the shape of a rugger scrum the captain, seeing that his scrum is well knit together, informs the opposing side that they may start. The object of the game is for the 'up' side to mount the backs of those 'down', without rolling off or touching the ground in any way whilst the aim for those 'down' is to be so strong that no one succumbs under the weight or sinks to the floor thereby losing the round. There is quite a lot to the game. The captain of the 'up' side must make a careful reconnaissance of the enemy's dispositions, pick out the weakest point and direct his heavy stuff on to that point. This usually means sixteen stone hurling itself across the room at top speed, leaping as hard into the air as possible, and descending with no mean velocity on the back of some herring gutted young man of ten stone. On the other hand, you might have a real enemy on whom you decided to pay off a score. This was a wonderful opportunity![39]
Captain Eric Routh, 16 Squadron, RFC

Then again, some pilots showed enormous imagination and considerable personal courage amidst the mayhem triggered by a new 'game'.

Harvey-Kelly had seen the first tanks in action and was very enthusiastic about their performances. On one occasion in the mess, some 'Doubting Thomas' expressed the opinion that they would not be much use against entrenched infantry as soon as their novelty had worn off. This proved too much for Harvey-Kelly, who proceeded to arrange a demonstration to prove his point of view. Protected with the coal-hod – a large iron one – he enacted the part of the tank, while the rest, armed with coal, were the infantry. The tank attacked from the end of the mess and made excellent progress until it came into contact with the big stove, which, surmounted by a long length of piping, stood well out into the room. The tank, true to tradition, and despite a heavy and accurate fire of coals, boldly tackled the stove, which overturned, and the piping came down and scattered the infantry in all directions. There was no doubt the tank gained a great tactical and moral victory – though it and the infantry had together to make good the damage next day.[40]

Lieutenant Thomas Marson, 56 Squadron, RFC

All in all, the mess served its purpose, not to all pilots but to a great many of them. It helped them get through the horrors that surrounded them, helped them survive the loss of close friends. Eccentricity was treasured and there were many cherished and beloved characters. But what happened when they were shot down? Consider the case of Captain Philip Prothero of 56 Squadron.

A Scotsman by birth, who insisted on wearing his kilt at all times, he was in many ways typical of this race, with the reddest of hair and a burr hard to understand after a drink or two. When he returned from an OP, his knees would be blue with cold and the hair thereon would stick out like bristles on a hog. One day I asked him why he so punished himself, to which he replied, 'You wouldna have me taken prisoner in disguise, would you now laddie?' On one occasion Prothero returned from leave. Several of us were in the mess when we heard him coming down the road, singing completely out of tune a Scots song, *'The Road to the Isles'*, which no one could understand. As he entered the mess, he was a picture, carrying a bottle of Drambuie, and with a haunch of venison over one shoulder, an overstuffed knapsack over the other, and swinging his swagger stick in time with his tune.[41]

Lieutenant Vershoyle Cronyn, 56 Squadron, RFC

Prothero would later be seen falling from 14,000 feet in SE5 A8924 after the starboard wings had fallen off on 26 July. It could have caused depression and a loss in morale, but Trenchard had long realised the importance of not allowing time for people to brood on their missing friends and had introduced a firm policy of 'no empty chairs for breakfast', by which means any squadron losses were to be instantly replaced.

> I always looked on the RFC as a family. I tried to put myself in the others' places and to consider the feelings of those who flew as if they had been my own. If as an ordinary pilot you see no vacant places around you, the tendency is to brood less on the fate of friends who have gone forever. Instead, your mind is taken up with buying drinks for the newcomers and making them feel at home. It was a matter of pride and human understanding.[42]
> Brigadier General Hugh Trenchard, Headquarters, RFC

Many of the squadrons on the Western Front were the recipients of visits from Trenchard and Baring. Opinions of Trenchard varied, but most of his men seemed to appreciate his visits.

> The effect that Trenchard's visits had on the morale of those in the squadrons was almost magical. He was a tall man of a commanding presence which was coupled with a personality that was extraordinarily inspiring. And yet that personality in itself, or perhaps I should say the quality of it, is difficult to analyse. He was far from being what could be called articulate, and on paper he was almost chaotic. When he spoke it was nearly always in a manner that was strangely disjointed, and sometimes it appeared that what he did manage to say was quite off the point. Perhaps it was the spirit and the great humanity of the man that counted, for those qualities shone through all the awkwardness. It gave him the unique ability of being able to raise the morale of those with whom he came in contact in a manner that was out of all proportion to the visible or audible manifestations of the spirit of the man.[43]
> Major William Sholto Douglas, 43 Squadron, RFC

But there were those who reacted badly. A more trenchant view was taken by Edward Mannock.

> General Trenchard came to see us, and 'hot-aired' for about half an hour. Talked 'bilge'! Don't like him. Too 'schoolmastery'.[44]
> 2nd Lieutenant Edward Mannock, 40 Squadron, RFC

Vital to the success of these visits was the presence of Baring. He was the man who kept the whole thing on track, and smoothed any ruffled feathers caused by his inarticulate gruff superior.

> If Maurice Baring ever considered that 'Boom' had been a little too severe or harsh with some squadron or individual during an inspection, he would take it upon himself to soften up his master through one of what he called

'Field Punishments for the General.' As they drove away in Trenchard's car from the airfield, Baring would lean forward in his seat and look out of the window and up into the sky as if he were watching an aeroplane. 'What is it, Baring?' Trenchard would demand, his curiosity aroused by Baring's almost open-mouthed interest. 'What is it? What's happening up there?' 'Oh, nothing!' Baring would reply. 'I was only watching some birds!' Then Trenchard would know that, in the eyes of those whom he had just visited, he had behaved badly, and that Baring was telling him as much.[45]

   Major William Sholto Douglas, 43 Squadron, RFC

Others remembered these 'field punishments' inflicted on the hapless general.

He instituted a series of punishments numbered from 'One' to 'Five X' and varying in that order in degree of severity. Punishment No. 1 consisted in taking away or hiding 'Boom's' pipe. The aggrieved party was always rung up and informed, 'The general behaved very badly today. He had Punishment No. 1 all the way home. He almost cried for his pipe; but I was adamant. I had it in my pocket, but I said I could not think what he had done with it. At dinner he was very penitent, so he was allowed to find his pipe afterwards, I think he is really sorry and will be better now!'[46]

   Lieutenant Thomas Marson, 56 Squadron, RFC

Baring's talents were not only in tormenting Trenchard. He was also accomplished at a range of tricks which could keep any mess entranced.

One of the star performers at those parties was Maurice Baring; and one of his turns was to balance a glass of port on his bald head and to lie down flat on the floor and get up again, keeping the glass in position and without spilling a drop. On very special occasions he was known to perform his little trick with a bottle of champagne instead of the port, while at the same time proceeding to undress while keeping the bottle balanced on his head.[47]

   Major William Sholto Douglas, 43 Squadron, RFC

But it is worth remembering, even amongst these jolly japes, that the young men Trenchard and Baring visited were leading a here today, gone tomorrow existence. On 29 April, they visited Major Harvey-Kelly, the first RFC pilot to land in France back in August 1914, who had now risen to the command of 19 Squadron based at Vert Galand airfield.

When we got there, we were told he had gone up by himself and one other pilot for a short patrol. We stayed there all the morning. By luncheon time he had not come back. He was due and overdue. When we went away the general said, 'Tell Harvey-Kelly I was very sorry to miss him,' but I knew quite well from the sound of his voice he did not expect this message would ever be delivered. Nor did I. Harvey-Kelly never came back. He was the gayest of all gay pilots. He always took a potato and a reel of cotton with him when he went over the lines. The Germans, he said, would be sure to treat him well if he had to land on the other side and they found him provided with such useful and scarce commodities.[48]

Captain Maurice Baring, HQ RFC

Harvey-Kelly had taken off in his French-supplied SPAD VII A6681, which was shot down in a confused dogfight by Leutnant Kurt Wolff, a rising German star flying with Richthofen's Jasta 11. Kelly suffered severe head injuries and died shortly afterwards. Baring and Trenchard, as both had suspected, were waiting in vain.

* * *

By 1917, the RFC were not alone on the Western Front, as they were reinforced and backed up by the RNAS, in particular the 3 and 8 (Naval) Squadrons. Inter-service rivalry is, of course, not a new phenomenon, but back in 1916, before the RNAS deployed to assist the RFC, there was a very real edge to complaints that the RNAS did little of the fighting but got much of the glory.

We were really rather embittered. In the first place, they had the pick of any aircraft that was worth anything, and we had to deal with the second-grade aircraft. Secondly, the only active service squadron they had was based at Dunkirk. It used to do raids going out into the Channel and into Ostend, out into the Channel and back again home; whereas the RFC were going up and down the trenches wth the anti-aircraft at them all the time. The attitude of the British public annoyed us – the RNAS were based in England, and they were the people who, when the Zeppelins started, seemed to the British public to be the only people who were defending them. They didn't see the RFC – we were out in France. As a result, we got rather bitter. On one of my seven-day leaves I was actually hissed and booed in going into the Savoy in London, merely because I was RFC. Presumably, according to those people, the RFC was not trying to protect them at all.[49]

Lieutenant Frederick Powell, 40 Squadron, RFC

Such views from a young man risking his life over the trenches were understandable, but unfair on the RNAS, which had many roles, but could point with justification to their core work in naval aviation: deploying a variety of airships, seaplanes and aircraft to carry out long-range reconnaissance for the fleet, endless patrols in an effort to suppress German U-Boat operations, and making the first – faltering – attempts at strategic bombing. The RNAS aircraft were sourced from private aircraft manufacturers, particularly Thomas Sopwith, and they were not as dependent on the Royal Aircraft Factory as the RFC. Supply chain difficulties are what led to Powell's claims that the RFC got second-grade aircraft.

Once the RNAS had scout squadrons engaged over the Western Front, the situation calmed down to relatively harmless 'chuntering'.

> We went to the naval squadron which is now attached to us, and which is on the same aerodrome as No. 32. They said they would like the oil used by No. 32 for machine-guns. It was better than their own naval oil. We then went on to No. 32. They asked if they might have the naval oil, which they said was better than their military oil. When the matter was investigated later there was found to be not the slightest difference between the naval and the military oil.[50]
>
> Lieutenant Colonel Maurice Baring, HQ, RFC

This is not their story, but we should recognise the determination and heroism of the RNAS pilots. They had their own raft of heroes and great aces, but perhaps we could pay tribute to the Australian-born ace Robert Little and let him stand for a very gallant group of gentlemen.

> Judged from the standpoint of actual flying, Little was just an average sort of pilot with tremendous bravery and a flair for finding his way about. There was nothing particularly accurate or finished about his flying, but for getting the last ounce out of an aeroplane as an offensive weapon, he had few equals. Air fighting seemed to him to be just a gloriously exhilarating sport, and he had been doing regular work over the lines for many months before I can remember his showing any sign of fatigue or nervous strain. When out on a job of work he never ceased to look for trouble, and very little escaped those keen eyes of his. In combat, his dashing methods, close-range fire and deadly aim made him a formidable opponent, and he was the most chivalrous of warriors. As a man, he was a most lovable character, and a sportsman in the truest sense of the word. When not flying his greatest joy was to go out after rabbits or rats with those other two great sportsmen, our fox terriers Maurice and Tich, who adored him.[51]
>
> Squadron Commander Geoffrey Bromet, 8 Naval Squadron, RNAS

Little was a remarkable shot, which is what made him a truly deadly opponent.

> Little was not so much a leader as a brilliant lone hand. I feel safe in saying that there have been few better shots, either in the services or outside, than this man. I have seen him bring down a crow on the wing with a .22 rifle and break bottles thrown into the air while they were still travelling upward; what more deadly foe could be found than such a man, armed with two machine guns firing at the rate of 2,000 rounds per minute? Once Little came within range of an enemy he did not give up until (1) the enemy was shot down, (2)

his own engine failed, or (3) he ran out of ammunition. He had in human guise the fighting tendencies of a bulldog – he never let go.[52]
      Captain Robert Compston, 8 Naval Squadron, RNAS

He would shoot down many Germans, but his contemporaries could not resist a reference to his less-than-stellar flying abilities.

The great Bob Little was credited with a net total of forty-seven Huns brought down – [but] he was the most ham-handed pilot. There was a joke that he'd written off more English aeroplanes than he'd written off Germans![53]
      Sub Lieutenant Herbert Thompson, 8 Squadron, RNAS

The RNAS pilots were subject to the same terrible stresses as the RFC men. Even if they survived a 'close shave', the circumstances could lead to a mental trauma and nightmares that haunted them for weeks or even months.

The whole flight was in patrol and Booker decided to dive on two German aircraft which were some way over the lines. I obediently followed, quite excited because they appeared to be dead ducks! I didn't realise Booker knew that they were a decoy for a considerable flight – there were eleven of them he counted in the end – of the 'Travelling Circus' up above. While I was busily engaged in shooting down one of the decoys, there was suddenly a frightful uproar behind me – two Spandau guns going full out! I panicked and dived away, which I shouldn't have done, because I couldn't out-dive an Albatros DIII in a Triplane. But the noise stopped immediately, and so I pulled out of the dive. When I looked around to see if I'd been damaged, I saw the main spar of my top plane had been shattered only it hadn't folded up. I decided the only thing I could do was to go home. Although I managed to land back at my own aerodrome it really was a technical shoot-down. Booker when he came back, said, I didn't think you'd get home!' He had come behind and shot an Albatros man off my tail. I think that was the cause of the bad dreams and the sleep-walking. After I'd been shot down, I found myself one night out on the cold grass! I'd crawled out under the brailing of the tent and I was sleep-walking. I'd never sleep-walked before, but for a whole week, every night I got out of bed and was sleep-walking. More than once I was collected by the sentry and brought back. It just sort of disappeared.[54]
      Sub Lieutenant Herbert Thompson, 8 Squadron, RNAS

* * *

The Battle of Arras had begun well, but it degenerated into a disaster. Why was this? Some cataclysmic failure by stupid British generals? Not really. The French offensive had started badly on 16 April. Although not a total failure, the promises by Nivelle of success in forty-eight hours were demonstrably over-exaggerated – and the hard-pressed *poilus*, who had suffered so much in the first three years of the war, began to mutiny. Nivelle was swiftly replaced by a safe pair of hands in General Philippe Pétain – and Haig was given operational independence once again. Not that he could immediately turn to his long-planned Flanders offensive. First, he had to support his allies; so he must continue battering away at Arras – and he had to do it as soon as possible. With no time for lengthy preparation, they had to resume the attack in just days. The battles that followed were painful in the extreme, resulting in the highest daily average of army casualties of any other British battle in the Great War. From 23 April, the Battle of the Scarpe would be swiftly followed by the Battles of Bullecourt in early May. All were miserable disasters.

Up above them, the RFC was fast approaching the end of its tether as the strains and stresses of 'Bloody April' were followed by more hard fighting in May. It just never seemed to end. Once again, for tragedy we need look no further than the crews of the Sopwith 1½ Strutter squadrons. Mannock remembered escorting them on yet another long-range photographic reconnaissance on 1 May.

'C' Flight escorted four Sopwiths on a photography stunt to Douai Aerodrome. Captain Keen, the new commander, leading. We were attacked from above, over Douai. I tried my gun before going over the German lines, only to find that it was jammed, so I went over with a revolver only. A Hun in a beautiful yellow and green 'bus' attacked me from behind. I could hear his machine-gun cracking away. I wheeled round on him and howled like a dervish (although of course he couldn't hear me) whereat he made off towards old Parry and attacked him, with me following, for the moral effect! Another one (a brown speckled one) attacked a Sopwith, and Keen blew the pilot to pieces and the Hun went spinning down from 12,000 feet to earth. Unfortunately, the Sopwith had been hit, and went down too, and there was I, a passenger, absolutely helpless, not having a gun, an easy prey to any of them, and they hadn't the grit to close. Eventually they broke away, and then their 'Archie' gunners got on the job, and we had a hell of a time. At times, I wondered if I had a tailplane or not, they were so near. We came back over Arras with the three remaining Sopwiths, and excellent photos, and two vacant chairs at the Sopwith squadron mess! What is the good of it all?[55]

2nd Lieutenant Edward Mannock, 40 Squadron, RFC

This was yet one more painful loss suffered by 43 Squadron. The pilot of Sopwith 1½ Strutter A8252, Lieutenant C.R. O'Brien, was wounded in the leg, while his observer, 2nd Lieutenant E.L. Edwards, was unhurt, but both were taken prisoner. Collectively, the Sopwith 1½ Strutter squadrons had no real choice but to keep on keeping on, and Norman Macmillan left a wonderful account of how a crew would prepare for take-off, every time knowing that this mission might be the last.

As the pilot and observer walked down the cinder-track to the aerodrome, they buttoned up their leather coats, strapped their fur-lined helmets tightly underneath their chins and pulled on great gloves; their feet and legs were encased in monstrous, sheepskin thigh-boots. Their appearance was grotesque. They looked like the bloated shadows of men that a candle sometimes throws upon a wall. Yet no one appeared to notice that; it was far too commonplace. They climbed into their seats – the pilot in front and the observer behind. The latter tested his gun-mounting for freedom of rotation and glanced round his cockpit to see that everything – ammunition-drums, Very pistol and flares, and revolver – was in its proper place. The pilot loaded his Vickers gun, then wriggled himself comfortably down into his seat. He tested the aeroplane's controls and looked quickly over his instruments. Then he glanced up. A watchful 'Ack Emma' [Air Mechanic], awaiting this moment, called out, 'Switch off, petrol on, suck in, sir!' From the pilot's cockpit came the sound of an air pump, the clicking of levers, and then the gruff reply, 'Suck in!' The mechanic swung the propeller round while the excess petrol dribbled out on to the ground from a pipe beneath the engine. The mechanic stopped swinging the propeller and wiped his oily hands upon his overalls. He scraped his feet on the ground to make sure of his foothold. Then striking a somewhat graceful attitude with his legs and body inclined forward, his arms upraised, his hands resting on the trailing edge of the propeller's horizontal blade, he tried his balance before calling out, 'Contact, sir!' A moment of pause was followed by the click of a switch. 'Contact,' replied the pilot. The 'Ack Emma' balanced on one foot, then swung lustily backward on to the other, driving the propeller round with the pull of his arms; until the engine tremored into life. For a full minute the pilot ran her steadily with his head inside his cockpit, the while he watched the engine revolution counter, the pulsator glass which recorded the oil beats in the lubrication pump and listened to the hum of the engine. He moved a lever and turned a petrol tap. The engine roared while the aeroplane quivered with the pride of its power. But the wooden chocks under the wheels, the 'Ack Emmas' at the wing-tips, and the grim-faced individuals hanging on to the tail-plane in the full blast of the slipstream checked its impetuous desire. The roar changed to a gentle hum as the pilot throttled down. A hand waved above his head gave the mechanics the all-clear signal. They withdrew the chocks. The long-suffering individual on the tail crawled from inside the elevator control-wires and went off to retrieve his cap from the cornfield. The pilot adjusted his goggles comfortably over his eyes.[56]

2nd Lieutenant Norman Macmillan, 45 Squadron, RFC

And off they went to who knew what.

*   *   *

Albert Ball was not only flying his rostered patrols as flight commander in his SE5; he was also undertaking a series of solo missions in his trusty Nieuport Scout. Right from the start, he had considerable success in advancing his score.

Am so fagged tonight, but feel that I must send you a line. We did our first two real jobs today, and I got two Huns – one I crashed, and the other I set on fire. I had six fights altogether. One of the Huns I got with a Nieuport, and one with a S.E.5. My machines were very badly hit about, and are having new planes tonight. Well, now I am on a job at 5am, so simply must sleep.[57]

Captain Albert Ball, 56 Squadron, RFC

Ball took incredible risks. There was no calm appraisal of the odds, of the chances of survival; if he saw German aircraft, he went at them bald-headed, come what may.

I had three fights, and managed to bring one down, crashed in a road. This I did with my Nieuport. After coming down I had to have five new planes, for the Hun had got about fifteen shots through my spars. Well, next I went up in my S.E.5 and had a very poo-poo time – five shots in my right strut, four in the planes, and two just behind my head. This was done by five Albatros Scouts, but I got one of them and set it on fire at 14,000 feet. Poor old chap inside. I should simply hate to be set on fire.[58]

Captain Albert Ball, 56 Squadron, RFC

This was not an isolated occurrence. Ball was certainly providing plenty of work for his hard-working ground crew.

I was attacked by twenty last night and had to fire all my ammunition, getting two of them. It was dark when I returned, and everyone thought that I must have been done in, but I had to stop on their side until it was dark, for I could not fight my way through without ammunition. My right plane was hit a few times, and I had to have a new one. I have now got another two Huns making four this time, and my total is thirty-four. Only three more to be got before I am top of England and France again. In order to whack the German man [Boelcke], I'd love to get about ten more. If it's God's will that I should do it, then I will come home; oh, I do so hope it can be managed. Tonight, if it clears up, I am taking all my flight out for a real good smack. I am off on my Nieuport then and at 5.30 I come back and do a job on S.E.5 with my Flight. You see they do one or two jobs each day, and I lead them, but during the remainder of the day I go up in my Nieuport and have a try myself. This is the only way to get them. Just keep at them all day.[59]

Captain Albert Ball, 56 Squadron, RFC

It is evident from Ball's correspondence that he was becoming obsessed with overtaking Oswald Boelcke and with topping the notational 'league table' of aces. It would lead him to ever-greater efforts.

He was the quietest young kid you ever saw, the most inoffensive youngster – you'd think he wouldn't punch anybody on the nose if he could duck him. But when he got into the air he was all hair-and-teeth! He was an excellent shot! He spent a great deal of time on the ground test-firing his guns in the pits.[60]

2nd Lieutenant Reginald Hoidge, 56 Squadron, RFC

But Ball was also beginning to display the signs of combat fatigue. Indeed, it is doubtful if he had really recovered from his efforts the year before.

On his return to the aerodrome, his engine was found to have been shot through, and there were several bullets through the back of the pilot's seat. Flushed in face, his eyes brilliant, his hair blown and dishevelled, he came to the squadron office to make his report, but for a long time was in so over-wrought a state that dictation was an impossibility to him. 'God is very good to me.' 'God must have me in His keeping!' 'I was certain that he meant to ram me!' The possibility that his opponent, finding himself mortally hit, had determined to have a life for a life occurred to him. In that event his nerve failed him at the last – Ball did not flinch. But in nervous exhaustion he paid the price.[61]

Lieutenant Thomas Marson, 56 Squadron, RFC

It could not last; and it did not last. On 7 May, Ball was involved in a sweep over Douai and Cambrai by eleven SE5s of 56 Squadron and another six French-supplied SPADs from 19 Squadron, with the bold intention of sweeping Jasta 11 from the skies. Amongst them was Arthur Rhys Davids.

After cruising around a bit we saw a Hun, a bright red beggar below us; this was about 5–10 miles over the lines. Down went the flight commander and down went I after him, but thank goodness that somehow I managed to remember to look behind me first, and saw another bright red and green beggar coming down on to my tail. So I came up again and we began turning round and round, he diving and firing at me, and then climbing up again, while I had all my work cut out to get out of the light and to climb up to him gradually. Meanwhile I had heard one bullet go into my undercarriage with the deuce of a wonk, one or two others were making themselves unpleasant by spoiling the appearance of my immaculate planes, and the tiresome young man in the red bus finally was unkind enough to plonk one into my engine, which we found out afterwards made a hole six inches square in the water jacket. Then for some curious reason he completely sheered off, or in other words, cleared off towards Hunland i.e. the east. And I, knowing very well my engine was wounded, proceeded to turn west, and after about five minutes, during which time I must have covered about 10–12 miles (aided by a strong east wind) the engine stopped altogether. So, after gliding as far as I could – from 7,000 feet – I perched neatly in a field not far from another aerodrome. I'm jolly lucky to have got off so light, the man up against me was obviously a far better pilot and fighter than I was – one of the few Hun 'pros' I expect. I can't think why he left me when he had me 'stony' as if I had had to go on turning much longer I should not have been able to get so far over the lines with my glide.[62]

Second Lieutenant Arthur Rhys Davids, 56 Squadron, RFC

The sequence of events in a convoluted series of dogfights that evening is somewhat confusing, but at some point Ball found himself facing the Albatros DIII flown by Richthofen's brother – Lothar von Richthofen – who was also an accomplished ace. Shortly afterwards, Ball's SE5 A4850 crash-landed on the outskirts of the village of Annouellin, where he died a few minutes later. Lothar von Richthofen claimed the 'kill', but his account is riddled with errors. Indeed, the one certainty is that his own engine was damaged, and he had to make a forced landing. The British were no better. As the last British sighting of Ball was of him flying into a dark thundercloud, this added an Arthurian legend element to the tragedy of his death. The impossibility of admitting the British hero had been vanquished meant that – with no evidence – they claimed Ball must have been hit by anti-aircraft fire. However, researchers have since uncovered a more convincing account from a German officer who witnessed the crash from nearby on the ground.

The aircraft was upside down with the wheels 'sticking up'. It was leaving a cloud of black smoke and this I considered was caused by oil leaking into the cylinders. We examined the wreckage, and we all came to the conclusion that the aircraft had not been either shot down in an air fight or anti-aircraft fire as the dead pilot had no marks or scratches and had not been wounded. I looked through his papers and found it was Captain Ball. We called him the English Richthofen. We were very disturbed by it all. I took his dead body to the field hospital. The doctor couldn't find any bullet wounds on the body, although the back and one leg were broken. My own opinion, and you will appreciate I was not in the air at the time, covers just two possibilities: 1) The odd chance that Lothar von Richthofen, in exchanging shots with Captain Ball's SE5, hit the aircraft with a stray shot - the breech of the Vickers gun carried a bullet hole. 2) I have thought that Captain Ball, flying into a cloud, turned the aircraft over and was unaware of this until he broke cloud, then so low that he could do nothing, and the aircraft flew into the ground. Again, when the SE5 crashed, it did not fire, and he must have been very low on fuel.[63]

Hauptmann Franz Hailer, Flieger-Abteilung 292

On 3 June, Albert Ball was awarded a posthumous Victoria Cross. His final score was some forty victories. The heroes of 1916 were now mostly dead: Ball, Hawker, Immelmann, Boelcke. A new generation of aces would have to step forward in the summer of 1917.

Chapter 8

Ypres of Trouble, 1917

I suppose I ought to be excited, sleepless, imagining myself in the throes of an air fight – the swift leap through space, the rattle of guns, the dive to earth of the stricken Hun, the triumphant loops of the victor – me! And all that kind of thing. Or else I ought to be brooding over the dangers ahead, especially after being greeted with a fatal casualty, which I'm detailed to attend as a pallbearer tomorrow. But to tell you the truth, apart from the thrill of just being here, I don't have any unusual emotions at all, except of anticipation of what I shall see on my first trip tomorrow, and maybe one little nagging worry – do we ever get eggs and bacon for breakfast?[1]

2nd Lieutenant Arthur Gould Lee, 46 Squadron, RFC

Flanders was always at the centre of Haig's mind. It offered the possibility that a short advance would reach Roulers rail junction, at a stroke disrupting a main pillar in the German logistical rail infrastructure. Not much further and they would clear the German submarine bases lurking in the Belgian ports of Zeebrugge and Ostend. Looking the other way, an advance would help clear the German threat to the Hazebrouck rail junction and the Channel ports, both vital to the continued existence on the Western Front of the BEF. Even just straightening the line a bit would help reduce the constant drain of casualties in the Ypres Salient, where the defenders were being shot at from three sides. Haig and the local Second Army commander, General Herbert Plumer, had been planning an offensive for years, with deep mines already tunnelled under the key tactical locations on the Messines Ridge which dominated the ground south of Ypres. But one way or another, Haig had been bound to the French: first by Kitchener's request to comply with Joseph Joffre's overall strategy; then when, through the machinations of David Lloyd George, he was placed under the control of Robert Nivelle. Now he was free, but he was obliged by the burgeoning French mutinies and the duties of alliance to launch a major campaign to distract attention and draw in German reserves. Of course, his eyes turned to Flanders. First, Plumer's Second Army would detonate the huge mines and strike home at the Battle of Messines on 7 June 1917. The attack was initially a great success, although the exploitation phase did trigger severe casualties. Haig then appointed General Hubert Gough and the Fifth Army to lead the advance to Passchendaele Ridge and beyond to Roulers. The Third Battle of Ypres would commence on 31 July, and of course the RFC would be crucial to the effective deployment of the preliminary barrage and all of the counter-battery work.

Indeed, the air offensive would begin some twenty-one days before the infantry went over the top. There would be no rest for the RFC.

In these circumstances, it was fortunate for the RFC that the intensive aerial fighting triggered by the onset of the Flanders offensive coincided with the arrival of another new British scout: the Sopwith Camel, so called because of its strange appearance. It was a powerful, stubby aircraft which could reach 110mph and had a ceiling of about 18,000 feet, while it was armed with – at last – two synchronised Vickers machine guns firing through the arc of the propeller. It had a rotary engine and was inherently unstable, as most of its weight was packed into the first 7 feet of the fuselage. As a result, it could turn like lightning in a dogfight – a useful characteristic – but it was also a difficult aircraft to control and as a result there were many accidents when flown by inexperienced pilots. There was a great deal of debate between pilots from Camel and SE5a squadrons as to which aircraft was the more deadly scout. Neither camp would ever concede the point, but Major William Sholto Douglas was certainly a fan of the SE5a when he flew them with 84 Squadron.

That will cause howls of anguish from the pilots who flew the Sopwith Camel; but it was a fact that the SE5 retained in a large measure its performance at high altitudes, which the Camel did not. And since the SE5 was very steady in a fast dive – which nine times out of ten was our way of making attacks – this was an additional advantage over the Camel. The faster we dived in the SE5, the steadier the aircraft became as a gun platform. The Camel, on the other hand, being an unstable machine, would vary in its angle of dive at high speed in spite of all the pilot's efforts to keep it steady; and because of its rotary engine there was also a good deal of vibration when diving fast, which made good shooting difficult.[2]

Major William Sholto Douglas, 84 Squadron, RFC

By the summer of 1917, as aircraft like the Camel and the SE5a arrived, there was the first stirrings of a change as such single-seaters were now not only being referred to as 'scouts' but increasingly being called 'fighters'. Terms like 'fighter patrol' or 'fighter escort' were also beginning to creep in. It represented their change in function and would ultimately entirely replace the old terminology.

The German Air Service had always been outnumbered on the Western Front, facing as they were the combined strength of the RFC, elements of the RNAS, and the French and Belgian air forces. To offset their numerical disadvantage, the Germans sought to ensure that they could secure local superiority by increasing the size of their scout formations. Thus, Jastas 4, 6, 10 and 11 were combined into one elite body – Jagdgeschwader No. 1 (JG 1) – commanded by Manfred von Richthofen himself. His pilots adopted in part Richthofen's all-red colour scheme, resulting in a colourful variety, which, combined with the fact that JG 1 moved up and down the front as the situation required, was the origin of the nickname 'The Flying Circus' amongst British pilots. In response, the RFC continued to fly in multiples of flights, but operating in tandem at layered heights, so that if they should encounter a large German formation, then they could all coalesce to join the battle. Both sides were becoming adept at setting complex ambushes, with seemingly unprotected aircraft covered by unseen higher predators ready to rush down and overwhelm any scout unwary enough to accept the 'lure' without due care and attention.

The Third Battle of Ypres proved to be a titanic clash which would rage on until deep into November 1917. With typical bad luck, the offensive seemed to trigger heavenly retribution, the infantry assault on 31 July marking the beginning of some four weeks of rain and the low cloud formations wrecking plans for close air cooperation. The RFC just had to do what they could: this was serious; this was war. Any and all risks had to be taken for the greater good of their comrades on the ground. Thus, 2nd Lieutenant Jack Walthew and his observer found themselves carrying out contact patrols in their RE8 under dreadful circumstances.

> There was, so experts tell me, the worst barrage that has ever been known, and I had to fly through it! I could hear, and occasionally see, the shells and every minute I was expecting to see one of my wings vanish. However, nothing hit us until we got over the line – which had been pushed forward considerably – and here in 8 minutes we got thirty holes through the machine from machine guns. Ten of them passed within a few inches of Woodstock; the wireless transmitter valued at £200 disappeared; three spars on the wing were broken; and lastly a bullet went through the petrol tank. I smelt a smell of petrol and in a few minutes, it all came rushing over my feet and legs. How we got back I don't know, it seemed the longest journey I have ever made; but eventually we landed safely. I had to write out a report on the flight and then had a shave, and was just going in to have some breakfast when I got orders to take up another machine to try and find the 30th Division who had got lost. So, off I went again and tootled over our lines for an hour. The first thing that happened was that the wireless transmitter again disappeared, leaving only a big hole in the fuselage. After this we weren't hit quite so much as before. Meanwhile we called to the infantry to light flares for us; but as they wouldn't do this, we had to draw the fire of the Huns into ourselves so as to discover where the enemy line was, and deduct ours from it. We managed to do this fairly successfully and came back unhurt.[3]
>
> 2nd Lieutenant Jack Walthew, 4 Squadron, RFC

The RE8 pilots and observers were real heroes in this battle. The conditions were awful, the German scouts were lethal and 'Archie' was as pesky as ever. But still they kept their sense of humour.

> This bad weather has just come at a very opportune moment as we have been having a very hard time lately and needed a rest very badly. Just at present I

am fostering an aggressive spirit by chasing and killing the numerous earwigs which have their being in my tent. So even when we are prevented from flying my love of war prompts me to acts of slaughter.[4]

Lieutenant Jack Walthew, 4 Squadron, RFC

This jocular letter was written on 31 August. Sadly, just a few days later, on 19 September, Jack Walthew would die in action at the tender age of 19 alongside his observer, on this occasion Lieutenant Michael Hartnett, when they were shot down in their RE8 B3427 during a photographic reconnaissance over the ANZAC Corps frontage at Ypres. This was the grim reality of life in an RE8 squadron. It was an unremitting diet of danger, past, present and future.

*   *   *

In retrospect, the summer and autumn of 1917 can be seen as the golden age of the great aces. We may intellectually appreciate that the most important aerial duties were carried out by the humble RE8 crews on their countless photographic reconnaissance and artillery observation missions, but even then, the eye is continually drawn to the glittering exploits of the scouts – the fighter aircraft. The cliché of the dawn patrol has woven its spell over the years, and who are we to resist its siren call? A whole new generation of RFC aces would rise to prominence, amongst them Edward Mannock, William Bishop, James McCudden and Arthur Rhys Davids, to mention but a few. But the Germans too had their paladins: Manfred von Richthofen still survived, though he was put out of action for a while after a bad head injury when he was shot down by Captain Donald Cunnell and his observer, 2nd Lieutenant Albert Woodbridge, on 6 July 1917. This crew, in their 20 Squadron FE2d A6512, would lodge a claim for four of the enemy shot down that morning, but although describing the fifth aircraft they had hit as a 'Red Albatros', they did not claim it as they did not see it crash. There was also Lothar von Richthofen, Kurt Wolff, Werner Voss, Karl Emil Schäfer and Karl Allmenröder – few of these would survive long, but they were deadly while they lasted. Soon, the qualification to becoming an ace, which was still set at five, came to seem inadequate as the scores rose exponentially. But the reality was that to secure one victory was difficult, and many pilots never managed to 'open their account'. The problems are illustrated by the experiences of 2nd Lieutenant Arthur Gould Lee. Upon his arrival at 46 Squadron, he was sent on a familiarisation flight in his Sopwith Pup to get the lie of the land behind the front line. He didn't realise that the westerly wind was carrying him over the lines, until the puffs of black smoke from the German 'Archie' brought him to his senses. It was only later that he saw how stupid he had been.

I got a sharp tick-off from Pratt for going too near the lines, where I would have been easy meat for a prowling Hun. I pointed out that the only machines I'd seen were the distant ones being 'Archied', and he said that newcomers never did see anything until they were being shot at, and often not even then. I said, 'Sorry, Skipper!' very meekly, for I suddenly remembered that I'd done the trip without for a moment thinking of loading my gun.[5]

2nd Lieutenant Arthur Gould Lee, 46 Squadron, RFC

The Sopwith Pup had come on stream in November 1916 with the RNAS, with 54 Squadron arriving at the front with them just weeks later. It was a beautiful aircraft to fly, with excellent manoeuvrability. Unfortunately, it was also underpowered and could only reach 100mph, while its single forward-firing Vickers machine gun left it outgunned by the Albatros. It could compete with the Albatros, but only at a disadvantage. Yet this was all in the future for Arthur Gould Lee as he was finally ready for his first real patrol, which he made alongside veterans Captain Charles Courtneidge and Lieutenant Clive Brewster-Joske on 24 May.

There were three of us on my first patrol, the others being Courtneidge and a tall slim fellow called Joske. Although I'd been looking forward to the thrill of this great occasion, I was so busy getting everything ready, such as loading my Vickers, running up the engine, and memorising Joske's instructions for signals, that before I knew what was happening, the others were taxiing along the track to the central take-off areas. I scurried after them, and we 'unstuck' in succession, me last, and as soon as we had taken up formation, me on Joske's left rear, he started climbing full out northwards. Once this began, I was so occupied in setting the fine adjustment – the lever controlling the mixture of petrol and air according to density and humidity – and keeping exactly in formation, that I quite forgot to notice how I felt about it all. Keeping formation is not all that easy until you have the knack, you're apt to overdo your efforts to get into position and to stay there. The Pup is so sensitive on the controls that any abrupt movement of the joystick or rudder makes her jump like a startled cat, and a ham-fisted pilot can skid off 50 yards to a flank at one moment and nearly collide with the whole formation the next. And, of course, you have to avoid getting in the slipstream of the machines in front. The patrol height was 17,000 feet. Up we climbed, with my throttle wide open to 6,000, 7,000, 8,000, still not halfway, and I wasn't thinking of anything much except keeping my place in this steep climb, and certainly not of Huns, when suddenly I saw three large specks in the sky ahead. They were diving towards us – and getting larger every second! My heart bounded. A Hun attack already! But Joske hadn't rocked his wings – the signal for Huns. Maybe he hadn't seen them. Should I dive forward in front and give the signal, as per instructions? But wouldn't that be a bit too cocky on my first patrol? My heart was still thumping as though I'd run up a cliff. I looked along my Aldis telescopic sight and could just get the outside Hun on the bead. Why didn't Joske give the signal, or fire, or do something? All he did was to climb even more steeply. Meanwhile the Huns were sinking beneath us, and in a

flash had passed behind. But not before I caught a glimpse of the three pilots waving to us. They were the Pups of 'A' Flight coming off patrol![6]
2nd Lieutenant Arthur Gould Lee, 46 Squadron, RFC

When they crossed the lines, there was a shock for the somewhat hapless Lee.

'Crack! Crack! Crack! Crack!' My heart nearly stopped for good and all! A Hun firing at me! I swung clear of the others and looked behind. Nothing there. Then I heard, 'Crack! Crack! Crack!' again, and this time saw tracers flashing from Courtneidge's Pup. They were testing their guns by firing short bursts into Hunland. So, I pooped off twenty rounds too, not awfully heroic, but maybe one of the bullets found its billet in some fat Boche well behind their lines.[7]
2nd Lieutenant Arthur Gould Lee, 46 Squadron, RFC

Then yet another alarm. But Lee really had little or no idea of what was happening.

There weren't any Huns around – or so I thought. But just as I was taking another long look at Ypres, Joske suddenly gave the signal and began a dive. Courtneidge and I followed. It got steeper and steeper, then they started firing their guns in bursts. Their tracers were converging on something, but for the life of me I couldn't see what. Surely this wasn't another gun test? No, Joske had signalled Huns. I stared intently ahead as the dive continued, but could spot no Hun, in fact nothing except the ground. So, not to be out of the party, I loosed off 100 rounds at a big tented camp that happened to come into my sights. It was on the German side, of course. At least, I hope so![8]
2nd Lieutenant Arthur Gould Lee, 46 Squadron, RFC

The patrol continued, but Lee suffered a machine-gun failure, at which he made what could have been a serious error of judgement.

We were now up at 16,000 [feet] again, and Joske turned east, and tried his gun, and so did Courtneidge. I followed suit, but after twenty rounds my gun jammed. I pulled out the hammer from its retaining strap and tried to knock down the cocking handle, to force the faulty round home into the breech of the gun. But the handle just wouldn't go down, and for the next 10 minutes I kept formation with my left-hand while I hammered away with my right at the gun, until I became so puffed I had to stop. At 16,000 the air is rare enough for continued exertion to make you gasp. So I followed the others around for another half-hour without a gun, which was stupid, for had we met any Huns I would have been for it. I should have dived ahead of Joske, switch-backed the machine to signal trouble, then gone home. But, somehow, I didn't want to end my first patrol that way. When we got back and I opened

my big mouth about it, I was for the high jump – both Joske and Pratt tore me off a strip for staying on, and being a liability had there been a scrap.[9]
2nd Lieutenant Arthur Gould Lee, 46 Squadron, RFC

There was a debriefing of sorts, where Lee found nothing was as he had thought.

You can imagine what a fool I felt when Joske and Courtneidge started talking about the Huns we'd attacked. It seemed that when we dived, we went after three Halberstadt scouts which Joske spotted over Houthulst Forest, north of Ypres, and which dived away south-east, and as they were quicker on the dive, they soon drew away. What was more, when the others tested their guns, the time I had my jam, it was because they'd seen a couple of two-seaters well to the eastwards, but on being fired at, they sheered off quickly. As for me, I never saw a thing. But apparently this happens with every new pilot. In fact, talking about it later in the Mess, Captain Heath, 'B' Flight Commander, told of a fellow in some other squadron who did the same as me, saw no Hun but fired when the others fired, and who, when they returned, was congratulated on having sent an Albatros down out of control! Still, on the whole, I'm pleased with today's efforts. I've shown I can fly a Pup, I've clocked up my first patrol, been over Hunland, been 'Archied', and fired at enemy scouts – not knowing they were there, admitted, but I might have hit one. Anyway, it was my first taste of powder. And I wasn't shot down![10]
2nd Lieutenant Arthur Gould Lee, 46 Squadron, RFC

Lee was still 'air blind', and as such unable to see anything that was going on in the three-dimensional world of aerial operations. Where more experienced pilots could spot the tell-tale glint of sun on the wings, or the tiny specks in the sky that were German aircraft, he saw nothing but the aircraft close alongside him. As such he was vulnerable – imagine how easy it would have been to surprise him and shoot him down before he knew what was happening if he had been on a solo mission. Which is, of course, why he was chaperoned closely on that first flight over the lines. As well as the advice and protection of his comrades, Lee was also the 'beneficiary' of helpful missives from higher authorities.

On the order of Headquarters, RFC, we have to stop calling Huns 'Hostile Aircraft' (H.A.) in our combat reports. Instead, we must always call them 'Enemy Aircraft' (E.A.). Of course, this will make a lot of difference to our lives out here. My hat, do you realise we've been calling Huns hostile all this time! No wonder we've not shot many down! But now we know they're enemy, maybe we'll do better.[11]
2nd Lieutenant Arthur Gould Lee, 46 Squadron, RFC

Scout pilots flew at altitudes which subsequently would be considered to require oxygen to avoid suffering from hypoxia, a condition then unrecognized which could scramble the brain. What was recognised was the effect of cold.

As no warmth came back from the rotary engine and there was no form of heating, one could get very cold on patrol. At that time there was no specially designed flying clothing, except that sheepskin boots and silk under-gloves were provided, on top of which we wore leather coats, gauntlet gloves and flying helmets. We were also given special oil to smear on our faces as above, say, 15,000 feet there was a chance of frostbite. My recollection is that one's fingertips were the parts to feel the cold most, and the pain in them when one came down into warmer air was excruciating, so much so that we sometimes climbed back into the cold again to get relief and descended gradually in order to restore circulation.[12]

2nd Lieutenant William Fry, 60 Squadron, RFC

Some pilots even resorted to a highly unofficial method of keeping warm.

One day there was a commotion because the C.O. had by chance discovered that one of the pilots was taking a small flask of spirits with him on patrols. We were all warned that anyone found doing this would be in serious trouble. While it didn't occur to most of us to do such a thing, it is understandable in the case of a pilot whose nerve was beginning to go. Though the consequences of making a habit of it would have been disastrous in the end, I have sometimes since felt that a little Dutch courage — rather like a soldier's rum ration before going over the top — on a cold and nerve-racking patrol might have made all the difference.[13]

2nd Lieutenant William Fry, 60 Squadron, RFC

There is no doubt that all-told, the skies above the Western Front were a difficult environment to thrive in, as Edward Mannock had discovered during a flight in his Nieuport Scout in May 1917.

Captain Keen, Rastus, and myself on second patrol. Rastus left us early owing to engine trouble so we went on without him. We engaged a Hun over Henin Lietard and chased him over towards Courcelles. I turned east and Keen turned west. I was inevitably attacked by three Huns. My gun jammed – Keen was almost out of sight. 'Aldous' [*sic*] sight oiled up, and the engine failed at the crucial momen. I thought all was up. We were 16,000 feet up at the time. I turned almost vertically on my tail – nose-dived and spun down towards our own lines, zig-zagging for all I was worth with machine-guns crackling away behind me like mad. The engine picked up when I was about three thousand feet over Arras and the Huns for some reason or other had left me. I immediately ran into another Hun – after I had climbed up to 12,000 again – but hadn't the pluck to face him. I turned away and landed here with my knees shaking and my nerves all torn to bits. I feel a bit better now, but all my courage seems to have gone after that experience this morning. The C.O. was very good and didn't put me on any more line jobs for the rest of the day. I hope I feel O.K. again in the morning, as I am on the 5.45am offensive patrol.[14]

2nd Lieutenant Edward Mannock, 40 Squadron, RFC

It will be noticed that both Lee and Mannock had problems with their machine guns jamming. This was an endemic problem.

It does seem darned silly not to have guns and ammo that work. We design and make a good aeroplane, we train and pay a pilot, we send him up into the air, he meets a Hun and has a fight, and after a lot of hot flying, if he's not shot down first, he gets the Hun in his sights, presses the trigger and then, after five shots, that infuriating blankness. Another jam, another priceless chance gone.[15]

2nd Lieutenant Arthur Gould Lee, 46 Squadron, RFC

Mannock was a thoughtful man who had put his mind to mastering the essentials of air warfare, working out the tactics that would save his own life, while bringing death to his opponents.

I brought my first dead certain Hun down this morning – over Lille – north. We escorted F.E.'s over Lille on bomb-dropping business – and we met Huns. My man gave me an easy mark. I was only 10 yards away from him – on top so I couldn't miss! A beautifully coloured insect he was – red, blue, green and yellow. I let him have sixty rounds at that range, so there wasn't much left of him. I saw him go spinning and slipping down from 14,000 [feet]. Rough luck, but it's war, and they're Huns.[16]

2nd Lieutenant Edward Mannock, 40 Squadron, RFC

It is noticeable that Mannock may have been thoughtful, but he was not overly sensitive, as is revealed by what he considered to be a practical joke on artillery observation aircraft.

Went out with Thompson this evening in search of scalps but nothing doing. Amused ourselves by dodging about the low clouds and frightening the engine out of sundry crawling 'Quirks' doing artillery work. Great sport. You come down vertically at approx. 160mph on a poor unsuspecting observer and bank away to the right or left when almost cutting off his tail. You can almost hear him gasp. They're always pleased to see us about though, and they forgive a little 'skylarking' occasionally.[17]

2nd Lieutenant Edward Mannock, 40 Squadron, RFC

I think one can imagine the pithy remarks of the long-suffering observer.

Another younger pilot who was beginning to prosper was Arthur Rhys Davids. As his 'air vision' improved, as he got used to the mental agility required in swirling dogfights, the technical difficulty of deflection snap-shooting, he also began to fall foul of that other harbinger of doom for a young pilot – over-confidence.

> I have an angel over me all the while I am flying with the great golden wings of LUCK spread over my head. The confession I referred to is that I have been an unholy dangerous fool, that I have taken four times the risk I ought to have done, and that by sheer luck I have come through with a whole skin, a great joy in life and five and a bit Huns brought down to my credit. In fact, I have been going on [Albert] Ball's lines. But I think I have had enough of that for a time. I started off being ultra-cautious, to say the least of it and that riled me; then I began being a mad dog in so much that one evening after a show – the one where I tackled the three two-seaters – the C.O. said, 'You put up a damn good show and I'm proud of you!' and after my last and silliest effort, my flight commander asked me not to do it again. The dear old adjutant gave me a fatherly piece of advice and beseeched me not to take undue risks, said it didn't pay, which I knew before was true, and which advice I intend to follow if I can. But, one can't lay down rules while on mere earth for people on fighting patrol in the air. You are a different man – at least you aren't a man at all, that is I am not – you are a devil incarnate filled with the dazzling thrill of playing the best game God ever created, mad after Huns and just forget everything else but showing the old Hun that there's only one man fit to be in the air and not two. And the only way you are sobered down is when you see fifteen red beggars coming for three of you, on which occasion you beetle off for dear life. And I can say that if I have been a fool, I have been a cunning fool, and I have given the 'Old Hun' jolly little chance of shooting straight.[18]
>
> 2nd Lieutenant Arthur Rhys Davids, 56 Squadron, RFC

But even experienced pilots could find themselves in dreadful straits. Captain William Molesworth had a narrow escape in his Nieuport Scout, which he recorded in true 'Boy's Own' fashion.

> Yesterday I had the narrowest shave I've ever had since I first started Boche-strafing. I was properly caught out this time, and really thought things were all up. We were just over the Drocourt Switch, near Vitry, when a dozen Huns got what you might call 'uppish'. We tumbled into a proper mix-up and, as there were only five of us, the Huns managed to break up our formation. We had arranged that, should this happen, we were to return to the line independently and re-form, so I started towards Arras, following the Scarpe. Just as I was passing over Gavrelle I espied three fat Hun two-seaters making south-east. 'Here we are, my son!' says I to myself. 'We'll just hop down and put the gust

up one of these Huns.' No sooner said than done. I pushed my nose down and, when within range, opened fire. The next thing I knew was a perfect hail of bullets pouring round me. Here is a rough description of my thoughts during the few minutes that followed: 'Crackle! Crackle! Crackle! My cheery aunt! There's a Hun on my tail. By jove! The blighter is making my grid into a sieve. Confound him! Let's pull her up in a good climbing turn and have a look at him. Heavens! It's the 'Circus' – I wonder if old Richthofen is the leader. The dirty dog nearly caught me out this time. Silly ass! Didn't hold his fire long enough, or he'd have made me into cold meat by now. Let's give him a dose and see how he likes it. Here he comes straight at me, loosing off with both guns. I hope we aren't going to collide. Missed! Bon! Everything's A1. Wish I'd hit him, though! I must pull her round quick, or he will be on my tail. Hang! I can't shoot for toffee, but he's pretty dud, too, thank heavens! Once again, boys, round with her. Let him have it hot. No good. Try again. Confound it! There's my beastly drum empty. I must spin and change it. Good enough! Now where's the blighter? My Harry! He has got me stiff this time; here he comes down on me from the right. Crack! Crack! Crack! Bang! Zip! Zip! There goes my petrol tank, now for the flames! Cheerio! No luck this time, you old swine. Wait till I get you next show. Here goes for the ground.' Luckily for me, my friend, and his pals, who had been watching the scrap, thought I was done for. They therefore chucked up the sponge and departed. I managed to pull the machine out, just scraping over the trenches. The engine was still running, although the petrol was pouring out all over my legs. A few minutes afterwards the engine conked out altogether, and I had to land in a field. I was immediately surrounded by a crowd of men, who had seen the fight. Amongst them were some artillery officers, who took me off to their mess and offered me a 'tot' which was very thankfully received, while they sent off a message to the squadron. The following is the official list of damage done to my machine. Six bullet holes in propeller. Cowling shot away. Large holes in bottom of petrol tank and sides. Main spar right-hand top plane broken. Rear right-hand under-carriage strut badly damaged. Twenty-eight holes in fuselage and ten in the planes – two or three missing the pilot's seat by less than an inch.[19]

Captain William Molesworth, 60 Squadron, RFC

It seemed unbelievable that so many bullets could be poured into such a small target without hitting something vital – or the pilot!

A great deal of an aeroplane could be holed without affecting its ability to fly. Wings and fuselage could be – and often were – pierced in fifty places, missing the occupants by inches – blissfully unaware of how close it had come until they returned to base. I have had bullets through my engine, bullets through my tanks, bullets through my windscreen and up through the floor of the cockpit between my knees and out over my shoulder and even, on one occasion, had the control stick knocked out of my hand by a splinter of wood chipped off the floorboards by a chance shot – yet never, such is the mystery of destiny, that one bullet which would have been enough to settle my account.[20]

Lieutenant Cecil Lewis, 56 Squadron, RFC

However, some pilots took such damage inflicted on their beloved aircraft extremely personally.

Back at Vert Galand, old Long 'Un' [Lieutenant F.A. Smith] was livid. Normally the most good-tempered, kindly sort of man, he had never been known before to lose his temper. But now he was literally incoherent with rage at the Hun who had shot up his aeroplane [a Sopwith Pup]. And it was quite a mess; holed like a sieve. The fact that he himself had escaped by a miracle did not concern him at all. It was his beautiful aeroplane; his own, personal steed upon which he rode to the hunt, which had been shot up by this blasted Hun; this bounder with the black and white checks on his fuselage.[21]

2nd Lieutenant Gordon Taylor, 66 Squadron, RFC

But it wasn't all lucky escapes, and pilots were aware that they could be shot down in flames. Mannock himself inflicted such a death on his opponents many times.

I met this D.F.W. at about 10,000 feet over Avion coming south-west, and I was travelling south-east. I couldn't recognise the black crosses readily – he was about 300 yards away and about 500 feet above me – so I turned my tail towards him and went in the same direction, thinking that if he were British, he wouldn't take any notice of me, and if a Hun, I felt sure he would put his nose down and have a shot thinking I hadn't seen him. The ruse worked beautifully. His nose went down – pointing at me – and I immediately whipped round, dived and 'zoomed' up behind him, before you could say 'Knife'! He tried to turn, but he was much too slow for the Nieuport. I got in about 50 rounds in short bursts whilst on the turn, and he went down in flames, pieces of wing and tail, etc. dropping away from the wreck. It was a horrible sight and made me feel sick. He fell down in our own lines, and I followed to the ground, although I didn't land. The boys gave me a great ovation.[22]

2nd Lieutenant Edward Mannock, 40 Squadron, RFC

It was the most painful and horrible death many of them could imagine. For some, it came to haunt their dreams. Mannock even began to carry a revolver aloft, as did Arthur Gould Lee. The reason was chilling – but obvious.

Why do I carry a Colt in the cockpit? For the reason we all do. Not to stage a one-man battle against a platoon of Boche soldiery if forced down the other side – I'd be butchered instantly. No, it's the fear of being set alight. It's something nobody talks about, but it's at the back of everybody's mind, and each of us knows he couldn't take it. To be burned alive, however soon it's over, is the one thing we can't face. Better to use the gun and end it in a split second.[23]

2nd Lieutenant Arthur Gould Lee, 46 Squadron, RFC

But there was still a black humour lurking within them that could bubble to the surface.

A few days later Wickett, the big genial Canadian, was missing. There was no news of him for several days. Then we heard from him, from near Abbeville. He had got lost in thick weather coming back from a patrol, couldn't identify the country, so had flown west till he was certain he was on the right side of the lines: then he had put his machine down in a field as his fuel was running out. Wickett had landed almost literally into the arms of a very attractive girl who had instantly fallen for him. According to him she knew only three words of English, but these were apparently adequate. He privately explained, though it inevitably got round the Mess, that all she could say was, 'Kees me queek!' So, it had taken him three days to find the way back from Abbeville![24]

2nd Lieutenant Gordon Taylor, 66 Squadron, RFC

Lieutenant T.H. Wickett was flying Sopwith Pup A6178 when he was subsequently shot down, wounded and taken prisoner on 10 May 1917. One can only hope his tender memories kept him warm during his long sojourn in a German POW camp.

The scout pilots measured their progress and status by the simple means of counting their victories. This was the be all and end all, and as we have seen it could lead even the best to take risks that were unsupportable. One 'elephant in the room' was the question of spurious claims. With most of the fighting over the German side of the lines, German claims could usually be confirmed, but the RFC had to rely on other air crew observing a German aircraft fall to earth, or the reports of artillery/balloon observers. It was not an exact science and there was considerable scope for error – and exaggeration. A dogfight was a whirlwind experience, where joined-up thinking was all but impossible. If you had to be in a dogfight, then the fast-turning Sopwith Camel was at its best – as Norman Macmillan discovered when 45 Squadron had at last got the dreaded Sopwith 1½ Strutter replaced by the Camel in August 1917.

In combat we flew like goldfish in a bowl swimming around the sky in all directions sometimes standing on our tails, sometimes with our heads right down, sometimes over on our backs, sometimes at right-angles to the ground – any attitude which enables the nose of the aircraft to point where we wanted it to point – in the direction of the enemy so that the guns could register hits. It was a fantastic type of flying and our machines could turn in such tiny circles that we simply swerved round in an amazingly small space of air, missing each other sometimes by inches. Missing enemy aircraft, missing our own aircraft, dodging in and out amongst the others in the sky, weaving the most fantastic patterns.[25]

Captain Norman Macmillan, 45 Squadron, RFC

In the confusion of such a dogfight, it is understandable that multiple claims could be made for shooting down the same aircraft, while sometimes an 'out of control' German would miraculously 'recover' once out of sight below the clouds and fly back to base.

We were at luncheon in the mess when a message was brought into the C.O. that a German two-seater was operating and taking photographs on the front of the right-hand corps of the Third Army on the Arras front, and would we drive it away or shoot it down. The C.O. asked Bishop and myself to go up after it and we were in the air within a few minutes. On getting up to the trench lines, we saw at once the German machine, straight in front and slightly higher than we were. I can see it now, after all these years, a black blob, and slightly above us. It turned away as we approached and we both let fly at it at long range, too far away to have any chance of hitting him. Having driven him off, we turned for home. On landing, Bishop came up to me and, to my surprise, said, 'We got him all right. Did you see him go down and crash?' Or something like that. Now I had not seen a German machine go down. The machine which I had taken to be the one we were attacking, and at which I had fired a burst at very long range, had turned back, deep into the German lines. But such was Bishop's reputation in the squadron that I thought he must have attacked and brought down another, closer, machine which I had not seen. I was certainly not going to contradict him. I was young [aged 21] and unsure of myself, feeling very much on trial under new management, and was not going to jeopardise my place in the squadron. This was the occasion on which we did the job and went back and finished our luncheon. Ever since, and over all the years, I have had that flight on my mind, and can still recollect the sight of the German two-seater turning sharply away and giving me the first suspicions as to my flight commander's credibility. But at the time it would not have entered my head to express any doubts. I did not make out a combat report, but Bishop, in his, gave me credit with him, so I shared the credit in Major Scott's report.[26]

2nd Lieutenant William Fry, 60 Squadron, RFC

Pilots were often encouraged by their commanding officers to be 'optimistic', and there is no doubt that some took advantage of this. William Bishop finished the war with some seventy-two acknowledged kills, but controversy still burns bright in some quarters as to how many he really shot down – indeed, there are questions over his veracity concerning the unwitnessed 2 June raid on a German airfield for which he was awarded the Victoria Cross on 30 August. Whatever the truth of this, there is no doubt Bishop was a brave man, flying dangerous missions over the lines, time and time again. Also, bear in mind that while some like William Fry may have been sceptics, many others within 60 Squadron were convinced he was genuine.

> There was tremendous excitement in the squadron yesterday, as our 'stunt merchant' [William Bishop] has been awarded the VC for that aerodrome show. We celebrated it last night by one of the finest 'busts' I have ever had. There were speeches and lots of good 'bubbly,' consequently everyone was in the best of spirits. After dinner we had a torchlight procession to the various squadrons stationed on the aerodrome. This was led by our Very light experts. Luckily for us, the night was very dull and cloudy, or else I expect old man Boche would have had a hand in it too. We charged into one mess and proceeded to throw everyone and everything we came across out of the window. We then went over to the other squadron. The wretched lads were all in bed, but we soon had them out, and bombarded their mess with Very lights, the great stunt being to shoot one in through one window and out at the other. I can't imagine why the blessed place didn't go up in flames. After annoying these people for a bit, we retired to our own mess, where we danced and sang till the early hours of the morning.[27]
>
> Captain William Earle Molesworth, 60 Squadron, RFC

Whatever the reality of the claimed 'victories', the scout pilots were the 'glamour boys' of the RFC. But most understood their real role – to clear the way for those who would do the essential work and deny any opportunities for the Germans.

> Our job is to see that the Boche does not get a chance to do any work in the air at all – I mean useful work like bombing and observation. What advantage do we gain? We just gain the supremacy of the air, bless you, that's all: we'll 'ave a notice board put up to the effect.

> AERIAL PARK.
> PRIVATE.
> HUN TRESPASSERS WILL
> BE PROSECUTED.

> And we keep our own machines safe.[28]
>
> 2nd Lieutenant Arthur Rhys Davids, 56 Squadron, RFC

And for all the horrors, there was a rare quality about aerial combat which could be almost addictive.

> Looking back on this scrap, I realise that however much you're scared before you start, once you're in it you don't feel excitement or fear, you fight in a sort of daze. When it's over, and you find you're still alive, you feel both exhausted and exhilarated. In fact, what with the sun shining, the blue sky above, and the white clouds below, and your engine running smoothly, and the Pup handling like the spirited thing she is, you can feel that you've enjoyed it. Like you enjoy a plunge in an icy-cold mountain pool – once you get out of it![29]
> 2nd Lieutenant Arthur Gould Lee, 46 Squadron, RFC

But then again, who in their right mind really enjoys a plunge into an icy mountain pool?

There was a very real element of the mythical Wild West gunfighter about the aces. No matter how good you might think you were, there was always somebody better. Cecil Lewis had become a very competent and confident young man by the summer of 1917. But his confidence was a little dented during a friendly encounter with the great French ace Capitaine Georges Guynemer of Escadrille No.3, who paid a visit to 56 Squadron flying his SPAD XII Scout.

> I do not want to appear conceited, but at that time I was considered one of the best pilots in 56 Squadron, so when Guynemer challenged me to a mock combat over the airfield I accepted with alacrity. I knew our machines were fairly evenly matched and judged that my own flying skill would give me the edge over the Frenchman. But I soon found it was otherwise. Guynemer's little SPAD was smaller and more manoeuvrable than the SE5. He had a better climb and could turn in a smaller circle. The result was that as I sat in a vertical turn with the stick right back circling as tightly as the SE5 could go, Guynemer just sat right on my tail turning in a slightly smaller circle so that he always kept his sights on me. Had I been an enemy, I should have been dead five times in the first minute. Do what I would, spin, half-roll, dive, climb, there he sat – just as if I had been towing him behind me. So I returned to the squadron that evening with a great respect for the SPAD and for the boy who piloted it with such skill. Only a few weeks later, stalking an unsuspecting Hun two-seater with his cannon, Guynemer was just too much preoccupied, and an Albatros, coming down out of the morning sun, shot him out of the sky.[30]
> Lieutenant Cecil Lewis, 56 Squadron, RFC

On 11 September 1917, Guynemer was shot down and killed, with his final accredited total standing at fifty-four victories. Perhaps he was tired; perhaps he had just lost concentration. We will never know.

On 15 August 1917, the ranks of 56 Squadron received a notable addition with the arrival of James McCudden. When we last encountered McCudden, he had been an accomplished air mechanic, flying occasional missions as an air gunner with 3 Squadron. To say he had 'moved on' would rather understate his progress. He had undergone pilot training early in 1916, after which he had a brief stint flying the FE2b with 20 Squadron, before a full tour on the DH2 as first a sergeant pilot, and then as a commissioned officer, with 29 Squadron. McCudden's career can be seen as a sign that Britain was beginning to run out of public schoolboys of the 'right type', and in consequence the RFC was gradually changing as merit and experience began to be more important than class. In this, the RFC was mirroring the experience of the officers' messes elsewhere in the British Army. By February 1917, McCudden had secured the five victories to qualify as an ace before a period on home service as an instructor. Upon arrival at 56 Squadron, his leadership qualities had been recognised and he was promoted to be a flight commander of 'B' Flight, which contained the irrepressible Arthur Rhys Davids. McCudden, ever the professional in everything he did, embarked on a programme to bring discipline to his flight, drilling them to fight as a unit and carrying out simple tactics designed to maximise pain to the Germans at the minimum of cost to his flight. It soon began to pay dividends. Perhaps his greatest challenge came on 23 September, when McCudden's flight was on an offensive patrol in the skies above the Ypres Salient and encountered the great German ace – ranked second only to Manfred von Richthofen, having claimed some forty-nine victories – Leutnant Werner Voss of Jasta 10, who was flying one of the new Fokker Dr 1 Triplanes. What happened next was the stuff of legend.

> Down we dived at a colossal speed. I went to the right, Rhys Davids to the left, and we got behind the triplane together. The German pilot saw us and turned in the most disconcertingly quick manner, not a climbing nor Immelmann turn, but a sort of flat half-spin. By now the German triplane was in the middle of our formation, and its handling was wonderful to behold. The pilot seemed to be firing at all of us simultaneously, and although I got behind him a second time, I could hardly stay there for a second. His movements were so quick and uncertain that none of us could hold him in sight at all for any decisive time. I now got a good opportunity as he was coming towards me nose-on, and slightly underneath, and had apparently not seen me. I dropped my nose, got him well in my sight, and pressed both triggers. As soon as I fired up came his nose at me, and I heard clack-clack-clack-clack, as his bullets passed close to me and through my wings. I distinctly noticed the red-yellow flashes from his parallel Spandau guns. As he flashed by me, I caught a glimpse of a black head in the triplane.[31]

Captain James McCudden, 56 Squadron, RFC

Voss should have tried to escape, but he took them on, using the superb manoeuvrability of the Fokker Triplane to flummox his opponents as they tried to get a clear shot at him. Indeed, his own chattering machine guns took a toll and two of the SE5as were forced to retire from the fight, badly damaged. Then, finally, Rhys Davids got on the Fokker's tail.

> Eventually I got east and slightly above the Triplane and made for it, getting in a whole Lewis drum and a corresponding number of Vickers into him. He made no attempt to turn, until I was so close to him, I was certain we would collide. He passed my right-hand wing by inches and went down. I zoomed. I saw him next with his engine apparently off, gliding west. I dived again and got one shot out of my Vickers; however, I reloaded and kept in the dive. I got in another good burst and the Triplane did a slight right-hand turn, still going down. I had now overshot him (this was at 1,000 feet), zoomed, but never saw him again.[32]
> Lieutenant Arthur Rhys Davids, 56 Squadron, RFC

McCudden was witness to the end. Voss had clearly been badly hit, as his flying became erratic before his Fokker Triplane smashed into the ground. Voss was dead, and at a stroke Rhys Davids became a hero of the RFC. But in this cruellest game, success was transitory; on 27 October, young Arthur Rhys Davids was himself killed in combat in his SE5a B31.

In circumstances like these, it is not surprising that men sometimes felt the need for release from the ever-growing tension. Wild drinking binges were still not the norm, but they seem to have become more regular than hitherto.

> We had more binges in the mess than we had at Vert Galand Farm; and this, I think, was a reflection of the stresses imposed by the war as it now had developed. More than once the whole place was wrecked as the pilots let go and the evening developed into a violent release from the tensions of the day. Major Henderson, the C.O., was a great man in these melees. He had a theory that no officer in the mess should be able to hold him down on the floor, and this was a challenge which resulted in the most terrific struggles and wreckage. 'Sticky' Hunter, a one-legged pilot who usually got into the centre of these contests, always took off his artificial leg and left it in his tent so that it wouldn't be broken. His one remaining leg had to take its chance.[33]
> Lieutenant Gordon Taylor, 66 Squadron, RFC

And then there was, as usual, the piano, the songs, different favourites for each squadron, but often imbued with a strange fatalism that was understandable when you realise that some of the drunken singers could easily be dead the next day.

We had a binge last evening, which started casually before dinner. Somebody was mixing some pretty potent cocktails, as we realised later. There was one drink, not deadly at all, which is prepared as a ritual before a binge dinner. It's a sort of squadron cocktail called 'Health and Strength', which everyone has to like whether he does or not. It's made of eggs, brandy, port and several kinds of liquor, and I found it rather cloying. We drink it at the dining-table, one foot on the chair, the other on the table, to the toast, 'Cheerio, Forty-Six!' yelled very, very earsplittingly. After dinner we had a noisy sing-song in the ante-room, with Dimmock strumming at the piano, and everyone gathering round him, bellowing to beat the band. The songs were either about women, 'She was poor but she was 'onest' kind of thing, or about aeroplanes and air fighting, in parodies of well-known ditties. Some I'd met before, others were new to me. The one I liked was sung to the tune of John Peel, it goes:

> *When you soar into the air on a Sopwith Scout,*
> *And you're scrapping with a Hun and your gun cuts out,*
> *Well, you stuff down your nose 'til your plugs fall out,*
> *Cos you haven't got a hope in the morning.*

Then comes the chorus:

> *For a batman woke me from my bed,*
> *I'd had a thick night and a very sore head,*
> *And I said to myself, to myself I said,*
> *'Oh, we haven't got a hope in the morning!'*

There were lots of other songs, and we went from one to another and back again, with a terrific din going on, everyone yelling for more drinks, and the waiters whizzing round, and everybody getting more and more tight.[34]
    2nd Lieutenant Arthur Gould Lee, 46 Squadron, RFC

Then of course, being young daft men, there were the practical jokes.

Early this morning, I was awakened by strange snorting noises, to which I listened for some time, half asleep. Then I came to with a start to find a cow's head 5 feet away from mine! She was stuck in my doorway, and I jumped up to find, behind her rump, Charles and Armitage puffing and blowing, and doing their damnedest to push her right into my cubicle. For one priceless moment we all stared at each other, then I seized my water jug and soused the three of them. This was all tit-for-tat for Odell and I throwing half a dozen chickens into their cubicles a few mornings back when we were on early patrol.[35]
    Lieutenant Arthur Gould Lee, 46 Squadron, RFC

Amidst it all, the poor old army cooperation RE8s were busy doing their bread-and-butter work. Every time the battleground inched forward, there was a new tranche of ground to be photographed, new targets to be registered. Every time they took off, the pilots and observers knew that there was a chance that this might be the day that they met the German scouts that would shoot them down. On 5 November, Sergeant George Eddington and his observer, 2nd Lieutenant F.A. Dormer, of 6 Squadron RFC, were carrying out an artillery observation mission in their RE8 C5028 when it finally happened. It was something that had perhaps haunted their nightmares for weeks before.

It was quite an interesting shoot – to watch the shell bursts as they corrected their range to as near as they could to the centre. All of a sudden, I heard a burst of gunfire. Eight Albatros [scouts] had crept up on me. I looked round and there was Mr Dormer lying flat out on the floor – they'd got him with the first burst. I thought, 'That's it!' I tried to avoid combat by making a series of wide flat circles which deprived the enemy of any chance of getting a straight line on me. All the time I was losing height because I knew that in the end they'd get me. Then I glanced round to see an aircraft diving down – out to make a proper job of it! I had to do something pretty quickly! I decided to do an Immelmann Turn: nobody had ever heard of anyone doing that in a RE8, but it was the only way out! I stood her up on her tail – pulled the stick right back, kicked the left rudder just as she was coming up and she started spinning! I was quite cool and even at that stage one doesn't think of death. Down she went and the firing stopped. They could see me spinning down and I suspect they were just waiting to see the shower of sparks. I centralised everything and, just as I was coming out of the dive into the straight, I heard two sharp bangs. Both the wing extensions had broken off against the struts and been carried right away. That left me with no lateral control at all. I was going down quite fast and there was nothing I could do about it. I looked round and shouted to Dormer, 'We're going to crash!' but of course he was still out. I switched off the engine because they always caught fire. I waited until we got to about 30 foot off the ground and then – very heavy on the controls – I pulled back with both hands on the stick into my stomach. It pulled her back a bit, but she dived into the ground with one colossal bang. I remembered no more – I'd landed in Sanctuary Wood and an artillery officer dragged me out – they'd already got the observer out.[36]

Sergeant George Eddington, 6 Squadron, RFC

Eddington had survived, but his nerve was gone and he was sent home to become an instructor.

The RFC had been developing a new role over the previous two years. Early attempts at ground strafing had been stymied by the weight of the weapons that the aircraft could carry, and the paucity of numbers available. But now there were hundreds of machines that could carry twin machine guns and small 20lb bombs to boot. The aircraft attacked the Germans in their trenches, but also roamed far and wide behind the lines, attacking gun batteries, transport and any worthwhile target of opportunity that appeared before them. By this time, Arthur Gould Lee and 46 Squadron had been equipped with the Sopwith Camel.

This trench-strafing is becoming rather a strain. In air fighting, what counts, apart from having an efficient plane, are things like experience, skill, tactics, good flying, good shooting. Plus luck, of course, though chance is only one of the factors. But trench-strafing is all chance, no matter how skilled you are. To make sure of your target you have to expose yourself to the concentrated fire of dozens of machine-guns and hundreds of rifles. Compared with this, 'Archie' is practically a joke. Of course, strafing behind the lines is different, the odds against you aren't nearly so great, and you can usually observe results, which is seldom possible in trench-strafing. I've got to admit it gives me the shakes, with so many guns firing you feel every time you dive that it's bound to be your last. Even Thomson [Captain George Thomson] is feeling it, and nobody in the squadron has more guts than him. He lives in the next cubicle to me, and last night, about midnight, I was awakened by awful screeching noises. It was Tommy. I took a torch and went into him. He was struggling and sweating and shouting, in the throes of a nightmare. The chaps in the other two cubicles heard, and came in, and we awakened him. He was very shamefaced. He'd just been shot down in flames, he said. It's not 'wind up', just nervous strain.[37]

Lieutenant Arthur Gould Lee, 46 Squadron, RFC

Even when sent home on leave, Lee could not shake off a feeling of overall malaise.

Looking back on leave, I have a mood of depression and disillusionment. I enjoyed every minute of it, yet now I'm back here among the chaps, I see things more clearly. I see all those lousy types in London, in fact all over the country, for whom the war is the big chance to make money and enjoy life. They don't want it to finish. You see all those fit men in bolt-holes, many of them in uniform, and you know that not one of them has any conception of what the people out here who do the fighting go through, especially the P.B.I. [Poor Bloody Infantry] They talk glibly about danger and bravery and so on, but these are just words, they don't mean a thing. They ask you how many Fritzes you've shot down, old bean, as though it's a cricket score. They just don't realise that a machine destroyed means a life ended, some unfortunate devil, British or German, smashed to pulp, or burned alive. Somehow, the air smells cleaner out here.[38]

Lieutenant Arthur Gould Lee, 46 Squadron, RFC

Lee's moodiness would prove to be the first signs of an imminent mental breakdown.

On 20 November, the Battle of Cambrai commenced. The British opened up a thunderous predicted barrage, using the new sciences of shooting 'off the map' and the diligent calibration of the guns, which removed the necessity of pre-registration. At the same time, the new tanks rolled forward to clear a path through the German barbed wire and the infantry were able to advance almost unopposed. But then the attack stalled on Bourlon Ridge. On 26 November, Arthur Gould Lee was leading his flight of Sopwith Camels on a ground target and bombing raid in the Bourlon Ridge sector. Diving down to attack some Germans, his aircraft was hit by flak and he was forced to land. This truly was a dangerous business.

There was a terrific metallic clang behind, and I felt the thud of bullets. A burst had gone through the petrol tank just behind my back. I looked over my tail, and my heart positively stopped. Trailing out 30 feet behind me was a wide plume of bluish-white vapour. It was petrol! Pouring out of the tank and being vaporised by the hot exhaust gases from the revolving engine. Exactly as I'd seen happen to planes in air fights just before they burst into flames. Instantly, I switched off and dipped my nose steeply towards the ground. I didn't care where I came down, scarcely even looked – all I craved for was the solid earth before some spark set everything alight. The ground rushed up. I flattened out, held her off for what seemed a long time until she slowed down to landing speed, touched wheels, ran into a trench, and tipped over into it. I was upside down, hanging on my straps, half concussed – and the petrol was pouring over me. In a sudden panic I unbuckled my harness, dropped head-first into the trench, and crawled along it until I was clear. I climbed out of the trench and took a very deep breath. I was soaked with petrol, but I was alive. A shell burst 30 yards away and although it didn't worry me, for I felt safe on the ground, the bombs were still on the machine, very obvious in the upside-down position, and a shell on those would make quite a bang, so I moved away. As I did so, a head appeared out of a trench, 10 yards off. 'You all right?' it asked. 'I think so,' I answered, 'so long as you keep your distance with that cigarette. I'm soaked with petrol!'[39]
Lieutenant Arthur Gould Lee, 46 Squadron, RFC

On 30 November, any initial successes at Cambrai were soon forgotten when the Germans trialled their own new stormtrooper tactics to considerable effect. Once again, the Camel pilots were called into action to try and stem the tide of field grey.

As I was making my fifth dive on trenches sloping down from the wood to Fontaine, with gusts of rifle fire coming up at me, I felt the thud of a bullet, then my engine petered right out. Not a sound from it – but plenty from below – a hell of a noise, dozens of guns. I was only 100 feet up, having dived from 500, and I gave myself up as a goner. My mind was a blank, there was nothing I could do except crash. Moving automatically, without any conscious reasoning, I switched on the gravity tank. At once the engine roared into life – wonderful music! I pulled out level, sickeningly close to the ground, barely 3 feet above a parapet. All I remember noticing was a baby faced Boche wearing spectacles, mouth open, gaping up at me from a deep trench. Back home, I found they had hit me, an engine bearer, but it was the pressure pump that had packed up, through the cold, I suppose, or the dive. I still don't know what instinct made me switch to gravity, but thank goodness I did. I felt exhausted for quite a time afterwards. This escape makes me disapprove of trench-strafing more than ever. To fly along a winding trench, bristling with successive nests of machine guns and mortars, and rifles by the score, all blasting at you every time you lift up to dive, and fired by people largely hidden and protected by traverses, really makes my hair stand on end. The strain of waiting for that one bullet with your name on it, knowing that you can't dodge it like you can 'Archie', is quite petrifying. Trench-strafing can be a suicidal job, especially if you're rash, and the staff types who so casually order it can have no conception of what it demands from a pilot. They ought to try it occasionally.[40]

Lieutenant Arthur Gould Lee, 46 Squadron, RFC

Lee was becoming more and more morbid, a sure sign that his nerve was going.

We had another Battle of Cambrai casualty today, but a different sort of casualty – a dog. Little Sandy, the melancholy-eyed mongrel that MacLeod adopted and took everywhere with him. Sandy became Mac's shadow and had no use for anybody else in the squadron. He slept on his bed, waited patiently for him outside the mess door, trotted after him to the hangar when Mac was on a job, and hung around there until he returned. On the day Mac crashed, Sandy stayed up at the hangar until it was closed, when the flight sergeant brought him down to our mess. For days he's been wandering round the huts and cubicles, refusing food, just looking for Mac. He avoided anybody who tried to stroke him, including me, and has just sickened away. This morning we found him lying outside Mac's old cubicle, almost unable to move. We knew he had to be put out of his misery, but nobody had the heart to do it. At last Robeson took him away into the orchard and put a bullet through his poor little head.[41]

Lieutenant Arthur Gould Lee, 46 Squadron, RFC

A few nights later, Lee woke up screaming.

I had proof last night that this darned trench-strafing had begun to get on my nerves. Apparently, I was yelling in a nightmare, and he had to come into my cubicle and waken me. I was shaking and sweating with it. I was diving,

diving, into a black bottomless pit with hundreds of machine-guns blasting up endlessly at me. I didn't like it a bit![42]

Captain Arthur Gould Lee, 46 Squadron, RFC

Hundreds of RFC pilots and observers were facing these terrors. The answer – it seems trivial – was often more jolly japes in the mess.

Then I proposed a bullfight. Turnbull was the matador, Rusby was the 'bull' and the others took part as picadores, horses, bandilleros etc. I was the beauteous lady who sits in a box and is Queen of the Festival. We all dressed up. Rusby put on a woolly fur coat and snow boots on his hands and feet, Turnbull wrapped our beautiful curtain round his middle and draped a tablecloth over his shoulder. Of course, he carried a red cloak and a sword (stick). All the others had various coloured cloths draped round them and Hamilton looked perfectly priceless in a piece of old sacking and a flying glove stuck on his head as a hat. He really is the ugliest man I have seen. First of all, we had the parade to appropriate music played by Poole. That ended with a flourish and from my box – the top of the piano – I flung the key into the arena, the parade continued, and the door of the bull's den was opened. Out rushed the bull and I nearly fell off the piano with laughter. The matador played with him first of all in the approved style and then the picadors on horseback plunged in. As it looked like becoming a most awful schmozzle I called off the gee-gees and sent in the bandilleros. Then came the kill. The pianist rose to frenzied efforts, I beat the drum, Payne blew the clarinet and everyone was dancing wildly round the room. Suddenly the door opened and in walked the general. The sight that met his eyes must have been perfectly priceless. There was a hideous silence, which Turnbull and the bull didn't pay any attention to because Turnbull chose that particular moment to kill the bull. I leaped from the piano and confronted the general. He was highly amused and insisted on us finishing the show, which we did.[43]

Major Charlie Dixon, 29 Squadron, RFC

It may seem childish, indeed it was childish, but it helped keep them going.

It was dud all yesterday for which many thanks! We had a great guest night last night. I went to the concert in the town before dinner; it was quite a good show. Then I came back and found three Royal Army Medical Corps captains and two colonels of other regiments into dinner. After dinner we all sang songs and most people got a bit merry. I sang 'A Wee Deoch an Doris' and 'Annie Laurie' amid loud applause. Then we sang 'Do You know the Muffin Man that Lives in 65?' One man goes up to another and sings that line, then that man sings, 'Yes I know the Muffin Man!' and he links arms with the first and the two go round to someone else. Finally, the whole room has joined up and I found myself with one arm in the C.O.'s and the other in a colonel's capering madly round the room all shouting, 'We all know the Muffin Man that lives in 65!' It was simply priceless.[44]

2nd Lieutenant Guy Knocker, 65 Squadron, RFC

The end came quickly for Arthur Gould Lee, although he continued to struggle on as best he could. He began to suffer from severe stomach cramps as his body started to send him unambiguous messages that he was 'done'.

The wing medical officer came to see me again this evening, ostensibly about my appendix. He was very chummy, and said that maybe I didn't know it, but I'd had enough. Being shot down three times had done me no good, apart from other things, such as shell bursts. He told me that even though I wouldn't admit I was on the way to cracking up, my body knew it, hence the tummy pains and other symptoms. I said there was nothing wrong with me that another good binge wouldn't cure.[45]

Captain Arthur Gould Lee, 46 Squadron, RFC

Lee was the only one left of the squadron he had joined just a few months ago. The rest were dead, wounded, prisoners of war or sent on home service to recuperate. His time had come to leave.

At 11.55 last night I stood with some of the old-timers outside the mess, waiting for the New Year. Scattered in the orchard around us were the others, Colt in one hand, Very pistol in the other. We waited in the darkness for the major, who kept an eye on his watch with a torch. Twelve o'clock! The major fires a red Very light, and instantly all the others go soaring up into the air. Then comes a fusillade of shots as the automatics are emptied, also upwards! Then hoots and catcalls, followed by prolonged cheering. As it peters out, we hear a similar din coming from 64 Squadron next door. We go into the mess, drink 'toddy', sing *Auld Lang Syne*. We're visited by some of the chaps from 64, go through it all again, and eventually stagger off to bed. It's 1918, and we're all still alive![46]

Captain Arthur Gould Lee, 46 Squadron, RFC

He had seen out the old year, but he would not see in 1918. Finally, the medical authorities intervened and sent him home for his own good.

New Year's Day, the medical officer has reported that I am run down physically, and won't be able to do any more useful flying until I've had a good spell of leave. Now that the decision has been made, I think maybe they're right. While I was on leave, I had that queer urge to get back here, and as I mentioned before, when I arrived at the Mess it seemed like

coming home. But now things have changed so much, so many chaps have gone, and half the people in the mess are strangers. I've been longer in the squadron than anybody and now I realise I've had enough. I feel a sort of waning of the spirit, and I shan't grumble if I'm now for home. I spent a lazy and interesting hour going through my log-book. I've done 260 hours in France, of which 222 were over the lines. I've done 118 patrols and ground strafings, been reported missing four times, had 56 combats, and shot down eleven Huns, five by me solo, the rest shared. Not wonderful compared with people like Ball, Bishop, Collishaw and McCudden, and I'm miles from being an 'ace', but at least I'm not a pigeon any longer, in fact I think I can consider myself practically a hawk![47]
Captain Arthur Gould Lee, 46 Squadron, RFC

He would not return to the front.

Chapter 9

Could It Get Any Worse? 1918

The feeling of safety produced an amazing reaction of fear, the intensity of which was terrific. Suddenly I experienced a physical and moral depression which produced cowardice. I suddenly felt I was totally unsuited to air fighting and that I would never be persuaded to fly over the lines again. For quite 5 minutes I shivered and shook.[1]

Lieutenant Ira Jones, 74 Squadron, RAF

The times they were a-changing on the Western Front. The strategic situation was affected by two major factors: Russia had collapsed and fallen out of the war, while on 6 April 1917, the United States had joined the Allies. One in; one out; but there was a window of opportunity for the Germans to switch divisions from the Eastern Front to concentrate them on the Western Front for one last *Gotterdammerung* to break the British and French before the Americans arrived in great strength in the summer of 1918. For three long years, the RFC had been at the forefront of planning and enabling the next 'Big Push'; now they had to fit into the defensive battle that would be fought in the spring of 1918. With the exception of Prime Minister David Lloyd George, who was busy denuding the Western Front of troops, everyone in authority knew what was coming. Even the ever-offensive Major General Hugh Trenchard prepared a pamphlet, 'The Employment of the Royal Flying Corps in Defence', and hammered home the point that its most important role was now to detect the location of the German offensive. Photographic reconnaissance was crucial and there was a renewed effort to educate the army as to what could be achieved. It did not always go to plan.

I started my course of 'Interpretation of Aeroplane Photographs' this morning. There were eight infantry officers – I rather think they were battalion intelligence officers – assembled round the table in the conference room at the corps, where Sergeant Cowley, Second Aircraftsman Ripley and I arrived with the component parts of a magic lantern. After a bit of business getting the light to work, I got under way with my celebrated lantern exhibition and was getting along quite nicely when the door behind the screen opened and the corps commander shuffled in, tripped over the electric light wire, put out the light and fused the arc lamp. The corps commander then fell over a chair, and I felt it was time to pull up a blind, which I did. He then told me to carry on as if he wasn't there.[2]

Lieutenant Thomas Hughes, 53 Squadron, RFC

Once the area of the great German Spring Offensive had been determined, what was the RFC to do then? Trenchard had the answer, although it was obvious – the RFC was to interfere with their preparations by – an old favourite – artillery observation, extensive bombing and ground strafing attacks. They were also to continue their eternal air offensive to take the battle to the German Air Service, even though Haig's armies as a whole were temporarily on the defensive. However, the RFC would have to face this looming campaign without their leader, for Trenchard was sent back home to become Chief of the Air Staff back in London. He was replaced by Major General John Salmond, a man who was imbued with the same basic principles as Trenchard. In effect, nothing changed.

One symbol of the continued attacking intent of the RFC was the return to France of Frederick Powell, who arrived to command 41 Squadron as a major at the age of just 22, after completing stints on home service as a chief fighting instructor and then in command of a reserve squadron. Now he was back, this time flying the SE5a – and he was determined that his new charges should follow his aggressive example. However, he was frustrated by what he considered their all-pervading timidity.

> The difficulty was to get them to see hostile aircraft. When they'd come back from an offensive patrol one after the other, they reported no hostile aircraft. By that time my own experience was that if you put your nose over the lines, you'd certainly within a few minutes be surrounded by the Albatros DV as Mr Richthofen's circus was busy on the other side of the lines – and I couldn't understand it. I only imagined that they weren't going over the lines, they were keeping too far this side.[3]
> Major Frederick Powell, 41 Squadron, RFC

He decided the best course of action was to lead an offensive patrol himself and show the way by example – he promised them they would have a fight before they got back. He was as good as his word, though not perhaps in the manner he intended. On 2 February, they took off in two flights. Powell himself led one, flying at 14,000 feet in his SE5a B8273, while the other flight of four SE5a would fly higher at 17,000 feet.

> The object being that when I was attacked by the Albatros, then the top flight would be able to dive down on the German. In effect, I was the bait. I put a six-foot yellow streamer on my rudder and two red, yellow and blue streamers on the wings. My flight commander just had a streamer on his rudder. I crossed over the lines at Amiens, turned left, and flew up to Douai going further over the lines. I had told the officers, 'We will go on and on, and if we don't get any Germans at all we'll gradually lose height, and if they don't come up, we will go down to the German aerodromes and shoot the blinking things on

the ground!' That was just sheer bravado, but I was so certain that as soon as we crossed we would soon be into the midst of it.[4]

Major Frederick Powell, 41 Squadron, RFC

Nevertheless, nothing happened. Powell couldn't believe it, but he wasn't going to back down.

I got to Douai and to my horror we had not been attacked! I thought, 'Oh damn, I'll have to lose height and carry out this hazardous trip to shoot the people in the aerodromes behind the lines!' I had only just turned about, and the sky seemed filled with black crosses. There were Germans everywhere! I got down on to the tail of a German, and I got him in my Aldis telescopic sight, but I thought, 'No, I'm not going to pull the trigger and blast off a lot of ammunition, I'll get this fellow so easily through the back of the head with the first three rounds!' But first I had to get him right in the centre of the sight. As the gun was fixed, you see, you had to steer the aircraft rather than the gun. This fellow, he just slipped out of the Aldis sight to one side. I counter-ruddered and brought him back – and I was just about to fire when another German, who was on my tail, fired and hit the instruments board, he hit me through the leg and through the arm. At the time I didn't notice this except that I felt a bang – and that was my first experience of getting a bullet through me. I had often visualised what the heck was it going to feel like, but of course one doesn't feel it; it is just a blow. He was using armour-piercing bullets, of which one went through the engine – it cut out one entire block of cylinders. There was a cloud of steam and water that went up: it had gone through the radiator. My first reaction was, 'My God, fire!' I knew I was at 14,000 feet, and I had to get down to the ground before the thing disintegrated entirely in flames, remembering we had no parachutes![5]

Major Frederick Powell, 41 Squadron, RFC

With no engine, he was in real trouble, well over the German lines and just waiting for the first smouldering flames that would signify a terrible death. Meanwhile, his German adversaries had by no means finished with him.

I dived down as hard as I could go, and looked back, and saw that I had got three German Albatros [scouts] on my tail. Well, they were heavy machines, the Albatros, with a big engine – they weren't so manoeuvrable as the SE5a. I was able to turn quickly in what we called an Immelmann turn, quickly, and go underneath them on my way down with no engine. They took a long time to get round before their guns came on to me, when I whipped round quickly the other way and went down. After I had seemed to be going down for about four weeks, I had to drag my eyes away from these Boche and look where I was. I was about 400 feet up in the air only, and passing over a marvellous

field, which turned out eventually to be a German aerodrome, where I landed. The German who shot me down, came in and landed on the aerodrome as well, and another two went round and round in circles, leaving a gun on my machine all the time: it was rather well done.[6]
Major Frederick Powell, 41 Squadron, RFC

He had been shot down by Leutnant Max Kühn of Jasta 10.

I got out of the machine, went to the little locker at the back, pulled off my flying helmet and put my cap on. Then I walked across to the German who was sitting there in his machine with the engine ticking over. The excitement had been so intense, I had forgotten that I had been hit. I went up to him and I put my hand out, and he leant out to shake my hand, because there was that sort of friendship. As he did so, he suddenly said, 'Verwundert?' That sounded like 'wounded' and I looked down and I saw blood running out of my sleeve. Then of course I felt it. I was then taken by two German soldiers wearing pickelhaubes and they bandy-chaired me and carried me across the road and into a casualty clearing station. As I was going into the casualty clearing station there was a feldwebel and he said, 'Your name?' I said, 'Powell!' 'Your regiment?' I said, 'Royal Flying Corps!' And he said, 'Your rank?' I said, 'Major!' He looked at me and said, 'Nein, nein, Feldwebel!', because at that time a German major was an elderly man with a white moustache, and he couldn't understand how a boy could call himself a major! They didn't believe it![7]
Major Frederick Powell, 41 Squadron, RFC

His war was over. Powell would live to die an elderly man – perhaps with a white moustache – in 1992.

*   *   *

The RFC soon discovered that the German Spring Offensive would be launched in the Somme area; as the British had found back in 1916, it was difficult to disguise the location of a major attack. There were improvements to rail and road communications to the sector, massive supply and munitions dumps, new camps to house the men and new airfields. The RFC now had to determine when exactly the blow would fall. The FE2b were employed on night missions, probing deep over the area in question to try to track rail activity and the movement of assault divisions.

It's surprising what you can see from the air at night – even on a very dark night. Objects like woods, which are a black blob on the landscape, they're extremely prominent and easy to pick out. Railway lines you can see because with the small amount of light that there is, even on a dark night, you get a glint off the rails and if there's a long straight stretch you can know it's a railway. On your map you can see a railway marked – and with the aid of landmarks such as woods, lakes, rivers – which all show up – you can then navigate almost as you do in daylight by following the landmarks.[8]

   Lieutenant John Hopkins, 83 Squadron, RFC

They also used a system of beacons at known locations; indeed, both sides had them, and tended to leave those of their opponents alone as they too were useful. At night, the bombers were relatively safe from German scouts, but there were plenty of other dangers.

Reconnaissance was accomplished by flying at about 4,000 feet over a particular area that had been indicated and then dropping parachute flares. They were launched through a tube and an electrical contact fired the magnesium compound. It dropped about 500 feet or less, the parachute opened, and at the same time the flare caught light. Well, if we were looking for traffic on the railway, we would fly along the railway, drop these parachute flares in a line and then turn round and come back over the top of the flares, to observe anything that we could see underneath. This was not a pleasant business because it was quite obvious to the Germans that having dropped the flares, we were going to come back over the top of them again – and they were waiting for us. Well at the height we flew we were within machine-gun range, and they had machine-guns there all right. Then they had these things they called 'flaming onions', which were balls of fire on wires and shot into the air – they looked like enormous Roman candles. They were quite terrifying, but as far as I know they never did any damage at all – except to put the wind up you. But the machine-gun was definitely a danger.[9]

   Lieutenant John Hopkins, 83 Squadron, RFC

The FE2b night squadrons also made attempts to bomb German trains that were bringing up divisions to the front.

Bombing a moving train has many of the characteristics of big game hunting and is perhaps the most sporting target in the whole of night bombing work. The results, too, especially just before an offensive, often have far-reaching effects, for it impedes the work of massing together both men and material, and delays food and ammunition in being brought up to the front line. An offensive by the Germans was expected, and the orders for the night were to bomb and machine gun a variety of targets behind the lines, which doings were calculated to harass the enemy and upset his plans. We were told to pay particular attention to trains running towards the lines, for these would undoubtedly contain men and munitions that were being massed for the attack. Leaving the aerodrome with a full load of small, high-explosive bombs, each of which was capable of derailing a train, we headed straight for a railway junction, some 10 miles behind the lines. We were well acquainted with the whereabouts of this junction, from experience of former raids. Arriving over it at 4,000 feet, we could see the rails quite plainly as they shone in the moonlight, and we circled round it to wait and watch events. We had not long to wait before down below we saw a faint glow and a trail of white smoke, which showed up well against the black background of earth. It was a train and travelling towards the lines. With engine cut completely off, we dived swiftly towards it, and, as we neared it, turned quickly round and took up a position behind it. Lower and lower we glided until the carriages became quite visible. We continued to glide down, however, until we were low enough to be absolutely certain of obtaining direct hits. Switching on the engine and throttling back, until the speed of our machine was only a trifle faster than that of the train, we flew parallel above it, and gradually overtook it. As the carriages slowly passed beneath us, we released three bombs in quick succession, and the force of the resulting explosions shook our machine from head to stern. With throttle full open we quickly climbed to a height and let off a parachute flare to aid us in observing the result. This was hardly necessary, for the clouds of smoke and sparks that were arising from the ground told their tale. By the light of the flare, however, we saw a heap of burning wreckage that had once been a train.[10]

Lieutenant W.A. Barnes, 100 Squadron, RFC

Other important targets were selected; anything to cause embuggerance to the German military effort.

The target given us was a German ammunition dump. Although dumps are usually situated but a short distance from the lines, they are by no means easy targets to find at night, for they are seldom situated near any definite landmarks and are invariably well camouflaged. After gaining height we struck a compass course for our objective, and at the end of about 30 minutes' flying, could just make out the faint outline of sheds. From the landmarks we had noted, we were practically certain we had arrived over our objective, but to make absolutely sure we let out a parachute flare to light up the ground. This promptly dispelled all doubt, for searchlights opened up, and a hail of machine gun bullets and 'flaming-onions' leapt up from the ground. 'Archie' had been active for some time, but the shells were bursting well above us and we were in little danger, save from a direct hit. The parachute flare proved a friend indeed, for both searchlights and machine guns concentrated upon it, giving us just time to dive swiftly, release our bombs, switch on the engine and climb away. When clear away and turning to observe results, we were spectators of one of the finest firework displays I have ever seen. Ammunition was exploding at a record speed, dense clouds of smoke were rising, and highly coloured flames were leaping up to a great height from the ground. We watched this fascinating exhibition for some minutes, until the 'cough' of an 'Archie' burst nearby reminded us that we were still in the danger zone, when with one last look, and a grin of satisfaction from pilot to observer, we turned and made for home.[11]

Lieutenant W.A. Barnes, 100 Squadron, RFC

Meanwhile, the RFC was also charged with stopping any German reconnaissance aircraft from photographing the British rear areas; photographs that would be crucial to their planning process. It was here that James McCudden came into his own. He had always been a competent and dedicated flight commander, acting as the cutting edge in combat fought where possible in a tight formation, but here was a role where he developed an additional 'lone wolf' persona in the interception of the German LVG and Rumpler high-level reconnaissance missions. Using his own engineering experience, he had modified his SE5a engine to achieve an improved performance which served him well in combat at extreme altitudes. He was a ruthless harbinger of doom for German air crews and reached the fifty-victory milestone as the top-scoring British ace on 16 February.

I saw a Hun two-seater running away east. For he had apparently seen me before I had seen him, for I was not expecting Huns over, for the visibility was not too good. But I suppose he was out for some urgent information. I now opened the throttle of the high compression Hispano and I overtook the L.V.G. just as though he was going backwards, for I should judge my speed to be 20 miles [per hour] faster level than his. I quickly got into position and although the L.V.G. tried hard, I presented him with a very excellent burst from both guns, and then he went down in a vertical nose-dive, and then past vertical onto his back. The enemy gunner shot out of the machine for all the world like a stone out of a catapult and the unfortunate rascal seemed all arms and legs.[12]

Captain James McCudden, 56 Squadron, RFC

McCudden was often flying at above 20,000–21,000 feet, and the effects of oxygen deprivation and the freezing cold were beginning to have a severe physical impact which even he could not ignore.

I felt very ill indeed. This was not due to the height or the rapidity of my descent, but was due to the intense cold that I experienced up high, so that when I got down to a lower altitude, I could breathe more oxygen, with the result that my heart beat more strongly and was trying to force my sluggish and cold blood around my veins too quickly. The reaction of this caused me a feeling of faintness and exhaustion that can only be appreciated by those who have experienced it. My word I did feel ill and when I got on the ground: the blood returning to my veins, I cannot describe as anything but agony.[13]

Captain James McCudden, 56 Squadron, RFC

Even McCudden was beginning to lose his way. On 26 February, he scored two more victories, but the contrasting methods illustrate that he was starting to fall victim to target fixation. The first 'kill' was typically efficient.

> What a beautiful day it was, but I felt so bad, for my throat was very sore and the cold and height were affecting it. But there were a lot of the enemy to be fought, and so I stayed up and very soon saw a Rumpler a few hundred feet above me returning to his lines from above Arras. I followed him in the direction of Douai, and finally got to close range and fired a good burst from both my machine guns, and at once the two-seater burst into flames and then fell to pieces, the wreckage falling east of Oppy.[14]
> Captain James McCudden, 56 Squadron, RFC

Then he fell victim to frustration in attempting to shoot down his second victim.

> I said to myself, 'I am going to shoot down that Hannover or be shot down in the attempt!' I secured my firing position, and placing my sight on the Hannover's fuselage, I fired both guns until the two-seater fell to pieces and the wreckage fell down slowly, a fluttering monument to my fifty seventh victory and my last over the enemy for a time. As I looked at the machine, I saw the enemy gunner fall away from the Hannover fuselage, and I had no feeling for him for I knew he was dead for I had fired three hundred rounds of ammunition at the Hannover at very close range and I must have got 90% hits.[15]
> Captain James McCudden, 56 Squadron, RFC

It was time to go home for a period of home service, and his somewhat emotional state after the dining-out organised by his fellow officers on 2 March showed that it was not before time.

> In bed that evening I thought over it all and I now more than ever regretted that I had to leave a life that was all; my everything to me, and I confess I cried.[16]
> Captain James McCudden, 56 Squadron

Another pilot approaching the end of his tether was Harold Balfour. This was his third visit to the Western Front, and he had striven manfully to overcome his demons. But now, once again, they were knocking at his door.

> For some weeks before the end of March I had felt the same old troubles coming back; unable to sleep at night, a general desire to shirk battle, and a complete inability to eat a decent meal. One day in the mess I half-fainted. The wing doctor happened to be lunching with us that day and insisted on examining me after lunch. He told me that my heart, which had a murmur as a result of diphtheria, was enlarged and in a bad state, and that I should have

to go to hospital. With nerves near to breaking strain I will admit that in the doctor's verdict I found nothing unpleasant, as perhaps I should have done had I been a tougher warrior, without any feelings, imagination, or temperament.[17]
    Captain Harold Balfour, 43 Squadron, RFC

Against all the odds, Balfour had claimed nine victories in combat. He had more than done his bit – who can blame him at being relieved to finally leave the Western Front?

*   *   *

On 21 March 1918, the German Spring Offensive commenced with Operation Michael on the Somme front. The RFC squadrons had been forewarned; the previous night, the pilots and observers of 48 Squadron had been carefully briefed by their C.O, Major H.S. Shield, as to the role they would play in their Bristol Fighters come the dawn. It was a dramatic call to arms that must have been repeated in messes up and down the front.

At dinner that evening, the C.O. addressed us. 'From now on,' he said, 'our job is to hamper the Boche advance. I need not tell you that this squadron has as fine a reputation as any in France, and it is up to all of us now to maintain that reputation. The whole Squadron will go up at five ack emma [AM] to-morrow. Each machine will carry bombs. Wherever you see Boche troops or transport, dive on 'em, and give 'em hell! We can do an appalling amount of damage in this way. The Bristols will go over as low as possible and strafe debussing points, and all cavalry, infantry and motor transport on the roads. The Bristols will be the lowest machines as they can do most damage with their two guns and bombs. Camels and SE5s will sit above you to deal with the enemy. Directly you have emptied your ammunition-belts come back, fill up and go over again. I do not wish to be maudlin about it, but this is literally a time when England expects every man to do his duty. If the Boches get us on the run now, it will be the end of all things, and Germany will have won the war. We are not going to allow that!' When the C.O. sat down the cheering nearly lifted the roof.[18]
    2nd Lieutenant Vivian Voss, 48 Squadron, RFC

On a more ominous note, Major Shield warned them that they would be moving lock, stock and barrel from Flez back to a new base at Champien, as it was accepted that the Germans would make considerable inroads into the lines.

The bombardment started. I had never conceived of such a racket. It was just one continuous deafening roar. No individual bursts from the greater guns could be distinguished, but this continuous roar waxed and waned, and kept on without a break. We wondered how the poor bloody infantry in the trenches were faring. It seemed impossible that a single man could escape with his life from that inferno. All of us were wildly excited. It did not take us long to collect our few possessions and put them next to our stretchers, ready to be stuffed into our valises in the morning. Captain [William Wells] was looking round the hut regretfully.

'Look here,' he said, 'do you think we should leave all this luxury for the Boches?' We did not, and, in a few minutes, we had ripped off all our decorations from the walls and ceiling and windows. 'I'm damned if they get my cupboard either,' said [Thomas], and proceeded to kick it to bits. At half-past ten the revellers returned from Peronne. We advised them to get to bed, as everyone had to leave the ground at five the next morning. 'Oh, I can't do that,' protested [Colin Gibson], with a comic gesture, 'I don't get up till nine!'[19]

2nd Lieutenant Vivian Voss, 48 Squadron, RFC

For all their determination, when hell and damnation broke all along the Somme front, the RFC squadrons were at first almost totally neutered by the terrible foggy weather conditions. Blinded, they could not call down any concerted response from the British artillery batteries, which also had their own problems as they were deluged by gas and high explosive shells. By the afternoon, most of the surviving gun batteries were in headlong retreat, so the RFC role was simplified to carrying out mass strafing attacks.

After lunch, I was ordered to lead a formation along the St Quentin–Estrees road and bomb and fire at the enemy infantry and transport. We had never undertaken this sort of 'job' before. We carried two 20lb bombs and about eight hundred rounds of ammunition. Our object was to get rid of our bombs at the earliest opportunity, as they were a handicap on a Camel owing to the weight. I led the formation along this road until we could see our infantry in action, then I dived down to 500 feet and looked for a good target. Enemy infantry were everywhere as usual, advancing in the open and in large columns on the road. I gave the sign to release the bombs when we were well over them. We were so low that their uniforms could easily be seen, especially their large helmets and long bayonets. I dived first and released both bombs at once; they must have hit the road squarely in the centre. I could hear the explosions and see the smoke. One by one the rest of the formation followed, dropping each pair of bombs and scattering the enemy. I turned and led the formation west and dived on the Huns in the open. At one time I must have been at the level of their heads, they lay down on the ground when they saw us coming. We continued to dive and fire at them in turn until our ammunition was exhausted, when I led the 'flock' home.[20]

Lieutenant Ewart Stock, 54 Squadron, RFC

The venerable FE2b continued to provide vital service as night bombers, where darkness nullified their relative slow speed and lack of manoeuvrability and they were rarely to be troubled by the modern German scouts. They carried out night attacks on the main lines of communication, flying at only 1,500–2,000 feet.

> The principal target for attack just for the first few days was the Bapaume–Albert Road on which the Germans were advancing rapidly. We simply concentrated on that. The weather was very fine; bright moonlight nights – we could see almost individual vehicles on the road and troops. The road showed up almost white in the moonlight and you'd see an obvious column of troops marching along – a long black blob along the road. You could pick out the individual vehicles. We dropped as many bombs as we could. Most were anti-personnel bombs as against the larger high explosive ones used for buildings. We'd return as quickly as we could to our aerodrome and there'd be intense activity, loading up the machine, filling up with petrol, oil, getting ready for the next show. We did a great deal of damage.[21]
>
> Lieutenant John Hopkins, 83 Squadron, RFC

Taken as a whole, tens of thousands of machine gun bullets were fired at targets of opportunity and tons of small bombs were dropped by the RFC aircraft – and it did make a difference. Teams of horses and carts were shot up, which could effectively block a road for hours. Ground strafing was a dangerous business, as it brought them within range of vengeful return fire. There were, however, occasions for levity.

> Had rather a priceless flip today! I saw a Hun officer on a horse in a field, so I dived at him – the horse pranced about and the officer promptly fell off! However, he got up again and when I dived and fired at him again, he hove off with all speed. Then I looked round and saw four Hun soldiers walking across a field, so I dived at them and shot at them and zoomed up. When I came round again, I saw all four lying in grotesque attitudes on the ground. I went very low and could see their steel helmets, grey uniforms and packs as they lay there. I think I killed all four of them. This low strafing which the squadron is on at present certainly is frightfully exciting and mostly amusing – I laughed like anything when that Hun fell off his horse![22]
>
> 2nd Lieutenant Guy Knocker, 65 Squadron, RFC

In the rampant confusion, there was also a return to the old 1914-style reconnaissance missions as there was a need to establish exactly where the German advance had reached, with nearly all communications with the front severed. Sadly, Lieutenant Robert Best also encountered 1914-style intransigence after he had sighted and reported formations of German troops pressing deep into the Fifth Army lines.

I must explain that the messages were put in bags, and these were wrapped up in long streamers so as to make them easy to see when we dropped them from the air. Unfortunately, Whitey threw the message bags overboard without rolling up the streamers, and they got caught up with some of the tail wires, so there was nothing for it but to land at Villers-Bretonneux. As soon as we examined the machine, we saw that this one wire had been shot through. While it was being repaired, Whitey and I went off for lunch, where we had one or two glasses of wine. Thus fortified, we thought we ought to deliver the message bags ourselves at Fifth Army headquarters, and so off we went. Immediately, we were overwhelmed by red tabs. (The music-hall song 'I'm on the Staff' kept running through my head!) We were told that we should report our story to General Gough in person, and we were shown into his office. After some heavy saluting, I explained to the general that while we were in the air, I had seen the German troops advancing perfectly clearly and marked their forward line on my map. He heard me courteously and patiently, but this did not prevent him from smacking me cheerfully on the back and telling me that I was mistaken. It seems we had counter-attacked in the morning, and I had probably mistaken the blue of the French uniform for the field grey of the Germans. But the general was soon to find out who had been mistaken.[23]

2nd Lieutenant Robert Best, 53 Squadron, RFC

In the end, with massive assistance from the French Army, the German advance both on the Somme and in a second assault in the Arras sector was stopped in its tracks. The vigorous response was coordinated in part by the new Allied commander-in-chief, Ferdinand Foch, a man who had already established a good working relationship with Haig. The Germans had gained nothing of strategic importance, merely created a large and vulnerable salient. The clock was ticking.

* * *

At the height of this decisive battle on the Western Front, the RFC and RNAS were rammed crudely together to form the Royal Air Force (RAF). This was at the behest of a hastily convened committee chaired by Lieutenant General Jan Smuts in response to the Gotha raids on London in July 1917. The result was a foolish knee-jerk recommendation to create one air force, and the final decision ended up in the hands of know-nothing politicians. The men who understood the situation – Haig and Trenchard – were too busy fighting the real war. And so it was that on 1 April 1918, a date much remarked upon, the RAF was born. It seemed no-one was happy.

All that happened was a complete hotchpotch. They were trying to join together two disparate forces. The Navy tradition was very firmly embedded, and the Army had a regimental tradition. The ex-RNAS rating would take off his hat to receive his pay; the Army man would keep his on. Where the ex-RNAS man would double across the parade ground the ex-RFC man would march across it. There were all sorts of incongruities of this nature. Of course, there was no uniform to distinguish them as a complete corporate force. We still wore RNAS uniforms – they still wore the old maternity jacket. The biggest possible pot mess that I ever came across, absolutely terrible. In the officers' mess ex-naval squadrons still sat down to toast 'The King' whereas the Army people got up – where you got a combination in one mess it was absolutely ludicrous – 'Fred Karno's Army' – nothing else! Whoever thought that Jan Smuts was the fount of all knowledge in recommending this beats me![24]

Pilot Officer Thomas Thomson, 217 Squadron, RAF

On a trivial level, the unification meant even more confusion in the incongruous collection of uniforms on display in the typical squadron.

The variety of the uniforms covered those of different countries as well as the different branches and regiments of the Army from which we came, to say nothing of the Royal Navy. It was a common sight to see the pilots in a squadron wearing an astonishing variety of uniforms, all the way from the rather smart double-breasted wrap-over jacket of the RFC to the tartan trews and short jackets of the Scottish regiments, with caps ranging from the fore-and-aft of the Flying Corps to glengarries and even the boy scout hats of the Americans.[25]

Major William Sholto Douglas, 84 Squadron, RAF

Due to the great good sense and restraint of officers within both the RFC and RNAS headquarters and amongst the squadrons, the unification turned out to be mildly irritating rather than the disastrous interruption it could have been. However, this relative harmony did not reach back to London. Here, Trenchard's role as Chief of the Air Staff did not last long, as he soon fell into an acrimonious quarrel with the Air Minister appointed by Lloyd George. Who was this supremo? Some aviation expert? No, it was newspaper proprietor Lord Rothermere. The inevitable rows between two men blessed with autocratic *persona* soon forced the resignation of both. Trenchard was then appointed to command the Independent Force (IF), which was intended to carry out the strategic bombing of Germany. He was replaced by Major General Sir Frederick Sykes, while the industrialist Sir William Weir took over as Air Minister.

The Germans had not given up after the relative failure of Operation Michael; they were merely preparing their next hammer blow, this time directed on the Lys Valley to the south of Ypres on 9 April. Again, the German belt buckles emblazoned with '*Got mit uns*' seem to have worked their magic, as the Boche attacked in a lethal combination of thick fog and low clouds. British retaliatory aerial operations and artillery observation were fatally hampered as the Germans broke through and penetrated deep behind the British lines. When the Germans approached 208 Squadron's base at La Gorgue, the commanding officer, Major Christopher Draper, found himself trapped by dense fog, which would have made flying a lethal business.

The general did not wish me to leave La Gorgue, but said if it was to save the machines from shell fire, we could fly them away. I replied it was quite impossible to fly at all. I told him that I should act on my own as it was probable that the line would go at any moment. They intimated that this was possible as their other lines were down. As far as I could judge, practically all our guns had been captured, as they were not firing at all. On the other hand, the enemy artillery became increasingly active immediately in the vicinity of the aerodrome. After careful deliberation with my flight commanders I decided that I was not justified in risking personnel by flying away in the fog, though the majority volunteered to try. We then collected the machines in one bunch in the middle of the aerodrome, the idea being for everyone to clear out and leave one officer with a cycle and sidecar to stand by until the last moment with orders to destroy the machines if necessary. A British officer in a lorry which pulled up at the aerodrome asked to borrow a car as he wanted to waylay an ammunition supply column which was apparently coming up to La Gorgue. I was unable to help him as I had sent the convoy off to Serny. He informed me he was unable to get into La Gorgue owing to the machine-gun fire. I then decided to burn the machines and retire from the camp; as far as I can remember it was about 11 o'clock. The fog was as thick as ever and it was quite impossible to fly. I fully realised the seriousness of the situation but, being unable to communicate with any reliable authority, I had to act on my own.[26]

Major Christopher Draper, 208 Squadron, RAF

In all, he burnt sixteen Sopwith Camels. It sounds serious, but they were almost immediately replaced. Trained pilots were a far more valuable resource, and Draper had surely made the right – if embarrassing – decision.

Next day, the Germans broadened the front and attacked to the north, thrusting towards Ypres and Messines. For a while, the situation was desperate before the attackers were stopped short of any serious objective, leaving yet another purposeless salient jutting into the British lines. During the fighting, Australian Jack Weingarth was sent up in his Camel on a ground-attack mission – basically to kill as many Germans as possible.

When about 10 miles over the lines we dropped our bombs upon a wood full of Huns from about 200 feet. Then we saw some transports nearby, about twelve horse-wagons; we tore into these, firing our machine guns all the time we were diving on them. It nearly made me sick, killing the horses, but it had to be done. We did not have it all our own way, for there were a lot of Germans about with machine guns and rifles. Just after we cut up the transport one of my mates was hit; he glided down and hit a hedge along a road that he was trying to clear, turned over and crashed. I followed him down, but could see that I could not help him, so I turned back to find the leader, who was then firing into another line of transport, and was pulling up out of the dive when he was shot. He turned over on his back and dived straight into the ground from about 150 feet. You can imagine my feelings: two killed and myself well into German territory, absolutely lost in the thick mist and smoke, which made me keep low. If I kept low, they would get me sooner or later; machine guns were chattering all around, besides firing shrapnel at me. I thought I'd never get into the mist; it seemed like two hours, but it only took seconds. At last, I got into the mist, which was only 500 feet from the ground, and tried to steer by compass, but it was spinning round and round and I could not go straight. Of course, they kept firing at me all the way home, mostly at random. In the mist they can see sometimes, but one cannot see the ground at all; in fact, one has to rely on one's instruments to steer. I kept climbing until I got a hazy glimpse of the sun; I got this on my back and kept it there until I thought I was over our side. I nosed down to have a look at the ground but found that I had drifted over the lines again, and promptly got black 'Archie' at me. I steered west again, and eventually tacked onto some other machines going the right way home. The Boche threw everything at us except the grand piano; it was worth it though, as we did a lot of damage. I was just about done up when I got home; on an empty stomach too!²⁷

Lieutenant Jack Weingarth, 4 Squadron, Australian Flying Corps (AFC)

Like the Canadians, the Australians formed a vital strand within the British air war effort. Amongst them was a lone English pilot, who found himself made welcome; or as welcome as any 'Pommie' could be amongst rough, manly Australians.

To English ears that were sensitive their language was often crude in the extreme. The word 'bastard' was continually on their lips, but they thought no more of it than we should of 'blighter'. 'Had a good scrap this morning?' 'Waddy' would say as he climbed out of his Camel, loosening the chinstrap of his helmet. 'Get a Hun?' 'You bet!' was the reply. 'Fried the bastard!' meaning that he had seen the Hun go down in flames. Or there would be a group listening to Taplin, who specialised in stalking enemy two-seaters. 'And how did it finish, Tap?' 'Well,' he drawled, 'I went into the cloud again, and when I came out the bastard was just above me. So I pulled up the bus and blew the observer's bum through the back of his neck!' Yes, they were tough, but they had hearts of pure gold.²⁸

Lieutenant Jack Wilkinson, 4 Squadron, AFC

Beside their own units, the Australians also contributed a number of renowned pilots to the British squadrons. One of the best known was Major Roderick Dallas, who had taken over command of 40 Squadron. He ran into trouble during a ground attack on the advancing Germans.

> We became split up in the mist and low clouds, and I found myself over enemy country with German troops shooting at me from below with rifle and machine gun fire. I saw a long row of German motor wagons going along bringing up supplies, so I fired into the leading one and set him on fire. He crashed into the ditch at the side. Just then a bullet went through my leg above the knee and ripped my breeches and out through the machine. This did not worry me a great deal, so I flew on and later I saw a German officer and a lot of men marching below, then I saw our shells blow up a German gun and horse team. I was just getting my bearings when they got on to me again with machine guns and, by God, they riddled the machine but only hit me once. This time a bullet hit an iron bar and then splashed into my ankle and heel making three wounds. This made my foot stiff and filled my boot with blood and then I thought perhaps I had better go home.[29]
>
> Major Roderic Dallas, 40 Squadron, RAF

Dallas was capable of flamboyant gestures in the tradition of Robert Lorraine. Upon landing, he was surrounded by his concerned young pilots. Dallas recounted his adventures to this rapt audience, missing no dramatic trick, as Cecil Usher observed.

> While he was entertaining us with various descriptions in an amusing way somebody said, 'What did that, Sir – a bullet?' and pointed to a little strip torn from his leather coat. 'Yes,' said Dallas, 'they shot me!' And he lifted his coat to one side and the inside of his left thigh was all blood and raw meat and torn breeches. A bullet had come through the floor, hit a Lewis gun drum, spread itself and torn his thigh. 'Good God!' we said, 'You must get that dressed!' 'Yes', said Dallas in his quiet way, 'Yes, I must get that dressed!' And he began hobbling away towards the sick bay. Then, after going some distance he half turned back and said, 'There's one in my heel too!'[30]
>
> 2nd Lieutenant Cecil Usher, 40 Squadron, RFC

Lorraine would have been proud of him – a scene played to perfection. In fact, his wounds were relatively minor, and he insisted on staying to lead his squadron in the field. After a few days devoid of contacts with German aircraft, Dallas grew impatient and on 2 May, despite his wounds, had himself lifted into his SE5a, which was also loaded up with assorted pairs of boots and shoes. He then flew over a German airfield, as he subsequently related.

Flew over La Brayelle aerodrome and fired on hangars on south side of aerodrome to attract attention. Dropped a parcel with the following message inside, 'If you won't come up here and fight, herewith one pair of boots for work on the ground – pilots for the use of!' Then flew in the mist till a party of men had collected to examine the parcel, when two bombs were dropped, one burst being observed near target. Opened fire with both guns firing about hundred rounds when troops scattered. General panic ensued.[31]

Major Roderic Dallas, 40 Squadron, RAF

Dallas would claim some thirty-nine victories before he was shot down and killed in his SE5a D3530 a month later on 1 June 1918.

*   *   *

Another tragedy was now approaching its climax. On 12 April, Edward Mannock returned to action. He had achieved some sixteen accredited victories during his time with 40 Squadron in 1917, and after a short spell of just three months on home service he was posted as a flight commander to 74 Squadron, under the overall command of the ebullient New Zealander Keith Caldwell, almost always known as 'Grid' Caldwell. Perhaps we can get a feel of the months of intensive air action by looking at the effect the extraordinary Mannock had on the men around him. He certainly made an immediate impact on his new squadron upon joining them while they were still forming up in England in March.

While we were waiting for orders to proceed overseas, the C.O. detailed Mannock to give us lectures on air fighting. And what delicious dishes of the offensive spirit they were! He was a forceful, eloquent speaker, with the gift of compelling attention. After listening to him for a few minutes, the poorest, most inoffensive pilot was convinced he could knock hell out of Richthofen or any other Hun. Since Mannock's experience of air fighting was extensive, his talks were most valuable. His first lecture on single seater fighting began and ended with the axiom to which he rigidly adhered: 'Gentlemen, remember. Always above, seldom on the same level, never underneath!'[32]

Lieutenant Ira Jones, 74 Squadron, RFC

'Mick' Mannock, as he was nicknamed in the squadron, shared with Richthofen the quality of being a great teacher, even though their methods differed. Mannock had long mastered the basics of aerial warfare and had the 'easy' personality that could impart that knowledge in the form of simple-to-understand axioms, backed up by stern warnings when his strictures were ignored. He and Caldwell made a great team, their contrasting approaches providing all the guidance their young comrades could need. Pilots would make mistakes, but they were seen as learning experiences – and a trigger for cheerful abuse.

Chasing the Hun was great fun. Mannock was cross that I had followed the enemy down so low. It must never be done, he says. All the flights did three shows each, patrols of one and a half hours. Everybody felt pretty tired at the end of it. Clements, who developed a splitting headache on his last patrol – due to continuous high flying, I think – crashed on landing and wrote his machine off. I, too, was in the wars when my crankshaft broke during the evening patrol. We were then between Armentières and Lille, at 17,000 feet. Suddenly there was a cloud of smoke and the machine quivered. Slowly my propeller stopped, and so, I might almost say, did my heart! What a plight I was in! Far over enemy lines, while all around were bags of hungry Huns! Cairns and the flight protected me until I crossed the lines. It was an uncanny business. I could hear the roar of their engines, the violent detonation of the 'Archies'– not the muffled noise one hears when the engine is running – and even at times the cannonade of the artillery. On my way down, I tried to think what I had done to deserve all this bad luck. Skeddon escorted me back. His face was wreathed in smiles as he came alongside. He put up a couple of fingers at me. I replied by thumbing my nose at him. He got the final laugh, watching me go head over heels as I tried to land in a ploughed field not very far from the aerodrome. 'Grid' says I'm a hoodoo. 'Mick' goes even further. He says that the sooner I'm shot down in flames, the better. Well, today has been a great day for the squadron. Naturally, 'A' and 'B' Flights are very bucked at having shot down machines on their first patrol. Cairns is a little despondent, but the remainder of the flight are not. We all did our best. We could do no more. The boys who drink rightly uncorked the champagne bottles tonight, and we had speeches from the Hun-strafers. 'Mick', in particular, made a good speech. He has a flair for it. He gave all his flight, especially Dolan, a pat on the back. That we must kill as many Huns as we can, without being killed ourselves, was his main theme. Grid's theme, on the other hand, was, 'Kill the sods, the Hunnerinoes, at all costs. Anywhere and everywhere!' Grid got so close to his Hun today that, had he been carrying a stick, he could have put him out with a whack on the head. He's a fighter, all right.[33]

Lieutenant Ira Jones, 74 Squadron, RAF

On 21 April, Mannock had not been back long when the RAF's arch nemesis, Manfred von Richthofen, was finally shot down, having broken all his own rules of air fighting. At various points in that fateful flight, he was caught isolated, target fixated, ignorant of a British scout on his tail, and flying low well over the British lines under fire from multiple machine guns on the ground. There may be a dull controversy as to who fired the fatal bullet, but he had made so many mistakes that someone was going to 'get' him that day. Did a shadow cross the mind of the British 'Richthofen', as some have called Mannock? The short answer is 'no'. Like most in the RAF, he was simply glad Richthofen was dead. After all, Mannock had enough to worry about in his own life.

Throughout this phase of his career, Mannock seems to have been increasingly fixated with the fate of the German pilots and observers sent down to a grisly death in flames. His response was to laugh, to poke fun at his own fears, to try to deflect them away.

> Whenever he sends one down in flames, he comes dancing into the mess, whooping and hallooing, 'Flamerinoes, boys! Sizzle, sizzle, wonk!' Then, at great length, he tries to describe the feelings of the poor old Hun by going into the minutest details. Having finished in a frenzy of fiendish glee, he will turn to one of us and say, laughing, 'That's what will happen to you on the next patrol, my lad!' And we all roar with laughter.[34]
> Lieutenant Ira Jones, 74 Squadron, RAF

In the officers' mess, Mannock demonstrated his attractive livewire personality that usually made him the centre of attention.

> Mannock would organise sing-songs in the mess. Singing at the top of his voice, he would play on a collection of cans, tankards, pots and pans, and glasses, tied to the back of a chair. He also had a proper drum which he played loudly. Soon we would all join in and get a jam-session going. We developed into a family really, 'Grid' and 'Mick' saw to that, an efficient, happy team. They both threatened to shoot down the first man who left a chum in trouble with the Huns. On the rare occasions that gloom did settle on the mess, 'Mick' was just the man to handle it. He didn't give a hoot how he did it, as long as the men ended up happy and morale was maintained. He was always the life and soul of the party, although this never interfered with our respect for his authority.[35]
> Lieutenant Harris Chapman, 74 Squadron, RAF

In May, there was a splendid mess party to celebrate the award of a DSO to Mannock. They really pushed the boat out.

> It was a great 'do'. We had speeches galore and one of our boys, Richardson, who was called 'the Cocktail King' mixed up a vicious brew for our consumption called the 'Seventy-Four Viper'! These just about killed poor old 'Mick' who wasn't much of a drinker, but everyone else liked them. It was one of the few occasions that anyone actually got properly drunk. We didn't drink much as a rule. We were so excited most of the time that one or two would do the trick. But that night was different.[36]
> Lieutenant Andrew Kiddie, 74 Squadron, RAF

It was on nights like these that Mannock would play his favourite prank, one which truly warms the heart.

Mannock was always full of pranks; his favourite one was to enter a comrade's hut in the early hours of the morning after returning from a 'night out'. He would enter, usually accompanied by Caldwell, who would be carrying a jug of water. Once inside Mannock would pretend that he had wined and dined too well and would make gurgling noises as if he was going to be sick. As each 'retching' noise was made, Caldwell would splash an appropriate amount of water on the wooden floor. The poor lad asleep would suddenly wake up and jump out of bed to the accompaniment of roars of laughter as his legs would be splashed with the remaining water.[37]

Lieutenant Ira Jones, 74 Squadron, RAF

On the ground, the Germans were still flailing away, aware that in just a month or two the Americans would be arriving in real strength on the Western Front. On 27 May 1918, another gigantic offensive was launched, this time Operation Blücher, which tore a huge gap in the French and British lines in the Chemin des Dames sector. But then that too was stemmed, the result being just another salient.

Mannock seemed to be going from strength to strength. By the end of May, he had reached a total of forty-one kills. He seemed unstoppable. June saw no diminution in his efforts, and by 16 June he had shot down his fifty-first victim, behind only McCudden and Richthofen in the ranking of aces. His reputation was sky-high and he was seen as the finest patrol leader and tactician in the whole RAF. Yet inside, Mannock was falling apart.

Things are getting a bit intense just lately and I don't quite know how long my nerves will last out. I am rather old now, as airmen go, for fighting. Still, one hopes for the best. These times are so horrible that occasionally I feel that life is not worth hanging on to myself, but 'hope springs eternal in the human breast!' I had thoughts of getting married, but?[38]

Captain Edward Mannock, 74 Squadron, RAF

On 18 June, he went on a well-deserved leave. By this time, his close friends in the mess were beginning to notice that something was wrong.

Mick went off on a spot of well-deserved leave this afternoon. It is very noticeable to me, after an absence of ten days from his company, that his nerves are very much on edge. It is easy to spot when a pilot is getting nervy. He becomes very talkative and restless. When I arrived in the mess this morning, Mick's greeting was, 'Are you ready to die for your country, Taffy? Will you have it in flames or in pieces?'[39]

Lieutenant Ira Jones, 74 Squadron, RAF

The leave was a disaster: Mannock simply could not shake off his inner fears and torments. Most young officers thoroughly enjoyed themselves on leave. Here, for instance, is William Sholto Douglas with a happy tale of wine, women and song.

> I sometimes stayed at the Cavendish when I was on leave in London. Rosa Lewis was a wonderfully warm-hearted woman with a free-and-easy outlook on life, and every evening she used to have a party in her sitting-room on the ground floor of the hotel that she had started back at the time of the turn of the century. The champagne flowed, and she particularly liked having around her young officers of the Flying Corps and attractive young women, and she was always very generous if any of us happened to be hard up. There were occasions when Rosa refused, as she did with others, to let me have a bill for my stay in the hotel, and only very rarely were we allowed to pay for the champagne which we nearly always drank. Rosa used to tell us that she had charged it up to her wealthier and older customers, and she would assure us that they would not mind; but I always had an idea that she paid for it herself.[40]
>
> Major William Sholto Douglas, 84 Squadron, RAF

Or here are the simple, and not so simple, pleasures of young William Lambert.

> A good hot bath, a change of clothing and we were ready to take on anything that London might have to offer. Food first. I was hungry as were the others. Someone knew a good spot in Soho. So we found a cab and away we went. Our restaurant was Chinese, and the food was wonderful but I doubt if anything like it ever originated in China. Almost midnight. Another cab and we were off to the Cafe Royale. When we entered those doors a blast of heat, smoke, odours of alcohol and human bodies almost knocked us off our feet. A gas-mask would have been a useful item there. The few lights were so dimmed with smoke that one could hardly see one's hands in front of one. That place was packed with bodies, both male and female. The males were in the minority. Wild women, tame women, meek women, ferocious women and beautiful women. Amazons all. And out to conquer the male. I had been there several times before but had never seen it so crowded and have often wondered just how many human bodies were jammed into it. There must have been at least three hundred when we arrived but, as time passed, the crowd thinned out. Groups or just couples were seen going out. Their places were soon taken by newcomers. Drinks, drinks and more drinks. The four of us were not alone very long as our pilot's wings acted like a magnet during those adventurous days of flying. Soon we were being crowded. What a place! What a night![41]
>
> Lieutenant William Lambert, 24 Squadron, RAF

Compare these cheerful accounts with the grim reality of Mannock's last leave. Jim Eyles, an old friend of 'Pat' – as he called him from their days together in the

Wellingborough Labour Party – was shocked at the change wrought in Mannock over just a couple of months. Away from the hurly-burly of the mess, Mannock's true feelings seem to have been revealed.

> Gone was the old sparkle we knew so well; gone was the incessant wit. I could see him wringing his hands together to conceal the shaking and twitching, and then he would leave the room when it became impossible for him to control it. As the time for his return to the front came closer, he became a different man. On one occasion we were sitting in the front talking quietly when his eyes fell to the floor, and he started to tremble violently. This grew into a convulsive straining. He cried uncontrollably, muttering something that I could not make out. His face, when he lifted it, was a terrible sight. Saliva and tears were running down his face; he couldn't stop it. His collar and shirt-front were soaked through. He smiled weakly at me when he saw me watching and tried to make light of it; he would not talk about it at all. I felt helpless not being able to do anything. He was ashamed to let me see him in this condition but could not help it however hard he tried. Later he told me that it had just been a 'bit of nerves' and that he felt better for a good cry. He would not admit that it had been more than a cry, and he avoided any further discussions.[42]
>
> Jim Eyles

There was a feeling of 'the doomed warrior' about their final parting. This may have been amplified in retrospect, but Eyles claims to have discerned it at the time.

> When he left our home for the last time, there was something wrong. I could feel it. On previous leaves he would walk out of the front door and talk very quickly and excitedly about getting back to the war, the next leave and the presents and souvenirs he would bring back. But that last leave had something very final about it all. 'Pat' was a very sensitive chap, and I do feel that he knew he was saying goodbye. He was in no condition to return to France, but in those days such things were not taken into consideration.[43]
>
> Jim Eyles

Nevertheless, Mannock went back to his squadron, driven on by his sense of duty, his burgeoning hatred of Germans and his own insecurities, and encouraged, like so many aces before him, by his ever-increasing victory tally.

On 5 July 1918, Major Edward Mannock was posted to command 85 Squadron, which had previously been commanded by Major William Bishop. The Canadian ace had rather concentrated on solo missions and it was felt that the squadron needed a firmer hand and tactical guidance – and who better to provide that than Mannock? He soon got control of his new charges, introducing tightly controlled formations and leading from the front to great effect. Then, on 9 July, came a further destabilising factor: Mannock's former flying instructor, his friend and only real rival as the greatest British ace, James McCudden, was killed in a simple flying accident. McCudden had been promoted to major and was flying out from England to take over command of 60 Squadron, when he got slightly lost and landed to get directions at the airfield of Auxi-le-Chateau. Disaster struck as he took off.

> The aircraft took off into the wind and at about 100 feet did a vertical turn and flew back across the aerodrome by the side of the wood. The engine appeared to be running badly. The pilot rolled the machine which failed to straighten out, at approximately 200 feet. It crashed nose down into the wood.[44]
> Lieutenant L.M. Fenelon, 52 Squadron, RAF

His SE5a smashed into some trees. When the nearby pilots and ground crew reached the scene, they found McCudden, who was not wearing his safety belt, had been thrown out and was unconscious. Earlier in the war, his brother, fellow pilot William McCudden, had been killed in a crash whilst wearing his belt; McCudden had made the split-second decision to unclip his. His skull was fractured, and he never regained consciousness. He finished his amazing career with fifty-seven victories at the age of just 23, apparently the victim of the wrong pattern of carburettor fitted in error to his SE5a. It was a strange way for such a deadly ace to die.

Mannock carried on seemingly undaunted, at least on the surface, providing the perfect role model for his pilots in 85 Squadron, leading combat patrols, guiding them and teaching them. His new charges looked on with great admiration.

> He shot down what turned out to be one of the crack Hun airmen. It all happened 25 miles across the lines, over a Hun aerodrome; and it was a pretty sight to see the way the Boche handled his triplane, pretty little thing, all black with a white tail. Although he put up a good fight, he had somebody better after him, and it was not long before the major got his position for a few seconds and, with both guns going, shot off his tail.[45]
> Captain Malcolm McGregor, 85 Squadron, RAF

Mannock was not a selfish ace, interested only in his own record; he also was reputed to help feed first 'kills' to some of his new pilots who had yet to taste success in the air. The idea was to give them confidence.

> He was determined to win. He hated the Huns and he wanted to kill all of them. He wasn't interested in just killing them himself. He wanted a lot of them killed, and he trained us how to do it. That was why, on several occasions, Mannock made way for a new pilot to come in and finish off an enemy aircraft that he had already winged. It was to give the new boy confidence.[46]
> 2nd Lieutenant Larry Callahan, 85 Squadron, RAF

The frequency of this should not be over-exaggerated, and Mannock would also claim a share for his own total.

Then, suddenly, it was all over. On 26 July 1918, Mannock was patrolling with a young New Zealand pilot, Lieutenant Douglas Inglis. Mannock sighted a two-seater LVG, and after shooting the observer, left the *coup de grâce* of the now helpless machine to Inglis.

> A quick turn and a dive, and there was 'Mick' shooting up a Hun two-seater. He must have got the observer, as when he pulled up and I came in underneath him I didn't see the Hun shooting. I flushed the Hun's petrol tank and just missed ramming his tail as it came up when the Hun's nose dropped. Falling in behind 'Mick' again we did a couple of circles round the burning wreck and then made for home. I saw 'Mick' start to kick his rudder and realised we were fairly low, then I saw a flame come out of the side of his machine; it grew bigger and bigger. 'Mick' was no longer kicking his rudder, his nose dropped slightly and he went into a slow right-hand turn round, about twice, and hit the ground in a burst of flame. I circled at about 20 feet but could not see him, and as things were getting pretty hot, made for home.[47]
>
> Lieutenant Douglas Inglis, 85 Squadron, RAF

Mannock had broken his own rules, flying ridiculously low over a fallen victim while within easy range of German machine guns on the ground. 'Do as I say, not as I do!' may have virtues in the parental home, but in the hostile skies of the Western Front, everybody had to obey the rules all the time or be liable to pay the penalty. Mannock was gone, and his grave has never been found. His men were distraught.

> We have lost our squadron commander. Went down in flames after getting over seventy Huns, and so the Royal Air Force has lost the best leader of patrols, and the best Hun-getter it has had. In another month he would have had over 100. However, unlike other stars, he left behind all the knowledge he had, so it is up to the fellows he taught, to carry on.[48]
>
> Captain Malcolm McGregor, 85 Squadron, RAF

As was traditional, they tried to hold a celebration wake, but it was a flat affair, even though some of Mannock's old friends from 74 Squadron arrived to bolster the numbers. Ira Jones summed up the mood.

> It was a difficult business. The thought of Mick's charred body not many miles away haunted us and dampened our spirits. There was more drinking than usual on these occasions; the Decca worked overtime; we tried to sing, but it was painfully obvious that it was forced.[49]
>
> Lieutenant Ira Jones, 74 Squadron, RAF

Mannock was the archetypal 'unknown ace' as far as the British public were concerned, but he was highly regarded in the RAF as the greatest British patrol leader of the war. He died with some sixty-one victories to his credit, but these were mysteriously boosted to seventy-three, which coincidentally was one more than William Bishop's total. A vigorous post-war campaign also resulted in the award of a posthumous VC in July 1919.

The age of the great individual aces was over. Their work was done: the aircraft and the aerial tactics had been mastered and disseminated. Numbers, rather than skill, were what mattered as the war approached a crescendo on the ground. The aircraft manufacturing process was now a smooth, well-oiled machine, while the training provided the men required. Thousands upon thousands of aircraft and air crew were devoted to the performance of the various functions of the RAF: photographic reconnaissance, artillery observation, contact patrols, ground strafing, bombing and of course the fighter scouts. There was now little room for individuality in the crowded skies above France and Flanders. The Germans had developed a promising new scout aircraft in the Fokker D.VII, which had entered the fray in early May 1918. A chunky-looking aircraft, it had at first been somewhat underestimated by British pilots, but it offered a superb combination which matched much of the SE5a's ability to dive and zoom back up, with a manoeuvrability that almost matched the Sopwith Camel without any tendency to stall. This might have been a game-changer earlier in the war, but it was now too late in the day to turn the tide.

*   *   *

Although Mannock's death cast gloom over the RAF, it did not endure long. These were young men; they faced imminent death themselves; today, tomorrow, or whenever. They had their own preoccupations, when on the ground, that soothed their cares away. Happiness was in the moment.

We all went into Abbeville for a good bath and a lot of other things. The bathing completed we made for our cafe which we found was filled even at 4.00pm. Amongst the many uniforms, I spotted an American lieutenant with U.S. wings at a table by himself. He sure looked forlorn, so Daley and I went over to him. We lifted him up and carried him back to our table, poured a drink down him and watched the results. I said we all thought he had lost his last friend and needed some mourners to attend the funeral! He grinned and thanked us. He came from Alabama and was called Jackson. I told him I was from Ohio and from then on he was one of us. The drinks flowed again. That place was crowded; waiters loaded with trays of drinks; older women and younger girls, most of whom were entwined with officers. One half-dressed redhead tried to dance on a table surrounded by eight or ten Australians. Better leave her alone; those Aussies looked very tough to me. We had no need to worry; within a short time the RAF wings sent out their magnetic waves and we were soon covered with females, some young and fresh, others older and hard-looking. 'Buy me a drink!' 'Dance with me!' 'Take me to bed!' 'Give me dinner!' You name it, they all wanted it![50]

Lieutenant William Lambert, 24 Squadron, RAF

When the moment was spent, the men of the RAF would fly on.

Chapter 10

Bombs Away, 1917–18

ombing, what is it good for? 'Absolutely nothing' might be one answer, but in war, every development in the apparatus of killing and destruction is enthusiastically adopted. The urge to bomb had existed almost as long as the aeroplane, indeed the first bombs were dropped as early as 1911, when an Italian bombed the Turks in Tripoli – to minimal effect. Of course, things had developed during the Great War, with early makeshift bombs gradually improved and bombing sights developed. But for a while it seemed that only Zeppelins had the lifting power to take up a worthwhile bomb load. In the summer of 1917, however, the German Gotha daylight raids on Britain had created such an outcry that the British government had been forced to take action to calm down the outraged masses. The Smuts Committee set in motion the creation of the RAF and the IF, but a more immediate response was to create 41st Wing, from which the Independent Force grew, initially based at Ochey (near Nancy) under the command of Lieutenant Colonel Cyril Newall. It was not a homogeneous force, consisting as it did of the DH4 two-seater light bombers flown by 55 Squadron, RFC, the FE2b 'jacks of all trades' of 100 Squadron, RFC, and the British equivalent to the Gotha, the Handley Page O/100 heavy bombers flown by 7 (Naval) Squadron, RNAS. The Handley Pages were imposing brutes with a wingspan of some 100 feet.

There's the pilot and the observer sat side-by-side in the front, and a gun-layer at the rear. The gun-layer had two platforms, one higher and one lower. He had three Lewis guns, one at the bottom for firing back underneath the tail, and two at the top. The observer had two Lewis guns in the front cockpit, and he was responsible for the bomb dropping equipment. The method of dropping the bombs was he lay almost prone, and he had five pushes, like bell pushes, and five lights, two red, two green and one white. The white obviously being the centre one to guide the pilot to whatever the observer wanted him to do. The two green meant veer to the right and so on. By that method of course, the pilot was able to see exactly what the observer wanted to try and get him lined up on the target. One had to calculate the height, the wind drift, and the speed of the machine. It was all done of course by angles. We had fourteen bombs and used to drop, say six or seven, and come round for the second run, and straddle the bombs. We found that the most successful way of getting a hit. You wouldn't say seven bombs would hit the target; we didn't mind if one out of seven hit the vital target. We were all quite satisfied – it caused an explosion![1]

Leading Mechanic William Wardrop, 7 Squadron, RNAS

They were meant to be concentrating on revenge raids on Germany, but it was inevitable that they would be drawn into tactical bombing raids designed to assist the army operations. Thus, Wardrop was involved in a raid on Namur on the night of 29/30 September 1917.

If you look at the map, you'll find there's a railway bridge coming over the river where nearly all the ammunition coming from Germany used to come. Our army authorities wanted it smashed up to stop the armaments and extra ammunition coming through. It was 200 miles behind the German lines. Commander [Herbert] Brackley was the pilot, Paul Bewsher the observer, and myself. Fortunately, we hit the bridge! We managed to get there and back. I think we had one or two people shoot at us as usually, but that was one of those things that was just bound to happen – it didn't do any damage as far as we were concerned. We got back all right, and it was reported by our agents that we were successful.[2]

Leading Mechanic William Wardrop, 7 Squadron, RNAS

The long-range bombing operations were also disrupted badly by the winter weather.

The FE2bs, which had made their debut in numbers on the Western Front in early 1916, were still working hard in their role as night bombers with 100 Squadron. A squadron poet soon commemorated their reassignment to 41st Wing in a splendid – and lengthy – dirge, of which the following is just a short extract.

100 Squadron Lament
We landed on the Western Front,
From Isel le Hameau was our first stunt,
And we soon ken from Jerry's moans,
That he didn't like the Aeros with the skull and cross-bones.
For they blew up all his railways,
For they blew up all his railways,
For they blew up all his railways,
And ammunition dumps.
Our pilots got well known round there,
Then Jerry, just to show his spite,
Bombed London with his planes at night.
The people said, 'You silly clowns.
Why not go and bomb his towns?'[3]

Corporal J.R. Bird, 100 Squadron, RFC

Louis Taylor had good reason to remember the raid carried out by 100 Squadron on Trier (also known as Trèves) in Germany on 24 January 1918. His observer that night was Lieutenant Le Fevre as they set off in their FE2b A852.

> The lights of Trier were extinguished on our approach, and a very heavy anti-aircraft barrage was put up around the Central Station, which was the objective. After successfully dropping our bombs, we were unfortunate enough to be hit by anti-aircraft, which put our rudder controls out of action. I looked towards my observer, who was leaning over the side and pouring a stream of machine gun fire into the city, and seemed to be thoroughly enjoying himself, although he looked like the Devil framed in a curtain of flickering shrapnel bursts from the anti-aircraft guns. I tried to get the machine flying south, but failed, and finally by putting on a slight bank I got a straight course in a south-westerly direction but was slowly losing height. We travelled about 30 miles in this crippled condition. It was a maddening feeling to hear the roar of a perfect running engine and to be constantly losing height, but I kept on my course. I could at least fly as far as possible towards the lines and then, if opportunity offered, we could try to escape from the country without being captured.[4]
>
> 2nd Lieutenant Louis Taylor, 100 Squadron, RFC

Flying in this crab-like fashion, thwarted by the lack of rudder controls, they reached the small town of Esche in Luxembourg. Then, suddenly, there was a new threat.

> Hearing a shout from my observer, I followed his pointing arm and saw that the town was defended by a balloon barrage – a steel net held up by balloons at intervals of about 50 yards. The balloons were at a height of about 4,000 feet, and it was impossible to get over them in our crippled condition, and to try to get round was worse than useless, so trusting to good luck I kept straight on, hoping to pass through the barrage without hitting a wire. My observer immediately opened fire on the balloon above and straight in front of us, in the vain hope of setting it on fire, and dropping the net, but nothing happened. We were now passing underneath the balloons and for a moment I had the elated feeling that we must have missed the wires, but suddenly the machine gave a violent lurch, and was thrown backwards; I immediately put the nose down, but the speed indicator dial only registered 30 miles per hour, and then I knew that I was caught. I wondered why the machine did not stall and plunge to the ground.[5]
>
> Lieutenant Louis Taylor, 100 Squadron, RFC

They were in desperate straits, as the aileron controls were now broken and all they had left was the hinged elevator controls. It was worse than useless. They were going down – that was for sure – the only question now was how quickly.

Then followed a sickening 5 minutes, during which I tried to get down to the ground dragging the balloon and net round and round with me, and, thanks to a perfect engine we finally got close to the ground, which was heavily wooded. My observer placed his machine gun to one side and sat down to await the inevitable crash as calmly as possible, shouting a few encouraging words over his shoulder. We were only a few feet from the ground, the engine roaring, when I saw directly ahead a small quarry surmounted by a wood, while we were making direct for it. I frantically pulled back the control lever, the machine leapt into the air, hovering over the wood for a second, coming down with a crash in a small field just beyond. We fell on one wing which crumpled up beneath the weight: I saw the observer leave the machine, when something struck my head and I lost consciousness.[6]

Lieutenant Louis Taylor, 100 Squadron, RFC

He was only out for a matter of seconds.

When I came to my senses I found myself hanging out of the machine, while the wing which was sticking straight up into the air seemed to my dizzy brain to be toppling over on to me bringing the heavy engine with it. I tried to extricate myself from the wreck, and get away from the machine, but was too weak to do so. Eventually a voice roared into my ear, 'All right, old thing, out you come!' And a strong pair of arms went about me, when I was dragged clear. I staggered to my feet a few moments later to be met by a flash of rifle fire at about 20 yards distance by about ten or more Huns, who were running and shouting like maniacs. I felt my observer grab me by the shoulder and I was flung down on my face, he dropping beside me. The bullets were whistling by and it's a great wonder neither of us was hit. We were immediately surrounded by the Huns and taken prisoners in no gentle manner.[7]

Lieutenant Louis Taylor, 100 Squadron, RFC

They were soon incarcerated in a guard house, where they awaited interrogation.

After waiting for about an hour the door opened and a German officer swaggered in, followed by several gaudily dressed officials, one of whom was an interpreter, and the usual questioning started, 'Where did you come from?' 'The other side of the lines.' 'Yes; we know that, but whereabouts?' 'We can't tell you!' 'You must!' 'We refuse!'[8]

Lieutenant Louis Taylor, 100 Squadron, RFC

And so the interrogation went on, but neither of them cooperated in any way. They would see out the war in a POW camp.

A well-recorded night bombing raid was carried out by 100 Squadron on the railway junction at Courcelles sur Metz on the night of 9/10 February 1918.

Four FE2bs flew that night, of which one was piloted by 2nd Lieutenant Alfred Kingsford, accompanied by his observer 2nd Lieutenant Huw Edwardes-Evans, while his friend, 2nd Lieutenant Owen Swart, was with his observer 2nd Lieutenant Anthony Fielding-Clarke. Several missions had recently been 'washed out' by bad weather and Kingsford was both eager and anxious that night.

It is difficult to describe your feelings the first night going over the enemy's lines. I was eaten up with curiosity, anxious to put up a good show, yet not knowing quite what to expect. Old pilots had given advice not to take unnecessary risks, not to come down too low on a first flight to do your bombing, remember to switch off your navigation lights before going on the line, and I found their advice useful. The night was just as dark and cold as it could be, and in spite of thigh boots, fur coat and many other accessories, we literally froze. At 6pm there was activity everywhere at the aerodrome. Flares were out, mechanics dashing here and there, machines lined up, and punctually at that hour, Swart and I were strolling with the rest up to our own machines. It was to be our christening, so we shook hands and wished each other, 'Good luck!' Edwardes-Evans and I inspected the bombs, parachute flare, wingtip flares and all the rest of the gadgets, then climbed into our seats.[9]

    2nd Lieutenant Alfred Kingsford, 100 Squadron, RFC

At last the clock ticked round and it was time to take off, and they went into the time-honoured routine.

The mechanic was ready at the engine. 'Switches off, Sir!' he shouted. 'Switches off!' I replied, 'Suck in,' and he swung the propeller round a few times. 'Switch on, Sir,' he yelled. And away went the prop. 1,300 revolutions to the minute. We let the engine warm up and then tried her full out, OK, and waited for the signal to go. Our flight commander was leading, he taxied out and we were signalled to follow. Swinging her round into the flare path, I pushed the throttle forward and away we went, skimming on what was my first raid of destruction over enemy lines.[10]

    2nd Lieutenant Alfred Kingsford, 100 Squadron, RFC

After gaining altitude the four FE2bs began their long journey to their objective, crossing the front lines at some 3,000 feet.

We were now over enemy territory. 'Keep your eyes skinned!' my observer leant over and yelled to me. 'Can't see a damned thing!' I replied, and there was not a light to be seen anywhere, just blank, impenetrable darkness, broken only by the red glare of the exhaust and the glow of the dashboard. Keeping her nose to the north-north-west for 20 minutes, I peered over the side to try and distinguish something that might serve to assure us that we were on the right course, but the density of the night gave no sign, except the whistling of the wind as we speeded by. The drone of the engine kept us company, 'Purr, Purr!' It was running perfectly! In spite of warm clothing and the usual thigh boots, I was getting cold, the bitter stinging of the keen wind making my face tingle.[11]

2nd Lieutenant Alfred Kingsford, 100 Squadron, RFC

They flew on, keeping at a steady altitude of 3,000 feet. Suddenly there was a rude interruption as they were caught by a German searchlight beam.

I could see my observer leaning over the side, hand on machine gun. Every part of the machine was plainly visible. A searchlight had pierced the darkness and caught us first go. He was directly to the left. Evans stood up, both hands grasping the gun, and signalled to swing round. Kicking the rudder and pulling the joystick over, I throttled back and dived straight down the beam. The machine gun spit forth, a burst of ten or so, but he didn't shut down. I side-slipped and he lost us. We were now at 1,800 feet and he was hunting the skies for us, found us for a second and then let us go again. We turned and throttled back once more, taking another dive at him coming down to 1,000 feet, Evans gave two or three good bursts; he immediately switched off and did not light up again. Eventually we picked up our course and proceeded undisturbed. The excitement had warmed us, or else we had forgotten the cold![12]

2nd Lieutenant Alfred Kingsford, 100 Squadron, RFC

Soon they were approaching the target at Courcelles sur Metz.

The leader on dark nights carried a phosphorous bomb, which usually set fire to something and lit up the surroundings. Our instructions were to drop our bombs as near this signal as possible. Evans had scarcely re-seated himself when, over to our right, not more than 2 miles away, we saw this bomb burst and light up the surroundings. It must have been seen for miles, and we immediately swung around and made for it. Approaching and keyed up with excitement as we were, we saw another burst, then three in quick succession and only a few yards apart. It was good bombing and the five made an excellent group. The first had caused a fire and we flew round once to have a look, discerning a group of buildings. Guiding the plane over them, Evans let two go and the bursts were quite visible, close together. We turned back and he let drop the others. Looking down to watch the effect, another searchlight caught us, and realising that the place was well protected against aircraft raids, I turned to dodge him, and instinctively looking over the side, I noticed a whole string of machine gun fire making directly for us. Like a procession of glow-worms these phosphorous bullets approached, and I immediately turned the plane in the opposite direction, dodging one searchlight but running into another line of machine gun fire. We'd dropped all our bombs, so I turned her nose down and beat it![13]

2nd Lieutenant Alfred Kingsford, 100 Squadron, RFC

Alas, all did not go so well for Owen Swart. The FE2b was a tough aircraft with a (usually) reliable engine, which made them more suited than one might have expected to these operations. However, the word 'usually' can cover a multitude of sins, as Swart soon found out. The engine of his FE2b B439 was *not* running perfectly that night.

My machine did not climb well, and the engine occasionally showed signs of some unpleasantness, but being a new pilot I was ashamed to return. Pride again! We had a fairly quiet passage over the lines, and eventually came to the railway line which we followed up until we came to a junction and saw a small village next to it. This appeared to be the spot we were looking for, so we pulled off our bombs and my observer fired at targets beneath. I only saw one bomb, a Cooper, go off to the south of the line, and near some houses. I had turned to the north sharply and came past the station of Courcelles in order to give my observer a better chance of using his gun, and also to see the bombs go off. This was the juncture where my engine failed me, not completely, but as though two or three cylinders had stopped firing.[14]

2nd Lieutenant Owen Swart, 100 Squadron, RFC

A more experienced pilot would never have risked going on a mission with a 'dodgy' engine, but Swart had not wanted to appear scared, so had taken the chance. Now he and his observer were paying the price. Perhaps they could still make it back across the British lines, but unfortunately they had been bombing from low altitude, so the chances were slim.

I was hardly at a height of more than 1,900 feet, but I turned her head towards the lines and steered south-west as the wind was more or less from the west. I also had a look at all my instruments which recorded everything correct, except the revolutions per minute. The pressure was all right, but I tried her on gravity tank. No better, the vibrations were so bad I tried throttling back, but to no purpose. So we glided gradually nearer to the ground and also nearer to the line, but just when I thought we might do it the engine cut out completely. My observer behaved very well, firing at searchlights, and machine gun posts, though he knew what had happened to the engine. I was only a couple of hundred feet up now, and I decided to use my parachute flares, even if I was still in German territory, as it was rather misty, and I wanted to see what I had to land on.[15]

2nd Lieutenant Owen Swart, 100 Squadron, RFC

It was better for German eyes to catch sight of them than to smash into some unseen obstruction landing on unknown ground in the dark.

> The first one did not show me much, but those my observer sent out showed that I was going to land on some small trees beneath. I thereupon lit my wing tip flare, and by its light saw a small clearing to the east, which I turned for, and in 5 seconds I was sailing down to it and landed amongst hundreds of hares sitting bolt upright with the gleam of the reflected light shining out of their great big saucy eyes. The machine touched the ground without a jar and came to a stop within 30 feet. My observer and I were both very thankful for this, and after talking it over we decided that there was just a possibility of having come down just across the line.[16]
>
> 2nd Lieutenant Owen Swart, 100 Squadron, RFC

They were both clearly optimistic chaps, deciding that Swart should go off and look for a French telephone to get help.

> I walked about 100 yards from the machine and came to a road, and in the obscure distance I saw a cart. Not knowing if it was coming or going, I gave it a 'Holloa!' I drew nearer, and when only 5 yards away I spotted the four occupants wearing fur Jerry helmets. You can well imagine how I wished I could sink into the earth. I was absolutely flabbergasted and stood frozen to the spot. The Hun in charge gazed at me, and noticing my RFC cap which I always carried with me, and which I had already donned, he put two and two together and made five, with the result that he asked, '*Sind Sie ein Franzosischer Flieger?*' (Are you a French Flyer?) Fortunately, I had learnt a little German at school in South Africa, and so I summoned up my courage and answered him to the best of my ability in German, 'No, do you not know who I am?' and then asked, 'Have you seen my automobile?' This puzzled them immensely, and I did not wait to be found out, especially as the four of them were already half out of the cart, and each had a rifle, but I turned on my heel and walked into the darkness. Why they didn't shoot at me I know not. I had started off in the wrong direction to put them off the lie of the machine but doubled back to the machine when out of their sight.[17]
>
> 2nd Lieutenant Owen Swart, 100 Squadron, RFC

It was all in the best tradition of 'cunning plans', but it was not to be. The Germans soon realised what was going on, and after several more escape and evasion adventures they were both captured. Meanwhile, Alfred Kingsford was wending his relatively untroubled way back to Ochey, where they awaited the other FE2bs. After a while, they realised one had not returned.

Well, who's missing – it's Swart! We strained our eyes in the direction of the line, but no machine lights could be seen. I remembered how keen he was and how we had talked of what we hoped to do on our first show. He was determined to put up a good performance and I wondered if he had been tempted to get down too low and so caught some of those tracer bullets. We hung about until we knew his benzine must be exhausted and that he must be down somewhere, and not until then did we think of returning to the mess. There was no jubilation and one by one we crept to our huts, after a final look to see if the missing machine had turned up.[18]

2nd Lieutenant Alfred Kingsford, 100 Squadron, RFC

The raids carried out by 41st Wing must have irritated the Germans, for early on in their stay at Ochey airfield they began to be targeted by retaliatory bombing raids.

Our C.O. was full of ideas, and we did not stay there long. We deceived the Hun airmen for a long time before they discovered our whereabouts. Not a mile from the landing ground were the Ochey Woods, and we camouflaged new hangars and huts, made a good runaway, and lived in perfect serenity. We used to watch him at night, bombing our old aerodrome, where we had left the hangars and rigged up necessary gear to cause a fire by the mere pressing of a button from our grandstand. Fritz would appear, drop a few bombs, our button would be pressed, a fire would light up, and some lucky enemy airman would get the Iron Cross next morning. Then over would come the enemy daylight machines to take photographs, and we did our best to assist them by posing some old, scrapped machine, often more than one, on the landing ground near a bomb hole, thus verifying the previous night's work. More Iron Crosses would be handed round. But as time wore on, Fritz could not understand why we could continue raiding his towns and military centres. He wondered how we could carry on if his raids were so successful as pictured. We certainly never missed an opportunity, two shows a night, often eighteen machines; he was mystified. Soon after this, more daylight machines came over to know the cause, and it was not until new tracks began to show up on the landing ground of our fresh aerodrome that he discovered where we were. Then he let us have it but did no real damage. His bombing was only fair.[19]

2nd Lieutenant Alfred Kingsford, 100 Squadron, RFC

It seems that sometimes, 'cunning plans' did work.

*　*　*

One evocative witness to the bombing raids carried out on Germany in the spring of 1918 was Lieutenant Arthur Keep of 55 Squadron, who can guide us through the thrills and spills of these raids. On 16 March, 55 Squadron were ordered to carry out a daylight raid on Zweibrücken, an industrial town in the Rhineland, over 100 miles across the German border. Each DH4 was carrying a bomb load of two, or at most three, 112lb bombs.

> The start of a raid is an impressive sight: the twelve machines, six in each formation set out in battle flying order on the aerodrome; the propellers revolving easily with the engines throttled right back; the streamers of the leader and deputy leader fluttering from the struts; heavy ominous looking bombs slung under the wings; machine guns pointing upwards; pilots and observers tense and waiting for the signal to start. Last, but not least, Roger the squadron dog running excitedly round. The low note of the engines becomes a full throttle roar and the leader machine followed by the rest of the formations move forward and rapidly gaining speed leave the earth behind.[20]
> Lieutenant Arthur Keep, 55 Squadron, RFC

It was a long way to fly over hostile territory. First, and not least, they had to get past the German anti-aircraft batteries.

> Below we could see the shell pocked earth and the wiggling lines of trenches, here and there the smoke of a bursting shell. For the time being one seemed curiously detached and aloof from all this, but this feeling was quickly dissipated once the line was reached and showed that the people below were by no means unmindful of your existence. What had previously been clear air now became filled with puffs of black and white smoke preceded by a little flash of flame. We were in the 'Archie' barrage. The sensation was weird. The little round black puffs of smoke apparently appearing from nowhere with nothing to herald them as unless they are very near you can't hear the noise of the bursting shell above the roar of the engine. It's only when you see jagged rents appearing in the planes that their full significance is properly realised.[21]
> Lieutenant Arthur Keep, 55 Squadron, RFC

Surviving unscathed, the DH4s flew on towards Germany. As might be expected, the Germans had noticed the increasing numbers of raids and had assigned several Home Defence Squadrons to protect the 'Fatherland' from interlopers. If the bombers were intercepted by modern scouts, their only chance of survival lay in keeping their nerve and maintaining a strict formation. Easy in theory; difficult in practice.

> With a cold thrill I saw a red light soar into the air from the leader's machine. Red always means danger and a red light fired from the leader's machine meant enemy aircraft approaching; close in and prepare to fight. Away on our left were some little rapidly growing black specks which speedily resolved themselves into hostile aircraft bearing down on us and a few seconds later spurts of flame appeared from the leading machine. I heard the never forgotten

crackle of the machine guns and saw the streaks of blue smoke from the tracer bullets as they sped on their way. Before I realised it, I was mixed up in an aerial fight with a Hun who was coming up behind. My own observer was blazing away with his Lewis gun and other observers were doing the same. To put it mildly I was frightened.[22]

    Lieutenant Arthur Keep, 55 Squadron, RFC

In the face of the combined fire of the DH4 formation, the Germans failed to press home their attack. The DH4s pressed into the Rhineland and at last reached their objective, Zweibrücken. Now they would unleash hell and damnation on the hapless Germans below them.

The leader fired a white light warning us to prepare to drop our bombs. Shortly after I saw his bombs fall and with great joy released my own with a vigorous tug on the release gear. The worthy inhabitants of Zweibrücken did not let us have all our own way and vigorously plastered us with 'Archie' shells but without much effect. As we wheeled round for home, I experienced great satisfaction in seeing flames in various parts of the town where our bombs dropped.[23]

    Lieutenant Arthur Keep, 55 Squadron, RFC

The raid was considered a success, but the damage inflicted cannot have been that serious, although civilian lives must have been lost. On this occasion the German opposition had not been that strong, although still frightening enough.

    Other targets in Germany were known to be defended by a more focussed combination of anti-aircraft guns and scouts who would press home an attack. One such target was the German poison gas manufacturing plant at Mannheim. This proved a very different kettle of fish when 55 Squadron were ordered to bomb it on 24 March. At first all went well, but then in a moment everything changed.

The sky became black with bursting 'Archie' shells and above the shell bursts we could see the Hun scouts waiting. The feeling was intense. Personally, I always found the few minutes preceding a fight the most trying. One's nerves were strung to the highest pitch, and it needed no vivid imagination to picture one's machine going down in flames from an enemy shell or tracer bullet. Once the fight started however all this was forgotten – one saw red and cared for nothing. There was no time to be afraid. The air seemed full of machines circling round each other for position while above the roar of the engines one could hear the crackle of the machine guns and see the smoke trails from the tracer bullets. My observer was blazing away at a Hun while two other machines were doing the same. Suddenly the Hun stalled, turned over and went headlong down at a terrific speed and crashed into the middle of the town. Patey, my observer, was Irish and nothing pleased him more than a winged Hun so he, and I also for that matter, felt the fates had been kind. A few seconds later the formation dropped the bombs, and one and a half tons of explosives were spread over Mannheim. In a few minutes the effect was electrical. Huge clouds of grey smoke from the poison gas factory showed that we had hit a container. Other bombs fell on big store sheds along the river dock and the biggest fire it has ever been my lot to see started there. We saw the flames 40 miles away as we crossed the Vosges. The Hun scouts had not been idle during this time and were attacking some of our machines hard. Samson's observer was shot through the heart and Samson himself narrowly escaped the same fate.[24]

    Lieutenant Arthur Keep, 55 Squadron, RFC

That was not the end of it. It had been a long way to Mannheim, but it seemed an even longer way back. The Germans attacked again in force when the DH4s were still some 20 miles from safety.

Our tired formation ran into about thirteen Huns and a real hard fight followed. Four Huns were driven down but we also lost two machines, one containing two of our best men. Patey fought well and put in some good shooting.[25]

    Lieutenant Arthur Keep, 55 Squadron, RFC

It had been a hard battle, but most of them had survived. Yet two DH4s had been shot down with their crews taken prisoner, and one landed with the wounded pilot and dead observer. That was 25 per cent of the bombing force; not good odds when raids were frequent.

On 18 May, another raid meant another difficult challenge for the men of 55 Squadron. This time they were to bomb Cologne on the River Rhine, the outward journey taking two-and-a-half hours. Once again, all was well until they reached their target, then all hell broke loose. Keep was again accompanied by his observer, Lieutenant William Patey.

To the west of the river and at about our own height were four Hun scouts approaching us. Some little time before my engine had not been going very well and we were finding it difficult to keep up with the formation. The scouts were beginning to close in by the time we reached Cologne and we began to exchange shots. Cologne was partially obscured by fleecy clouds but not enough to seriously interfere with bombing. Our machine carried the camera for taking photos of the damage. Patey was determined to get his pictures whatever happened and did some splendid work bobbing up and down like a 'Jack in the box'; first taking photos and then up firing a few rounds at two Huns who were trying to close in. Williams the leader fired a white light and down went all the bombs all over Cologne, mostly small 20pdrs which we afterwards learned caused a great number of casualties.[26]

    Lieutenant Arthur Keep, 55 Squadron, RAF

Then it was time for home, but his engine was still running badly and they were still being pursued by the four German scouts. It looked bad for Keep and Patey.

> We had the helpless feeling of being left behind as the formation gradually drew away from us and upwards. The leader was doing the right thing as the safety of his formation depended on getting to the greatest possible height on the return trip; they could not risk the others for one machine. It was only a few minutes before two of the attacking scouts discovered we were being left behind and turned their whole attention to us. One swung round behind us right under our tail while the other took up his position to our left and about 50 feet above ready to turn and dive as soon as Patey was busy with the other. The first fellow opened fire – cut two struts nearly through and one landing wire and only a rapid swerve on our part saved worse following. Round came Patey's Lewis gun and he fired a burst at the second one hitting him badly in the radiator. Clouds of steam came out from him and down went his nose to get to earth before his engine seized up. Very glad we were to see the last of him. This also cooled the ardour of the other, who, much to our relief, turned to see the fate of his companion.[27]
>
> Lieutenant Arthur Keep, 55 Squadron, RAF

They were still in a world of trouble, having fallen more than a mile behind the rest of the formation, with 150 miles to go and the engine still showing no signs of making a miracle recovery. Keep decided not to follow them, but to take his own route back, hoping to avoid German scouts searching for the main body. This seems to have worked until they were above Trier (Trèves), when the bursting of anti-aircraft shells around their DH4 attracted the unwelcome attention of three scouts. Then it was just a race back to the lines.

> We had about 3 or 4 miles start and 60 miles to go. It was intense: mile after mile with the enemy gradually closing in. Suddenly without warning came the crackle of machine guns followed by the roar of an engine as a blue painted Albatros dived down past us. We had been so intently watching our pursuers that we had neglected to look for others above us. Fortunately, no damage was done, but he was at once followed by a yellow Albatros who swooped down firing as he came and put several holes in the wings. Then there was a splinter of glass as a bullet carried away the top of my windscreen, while two more bullets tore a big hole in the top of the petrol tank and a second afterwards the undercarriage was splintering. Patey could not fire at the fellow as he was obscured by our own tail. That Hun meant business and if we were not going to be shot down, we just had to put him out of action. We tried a trick which we had found successful before: stick right back, left bank and left rudder – brought us round and before the Hun realised it, we were alongside each other. Patey was waiting and let fly with our last half drum of

ammunition catching the Albatros right in the pilot's cockpit. I think he must have riddled him, anyway the machine went up, turned over on its back, spun away and one wing fell off. We made for home and 10 minutes later crossed the line. Inside half an hour we were back in our own aerodrome with a very battered aeroplane but feeling lucky to be alive.[28]
    Lieutenant Arthur Keep, 55 Squadron, RAF

Patey was credited with two German aircraft out of control. And there it was: one minute facing near certain death, thirty minutes later with their feet up in perfect safety in the officers' mess. Amidst the losses and stress, there was one surrealistic postscript to these operations.

There was also a presentation of *Croix de Guerres* by General Castelnau to four of our fellows. The presentation was carried out with appropriate ceremony and the recipients kissed on the cheek by the General – much to their disgust and the huge delight of everybody else. As the worthy general was about 3 feet nothing and Captain Collett, one of the victims, stood 6 feet 4 inches the kissing was worth seeing![29]
    Lieutenant Arthur Keep, 55 Squadron, RFC

A rare moment of humour in a grim business.

*   *   *

The creation of the Independent Force RAF in June 1918, under the command of Major General Hugh Trenchard, made little practical difference to the augmented bomber squadrons. It was undoubtedly a little strange that Trenchard, the high priest of army co-operation, should have been posted to command the strategic bombing effort. The Independent Force was intended to use the envisaged masses of surplus aircraft to create a force capable of doing real harm to German industry and infrastructure. It was always a bit of a pipedream, as the promised aircraft never arrived; just a few more squadrons would be added, in total less than Trenchard had requested years ago to augment the RFC force. These reinforcements nevertheless allowed a reorganisation, thus 41st Wing (55, 99 and 104 Squadrons) were devoted to day bombing raids, while the new 83rd Wing (100 and 216 Squadrons) were on night raids. Trenchard was tempted but resisted the French concept of concentrating all their resources to achieve the complete destruction of one industrial centre, believing it to be beyond the scope of his force. The limited number of aircraft available and the small bomb loads they could carry, coupled with the constraints on long-range operations imposed by bad weather, meant that he believed such policy was unfeasible for up to five years. Concentrated bombing would also allow the German defences to focus their energies. Instead, for the time being, Trenchard preferred a scatter-gun approach.

By attacking as many centres as could be reached, the moral effect was first of all very much greater, as no town felt safe, and it necessitated continued and thorough defensive measures on the part of the enemy to protect the many different localities over which my force was operating. At present the moral effect of bombing stands undoubtedly to the material effect in a proportion of twenty to one, and therefore it was necessary to create the greatest moral effect possible.[30]

Major General Hugh Trenchard, Headquarters, Independent Force

For the pilots and observers of the bombing squadrons, there was no respite. Reading their accounts, one is reminded of the traumas suffered by so many of their descendants serving in Bomber Command just twenty years later. Casualties were frequent, with the 'fickle finger of fate' finally settling on Albert Keep on 20 July. The target that day was a munitions centre at Oberndorf. Keep took off in his DH4 A7427, accompanied by his observer, 2nd Lieutenant James Pollock.

Our formation reached it [the target] without trouble, and we did some very destructive bombing. As we left the town our six machines were attacked by nine first-class Hun scouts and we fought as I have never fought before. Almost at once poor Young in the machine next to me went down in flames and his observer jumped out 15,000 feet up, sooner than be burnt alive and disappeared falling over and over. Another machine piloted by an NCO next went down out of control. Then came the rattle of a machine gun straight behind us, a splintering sound as the bullets tore through some of the woodwork, then a blow like a terrific kick – my right arm was useless and the machine in a spin. Fortunately, I managed to get straight with the left hand and Pollock who was my observer on that trip drove the Hun off and I believe put him down. By this time most of the fighting was finished and the Huns drew off having lost two if not three machines![31]

Lieutenant Arthur Keep, 55 Squadron, Independent Force

But the hard miles still lay ahead of them.

Then came that awful trip back – 70 miles to go before the line and safety could be reached, one arm out of action and pouring blood. Two tanks draining away through bullet holes and self feeling like nothing. I could not keep with the others in formation and gradually wandered away, a most fatal thing to do. At last, we reached the line, but not safety, as coming towards us was a patrol of three hostile scouts, one fortunately in front of the rest. Then the rattle of the machine guns once more with Pollock firing hard. To our joy the shots went home, and the Hun lost control and spun earthwards and we afterwards heard from French artillery observers crashed into a tangled heap 14,000 feet below. The other two seeing his fate kept clear but still fate was against us. There was an awful roar and concussion. The machine seemed to go straight up in the air as an 'Archie' shell burst just below us. The steel tank below my seat was crumpled out of shape and undoubtedly saved my life, but poor Pollock had his leg almost severed at the knee by a ragged piece of shell. Somehow, we glided over the line and got down in a field beside the French hospital. Stretchers were brought and we were got out of the machine. Poor Pollock was past help and died a few minutes later. I was bundled off to the operating theatre and woke up in bed feeling as if I had returned from another world.[32]

Lieutenant Arthur Keep, 55 Squadron, Independent Force

Amongst the bombing squadrons, the tensions could only increase with every raid they survived.

New pilots arriving about this time realised that it was a real war, while the old stagers tried their level best not to show any effects of giving way. One could always note, however, the anxiety with which operation orders were awaited each day, and the weather report would be studied time after time. The worst part was the waiting about before the show, when pilots and observers would congregate at their hangars at dusk, often not receiving orders to take off for an hour or so. The weather might be doubtful, in which case we'd patrol to and fro, lighting endless cigarettes. Once in the air we were all right, but the damned hanging about got on our nerves.[33]

2nd Lieutenant Alfred Kingsford, 100 Squadron, Independent Force

The trickle of casualties gradually eroded their ranks, but there were always new pilots and observers arriving to be made welcome. The IF was augmented during August by the arrival of the 97, 115 and 215 Squadrons, all flying the Handley Page O/400, and 110 Squadron, flying the DH9a. Ewart Garland had served above the Western Front in 1916 and 1917, but knowledge of the grim casualties suffered in daylight bombing missions over Germany affected him badly. Still, he was determined to do his best.

Rumour that we will start on raids in a couple of days' time. The time draws near to say goodbye! Damn me for a frightened fool! But not a coward – it is one thing to be in a funk and yet do your job, and another to shirk because you are frightened.[34]

Captain Ewart Garland, 104 Squadron, Independent Force

On the morning of 7 September, they were to attack the Badische Works at the dreaded Mannheim.

The adjutant gave the target on the phone in a sort of hushed tone: 'Mannheim!' It is like being under sentence of death. But now I am quite calm for some reason

and don't mind much, I will trust in God and all that, but at the same time I'll take with me spare socks, a cheque book and my vast pocket Shakespeare![35]
    Captain Ewart Garland, 104 Squadron, Independent Force

When he wrote his diary that night – always a good sign when he was able to do that after a raid – he could reflect on a success, and the fact that for the moment he had controlled his own fears.

Hurrah! We have bombed Mannheim and only lost three machines, two of them from my flight. We combined with 99 Squadron, twelve machines each, I led my flight of six, but two turned back with engine failure and two were shot down under control about 20 miles over, so that left Ross and I. Huns got up to us almost as soon as we crossed the lines, and we had the little coloured devils at us all the way. Over Mannheim the air became full of them, and they got right into us pumping incendiaries till the sky was a mass of smoke. We kept pretty good formation after dropping the bombs and started back attacked all the time – we were about twenty strong. We got back after 4 hours in the air. One observer was wounded and several machines, including mine, badly shot up and write-offs. However, it is considered a good show – maybe – but – Oooh – my head![36]
    Captain Ewart Garland, 104 Squadron, Independent Force

Another pilot who joined the fray in August would have a considerable impact on the fictional world of aviation. 'Captain' W.E. Johns, the author of the *Biggles* series of books, was a bit of a character. Not really a captain, just a 2nd lieutenant, he would nevertheless do his bit in the skies over Germany that autumn after joining 55 Squadron. He soon noticed that the mess was a wild place, tormented by their frequent casualties.

The strain of combat and the constant risk of death meant that the pilots often defied the strict conventions of acceptable behaviour and took enormous risks for a little boisterous fun which in a less forgiving time might equally be considered as rank hooliganism. We came upon two steamrollers, their funnels smoking gently while the drivers had their tea. In a brace of shakes two officers had climbed aboard, and away went the steamrollers down the hill, of all things. What a sight! One finished on its side in a ditch, minus its funnel. The other one hit a tree. No one was hurt.[37]
    2nd Lieutenant William Johns, 55 Squadron, Independent Force

Johns himself did not last long. On 16 September, six DH4s of 55 Squadron were sent to bomb Mannheim. Johns was flying with his observer, 2nd Lieutenant Alfred Amey, in their DH4 F5712. All was well until they got to Savern.

I was watching a string of what appeared to be gaudy butterflies crawling along the ground; now and then the sun flashed on their wings. It was a full squadron of Fokker DVIIs trailing us – and climbing fast. There was a bit of 'Archie' about, nothing to worry us, but the odd chance came off. There was a terrific explosion almost in my face, and a blast of air and smoke nearly turned my machine over. I tried the controls anxiously and all seemed well, but a stink of petrol filled my nostrils, and I glanced down; my cockpit was swimming with the stuff. I switched over to my near main tank – it was empty. A quick glance revealed the Fokkers now about 4,000 feet below and 2 miles behind. I could not go on with the formation for I had not got enough petrol, but I had just about enough to reach the lines if I could get through. Pulling my bomb toggle, I sent my single 230lb bomb on its last journey; where it fell I do not know, for there were other things I had to attend to.[38]

2nd Lieutenant William Johns, 55 Squadron, Independent Force

They were about 60 miles from home, but at least they had a good deal of altitude at around 19,500 feet. Yet flying alone above Germany was a dangerous business. They were soon spotted and assailed by some seven or eight German scouts. Johns' account is very detailed – and one may wish to recall his subsequent profession – yet it does convey the idea of what happened in that adrenaline-fuelled battle for survival.

I settled down for the race home hoping the enemy would not see me. What a hope! Within 5 minutes Amey's gun was talking; seven or eight Fokkers had not only caught us but had height on us. Toying with the compensator I climbed to 21,000 feet, but the coloured gentlemen were still with me. The leader came in with a rush and I touched the rudder-bar to let his tracer go by. A bunch of them came up under my elevators and I kicked out my foot, slewing Amey round without losing height, to bring his guns to bear. The Fokkers came right in and I give them credit for facing Amey's music. One turned over, a second spun out of it, but another came right in to point-blank range; Amey raked him fore and aft without stopping him. Others came down on us from above. My sky-light was ripped to shreds, the instrument board shed glass and sawdust, a bullet ripped my goggles off and another seared my hip. Wiping the blood out of my eyes I looked back. Poor Amey was sagging slowly on to the floor of his cockpit. Sick with fright and fury I looked round for help, but from horizon to horizon stretched the unbroken blue of the summer sky. Bullets were striking the machine all the time like whip-lashes, so I put her in a steep bank and held her there while I considered the position. For perhaps 5 minutes we tore round and round, the enemy getting in a burst now and then and me 'browning' the whole bunch of them, but I could not go on indefinitely.[39]

2nd Lieutenant William Johns, 55 Squadron, Independent Force

Picking his moment, he shot off at a tangent, but they soon overhauled him. By his own account, with little or no hope of survival, Johns then saw red.

> I yanked the machine round and went for them like a mad dog. The next few minutes were like a bad dream. Whichever way I looked I saw Fokkers, red, blue, yellow, orange, striped like tigers and spotted like leopards. You will believe me when I say I threw that old 'Four' about like a single-seater, not so much to fight as to try and dodge the hail of lead. How it held together I do not know. If anyone is doubtful about his ability to stunt, the situation I am describing provides an excellent test. There is nothing like a burst of machine-gun bullets to make you shake the stick. We lost height rapidly of course. Eighteen, fifteen, ten, eight thousand, and we were still at it. Wires trailed loose behind me, fabric stripped off, and the centre-section strut splintered at the fuselage junction. At 6,000 feet a striped gentleman put his gun nearly in my ear and sent a stream of lead over my shoulder and into the engine; she cut out dead, a cloud of white petrol vapour trailed aft, and I braced myself for the inevitable flames; I had seen the vapour and what follows it before. That was my worst moment. I switched off and literally flung the machine into a vertical side-slip, but she still smoked as the petrol ran over the hot engine. Suddenly the joystick went loose in my hand as the controls broke somewhere; we spun, half came out, and spun again. With my left hand I tried to wipe the blood and broken goggles off my eyes in order to see where we were going, while with my right I fought to get the machine under control, but it was useless.[40]
>
> 2nd Lieutenant William Johns, 55 Squadron, Independent Force

All that remained was a reacquaintance with the ground in what looked like none-too-favourable circumstances. It was a time for split-second decisions – and a wrong choice could be fatal.

> Below me a man who had been ploughing was running in one direction and his horse in another; bullets were still flicking up the dust around them. I knew I was going to crash, but curiously enough, I do not think I was afraid (I have been much more scared on other occasions). I hadn't time to be scared. My brain was whirling at full revs – should I jump as we hit the ground – should I unfasten my belt – and so on, and all the time I was automatically trying to get the machine on [an] even keel. Twice her nose nearly came up of her own accord as she tried to right herself, and it was in this position that we struck. A clump of trees on the edge of the field seemed to rush and meet me. I remember kicking out my foot instinctively, lifting my knees to my chin and covering my eyes. There was a crash like the end of the world. My next recollection is fighting like a madman to get out of the wreck before it fired. I still had the horror of fire on me, and I suppose every pilot would feel the same.[41]
>
> 2nd Lieutenant William Johns, 55 Squadron, Independent Force

He managed to get out, but the mortally wounded Amey was still helpless, trapped in the rear cockpit. Fortunately, the aircraft did not burst into flames.

> I leaned against the vertically poised fuselage and picked pieces of glass from the instrument dials out of my face. I was bleeding pretty badly, for my nose was broken and my lips smashed to pulp. In that frightful crash my feet had thrust the soles off my flying boots and the 8 inch deep leather safety belt went to pieces like tissue paper, ripping all the clothing and skin off my stomach as cleanly as if it had been cut with a razor. That rattle of a gun made me look up and bullets kicked up the earth around me. The German pilot afterwards told me he did this to drive me away from the machine as he thought I was trying to set fire to it. I tried to get Amey out of the wreckage, but couldn't, so I could not set fire to the machine although I had a Very pistol in the knee pocket of my Sidcot [one-piece flying suit]. A long line of grey coated soldiers with an officer at the head came sprinting down the field and I knew that as far as I was concerned the war was over.[42]
>
> 2nd Lieutenant William Johns, 55 Squadron, Independent Force

Sadly, Alfred Amey died later that day. Johns himself was black and blue all over, but he was treated to the traditional hospitality by his nemesis, Leutnant Georg Weiner.

> I realised that hitherto I had regarded him only in the abstract. With something like a mild shock, it slowly dawned upon my numbed brain that the fellow who had been in the red-nosed, black-crossed machine was an ordinary mortal like myself. Before, the aircraft and the occupant had been one, a hideous instrument – creature, if you like – bent on my destruction; the individual had never entered into my calculations. But there he was, saluting with the inimitable little German bow, his keen grey eyes smiling whimsically in a clean-cut face. He wore a perfectly streamlined blue-grey tunic of fine material, relieved only by a beautiful enamel cross at his throat which, I later learned, was the Pour-le-Mérite and a nifty little dagger on his hip. 'Well,' he said in French, 'you've had a bit of bad luck – but it might have been worse, eh?' He picked up a slip of paper from the things that had been taken from my pockets; it was a pass to Paris. He tipped me a knowing wink! Again, I felt that something was wrong somewhere. It was all very unreal. Far from hating the man, it would have been churlish not to have responded to the obvious friendly spirit with which he made arrangements for my immediate comfort. As far as he and the officers of his Staffel were concerned, I must give them their due, they were as cheery a crowd as I should have met had I gone down over my own side of the lines.[43]
>
> 2nd Lieutenant William Johns, 55 Squadron, Independent Force

The progenitor of *Biggles* was undone. He would be a prisoner for the rest of the war.

But the war went on. The FE2bs flown by 100 Squadron were finally replaced by the Handley Page O/400s, and they continued their night raids. Roy Shillinglaw flew in them as a navigator and was responsible for bomb aiming. Long after the war, he reflected on what he did over Germany.

I don't think anybody deliberately bombed civilian houses or people. So far as my colleagues and myself were concerned we were very, very keen to be on our target. There is no doubt that our raids on German towns – railway stations and factories in those towns – must have been demoralising to some of the civilian inhabitants. In our night bombing it was difficult to see our results – we would see a fire burning or the explosion in a works. But next day the day bombers would be over at dawn and as they passed over our targets they photographed them and within 24 hours we would see pictures of our targets and where perhaps we'd hit, or whether we'd just missed and so forth. So we were very keen to be on target because our errors were shown up on those photographs – there was no kidding the authorities. I think we were pretty accurate on the whole.[44]

2nd Lieutenant Roy Shillinglaw, 100 Squadron, Independent Force

Experience since has taught us that whatever they may have thought, bomb aiming was a fairly random 'science', and would remain so for decades. The civilians undoubtedly suffered casualties; nothing comparable to the Second World War, but painful all the same. Crudely put, the whole purpose of the Independent Force was to exact vengeance for the bombing of London.

The Independent Force was originally intended to comprise some forty squadrons, but such hopes were stillborn, given the many other pressures on resources. The men who flew the missions over Germany were certainly brave – surely we have established that – but what did they really achieve? The answer is: not much. Yes, the bombs caused some damage, but much of that could be repaired swiftly. There were too few bombers, too few bombs and they were too inaccurate to cause real, lasting damage. Was it all worthwhile? Well, they forced a huge diversion of German resources as squadrons of scouts and masses of anti-aircraft guns much needed at the front were diverted to home defence. As to the rest – as with the German bombing campaign over England – the main cause of damage to the German war effort was the wail of the air raid sirens. Factories then stopped work, iron foundries manufacturing steel were closed down, and the raids caused misery and despair amongst the civilian population. Their perception of what was happening did not match the results, but as Trenchard said so wisely: 'The moral effect of bombing stands undoubtedly to the material effect in a proportion of twenty to one.'[45] This was the real effect of the bombing campaign. Dreams of mass destruction would have to wait until the 'Thousand Bomber Raids' of the Second World War.

Chapter 11

Not Over Yet, 1918

Combat flying became such a vital part of my life that even now I relive the unforgettable days spent above the fields of France. Unlike some pilots of my acquaintance, I felt no desire to build-up a record of enemy aircraft and pilots destroyed, but in war the choice is: kill or be killed. During my time in hospital, I eagerly looked forward to rejoining No. 24 [Squadron] and it never occurred to me that I had flown my last patrol. That only became apparent with the signing of the Armistice. With a shock I realised that it was the end of another chapter of my life. But what is life without memories?[1]

Lieutenant William Lambert, Queen Alexandra's Hospital

In July 1918, the clock had stopped ticking for the German Army. The 'bonus' bequeathed them by victory on the Eastern Front had been frittered away in a series of increasingly desperate offensives on the French and British lines. Fittingly, it was the French who turned the tide, just as they had done in September 1914. On 15 July, the Germans launched Operation Marneschutz-Reims (also known as *Friedensturm*, the Peace Offensive), their final, last-ditch effort to break the Allies. The French stopped the Germans dead in their tracks in the Second Battle of the Marne, and then on 18 July initiated the Battle of Soissons, the first of a huge series of Allied counter-offensives that would eventually win the war. Careless chatter that the French were 'finished' after the 1917 mutinies was exposed as nonsense. The French Army was once again a formidable foe. The British were also ready to play their part. The 'All Arms Battle' had been tried and tested over the previous year and was now unleashed. As the name suggested, it was the flexible battlefield interaction of artillery, tanks, infantry, cavalry – and yes, the RAF – to achieve victory. The Germans were in no fit state to resist as their manpower resources had been severely eroded by four years of war and their own desperate offensives, while the advent of the American millions removed all hope and shattered morale. Everyone now knew who was going to win the war; the only question was when.

The next hammer blow came with the Battle of Amiens, launched on 8 August 1918, which all authors are contractually obliged to refer to as the 'black day for the German Army'. The new artillery techniques and proper gun calibration meant that shooting 'off the map' reduced that aspect of artillery observation – at least before the attack began. That and the advent of the tank had reintroduced the concept of surprise to warfare on the Western Front. The RAF were called on once more: they had to stop the German photographic missions probing behind the Allied lines and photograph every inch of the ground ahead of the infantry; and they had to do all this without making it obvious that an attack was imminent. However, there was no longer any need to move squadrons to the new focus point, as there were enough aircraft all along the front to cope with any requirements. In the end, some 1,900 British and French aircraft could be deployed, facing in the first instance just 365 German aircraft before reinforcements arrived – too late. The Germans had always been outnumbered, but this was getting desperate, especially as they were beginning to run short of aviation fuel.

When the attack began at 4.20 am on 8 August, Lieutenant William Grossart and his observer, Lieutenant J.B. Leach, were up aloft in their DH4 in a flight led by Captain Euan Dickson.

> We were flying in flights. Dickson led 'C' and I brought up the rear. Low clouds hung about and Dickson was soon leading us up between two banks. It was weird, mystic, wonderful. High grey walls towered above us on each side, [and] stars in the sky above were not yet obscured by the coming dawn. We wound our way between the banks of cloudland to the Somme which we followed for a while, its course marked by a grey winding ribbon on a dark featureless landscape. All the hollows below were filled by grey mist. At Amiens we cut off to the south-east for Chaulnes and the hellfire vision of the French barrage met our gaze. The landscape was a mass of flame, the stabs of fire from guns and shells only lighting up a haze of smoke. It was an inspiring sight and many were the shells that swept unseen past our planes. The greatest day of the war in the air had begun.[2]
>
> Lieutenant William Grossart, 205 Squadron, RAF

Perversely, misty weather conditions thwarted most of the RAF missions for the first few hours, but at least it helped the infantry and tanks on the ground. And what a day they had. The British and French cut through the enemy lines like a knife through German sausage. In the afternoon, the focus changed to trying to cut off the battlefield – to bomb the bridges over the Somme that would allow German divisions to reach the front – and if the successes continued, to leave them no means of escape. Hundreds of bombing missions were launched, with 57 tons of bombs dropped on the Somme bridges over the next few days.

> Flight succeeded flight as each arrived and left. Everyone was working hard and the hardest of all were our mess orderlies. Never from morning till night were the tables cleared; the orderly routine of early coffee, breakfast, lunch, and dinner gave way to a running buffet. Never during the day did many have off their flying suits. Leach and I were an exception, being held up for two hours for a new bit of petrol pump, one of which got a bullet through it when I was attacked by three Pfalz scouts upon our second raid. As soon as a flight landed, mechanics swarmed over the machines filling with petrol, oil

and water, bombs and ammunition, looking over shock absorbers, bracing wire and control wires. The day was one of enthusiasm, interest, and excitement, such as I never knew in France. These were enhanced greatly about mid-day when reports came in of the success of the Australians and Canadians. The surprise attack had succeeded beyond the most sanguine hopes.[3]
    Lieutenant William Grossart, 205 Squadron, RAF

On the ground, the air crew were released from the tension. The bridges were defended by the German scouts, and casualties were high amongst the bomber crews. Their continued existence hung by the slimmest of threads, but just a few minutes later they could be as safe as houses.

Finally, we got home to our aerodrome and were strolling over to our tents in the sylvan peace. Flying is a dirty business, and a good scrub was indicated. Our orderly had provided warm water and had our portable canvas wash buckets in position outside our tent all ready for us. We had just time to have a good wash and brush-up and get over to the mess for dinner. Everything at our table with its snow-white covering seemed so permanent. Even the solid construction of the mess, timber though it was, its walls decorated with pictures, the curtains giving access to the ante-room, all suggested peace, not war. And the mellow evening air coming through the open windows gave a never to be forgotten charm to the setting. What a glorious contrast to the war on land! Here we were little more than an hour after being in 'action' sitting down before a five-course dinner in the comfort and security of our mess – 30 miles from it all. The noisy, happy chatter gave me an impression of make-believe. It just didn't seem like war somehow. But it was, for we were front line soldiers. In effect we had the privileges, comforts and amenities of the 'base wallah', without his conscience; for we knew the thrill and satisfaction which only the front-line soldier knows.[4]
    Lieutenant William Grossart, 205 Squadron, RAF

That is not to say that when losses were heavy, a terrible depression could not grip a squadron on a bad day – it certainly could.

The few of us who were left sat down at mess that night and cried like children as we looked around at the vacant chairs. In two days, we lost fourteen men out of a complement of twenty-seven. As I write the names of my late comrades, it is hard to believe that they are dead. With me, they set out in possession of life and glorious health – within an hour or so they were charred and mangled remains. This is War![5]
    2nd Lieutenant George Coles, 107 Squadron, RAF

But what had they achieved? Perhaps it might be expected that the bridges were broken, the German Army trapped. Not a bit of it. What damage was done was swiftly repaired. Under the lethal pressure of buzzing German scouts and concentrated anti-aircraft fire, the bombing was not accurate; and even if they hit, the bombs were not powerful enough. Perhaps the Independent Force should have been diverted from raids on Germany to the bridges, although in all probability they would have made little or no difference.

The fighting rose to a frenzy, with aircraft of both sides tumbling from the sky like confetti. Amongst them was Oberleutnant Erich Löwenhardt, who had shot down some fifty-three victims and was the highest-scoring German ace alive. His fate mirrored that of Oswald Boelcke, as on 10 August, Löwenhardt collided with an inexperienced pilot, Leutnant Alfred Wenz, and both crippled aircraft plunged to the ground. The Germans had recently been issued with parachutes, so all was not lost as both pilots jumped. Wenz's parachute opened, and he landed safely; Löwenhardt's did not, and he was killed. One would not have relished facing the reception Wenz might have expected upon his return to the officers' mess. Another German ace was now dead.

On the ground, the Anglo-French offensive came to a halt as they ran out of steam and the Germans fell back to their defence works from 1916. In all, the Allies had advanced some 12 miles in the Battle of Amiens. But then came something new. Guided by their Supreme Commander, General Ferdinand Foch, the Allies began to launch a series of offensives switching the focus up and down the Western Front. The Germans could not react quickly enough to the series of hammer blows. The Battle of Albert, Second Battle of Noyon and Second Battle of Arras all followed, chained together, each driving the Germans back and culminating in four huge separate onslaughts in four days: the French and Americans attacked in the Meuse-Argonne on 26 September; the British struck across the Canal du Nord driving towards Cambrai on 27 September; the British and Belgians smashed their way across the old Ypres Salient on 28 September; and the British and Americans breached the Hindenburg Line on the Somme on 29 September. This was not one nation winning the war; this was all the Allies acting together to achieve victory.

*   *   *

It is no coincidence that the casualties of 'Bloody April' were dwarfed by the mayhem inflicted in the air in 'Black September'. There was never a separate 'air war'; it was always an adjunct to the war on the ground. As that boiled up and over in September, so did the fighting in the air. The German scouts still fought hard – heroes in defence of their country. And the necessity for ground attacks also increased the number of RAF casualties, as when they flew low they had to pass through a maelstrom of small-arms and machine-gun fire. The idea of strafing was simple: to keep the Germans off balance, under constant threat of attack in the line, harassed as they marched to and from the battlefield, even bombed in their rest camps. There was no rest for the Germans.

Neither was there any rest for those in the skies. When the Germans retreated, it meant that a whole new set of photographs would be needed to chart every detail of their new defensive lines, to allow the staff to probe their weaknesses. William Grossart had been promoted to captain and made a flight commander, which meant new responsibilities in the air and on the ground.

> Urgent demands came for photos, and more photos, to see what his [the Germans'] next stand was to be. I started now on the most difficult job I have ever succeeded in doing in my life: the photography of the Hindenburg Line from Cambrai to St Quentin. Jerry had his crack squadrons with their finest machines against our front and seemingly intent on preventing photography at all costs. Every day we were at it, Leach being my observer for the most part. On the 13th, 14th and 19th, 22nd and 29th we were attacked, trapped or chased until I began to think of packing my slippers, pyjamas and a toothbrush in the plane for the least pessimistic outcome of these shows landing me in Ruhleben [prison camp]. Time after time we ran the devils out of petrol, sneaked back and stole the photos.[6]
>
> Captain William Grossart, 205 Squadron, RAF

Fatigue began to gnaw away at Grossart, culminating in a farcical near-calamity when he managed to fall asleep while landing his DH4 at his Conteville base.

> Through the combined effects of the strain of the last few weeks, of the long shows at high altitude that day and of a confidence in landing born of much experience, I fell asleep to the conscious world around me. My sub-conscious mind sent my right hand mechanically to the incidence wheel low down on the right side of the cockpit and wound it fully back. It also pulled the throttle back and pointed the machine round into the wind against the wind stocking. It probably did everything but land her successfully, for we floated down with a forward speed which could not have been more than 50mph. It was a perfect pancake, sent the undercarriage up, burst the longerons and therefore completely 'wrote off' the machine, but left my observer and me smiling – me a little wanly perhaps – for about the whole damn squadron were hanging around sitting on whatever they could find and watching me. I felt very small and uncomfortable.[7]
>
> Captain William Grossart, 205 Squadron, RAF

The aircraft engaged in bombing missions could gain a real sense of the progress made on the ground.

Just recently our troops have been making a tremendous advance. Places which this squadron was bombing a fortnight ago – Bapaume and Peronne – are now in British hands. The troops are still advancing and are only 5 miles from Marquion now on the Arras–Cambrai road. Very interesting sight at night from above when a strafe is going on. To see the shells bursting, ammunition dumps blowing up; then, when the Hun spots us, searchlights, green 'flaming onions' and star shells, streams of tracer bullets coming up and going just in front of one; then bang an 'Archie' on your tail. Zip-zip-zip goes the machine gun at the nearest searchlight which wavers and goes out. Another springs up and then by throwing the machine about and shutting off engines – we are out of the searchlights. See them wavering and searching. One comes closer, closer and closer – will she find us? Yes–no–yes! It flickers across and then passes on; it has passed right over us and not seen us. On we go. The objective is sighted – Boom, Boom – go the sixteen heavy bombs and around we turn to come home as fast as we can, to run through a similar gauntlet as before. After crossing the lines we throttle back and come home on our own. The dummy aerodrome sighted, we signal our code letter which is answered and then the landing 'T' lights up and we land. Another raid over and done. Into the office to make a report, then to the mess for a hot drink and something to eat. Everybody is discussing the raid and finally after the last machine has returned to its lair, we turn in for a well-deserved rest.[8]

Lieutenant Leslie Semple, 207 Squadron, RAF

Bombing raids were also directed at the main German airfields. The thinking was obvious.

Why wait for him to come up into the air, blow him out on the ground? So No. 4 Australian and No. 2 Australian were ganged up with others from the wing and they took to the German aerodromes in turn – two names – Lomme and Haubourdin. We went straight in and as far as the SE5s were concerned our fellows carried six 25lb phosphor bombs and six 25lb Cooper high explosive bombs. The phosphor bombs were horrible damn things – when they burst if you got any of that on you then you burnt. The Huns got all their aircraft in the air if they could but they didn't have much to come home to afterwards![9]

Lieutenant Frank Roberts, 2 Squadron, AFC

By this time, it was evident that the later versions of the Fokker DVII, with even more powerful engines, were a real threat in the air. But although probably the finest scout aircraft of the war, it was still relatively limited in numbers compared to the buzzing swarms of Sopwith Camels, SPADs, SE5as and the powerful new Sopwith Dolphins. Most of all, it was helpless when caught on the ground in the bombing raids on the German airfields. This was the way forward in the air war; catch them on the ground – this was the future.

The British were, however, forced to modify their tactic of flying in smaller flight formation, which would join together as and when required. German tactics were based on larger formations securing a local numerical superiority in 'bouncing' RAF formations before reinforcements could arrive. One example occurred on the afternoon of 5 September, when five Sopwith Camels under Flight Commander Norman Trescowthick of 4 Squadron, AFC, were ambushed during a sweep of the Douai area by three strong formations of Fokker DVIIs. Arrangements to meet other RAF squadrons had broken down and the Australians were on their own. They tried to avoid action but were attacked from all sides, and only Trescowthick managed to escape. Lieutenant Leonard Taplin reveals what happened to the rest. He had taken the precaution of flying some 1,000 feet above the other Camels in his aircraft E1407.

We had to fight. No signal to avoid action could have had any effect. The escape of one machine (Trescowthick) was due to the Germans' attention being centred upon us four. However, that is neither here nor there. Two formations of about twelve to fifteen machines attacked almost simultaneously, one from high up in the west, and one from the north. Later a very much larger formation came in from the east, which I at first thought was our escort coming to our rescue. Trescowthick dived away under the formation coming from the direction of our own lines, but the others were cut off. No German attempted to follow Trescowthick, so evidently, he was unobserved. Meanwhile, I was gaining all the height I could, and, as the formation from the north closed in, I dived into the middle of them. I had not been seen, apparently, by reason of my height. The leader, a red-and-white-tailed Fokker, pulled up, and we went at it head-on. I got a good burst into his radiator, and he went down on a glide not out of control, just engine out of action. Next moment, I was right in the middle of them, and before I could do anything a German below me pulled his nose up and put a burst right through the bottom of my machine. One bullet went through my right hand, smashing it up and breaking the wrist. My Camel immediately stalled and half-rolled itself, and, to conform with poetic justice, came out of the stall right on the tail of my attacker, who was recovering from his own stall. I was now under control with my left hand and easily shot this German down. Just then I saw Lockley dropping past me completely out of control. I also saw during the fight two machines in flames, which I now suppose were Eddie and Carter. I was getting shot about and was firing at anything I saw, when a Fokker from somewhere – the sky seemed full of them – again got a burst into me. One bullet, an explosive, smashed the breech and crank-handle of one of my guns and sent a splinter through my nose. This dazed me and I fell out of control in an engine-spin. I spun down to about 1,000 feet and then recovered, to find two Fokkers had followed me down. I again had to fight, and luckily shot down one German easily; the other then left me alone. After this fight I was down to about 100 feet and started off towards home. My engine was just about done, from being shot about and from running full throttle through everything. I had only one hand and could not properly control the engine to gain height, so just staggered along. After running the gauntlet of ground-fire for several miles I was shot down from the ground when within a few hundred yards of the German front-line and taken prisoner.[10]

Lieutenant Leonard Taplin, 4 Squadron, AFC

When the Fokker DVII's superiority was factored in, it was evident that more organisation was required. Gradually, British formations followed the German trend, with multiple squadrons flying combat patrols to press the Germans well back over their lines. Less was left to chance and the sort of disastrous errors that had doomed Taplin's comrades. Such ambushes would gradually happen less often. The Camel squadrons would fly low, often strafing the German airfields, while the SE5a or Dolphin squadrons flew high above to protect them from surprise attack.

On 24 September, Lieutenant Yvonne Kirkpatrick was flying a Sopwith Camel when he was despatched on a ground strafing mission.

I told you that from 12 noon to 2 pm today would be pretty exciting, but I had no idea I would have experienced so much excitement and yet be able to write to tell you about it. I cannot tell you what the job was, but this is partly what happened. We broke up formation and dived on our objective. I dropped my bombs on something which I thought would appreciate them and then at a height of 100 feet charged about firing my guns at things on the ground till they would not fire any more. Then I decided to come home. The 'Archie' was awful and also the machine-gun fire from the ground. I was trying to climb up and join some of our machines flying westwards, when suddenly my engine stopped. I picked a field and was just going to land when I thought I would switch over to my gravity tank. The engine restarted and I decided to try to get home. I was about 11 miles east of the lines and none of our other machines were in sight, so I decided to hedge-hop near to the ground to avoid 'Archie'. My engine wasn't going very well and the west wind was against me. You should have seen the expression of people's faces. I flew over a sunken road and saw two fat old Huns walking calmly along with their hands in their pockets; they simply stared at me with mouths wide open. Then I saw two Fokkers diving on me. I simply tore round trees and church steeples with them firing at me. After what seemed like years, I saw some trees, which I thought I knew were on our side of the lines. The machine-gun fire got very fierce, then suddenly stopped. I looked over the side of the cockpit and saw some Scotsmen waving to me. Some relief, believe me. While I was hedge-hopping I saw one of our machines land under control on the Hun side of the lines and on arriving home I found we had three pilots missing. A bullet had gone through my tank and the petrol was pouring out.[11]

Lieutenant Yvonne Kirkpatrick, 203 Squadron, RAF

Casualties were all but inevitable in this kind of low-level work. Captain John Middleton and the SE5as of 40 Squadron were flying above the Battle of the Canal du Nord on 27 September. They were to drop four small bombs on the Sensée Canal bridges, just to the north of Cambrai.

> We set off at about ten o'clock. When we got as far as Arras we could see sights that made it obvious that the Boche was going back. Dumps were burning all over the place and Cambrai was in flames. It was a great sight. We were flying at about 4,000 feet and east of Cambrai there were some Huns. I messed about for nearly half an hour hoping they would go. It would be rotten flying up the canal at 3,000 feet with six Huns diving on us. The Huns did not go so there was nothing for it but to ignore them. They did not come for us at first and I began to think they had not seen us! We did our best with our bombs and then turned to come home. We were east of the Huns now. As soon as they saw we were going home they came for us, diving on us from the west. We flew for it as hard as we could. The leader picked me out and came for me and he was the last Hun I got to my credit! The 'Archie' people saw him crash. I looked back and saw that Drinkwater was all right, he was quite near to me. I saw Bruce with a Hun on his tail, he suddenly dived vertically and with the engine full on he flew from 3,000 feet smack into the earth on the outskirts of Cambrai. It was a rotten sight.[12]
>
> Captain John Middleton, 40 Squadron, RAF

Lieutenant Ronald Sykes of 201 Squadron was in his Camel engaged in ground strafing in direct support of advancing British troops.

> A shell burst below me and within a second the whole of the ground seemed to be turning over, boiling up in brown earth that had been thrown up and smoke from the bursting shells. I thought, 'Well nobody can live down there and I don't think I'm going to live long if I stay over the top of it!' I went straight to the clear air over the German support areas. There I found the sunken roads were full of German troops – within seconds they all vanished into the grass verges – so I strafed the verges. I got rid of three of my four little bombs. Then four Fokkers came down from above and attacked me. I saw them coming and I'd had quite a lot of practice at taking evasive action, so I went down to ground level round the trees and zig-zagged back keeping out of their way. We'd been told to attack troops and not go in for aerial combat as other squadrons were up above to do that. As I got back into the battle smoke they broke away to the east and left me. I went back to the German infantry and got rid of my last bomb. Then the smoke over the battle area was clearing and I could see the trenches. I spotted one advance trench with some Germans. I dived on it, fired, pulled up and did what I call a cartwheel over the far end and down again. I didn't shoot because they were running and

seemed to have their hands up as I got close to them – I pulled up again. Some British troops were just arriving, and the Germans started to climb over the parapet going off west as prisoners. Then I went back to our advance landing ground to rearm and refuel.[13]

Lieutenant Ronald Sykes, 201 Squadron, RAF

On another occasion, Yvonne Kirkpatrick was also attacked by the German scouts, who proved to be rather more persistent.

We dropped our bombs and started to come back, when umpteen Fokkers appeared from nowhere. I picked up the other two Camels and we came out hell for leather. They had us in a rather tight corner because there was a strong wind blowing us into Hunland the whole time. Wherever I looked round the sky was thick with Fokkers. We dived right down to the ground and they followed us. I looked round and saw a Camel with a Fokker on its tail. The Camel went round trees, over hedges, everywhere the Fokker followed him. If my engine hadn't had that tired feeling, I'd have turned round and taken a pot at him, but it felt as if it was going to seize, so I thought I'd better get home. How it was I never hit anything on the ground I don't know. I was watching my tail more than where I was going. Anyhow it's much harder to hit you from the ground when you're so low, and much harder for the Fokker, because he has to look where he was going as well as where I was. Anyhow, somebody shot the Fokker down that was chasing us. Several of our pilots had some holes in their machines, but we all got back except a sergeant pilot, who, we hope, has landed this side somewhere. It's raining now, and personally I don't mind if it continues for a bit. Things are rather too exciting now.[14]

Lieutenant Yvonne Kirkpatrick, 203 Squadron, RAF

James Gascoyne cheerfully recalled another rather more amusing incident in these final weeks of the conflict.

I discovered a line of infantry behind a hedge. I don't know how many troops there were there, but riding towards them going across a ploughed field was a big fat German on a horse. The horse was walking – there was plenty of mud and dirt about. It suddenly appealed to me to see what I could do about it. I didn't want to hurt the horse so I dived down and flew very close over the top of the horse. The German saw me coming down, jumped off the horse and got underneath its neck, holding the reins. I frightened this poor horse so much that it started to gallop across the field! The fat German hung on to the reins for 10 or 15 yards dragged through this mud and mire – and he looked a proper sight before I had finished with him![15]

Lieutenant James Gascoyne, 92 Squadron, RAF

By the end of September 1918, the German Army had reached the bottom of the hangman's rope. Peace negotiations began and the German high command turned to the business of avoiding and misdirecting blame. But still the battles raged on. Blow after blow was rained on the German lines. Throughout October, the British, the French, the Americans and the Belgians continued their series of bone-crunching offensives up and down the Western Front.

As the German lines crumbled, there was a pressing demand from the British generals and their staff for long-range reconnaissance missions to track the movements of the depleted German divisions through the main rail junctions and stations. Lieutenant Frederick Pargeter of 53 Squadron was sent on one such mission. He was a somewhat irritable character – always a delightful trait.

> The 'big wigs' ask us to find trains, trains and more trains. Skipper calls Dunlop and me, who are for pre-dawn flight take off so as to be over at first light. He says we have not found as many trains as the squadrons to the right and left. I reply if I see a train and report, 'Waterloo to Clapham Junction', I do not also report it at 'Vauxhall and Queens Road'. But we take off in the dark, rather piqued and in a, 'If they want trains they shall have them' mood! The result was we glued ourselves to the railways, find every train, engine, steam etc. and forget all else. So we were too far, too low, too light and we touch Jerry in a tender spot for up comes the kitchen sink and everything else. Shells, red tracers, flaming onions – a pretty display from outside but rather different inside. We dodge madly about. I watch pieces of airplane blown off, control wires cut, bracing wires snapped and we ponder on the least possible amount of plane that will keep us airborne. In defiance I keep on giving odd bursts, a sort of snap of the fingers, 'We are still here!'[16]
>
> Lieutenant Frederick Pargeter, 53 Squadron, RAF

Contact patrols were also in great demand, but the difficulties that had dogged them in 1915 were still there. It was difficult to discern the national origin of the uniforms of muddy troops as you flashed over them – and they were going a lot faster in 1918. All they could do was get down as low as possible, and hope that German ground fire was inaccurate and that the British troops had majored in snap aircraft recognition. Major William Sholto Douglas of 85 Squadron took his Camel as low as 20 feet.

> Visibility was only about 400 yards, and the cloud base was down to about 300 feet. I took off and flew just above the tree-tops down the long, straight road that ran from north of St Quentin to Le Cateau. There were three or four roads running out of Le Cateau to the east, and I flew along each of these in turn until I found myself shot at from the ground, at which point I rapidly turned around. After marking on my map the spot where I had been fired at, I made my way back to Le Cateau and repeated the process along the other

roads. Having collected this information, I then groped my way back to my own aerodrome by contour-chasing with my map on my knee. When I got there and gave the information to our intelligence people they were able to join up the points that I had marked, and through that they were able to gain quite a fair picture of the location of the German front line.[17]

   Major William Sholto Douglas, 85 Squadron, RAF

The fighting raged on. On 30 October, an old 'favourite', Louis Strange – now a distinguished lieutenant colonel – led a mass raid by sixty-two aircraft of the 80th Wing on Rebaix airfield north of Ath. Once he had struggled into the air with a Lewis gun; now he was in a Sopwith Camel armed with two Vickers guns. The raid was successful, and Strange even claimed a victim under somewhat unusual circumstances.

   To show how little one knows of what happens in an air fight, I may say that until I got back, I was blissfully unaware that I had shot down a Fokker. An observer in one of the DH9s who recognised the machine I flew, reported and confirmed that I had got this enemy when he was sitting on the DH9's tail. Personally, I had no idea this Hun had crashed, although I thought I got a good burst on him; but I was more worried about the question whether I had any undercarriage left, because I hit the Fokker's wing hard with my wheels when I pulled out of my dive.[18]

   Lieutenant Colonel Louis Strange, Headquarters, 80th Wing, RAF

Short of fuel, outnumbered in the air and bombed on the ground they may have been, but the German scouts still tried their best. Their tactics were cautious – they had little choice – but they were still trying to entrap victims, as Yvonne Kirkpatrick observed little more than a week before the end of the war on 3 November.

   Every time we go up, we meet these blooming Huns, about forty of them. They're very cautious and try to lure us over to their side where they could deal with us fairly comfortably. We sort of hare round, and they chase us, and we turn round and chase them back again. Today we had a sort of scrap. The clouds were at about 10,000 feet, at least one layer was. When we crossed the lines just below these clouds we saw about fifteen of them climbing and going south, so we went towards them, but they went east, then we did a turn to the left and went north and they chased us. This sort of thing went on for ages and no real dogfight developed. The Huns wanted to have it all their own way and we didn't see why they should. One came fairly close and I took a shot at him. Then we turned and one came down and took a shot at me. I tore the sky up with some colossal turns and he left us. I had a sort of feeling that if we went over after them we'd have all the German Air Service down on us from above the clouds – and I was right – because somebody who'd been above the clouds had seen a whole crowd more of them. The war news is good, but the Huns on this front, the aerial ones anyway, don't seem to be thinking about stopping fighting.[19]

Lieutenant Yvonne Kirkpatrick, 203 Squadron, RAF

The final British offensive, the Battle of the Sambre, began on 4 November, and within a few days they were approaching Mons, where it had all begun for them on 23 August 1914. The weather was grim, but many aircraft still struggled up to support the troops on the ground.

So interesting watching the Tommies strolling along the roads to Berlin, that one couldn't resist going to see how much further they had gone since the last time one was out. Then, too, it is so interesting getting lost and dodging trees and houses, although two chaps I knew in another squadron, one of whom flew into the side of a house, and the other into a tree perhaps have different ideas on the subject. However, once you find the lines – and you do that by flying east until you are shot at – [it] is wonderful the good that can be done by helping the infantry, knocking out machine guns, shooting up troops and transport, etc. It bucks up the troops to see aeroplanes flying about in front of them as they advance, as for one thing the fact of us being shot at and shooting back, gives a very good idea as to where the Hun is, and how strongly he holds the position. Whenever an aeroplane flies low over hostile troops, it seems to be the craze for anyone with anything that will shoot to let blaze, and they are getting pretty good too – as you perhaps would have thought had you been able to see my machine yesterday, and the hole in my pal's leg from an explosive bullet. Plucky little beggar: after being hit he turned back into Hunland and dropped his bombs on the people that fired at him![20]

Captain Malcolm McGregor, 85 Squadron, RAF

Not everyone was looking forward to the cessation of war. Duncan Grinnell-Milne had been taken prisoner way back in 1916. However, always an ingenious fellow, he had escaped in April 1918 and was now back in the fray, flying a SE5a with 56 Squadron, which he had emblazoned '*Schweinhund*' in a none-too-subtle personal message to his erstwhile captors. He would claim five victories in this late flowering as a scout pilot. And he wanted more.

I had just landed the '*Schweinhund*', after she had had the good fortune to bring down a couple of Fokkers with no more damage than a few holes through her radiator, [and] I found Bob in the tent office, where I had gone to make out my report. His boots were immaculate as ever, but his face was long as a winter's night. 'Any luck?' he asked gloomily. I told him the news, restraining my elation with difficulty. 'That's good!' he exclaimed grinning. 'Johnny has got one, too. The squadron record is going up!' His face grew sombre again. 'I'll have to hurry to catch up – it will soon be my last chance!' 'Why?' I asked in alarm. 'They aren't transferring you to another squadron, are they?' 'No, no – but it's all over now, bar the shouting!' 'What is? The squadron? They're sending us home to get the new machines?' 'No, not that either. We'll never get those new machines. It's the war – she's finished, done for. Fritz has thrown in the towel. Asking for peace!' I couldn't believe it. Nor could anyone else, not for days. It seemed impossible that it should be so. That great, strong German who had held us back for years – on his knees? True, since August he had been beaten everywhere, on all fronts, beaten so that he could not hope to attack again, but although he was now in full retreat, flight almost, he had not yet been pushed back as far as he had advanced. He still stood on French soil. And already he was crying for mercy? Couldn't stand up for the last round? Couldn't take as much punishment as the Belgians, the Serbians, even the Rumanians? No, it couldn't be true! It was just the usual peace talk, a trick on the part of the enemy. Had I believed it I think I should have stopped fighting then and there.[21]

Lieutenant Duncan Grinnell-Milne, 56 Squadron, RAF

Imprisonment had clearly not reduced his enjoyment of a 'good drink' in the officers' mess, but there was a strange febrile mood.

Eagerness, enthusiasm were still there, but blended now with something very like despair. It was the same with others. 'Where's that mess corporal?' 'Corporal, a round of drinks for these officers – yes, all of them!' 'Mine's a double whisky, hot – getting cold in the air these days!' 'Gin and Italian for me, and don't forget the gin!' 'What happened to you this afternoon?' 'Got a Hun in flames did you? Good for you!' 'Any further news of Jimmy? He's been missing for two days now.' 'Pulled his wings off in a dive, you say? Poor bastard!' 'Well, he's dead enough – dived from 18,000 – must have made a big hole in the ground – probably came out in China!' 'Better luck than his friend "K". He was burnt to a crisp!' 'Well, chaps, dawn patrol tomorrow – going up high, got to get some more Huns!' 'And for God's sake, Skipper, don't lead us under a bunch of Fokkers like you did last time – enough to make one's hair turn white!' 'How about having the band in tonight? Haven't had it for the last few days, what with fellows going west and all that!' 'I'll be there to meet you in a taxi, honey.' 'Seen that pair of dead Boches in the tank just beyond "C" Flight's office? Funny looking couple – no, they don't smell – roast meat, burnt to a cinder!' 'Passed through Doullens on my way back from leave. There's a peach of a girl at the Bon Air – Marguerite's her name!' 'Where's poor old "P" buried? We ought to stick a propeller-cross over his grave. A damn' good fellow!' 'Corporal, another round of drinks. And hurry up for the love of Mike!' 'Dawn patrol tomorrow – don't want me to die thirsty, do you?' Danse Macabre![22]

Lieutenant Duncan Grinnell-Milne, 56 Squadron, RAF

His kaleidoscopic account conjures up that strange atmosphere in the final weeks of the war.

Whatever the likes of Grinnell-Milne may have wanted, the Armistice negotiations were underway, but there was still no real let-up in the fighting when the weather permitted. Leslie Semple took considerable pleasure in carrying out his last bombing raid on the night of 10 November.

> Raid carried out on Namur. Owing to dud engines I was late in starting and consequently bombed 1½ hours after everybody else. Very good shooting obtained, but hundreds of 'flaming onions' all around me. Gave my observer, Boshier, control on the way home. He was quite good. Went to bed at about 11pm and at 1am news came via the wireless that the Armistice had been signed and cessation of hostilities from 11am today. Beautiful news. Lighted a tin of petrol and we kicked it all round the camp. This morning we all had a jolly good drink. Sent somebody to Rouen to buy as much as possible. Have discovered that I was the last pilot to drop bombs on enemy territory during this war. Very good.[23]
>
> Lieutenant Leslie Semple, 207 Squadron, ARF

It was all over at last, with the start of the Armistice at 11.00 am on 11 November 1918. Did they celebrate? What do you think?

> We were all sitting in the anteroom when somebody said they were ringing bells and blowing sirens in the town. We went outside and sure enough they were. The searchlights were swinging about all over the sky and thousands of Very lights going up from all the aerodromes and infantry and artillery people right up to the front line. We guessed what the news was and later confirmed it through our wireless. Then all the sergeants came up and proceeded to lap up our drink. Grid Caldwell brought his lot across and we had a jollification until all our drink had gone. Then we all went down to the aerodrome but all the Very lights had been fired off. Next, we trooped into Courtrai and assisted at the bonfire – even furniture was fed into it. Finally, we got to bed at 2am. Jolly good ending to the war.[24]
>
> Major Charlie Dixon, 29 Squadron, RAF

Chapter 12

At Last: the Fat Lady Sings

My brother officers said, 'Good Heavens haven't you seen enough planes come down in flames?' I said, 'Yes, but haven't you seen enough death in trenches?' That was one way of dying that was all. The real reason was I wanted to fly and with flying it would soon be over if you'd come to the end of your life. You didn't have to sleep in mud, night after night, day after day, in mud and water.[1]
  Lieutenant Thomas Rogers, 22 Squadron, RAF

And then it was all over. The airmen had flown into nerve-shredding danger in a new battle environment, high up amongst the clouds. Was it more dangerous than the trenches? Well, it all depends, as 'where' and 'when' are distinct factors to be considered. But there is no need for absolutism; it was dangerous. What was unique at the time was the contrast between the safety on the ground and the moments of excruciating terror aloft, to be caught in the sights of a swooping Fokker, with only their own split-second decisions and reactions to prevent being killed in terrible circumstances. Perhaps they would get a 'clean' death from a bullet through the head, but just as likely a crippled aircraft and nothing to look forwards to but a long fall to the welcoming arms of Mother Earth. And then there was fire – the prospect of the last moments screaming in agony as the flames scorched and melted flesh to the bone. Never was death so fervently wished for – no wonder many pilots and observers chose the last jump to eternity when their aircraft was burning. Then there was the joy of victory; the thrill of inflicting the self-same nightmare on the enemy; the meticulous counting of kills in the ultimate male competitive frenzy to be the top ace. But a few minutes later they were back on the ground, ensconced in comfortable living quarters, with the laughter and banter of the mess to look forward to. Their nerves were stretched tight and then loosened over and over again. Whatever the joys of the mess, however much they might drink or play hard in local townships, they always had dawn the next day to look forward to. Many came to dread the dawn – the symbol of rebirth, but which meant only the prospect of an imminent death from their jaundiced point of view.

Ours was a strain of a new and peculiar temper that even now is hard to analyse. In some cases, the abrupt change from the quiet of our way of life on the ground to the heat of being in a scrap in the air over the front lines, often in a matter of only a few minutes, led to a tension or strain that, I must admit, had severe effects on the nerves. Stomach ulcers became one of the hallmarks of our trade, and insomnia and nightmares sometimes made a mockery of sleep; and there were young pilots who broke under that particular strain and had to be sent home as unfit for further service at the front. They were casualties not listed as officially wounded, but they were nevertheless still casualties, and some of them were wrecked in health for the rest of their lives.[2]

Major William Sholto Douglas, 84 Squadron, RAF

Even the strongest began to suffer; if not obviously, then by the mistakes in their own carefully defined rules of survival that had kept them alive to that point. What else can explain the deaths of the likes of Edward Mannock and Manfred von Richthofen? Very different characters, but both committing elementary mistakes that contradicted every tenet they preached for survival.

Many had not considered a future after the war; they presumed they would have no future. For a while, things remained the same, as the Armistice did not end the war – that only came on 28 June 1919 with the signing of the Treaty of Versailles. For those airmen fortunate enough to have survived the Great War, there was a huge problem: what were they going to do now? The answer was obvious to some of the young men whom peace had released from the shadow of death. They would engage in stunt and low-level flying to vicariously recreate the thrill of combat. Why? Who knows – it seems to be something in the human condition.

It was silly, mad. People who had risked their lives, prayed that they lived – no sooner were they free of war then they did the most curious things in the air. Contour chasing was following the contours of the ground, going across towards a farm house and just zooming up over the top missing the chimney pots by a few feet. The cows would run with their tails stiff out behind them! The chickens would fly as though they were trying to take off going at a rate of knots running. Old ladies came to the door and shook their fists as you came along. We got amusement from that! This was sport. It struck me then that it was extraordinary what a kick one could get out of other people's uncomfortableness – these old ladies were infuriated with us – but it was rather fun.[3]

Lieutenant Thomas Rogers, 22 Squadron, RAF

After all, they were immortal – the war had proved that! What could go wrong? Quite a few found out the hard way.

One of our fairly new pilots went and brought himself to a sticky end the other day, diving on some soldiers he hit a telegraph pole when he was doing about 150mph. Jolly bad luck as he'd been right through the war with the infantry. Hedge-hopping is like drink: it's absolutely fascinating and a very hard habit to get rid of, but I hereby register a vow to stop it for at least a week.[4]

Lieutenant Yvonne Kirkpatrick, 203 Squadron, RAF

Lieutenant Leslie Sutherland managed to survive a post-war smash to write most amusingly on the base ingratitude of his favourite 'steed', which he considered had let him down by crashing.

> Personally, I've had only one favourite. It was an SE5a – No. A226, of the Royal Australian Air Force. I groomed and cared for that hussy in *deluxe* style. I spent hours and hours of my own time with her; and quite a lot of what would have been cigarette money was lavished on her appearance – varnish, metal polish, and little knick-knacks to improve her 'turn out'. Of course, I was very proud of her. But what did she do for all this loving care and attention? She bit the hand that fed her. Actually, it was more serious than that, for she broke my neck. Still, I recovered, and she did not. So there is some justice. Exit A226! But, although I never flew again, and never shall, worse luck, I have this consoling thought about A226 – I was the first and the last to fly her.[5]
> Lieutenant Leslie Sutherland, 1st Squadron, RAAF

The other thing they could do had nothing to do with flying – it was partying. One memorable shindig occurred after 206 Squadron had moved forward into Germany as part of the occupying forces. They were celebrating the imminent departure of their comrades in the Australian 4 Squadron.

> It developed into a wild party which reached its climax when the Australians decided to paint Kaiser Bill's gigantic equestrian statue, nearly opposite our mess, with white aircraft fabric dope. The Kaiser's charger, twice as large as life, was a stallion and the sculptor, with true Teutonic thoroughness had faithfully reproduced every detail of the animal's anatomy to scale. After the Aussies had finished the job, the stallion possessed zebra stripes and huge white bollocks! To crown all (literally) they borrowed our C.O.'s enamel chamber pot and wired it on top of the Kaiser's head. Like Queen Victoria, the Germans were definitely *not* amused when they beheld this ribald spectacle next morning, Furious protests were made, but the culprits were by then well on their way home. For several days afterwards the Germans had a party of charwomen with buckets of water and scrubbing brushes at work trying to clean up the statue. Alas the white dope was both water and petrol resistant and when I myself left Cologne the zebra stripes still showed up faintly despite all the efforts of the 'Seven maids with seven mops'![6]
> Second Lieutenant John Blanford, 206 Squadron, RAF

The conditions demanded to secure the Armistice had been designed to cripple the German armed forces – including the air force. Almost all their aircraft had to be handed over, leaving them nothing to fly into battle should war have resumed. Ironically, once peace had been signed, the British also set about dismantling the RAF, trimming it down to the very bone, amidst serious questions as to whether it should continue to exist as a separate service. The cuts left very few openings for officers and men who wanted to continue flying. Like it or not, most men would be returned to civilian life.

What on earth am I going to do? I certainly don't want to go to Oxford, or Cambridge, or any other place like that. In the first place it'll take them years to get those places going again, after all the cadet schools have cleared out. Two years ago, I'd have enjoyed that sort of life, but now I'm afraid it would bore me stiff. I don't want to learn Latin or any of those funny sorts of things again. I don't enjoy playing games so much that I should want to play football all day. I really haven't the foggiest idea what I do want to do and I haven't met anybody else out here who does.[7]

Lieutenant Yvonne Kirkpatrick, 203 Squadron, RAF

In sharp contrast, many more did not mind this severance from the world of aviation. Ewart Garland had done his bit, latterly with 104 Squadron of the Independent Force, and as far as he was concerned that was it – even when he was lucky enough to be offered the rare chance to stay in the RAF.

I refused a permanent commission immediately after the Armistice and never piloted an aeroplane again as long as I lived. Strangely enough, I lost interest completely the moment the war was over.[8]

Ewart Garland

Some hoped to gain work with the civil aviation airlines that were being set up all over the world, often using adaptations of bombers such as the Handley Page O/400. But again, there were very few vacancies – and thousands upon thousands of former pilots. If they wanted to fly, it seemed they would have to buy their own aircraft. This was not as difficult as it may seem, as the RAF were selling thousands of aircraft at knockdown prices. On a whim, Philip Townsend and another pilot chum both decided to purchase an aircraft when they attended a surplus sale at Hendon airfield.

We both thought it would be lovely to buy an SE5a, which were on sale for £5. We agreed to the price: he bought one; I bought one. We had them filled up with petrol and oil, tested them there and then for engine efficiency against the chocks, then took our aircraft up and flew around Hendon for about half an hour. We landed within 5 minutes of one another, stopped out props, climbed out and shouted to one another in joy at having enjoyed such a wonderful flight.[9]

Philip Townsend

What fun lay ahead of them. Or did it? All they had to do now was find somewhere to permanently keep the aircraft and someone willing to act as their ground crew; all that without a private income. Flying was still a rich man's game without the backing of the RAF.

> Both of us became very dejected at having to realise that we couldn't possibly afford them. We'd no hangar, no reason to believe that we had any place at home where we could even house the aircraft. So we talked to the air mechanics and we agreed to sell them back for £4-10s. It took us I should think half an hour in silent tears to walk away from Hendon aerodrome realising that we had been defeated in our objective of being civil flyers.[10]
> Philip Townsend

Many would return to the RAF in the Second World War, but by then they were often employed in an administrative capacity. War in the air was a young man's game – their time was done.

* * *

How did they cope? This is a question we have tried to answer, using the words of the men who were there. There was little to laugh at in the skies, although some still managed it, with a dark humour acting as a veneer to their doomed youth. But on the ground, it was very different. Here, they sought to forget the dawn patrol in laughter, in boozing and occasionally – whisper it – in fornication. Did it work? The honest answer is, not really. It may have helped for a while, but the pressures usually got the better of them in the end. However, it is their defiance that this book celebrates. And what better than an adaptation of a long-standing Great War masterpiece, egregiously claimed as his philosophy by William Johns, but extant in various versions long before he arrived at the front. Whoever the writer was, it sums up our message perfectly.

Philosophy

> Of two things, one thing is certain:
> Either you are on the ground or in the air,
> If you are on the ground there is no need to worry.
>
> If you are in the air, one of two things is certain:
> Either you are flying straight or you are turning over,
> If you are flying straight there is no need to worry.
>
> If you are turning over, one of two things is certain:
> Either you will crash or you will not crash,
> If you do not crash there is no need to worry.

If you do not crash, one of two things is certain:
Either you will be injured or you will not be injured,
If you are not injured there is no need to worry.

If you are injured, one of two things is certain:
Either you will recover or you will die,
If you recover there is no need to worry,
If you die you CAN'T worry![11]

2nd Lieutenant William Johns, 55 Squadron,
Independent Force

Acknowledgements

We would like to thank everyone who made this book possible. Our primary sources originate in the hard work of other people, not least the dedicated staff at the Imperial War Museum who preserved the interviews and documents at the heart of the book. We would particularly thank David Lance, Margaret Brooks, Rod Suddaby and Anthony Richards. Thanks also to the veterans who published their memories in books. We attach below a list of those books that we trawled through to greatest effect and which we urge every one of you to buy – they are fantastic. But our bible has been *The Sky Their Battlefield II: Air Fighting and Air Casualties of the Great War* by Trevor Henshaw. As a resource this is beyond brilliant, and without it we would have been lost. Hence, we are honoured that he has contributed a preface for us, checked the text and provided the majority of the photographs, he is a great friend to both of us. As young people used to say, 'We are not worthy!' We have had a wonderful team at Pen & Sword, and we would thank Tara Moran, our fabulous editor Harriet Fielding and our hard-working copy-editor Tony Walton. Special thanks to our indexing guru David Atlkinson. Our chums John Gilder, John Paylor (the Old Reliable) and Warren Smith were kind enough to check early versions of the manuscript. They are all lovely. And so are you for buying this book!

Highly Recommended Books

Balfour, Harold, *An Airman Marches* (London: Hutchinson & Co, 1933)

Baring, Maurice, *Flying Corps Headquarters 1914–1918* (Edinburgh & London: William Blackwood & Sons, 1968)

Beresford Ellis, Peter & Schofield, Jennifer, *Biggles! The Life Story of Capt. W.E. Johns* (Dorset: Veloce Publishing PLC, 1993)

Bott, Alan, *Cavalry of the Clouds* (New York: Arno Press, 1972)

Burge, Cyril, *The Annals of 100 Squadron* (London: Herbert Reiach Ltd, 1919)

Douglas, William Sholto, *Years of Combat* (London: Collins, 1963)

Fry, William, *Air of Battle* (London: William Kimber, 1974)

Grinnell-Milne, Duncan, *Wind in the Wires* (London: Grub Street, 2014)

Hawker, Tyrell, *Hawker V.C.* (London: The Mitre Press, 1965)

Henshaw, Trevor, *The Aircraft Manufacturing Company De Haviland D.H2 and the Men who Flew Them* (The Great War Aviation Society Monograph Series)

Henshaw, Trevor, *The Sky Their Battlefield II: Air Fighting and Air Casualties of the Great War* (London: Fetubi Books, 2014)

Lee, Arthur Gould, *No Parachute: A Fighter Pilot in World War 1* (London: The Adventurers' Club, 1969)

Lorraine, Winifred, *Robert Lorraine: Actor – Soldier – Airman* (London: Collins, 1938)

Jones, Ira, *King of Air Fighters* (London: Ivor Nicholson & Watson Limited, 1935)

Langham, Rob, *Bloody Paralyser: The Giant Handley Page Bombers of the First World War* (Croydon: Fonthill, 2016)

Lewis, Cecil, *Sagittarius Rising* (London: Greenhill Books, Lionel Leventhal Limited, 1993)

McCudden, James, *Flying Fury: Five Years in the Royal Flying Corps* (London: Aeroplane and General, 1918)

Mackersey, Ian, *No Empty Chairs* (London: Phoenix, The Orion Publishing Group Limited, 2013)

Money, Raymond, *Flying and Soldiering* (London: Nicholson & Watson, 1936)

Oughton, Frederick, *The Personal Diary of 'Mick' Mannock* (London: Neville Spearman, 1966)

Revell, Alex, *Brief Glory: The Life of Arthur Rhys Davids* (London: William Kimber, 1984)

Revell, Alex, *High in the Empty Blue: The History of 56 Squadron, RFC, RAF, 1916–1919* (Mountain View, CA: Flying Machines Press, 1995)

Strange, Louis, *Recollections of an Airman* (London: The Aviation Book Club, 1940)

Taylor, G., *Sopwith Scout 7309* (London: Cassell & Company Limited, 1968)

If you buy each and every one of these books, you will have the start of a marvellous Great War aviation collection – the rest is up to you. Follow your interests! Books are cheaper in the long run than wine, women and song!

Notes

Preface

1. R.R. Money, *Flying and Soldiering* (London: Nicholson & Watson, 1936), p.9.
2. IWM DOCS: H. Taylor, Typescript memoir, p.11.
3. A.S.G. Lee, *No Parachute: A Fighter Pilot in World War 1* (London: The Adventurers' Club, 1969), p.xvii.
4. I. Jones, *An Air Fighter's Scrapbook* (London: Greenhill Books, 1990), p.45.
5. R.J.O. Compston, quoted in *Naval Eight: A History of No. 8 (Naval) Squadron, RNAS* (London: Signal Press Ltd, 1931), p.96.
6. IWM SOUND: C. Lewis, AC 004162, Reel 1.
7. I. Mackersey, *No Empty Chairs* (London: Phoenix, The Orion Publishing Group Limited, 2013), p.186.

Chapter 1

1. B. Dickson, quoted by E. & J. Lawson, *The First Air Campaign, August 1914 – November 1918* (Conshohocken, P.A.: Combined Books Inc,1966), pp.21–22. Bertram Dickson said this in about 1912 – amazing prescience.
2. R. Miller, *Boom, The Life of Viscount Trenchard, Founder of the Royal Air Force* (London: Weidenfeld & Nicolson, 2016), p.80.
3. E. & J. Lawson, *The First Air Campaign, August 1914 – November 1918* (Conshohocken, P.A.: Combined Books Inc, 1966), p.31.
4. R. Miller, *Boom, The Life of Viscount Trenchard, Founder of the Royal Air Force* (London: Weidenfeld & Nicolson, 2016), p.84.
5. D. Henderson, quoted by W. Raleigh, *The War in the Air, Volume I* (Oxford: The Clarendon Press, 1922), p.202.
6. H.R.P. Reynolds, quoted by W. Raleigh, *The War in the Air, Volume I* (Oxford: The Clarendon Press, 1922), pp.194–95.
7. J. Grierson, quoted by W. Raleigh, *The War in the Air*, Volume I (Oxford: The Clarendon Press, 1922), p. 226.
8. IWM SOUND: E.J. Furlong, AC 00015, Reel 2.
9. IWM SOUND: E.J. Furlong, AC 00015, Reel 2.
10. W. Raleigh, *The War in the Air, Volume I* (Oxford: Clarendon Press, 1922), pp.128–29.
11. W. Raleigh, *The War in the Air, Volume I* (Oxford: Clarendon Press, 1922), p.129.
12. L. Strange, *Recollections of an Airman* (London: The Aviation Book Club, 1940), p.15.
13. L. Strange, *Recollections of an Airman* (London: The Aviation Book Club, 1940), p.20.
14. IWM SOUND: D.W. Clappen, AC 00009, Reel 1.
15. IWM SOUND: D.W. Clappen, AC 00009, Reel 2.
16. IWM SOUND: D.W. Clappen, AC 00009, Reel 1.
17. IWM SOUND: G. Donald, AC 00018, Reel 1.
18. IWM SOUND: G. Donald, AC 00018, Reel 1.
19. IWM SOUND: C. King, AC 00027, Reel 3 & 4.

20. IWM SOUND: C. King, AC 00027, Reel 4.
21. IWM SOUND: C. King, AC 00027, Reel 3.
22. IWM SOUND: C. King, AC 00027, Reel 3.
23. R. Miller, *Boom, The Life of Viscount Trenchard, Founder of the Royal Air Force* (London: Weidenfeld & Nicolson, 2016), p.95.

Chapter 2

1. IWM SOUND: S.S. Saunders, AC 00292, Reel 6.
2. L. Strange, *Recollections of an Airman* (London: The Aviation Book Club, 1940), pp.35–36.
3. IWM SOUND: J. Gascoyne, AC 00016, Reel 1.
4. IWM SOUND: E. Bolt, AC 00003, Reel 6.
5. IWM SOUND: J. Gascoyne, AC 00016, Reel 1.
6. P.B. Joubert de la Ferté, quoted by W. Raleigh, *The War in the Air, Volume I* (Oxford: The Clarendon Press, 1922), pp.293–94.
7. IWM SOUND: C.E.C. Rabagliati, AC 04208, Reel 1.
8. IWM SOUND: C.E.C. Rabagliati, AC 04208, Reel 1.
9. L. Strange, *Recollections of an Airman* (London: The Aviation Book Club, 1940), p. 43.
10. M. Baring, *Flying Corps Headquarters 1914–1918* (Edinburgh & London: William Blackwood & Sons, 1968), p.34.
11. IWM SOUND: J. Gascoyne, AC 00016, Reel 1.
12. L. Strange, *Recollections of an Airman* (London: The Aviation Book Club, 1940), pp.49–50.
13. M. Baring, *Flying Corps Headquarters 1914–1918* (Edinburgh & London: William Blackwood & Sons, 1968), pp.34–35.
14. P.B. Joubert de la Ferté, quoted by W. Raleigh, *The War in the Air, Volume I* (Oxford: The Clarendon Press, 1922), p.325.
15. L. Strange, *Recollections of an Airman* (London: The Aviation Book Club, 1940), pp.54–55.
16. R. Lorraine, quoted by W. Lorraine, *Robert Lorraine: Actor–Soldier–Airman* (London: Collins, 1938), pp.185–86.
17. J.T.B. McCudden, *Flying Fury: Five Years in the Royal Flying Corps* (London: Aeroplane and General, 1918), p.35.
18. R. Lorraine, quoted by W. Lorraine, *Robert Lorraine: Actor–Soldier–Airman* (London: Collins, 1938), p.186.
19. IWM DOCS: W. Read, Transcript diary, 30/9/1914.
20. Internet source: http://monologues.co.uk/George_Robey/Archibald_Certainly_Not.htm.
21. G.H. Raleigh, quoted by W. Raleigh, *The War in the Air, Volume I* (Oxford: The Clarendon Press, 1922), p.348.
22. L. Hawker, quoted by T. Hawker, *Hawker V.C.* (London: The Mitre Press, 1965), p.51.
23. D. Corbett Wilson, quoted by D. MacCarron, *Letters from an Early Bird: The Life and Letters of Denys Corbett Wilson, 1882–1915* (Barnsley: Pen & Sword Aviation, 2006), p.99.
24. IWM SOUND: S.S. Saunders, AC 00292, Reel 9.
25. IWM SOUND: C. King, AC 00027, Reel 6.
26. IWM SOUND: C.E.C. Rabagliati, AC 04208, Reel 1.
27. IWM SOUND: C.E.C. Rabagliati, AC 04208, Reel 1.
28. IWM SOUND: C.E.C. Rabagliati, AC 04208, Reel 1.
29. L. Hawker, quoted by T. Hawker, *Hawker V.C.* (London: The Mitre Press, 1965), p.52.
30. M. Baring, *Flying Corps Headquarters 1914–1918* (Edinburgh & London: William Blackwood & Sons, 1968), p.51.

31. C.R. Samson, *Fights and Flights* (Nashville: The Battery Press, 1990), pp.184–85.
32. Internet source: C.J. Burke, quoted https://rafmontrose.org.uk/wp-content/uploads/2016/03/Maxims1700.jpg.
33. R. Miller, *Boom, The Life of Viscount Trenchard, Founder of the Royal Air Force* (London: Weidenfeld & Nicolson, 2016), p.104.
34. W. Raleigh, *The War in the Air, Volume I* (Oxford: Clarendon Press, 1922), p.111
35. I. Mackersey, *No Empty Chairs* (London: Phoenix, The Orion Publishing Group Limited, 2013), p.62.
36. R.R. Money, *Flying and Soldiering* (London: Ivor Nicholson & Watson, 1936), p.9.
37. S. Douglas, *Years of Combat* (London, Collins, 1963), pp. 56–57, & I. Mackersey, *No Empty Chairs* (London: Phoenix, The Orion Publishing Group Limited, 2013), p.30.
38. IWM SOUND: A. Harris, AC 3765, Reel 1.
39. A.R. Kingsford, *Night Raiders of the Air* (London: Greenhill Books Limited, 1988), pp.15–17.
40. I. Jones, *King of Air Fighters* (London: Ivor Nicholson & Watson Limited, 1935), p.27.
41. G. Taylor, *Sopwith Scout 7309* (London: Cassell & Company Limited, 1968), p.15.
42. A. Rhys Davids, quoted by A. Revell, *Brief Glory: The Life of Arthur Rhys Davids* (London: William Kimber, 1984), p.68.
43. W.M. Fry, *Air of Battle* (London: William Kimber, 1974), pp.37–39.
44. D. Grinnell-Milne, *Wind in the Wires* (London: Grub Street, 2014), p.12.
45. C. Lewis, *Farewell to Wings* (London: Temple Press, 1964), p.2.
46. D. Grinnell-Milne, *Wind in the Wires* (London: Grub Street, 2014), p.13.
47. RAF Museum: J.C.F. Wilkinson, Typescript memoir, pp.195–97.
48. RAF Museum: J.C.F. Wilkinson, Typescript memoir, pp.198–99.
49. IWM SOUND: F.J. Powell, AC 00087, Reel 1.
50. D. Grinnell-Milne, *Wind in the Wires* (London: Grub Street, 2014), pp.15–16.
51. F. Chapman, quoted by J. Dudgeon, *Mick: The Story of Major Edward Mannock* (London: Robert Hale, 1993), p.54.
52. A.G. Graves, quoted by N. Franks & A. Saunders, *Mannock: The Life and Death of Major Edward Mannock* (London: Grub Street, 2008), pp.19–20.
53. IWM DOCS: T.C. Traill, Typescript account, p.41.
54. IWM SOUND: F.J. Powell, AC 00087, Reel 4.
55. H.H. Balfour, *An Airman Marches* (London: Hutchinson & Co, 1933), pp.34–35.
56. D. Grinnell-Milne, *Wind in the Wires* (London: Grub Street, 2014), pp.24–25.
57. D. Grinnell-Milne, *Wind in the Wires* (London: Grub Street, 2014), pp.25–27.
58. J. Brophy, *A Rattle of Pebbles: The First World War Diaries of Two Canadian Airmen* (Ottawa: Publishing Service, Canada, 1987), pp.25–26.
59. D. Grinnell-Milne, *Wind in the Wires* (London: Grub Street, 2014), pp.38–39.
60. W.M. Fry, *Air of Battle* (London: William Kimber, 1974), p.43.
61. IWM SOUND: G. Donald, AC 00018, Reel 3.
62. H.H. Balfour, *An Airman Marches* (London: Hutchinson & Co, 1933), p.31.
63. IWM SOUND: J.C.F. Hopkins, AC 00021, Reel 1.
64. S. Douglas, *Years of Combat* (London: Collins, 1963), p.88.
65. IWM SOUND: C.J. Chabot, AC 00008, Reel 4.
66. Internet source: C.J. Burke, quoted https://rafmontrose.org.uk/wp-content/uploads/2016/03/Maxims1700.jpg.
67. IWM SOUND: C.N.H. Bilney, AC 00002, Reel 5.
68. C. Bowyer, *Albert Ball, VC* (Wrexham: Bridge Books, 1994), p.35.

69. R.R. Money, *Flying and Soldiering* (London: Ivor Nicholson & Watson, 1936), pp.15–16.
70. A. Rhys Davids, quoted by A. Revell, *Brief Glory: The Life of Arthur Rhys Davids* (London: William Kimber, 1984), pp.74–75.
71. D. Grinnell-Milne, *Wind in the Wires* (London: Grub Street, 2014), pp.17–18.
72. R.R. Money, *Flying and Soldiering* (London: Ivor Nicholson & Watson, 1936), p.10.
73. RAF Museum: J.C.F. Wilkinson, Typescript memoir, pp.174–75.
74. A.J. Insall, *Observer: Memoirs of the RFC, 1915–1918* (London: William Kimber, 1970), p.44.
75. Ira Jones, *Tiger Squadron* (London: White Lion, 1972), p.36.
76. IWM SOUND: F.J. Powell, AC 00087, Reel 2.
77. H.H. Balfour, *An Airman Marches* (London: Hutchinson & Co, 1933), p.38.

Chapter 3
1. I. Mackersey, *No Empty Chairs* (London: Phoenix, The Orion Publishing Group Limited, 2013), p.30.
2. IWM SOUND: A. James, AC 00024, Reel 2.
3. S. Douglas, *Years of Combat* (London, Collins, 1963), pp.75–76.
4. D.S. Lewis, quoted by H.A. Jones, *The War in the Air, Volume II* (Oxford: Clarendon Press, 1928), p.86.
5. H. Trenchard, quoted by A. Boyle, *Trenchard: Man of Vision* (London: Collins, 1962), p.128.
6. W. Sholto Douglas, quoted by H.A. Jones, *The War in the Air, Volume II* (Oxford: Clarendon Press, 1928), p.137.
7. M. Baring, *Flying Corps Headquarters 1914–1918* (Edinburgh & London: William Blackwood & Sons, 1968), p.138.
8. L. Hawker, quoted by T. Hawker, *Hawker V.C.* (London: The Mitre Press, 1965), p.85.
9. D. Corbett Wilson, quoted by D. MacCarron, *Letters from an Early Bird: The Life & Letters of Denys Corbett Wilson* (Barnsley: Pen & Sword Aviation, 2006), pp.161–63.
10. L. Strange, *Recollections of an Airman* (London: The Aviation Book Club, 1940), pp.112–15.
11. IWM SOUND: A. James, AC 00024, Reel 5.
12. M. Baring, *Flying Corps Headquarters 1914–1918* (Edinburgh & London: William Blackwood & Sons, 1968), pp.105–06.
13. H. Trenchard, quoted by A. Boyle, *Trenchard* (London: Collins, 1962), p.199.
14. M. Baring, *Flying Corps Headquarters 1914–1918* (Edinburgh & London: William Blackwood & Sons, 1968), p.xvi.
15. T. Hawker, *Hawker V.C.* (London: The Mitre Press, 1965), p.109.
16. R.R. Money, *Flying and Soldiering* (London: Ivor Nicholson & Watson, 1936), pp.18–19.
17. R.R. Money, *Flying and Soldiering* (London: Ivor Nicholson & Watson, 1936), p.20.
18. R.R. Money, *Flying and Soldiering* (London: Ivor Nicholson & Watson, 1936), pp.35–36.
19. R.R. Money, *Flying and Soldiering* (London: Ivor Nicholson & Watson, 1936), pp.22–23.
20. R.R. Money, *Flying and Soldiering* (London: Ivor Nicholson & Watson, 1936), p.27.
21. R.R. Money, *Flying and Soldiering* (London: Ivor Nicholson & Watson, 1936), pp.30–31.
22. L. Strange, *Recollections of an Airman* (London: The Aviation Book Club, 1940), pp.127–28.
23. L. Strange, *Recollections of an Airman* (London: The Aviation Book Club, 1940), p.130.
24. L. Strange, *Recollections of an Airman* (London: The Aviation Book Club, 1940), pp.127–28.
25. R.R. Money, *Flying and Soldiering* (London: Ivor Nicholson & Watson, 1936), pp.33–34.
26. D. Grinnell-Milne, *Wind in the Wires* (London: Grub Street, 2014), p.52.
27. D. Grinnell-Milne, *Wind in the Wires* (London: Grub Street, 2014), p.69.

28. M. Immelmann, quoted by F. Immelmann, *Immelmann: The Eagle of Lille* (London: Heinemann, 1935), p.109.
29. Ira Jones, *Tiger Squadron* (London: White Lion, 1972), p.38.
30. IWM SOUND: F.J. Powell, AC 00087, Reel 3.
31. IWM SOUND: F.J. Powell, AC 00087, Reel 3.
32. R. Lorraine, quoted by W. Lorraine, *Robert Lorraine: Actor–Soldier–Airman* (London: Collins, 1938), pp.213–14.
33. E. Lubbock, quoted by W. Lorraine, *Robert Lorraine: Actor–Soldier–Airman* (London: Collins, 1938), pp.211–12.
34. R. Lorraine, quoted by W. Lorraine, *Robert Lorraine: Actor–Soldier–Airman* (London: Collins, 1938), pp.213–14.
35. E. Lubbock, quoted by W. Lorraine, *Robert Lorraine: Actor–Soldier–Airman* (London: Collins, 1938), pp.211–12.
36. E. Lubbock, quoted by W. Lorraine, *Robert Lorraine: Actor–Soldier–Airman* (London: Collins, 1938), pp.211–12.
37. R. Lorraine, quoted by W. Lorraine, *Robert Lorraine: Actor–Soldier–Airman* (London: Collins, 1938), pp.213–14.
38. IWM SOUND: A. James, AC 00024, Reel 8 & 10.
39. F.J. Powell quoted by W. Lorraine, *Robert Lorraine: Actor–Soldier–Airman* (London: Collins, 1938), p.220.
40. IWM SOUND: F.J. Powell, AC 00087, Reel 4.
41. IWM SOUND: F.J. Powell, AC 00087, Reel 2.
42. IWM SOUND: S.S. Saunders, AC 00292, Reel 6.
43. A character from the situation comedy *Only Fools and Horses*.
44. J. McCudden, *Flying Fury, Five Years in the Royal Flying Corps* (Folkstone: Bailey Brothers and Swinfen Limited, 1973), p.78.
45. D. Grinnell-Milne, *Wind in the Wires* (London: Grub Street, 2014), p.123.

Chapter 4

1. S. Douglas, *Years of Combat* (London: Collins, 1963), p.124.
2. IWM DOCS: T. Hughes, Transcript diary, 1/5/1916.
3. R.R. Money, *Flying and Soldiering* (London: Ivor Nicholson & Watson, 1936), pp.51–52.
4. IWM SOUND: A.B. Yuille, AC 00320, Reel 1.
5. T.M. Hawker, *Hawker VC* (London: The Mitre Press, 1965), p.182.
6. L. Rees, quoted by W.A. Williams, *Against the Odds: The Life of Group Captain Lionel Rees* (Wrexham: Bridge Books, 1989), p.63.
7. C. Lewis, *Sagittarius Rising* (London: Greenhill Books, Lionel Leventhal Limited, 1993), p.101.
8. C. Lewis, *Sagittarius Rising* (London: Greenhill Books, Lionel Leventhal Limited, 1993), p.104.
9. J. Brophy, *A Rattle of Pebbles: The First World War Diaries of Two Canadian Airmen* (Ottawa: Publishing Service, Canada, 1987), p.85.
10. L. Rees, quoted by W.A. Williams, *Against the Odds: The Life of Group Captain Lionel Rees* (Wrexham: Bridge Books, 1989), p.92.
11. G. Lewis, quoted by W.A. Williams, *Against the Odds: The Life of Group Captain Lionel Rees* (Wrexham: Bridge Books, 1989), p.92.
12. A. Bott, *Cavalry of the Clouds* (New York: Arno Press, 1972), pp.228–29.
13. A. Bott, *Cavalry of the Clouds* (New York: Arno Press, 1972), p.56.

14. A. Bott, *Cavalry of the Clouds* (New York: Arno Press, 1972), pp.vii–viii.
15. W.M. Fry, *Air of Battle* (London: William Kimber, 1974), pp.62–63.
16. J. Brophy, *A Rattle of Pebbles: The First World War Diaries of Two Canadian Airmen* (Ottawa: Publishing Service, Canada, 1987), pp.89–90.
17. IWM DOCS: A.M. Wilkinson, Typescript memoir, 'The Somme Battle'.
18. A. Ball, quoted by W.A. Briscoe and H. Russell Stannard, *Captain Ball VC* (London: Herbert Jenkins Ltd, 1918), pp.179–80.
19. A. Ball quoted by W. A. Briscoe and H. Russell Stannard, *Captain Ball VC* (London: Herbert Jenkins Ltd, 1918), pp.178, 184.
20. A. Ball, quoted by W.A. Briscoe and H. Russell Stannard, *Captain Ball VC* (London: Herbert Jenkins Ltd, 1918), p.185.
21. I. Mackersey, *No Empty Chairs* (London: Phoenix, The Orion Publishing Group Limited, 2013), p.31.
22. IWM DOCS: L. Horridge, Manuscript letter, 7/8/1916.
23. IWM DOCS: E. Garland, Typescript diary, 26/7/1916.
24. A. Bott, *Cavalry of the Clouds* (New York: Arno Press, 1972), pp.190–91.
25. R.R. Money, *Flying and Soldiering* (London: Ivor Nicholson & Watson, 1936), pp.84–85.
26. C. Lewis, *Sagittarius Rising* (London: Greenhill Books, Lionel Leventhal Limited, 1993), pp.87–88.
27. C. Lewis, *Sagittarius Rising* (London: Greenhill Books, Lionel Leventhal Limited, 1993), p.89.
28. C. Lewis, *Sagittarius Rising* (London: Greenhill Books, Lionel Leventhal Limited, 1993), pp.89–90.
29. C. Lewis, *Sagittarius Rising* (London: Greenhill Books, Lionel Leventhal Limited, 1993), pp.146–47.
30. IWM SOUND: F.J. Powell, AC 00087, Reel 4.
31. IWM SOUND: F.J. Powell, AC 00087, Reel 6.
32. IWM SOUND: F.J. Powell, AC 00087, Reel 6.
33. IWM SOUND: F.J. Powell, AC 00087, Reel 5 & 6.
34. H.H. Balfour, quoted by A.J. Scott, *Sixty Squadron RAF: A History of the Squadron, 1916–1919* (London: Greenhill Books, 1990), pp.11–12.
35. H.H. Balfour, *An Airman Marches* (London: Hutchinson & Co, 1933), p.46.
36. H.H. Balfour, *An Airman Marches* (London: Hutchinson & Co, 1933), p.47.
37. H.H. Balfour, *An Airman Marches* (London: Hutchison & Co, 1933), p.59.
38. J. Brophy, *A Rattle of Pebbles: The First World War Diaries of Two Canadian Airmen* (Ottawa: Publishing Service, Canada, 1987), pp.93–94.
39. A. Bott, *Cavalry of the Clouds* (New York: Arno Press, 1972), pp.57–65.
40. A. Bott, *Cavalry of the Clouds* (New York: Arno Press, 1972), pp.57–65.
41. A. Bott, *Cavalry of the Clouds* (New York: Arno Press, 1972), pp.57–65.
42. A. Bott, *Cavalry of the Clouds* (New York: Arno Press, 1972), pp.57–65.
43. A. Bott, *Cavalry of the Clouds* (New York: Arno Press, 1972), pp.57–65.
44. A. Bott, *Cavalry of the Clouds* (New York: Arno Press, 1972), pp.57–65.
45. A. Bott, *Cavalry of the Clouds* (New York: Arno Press, 1972), pp.57–65.
46. A. Bott, *Cavalry of the Clouds* (New York: Arno Press, 1972), pp.57–65.
47. A. Bott, *Cavalry of the Clouds* (New York: Arno Press, 1972), pp.39–40.
48. R.R. Money, *Flying and Soldiering* (London: Ivor Nicholson & Watson, 1936), pp.101–04.
49. E. Lewis, quoted by T. Henshaw, *The Aircraft Manufacturing Company De Haviland D.H2 and the Men who Flew Them* (The Great War Aviation Society Monograph Series), pp.86–88.

50. A. Ball, quoted by C. Bowyer, *Albert Ball, VC* (Wrexham: Bridge Books, 1994), pp.97–99.
51. A. Ball, quoted by C. Bowyer, *Albert Ball, VC* (Wrexham: Bridge Books, 2nd edn, 1994), p.91.
52. C. Bowyer, *Albert Ball, VC* (Wrexham: Bridge Books, 1994), pp.79–81.
53. IWM DOCS: Quinell Papers, 83/17/1.
54. W.M. Fry, *Air of Battle* (London: William Kimber, 1974), pp.81–82.
55. W.M. Fry, *Air of Battle* (London: William Kimber, 1974), pp.91–92.
56. W.M. Fry, *Air of Battle* (London: William Kimber, 1974), pp.64–65.
57. J. Brophy, *A Rattle of Pebbles: The First World War Diaries of Two Canadian Airmen* (Ottawa: Publishing Service, Canada, 1987), p.134.
58. C. Lewis, *Sagittarius Rising* (London: Greenhill Books, Lionel Leventhal Limited, 1993), p.154.
59. RAF Museum: W.J. Lidsey, Typescript diary, 25/12/1916.

Chapter 5
1. RAF Museum: F. Ortweiler, Manuscript diary, 13/4/1917.
2. G. Taylor, *Sopwith Scout 7309* (London: Cassell & Company Limited, 1968), p.19.
3. R.J. Brownell, *From Khaki to Blue* (Canberra: The Military Historical Society of Australia, 1978), p.138
4. G. Taylor, *Sopwith Scout 7309* (London: Cassell & Company Limited, 1968), pp.21–22.
5. A.R. Kingsford, *Night Raiders of the Air* (London: Greenhill Books Limited, 1988), pp.56–57.
6. IWM SOUND: S.S. Saunders, AC 00292, Reel 9.
7. P. Berresford Ellis & J Schofield, *Biggles! The Life Story of Capt. W.E. Johns* (Dorset: Veloce Publishing PLC, 1993), pp.35–37.
8. P. Berresford Ellis & J Schofield, *Biggles! The Life Story of Capt. W.E. Johns* (Dorset: Veloce Publishing PLC, 1993), pp.35–37.
9. P. Berresford Ellis & J Schofield, *Biggles! The Life Story of Capt. W.E. Johns* (Dorset: Veloce Publishing PLC, 1993), pp.35–37.
10. P. Berresford Ellis & J Schofield, *Biggles! The Life Story of Capt. W.E. Johns* (Dorset: Veloce Publishing PLC, 1993), pp.35–37.
11. H. Price, *A Rattle of Pebbles: The First World War Diaries of Two Canadian Airmen* (Ottawa: Publishing Service, Canada, 1987), pp.193–94.
12. H. Price, *A Rattle of Pebbles: The First World War Diaries of Two Canadian Airmen* (Ottawa: Publishing Service, Canada, 1987), p.204.
13. R.J. Brownell, *From Khaki to Blue* (Canberra: The Military Historical Society of Australia, 1978), p.138.
14. H. Balfour, quoted by F.D. Tredrey, *Pioneer Pilot* (London: Peter Davies Limited, 1976), p.88.
15. H.H. Balfour, *An Airman Marches* (London: Hutchinson & Co, 1933), p.113–14.
16. RAF Museum: J.C.F. Wilkinson, Typescript memoir, pp.191–92.
17. IWM SOUND: H. Andrews, AC 00984, Reel 1.
18. P. Berresford Ellis & J Schofield, *Biggles! The Life Story of Capt. W.E. Johns* (Dorset: Veloce Publishing PLC, 1993), p.37.
19. L.H. Rochford, *I Chose the Sky* (London: William Kimber, 1977), pp.133–34.
20. IWM SOUND: F.J. Powell, AC 00087, Reel 8.
21. G.M. Knocker (edited by C.M. Burgess), *The Diary and Letters of a World War One Fighter Pilot* (Barnsley: Pen & Sword Aviation, 2008), p.36.

Chapter 6

1. H.H. Balfour, *An Airman Marches* (London: Hutchinson & Co, 1933), p.70.
2. S. Douglas, *Years of Combat* (London: Collins, 1963), p.161.
3. H.H. Balfour, *An Airman Marches* (London: Hutchinson & Co, 1933), pp.70–71.
4. H.H. Balfour, *An Airman Marches* (London: Hutchinson & Co, 1933), pp.71–72.
5. S. Douglas, *Years of Combat* (London: Collins, 1963), pp.165–66.
6. G.M. Hopkins, quoted by B.J. Gray, 'Pusher Pilot with 22', *Cross & Cockade*, Vol. 3, No. 2, pp.48–49.
7. NATIONAL ARCHIVE: AIR 1/2386/228/11/21, D.F. Stevenson.
8. F.T. Courtney, *Flight Path: My Fifty Years of Aviation* (London: William Kimber, 1973), pp.102–03.
9. N. MacMillan, *Into the Blue* (London: Duckworth, 1929), pp.50–51.
10. IWM DOCS: N. MacMillan papers, including transcribed notes of Frank Courtney.
11. N. MacMillan, *Into the Blue* (London: Duckworth, 1929), p.46.
12. M. von Richthofen, quoted by F. Gibbons, *The Red Knight of Germany* (New York: Garden City Publishing Co. Inc, 1927), p.180.
13. RAF Museum: C.D. Smart, Manuscript diary, 9/4/1917.
14. H.H. Balfour, *An Airman Marches* (London: Hutchinson & Co, 1933), pp.76–77.
15. H.H. Balfour, *An Airman Marches* (London: Hutchinson & Co, 1933), p.80.
16. H.H. Balfour, *An Airman Marches* (London: Hutchinson & Co, 1933), p.80.
17. H.H. Balfour, *An Airman Marches* (London: Hutchinson & Co, 1933), pp.90–92.
18. H.H. Balfour, *An Airman Marches* (London: Hutchinson & Co, 1933), p.93.
19. RAF Museum: A.S.W. Dore, Transcript diary, 1/5/1917.
20. M. von Richthofen, *The Red Air Fighter* (London: Greenhill Books, 1990), pp.119–20.
21. W.B. Wood, quoted by Jack Wales, 'Ace from 29: Lieutenant W.B. Wood MC', *Cross & Cockade*, Vol. 2, No. 1, p.11.
22. A. Ball, quoted by W.A. Briscoe & H.R. Stannard, *Captain Ball VC of the Royal Flying Corps* (London: Herbert Jenkins Ltd, 1918), p.239.
23. A. Rhys Davids, quoted by A. Revell, *Brief Glory: The Life of Arthur Rhys Davids* (London: William Kimber, 1984), p.89.
24. F. Oughton, *The Personal Diary of 'Mick' Mannock* (London: Neville Spearman, 1966), pp.45–47.
25. S. Douglas, *Years of Combat* (London: Collins, 1963), pp.200–01.
26. W. Bovett, quoted by F. Oughton, *The Personal Diary of 'Mick' Mannock* (London: Neville Spearman, 1966), p.153.
27. D. De Burgh, quoted by F. Oughton, *The Personal Diary of 'Mick' Mannock* (London: Neville Spearman, 1966), p.49.
28. F. Oughton, *The Personal Diary of 'Mick' Mannock* (London: Neville Spearman, 1966), p.47.
29. G.I. Lloyd, quoted by N. Franks & A. Saunders, *Mannock: The Life and Death of Major Edward Mannock* (London: Grub Street, 2008). p.28.
30. E. Mannock, quoted by N. Franks & A. Saunders, *Mannock: The Life and Death of Major Edward Mannock* (London: Grub Street, 2008), p.28.
31. A. Rhys Davids, quoted by A. Revell, *Brief Glory: The Life of Arthur Rhys Davids* (London: William Kimber, 1984), p.102.
32. H.H. Balfour, *An Airman Marches* (London: Hutchinson & Co, 1933), pp.79–80.
33. A.S.G. Lee, *No Parachute: A Fighter Pilot in World War 1* (London: The Adventurers' Club, 1969), pp.12–13.
34. G. Taylor, *Sopwith Scout 7309* (London: Cassell & Company Limited, 1968), p.68.

35. L.H. Rochford, *I Chose the Sky* (London: William Kimber, 1977), p.68.
36. O. Stewart, 'Memorable Mess Nights', *Popular Flying*, 4/1939, p.35.
37. W.A. Bond, quoted by E. Bond, *An Airman's Wife* (London: Herbert Jenkins, 1918), pp.34–35.
38. A.S.G. Lee, *No Parachute: A Fighter Pilot in World War 1* (London: The Adventurers' Club, 1969), p.6.
39. IWM DOCS: E.J.D. Routh, Typescript account.
40. T.B. Marson, *Scarlet & Khaki* (London: Jonathan Cape, 1930), pp.134–35.
41. V. Cronyn, quoted by A. Revell, *High in the Empty Blue: The History of 56 Squadron. RFC, RAF, 1916–1919* (Mountain View, CA: Flying Machines Press, 1995), pp.106–07.
42. H. Trenchard, quoted by A. Boyle, *Trenchard* (London: Collins, 1962), p.190.
43. S. Douglas, *Years of Combat* (London: Collins, 1963), p.182.
44. F. Oughton, *The Personal Diary of 'Mick' Mannock* (London: Neville Spearman, 1966), p.103.
45. S. Douglas, *Years of Combat* (London: Collins, 1963), p.184.
46. T.B. Marson, *Scarlet & Khaki* (London: Jonathan Cape, 1930), pp.160–62.
47. S. Douglas, *Years of Combat* (London: Collins, 1963), p.184.
48. M. Baring, *Flying Corps Headquarters 1914–1918* (Edinburgh & London: William Blackwood & Sons, 1968), pp.219–20.
49. IWM SOUND: F.J. Powell, AC 00087, Reel 4.
50. M. Baring, *Flying Corps Headquarters* (Edinburgh & London: William Blackwood & Sons, 1968), p.189.
51. G.R. Bromet, *Naval Eight: A History of No. 8 Squadron RNAS* (London: The Signal Press, 1931), p.40.
52. R.J.O. Compston, *Naval Eight: A History of No. 8 Squadron RNAS* (London: The Signal Press, 1931), p.77.
53. IWM SOUND: H. Thompson, AC 00308, Reel 1.
54. IWM SOUND: H. Thompson, AC 00308, Reel 5 & 6.
55. F. Oughton, *The Personal Diary of 'Mick' Mannock* (London: Neville Spearman, 1966), pp.57–59.
56. N. MacMillan, *Into the Blue* (London: Duckworth, 1929), pp.92–93.
57. A. Ball, quoted in W.A. Briscoe & H.R. Stannard, *Captain Ball VC of the Royal Flying Corps* (London: Herbert Jenkins Ltd, 1918), p.244.
58. A. Ball, quoted in W.A. Briscoe & H.R. Stannard, *Captain Ball VC of the Royal Flying Corps* (London: Herbert Jenkins Ltd, 1918), pp.244–45.
59. A. Ball, quoted in W.A. Briscoe & H.R. Stannard, *Captain Ball VC of the Royal Flying Corps* (London: Herbert Jenkins Ltd, 1918), pp.246–48.
60. R.T.C. Hoidge, quoted by H.D. Hastings & L. Raidor, 'Captain Reginald T.C. Hoidge: 56 Squadron', *Cross & Cockade*, Vol. VII, No. 4, p.385.
61. T.B. Marson, *Scarlet and Khaki* (London: Jonathan Cape, 1930), pp.143–44.
62. A. Rhys Davids, quoted in A. Revill, *Brief Glory: The life of Arthur Rhys Davids* (London: William Kimber, 1984), p.99–100.
63. F. Hailer, quoted by D. Whetton, 'And not for Glory', *Cross & Cockade*, Vol. X, No. 3, p.228.

Chapter 7

1. A.S.G. Lee, *No Parachute: A Fighter Pilot in World War 1* (London: The Adventurers' Club, 1969), p.13.

2. S. Douglas, *Years of Combat* (London: Collins, 1963), pp.244–45.

3. IWM DOCS: J.S. Walthew, Letter, 31/7/1917.

4. IWM DOCS: J.S. Walthew, Letter, 31/8/1917.

5. A.S.G. Lee, *No Parachute: A Fighter Pilot in World War 1* (London: The Adventurers' Club, 1969), p.16.

6. A.S.G. Lee, *No Parachute: A Fighter Pilot in World War 1* (London: The Adventurers' Club, 1969), pp.20–21.

7. A.S.G. Lee, *No Parachute: A Fighter Pilot in World War 1* (London: The Adventurers' Club, 1969), pp.21–22.

8. A.S.G. Lee, *No Parachute: A Fighter Pilot in World War 1* (London: The Adventurers' Club, 1969), p.22.

9. A.S.G. Lee, *No Parachute: A Fighter Pilot in World War 1* (London: The Adventurers' Club, 1969), p.23.

10. A.S.G. Lee, *No Parachute: A Fighter Pilot in World War 1* (London: The Adventurers' Club, 1969), pp.23–24.

11. A.S.G. Lee, *No Parachute: A Fighter Pilot in World War 1* (London: The Adventurers' Club, 1969), p.61.

12. W.M. Fry, *Air of Battle* (London: William Kimber, 1974), p.126.

13. W.M. Fry, *Air of Battle* (London: William Kimber, 1974), p.125.

14. F. Oughton, *The Personal Diary of 'Mick' Mannock* (London: Neville Spearman, 1966), pp.73–77.

15. A.S.G. Lee, *No Parachute: A Fighter Pilot in World War 1* (London: The Adventurers' Club, 1969), p.49.

16. F. Oughton, *The Personal Diary of 'Mick' Mannock* (London: Neville Spearman, 1966), p.105.

17. F. Oughton, *The Personal Diary of 'Mick' Mannock* (London: Neville Spearman, 1966), pp.91–93.

18. A. Rhys Davids, quoted by A. Revell, *Brief Glory: The Life of Arthur Rhys Davids* (London: William Kimber, 1984), pp.118–19.

19. A.J.L. Scott, *Sixty Squadron R.A.F., A History of the Squadron 1916–1919* (London: Greenhill Books, Lionel Leventhal Limited,1990), pp.66–69.

20. C. Lewis, *Farewell to Wings* (London: Temple Press, 1964), p.ix.

21. G. Taylor, *Sopwith Scout 7309* (London: Cassell & Company Limited, 1968), p.90.

22. F. Oughton, *The Personal Diary of 'Mick' Mannock* (London: Neville Spearman, 1966), pp.139–43.

23. A.S.G. Lee, *No Parachute: A Fighter Pilot in World War 1* (London: The Adventurers' Club, 1969), p.60.

24. G. Taylor, *Sopwith Scout 7309* (London: Cassell & Company Limited, 1968), p.77.

25. IWM SOUND: N. MacMillan, AC 4173, Reel 1.

26. B. Greenhous, *The Making of Billy Bishop, The First World War Exploits of Billy Bishop, VC* (Toronto: The Dundurn Group, 2002), pp.96–97.

27. A.J.L. Scott, *Sixty Squadron R.A.F., A History of the Squadron 1916–1919* (London: Greenhill Books, Lionel Leventhal Limited,1990), p.104.

28. A. Rhys Davids, quoted by Alex Revell, *Brief Glory: The Life of Arthur Rhys Davids* (London: Kimber, 1984), pp.138–39.

29. A.S.G. Lee, *No Parachute: A Fighter Pilot in World War 1* (London: The Adventurers' Club, 1969), p.80.

30. C. Lewis, *Farewell to Wings* (London: Temple Press, 1964), p.62.

31. J. McCudden, *Five Years in the Royal Flying Corps* (London: Aeroplane and General, 1918), p.194.
32. A. Rhys Davids, quoted by H.A. Jones, *War in the Air, Vol. IV* ((Oxford: The Clarendon Press, 1922–1937), p.189
33. G. Taylor, *Sopwith Scout 7309* (London: Cassell & Company Limited, 1968), p.156.
34. A.S.G. Lee, *No Parachute: A Fighter Pilot in World War 1* (London: The Adventurers' Club, 1969), pp.25–27.
35. A.S.G. Lee, *No Parachute: A Fighter Pilot in World War 1* (London: The Adventurers' Club, 1969), pp.129–30.
36. IWM SOUND: G. Eddington, AC 00013, Reel 5.
37. A.S.G. Lee, *No Parachute: A Fighter Pilot in World War 1* (London: The Adventurers' Club, 1969), p.183.
38. A.S.G. Lee, *No Parachute: A Fighter Pilot in World War 1* (London: The Adventurers' Club, 1969), pp.154–55.
39. A.S.G. Lee, *No Parachute: A Fighter Pilot in World War 1* (London: The Adventurers' Club, 1969), p.178–79.
40. A.S.G. Lee, *No Parachute: A Fighter Pilot in World War 1* (London: The Adventurers' Club, 1969), p.193–94.
41. A.S.G. Lee, *No Parachute: A Fighter Pilot in World War 1* (London: The Adventurers' Club, 1969), pp.194–95.
42. A.S.G. Lee, *No Parachute: A Fighter Pilot in World War 1* (London: The Adventurers' Club, 1969), p.198.
43. IWM DOCS, C. Dixon, Microfilm typescript diary, 25/12/1917.
44. G.M. Knocker (edited by C.M. Burgess) *The Diary and Letters of a World War One Fighter Pilot* (Barnsley: Pen & Sword Aviation, 2008), pp.113–14.
45. A.S.G. Lee, *No Parachute: A Fighter Pilot in World War 1* (London: The Adventurers' Club, 1969), p.198.
46. A.S.G. Lee, *No Parachute: A Fighter Pilot in World War 1* (London: The Adventurers' Club, 1969), pp.207–08.
47. A.S.G. Lee, *No Parachute: A Fighter Pilot in World War 1* (London: The Adventurers' Club, 1969), p.198.

Chapter 8
1. I. Jones, *King of Air Fighters* (London: Ivor Nicholson & Watson Limited, 1935), p.180. Jones says that it is from the diary of a pilot named VanIra, but it is a pseudonym.
2. IWM DOCS: T. Hughes, Transcript diary, 1/1/1918.
3. IWM SOUND: F.J. Powell, AC 00087, Reel 8.
4. IWM SOUND: F.J. Powell, AC 00087, Reel 8.
5. IWM SOUND: F.J. Powell, AC 00087, Reel 8.
6. IWM SOUND: F.J. Powell, AC 00087, Reel 8.
7. IWM SOUND: F.J. Powell, AC 00087, Reel 8.
8. IWM SOUND: J.C.F. Hopkins, AC 00021, Reel 2.
9. IWM SOUND: J.C.F. Hopkins, AC 00021, Reel 4.
10. W.A. Barnes, quoted by. C.G. Burge, *The Annals of 100 Squadron* (London: Herbert Reiach Ltd, 1919), pp.48–49.
11. W.A. Barnes, quoted by. C.G. Burge, *The Annals of 100 Squadron* (London: Herbert Reiach Ltd, 1919), pp.43–44.

12. RAF Museum: J.T.B. McCudden, *Five Years in the Royal Flying Corps* (original manuscript), p.148.
13. RAF Museum: J.T.B. McCudden, *Five Years in the Royal Flying Corps* (original manuscript), p.161.
14. RAF Museum: J.T.B. McCudden, *Five Years in the Royal Flying Corps* (original manuscript), p.172.
15. RAF Museum: J.T.B. McCudden, *Five Years in the Royal Flying Corps* (original manuscript), pp.173–74.
16. RAF Museum: J.T.B. McCudden, *Five Years in the Royal Flying Corps* (original manuscript), p.178a.
17. H.H. Balfour, *An Airman Marches* (London: Hutchinson & Co, 1933), pp.144–45.
18. V. Voss, *Flying Minnows, Memoirs of a World War One fighter pilot from training in Canada to the Front Line, 1917–1918* (London: Arms and Armour Press, 1977), pp.131–32.
19. V. Voss, *Flying Minnows, Memoirs of a World War One fighter pilot from training in Canada to the Front Line, 1917–1918* (London: Arms & Armour Press, 1977), p.132. Voss used pseudonyms, so the real names are in square brackets.
20. IWM DOCS: E.E. Stock, Manuscript diary account, 21/3/1918.
21. IWM SOUND: J.C.F. Hopkins, AC 00021, Reel 4.
22. G.M. Knocker (edited by C.M. Burgess), *The Diary and Letters of a World War One Fighter Pilot* (Barnsley: Pen & Sword Aviation, 2008), pp.177–78.
23. L. Macdonald, *To the Last Man, Spring 1918* (London: Penguin Books Limited, 1998), pp.221–22.
24. IWM SOUND: T. Thomson, AC 00309, Reel 6.
25. S. Douglas, *Years of Combat* (London: Collins, 1963), pp.287–88.
26. C. Draper, *Naval Eight: A History of No. 8 Squadron RNAS* (London: The Signal Press, 1931), pp.52–53.
27. J.H. Weingarth, quoted by G. Weingarth, 'Camel Pilot', *Cross & Cockage*, Vol. 27, No. 1, p.8.
28. RAF Museum: J.C.F. Wilkinson, Typescript memoir, pp.272–73.
29. R.S. Dallas, quoted by A. Hellwig, *Australian Hawk over the Western Front: A biography of Major R.S. Dallas* (London: Grub Street, 2006), pp.156–57.
30. C. Usher, quoted by A. Hellwig, *Australian Hawk over the Western Front: A biography of Major R.S. Dallas* (London: Grub Street, 2006), p.149.
31. R.S. Dallas, quoted by A. Hellwig, *Australian Hawk over the Western Front: A biography of Major R.S. Dallas* (London: Grub Street, 2006), p.153.
32. Ira Jones, *Tiger Squadron* (London: White Lion, 1972), p.65.
33. Ira Jones, *Tiger Squadron* (London: White Lion, 1972), pp.79–80.
34. Ira Jones, *Tiger Squadron* (London: White Lion, 1972), p.108.
35. H.G. Clements, quoted by J. Dudgeon, *Mick: The Story of Major Edward Mannock* (London: Robert Hale, 1993), p.124.
36. A. Kiddie, quoted by J. Dudgeon, *Mick: The Story of Major Edward Mannock* (London: Robert Hale, 1993), p.138.
37. Ira Jones, *King of Air Fighters* (London: Ivor Nicholson & Watson Limited, 1935), pp.208–09.
38. E. Mannock, quoted by N. Franks & A. Saunders, *Mannock: The Life and Death of Major Edward Mannock* (London: Grub Street, 2008), p.118.
39. I. Jones, quoted by N. Franks & A. Saunders, *Mannock: The Life and Death of Major Edward Mannock* (London: Grub Street, 2008), p.122.

40. S. Douglas, *Years of Combat* (London: Collins, 1963), p.257.

41. W. Lambert, *Combat Report* (London: William Kimber, 1973), p.150.

42. J. Eyles, quoted by J. Dudgeon, *Mick: The Story of Major Edward Mannock* (London: Robert Hale, 1993), p.154.

43. J. Eyles, quoted by J. Dudgeon, *Mick: The Story of Major Edward Mannock* (London: Robert Hale, 1993), pp.154–55.

44. J.T.B. McCudden, quoted by C. Cole, *McCudden VC* (London: William Kimber, 1967), pp.191–92.

45. G.H. Cunningham, *Mac's Memoirs, The Flying Life of Squadron-Leader McGregor* (Wellington: A.H. & A.W. Reed, 1937), p.63.

46. L. Callahan, quoted by S. Douglas, *Years of Combat* (London: Collins, 1963), p.311.

47. D. Inglis, quoted by Ira Jones, *King of the Air Fighters* (London: Greenhill Books, 1989), pp.248–49.

48. G.H. Cunningham, *Mac's Memoirs, The Flying Life of Squadron-Leader McGregor* (Wellington: A.H. & A.W. Reed, 1937), p.63.

49. Ira Jones, *King of the Air Fighters* (London: Greenhill Books, 1989), p.251

50. W. Lambert, *Combat Report* (London: William Kimber, 1973), p.131.

Chapter 9

1. IWM SOUND: W.E.D. Wardrop, AC 00029, Reel 4.

2. IWM SOUND: W.E.D. Wardrop, AC 00029, Reel 6.

3. J.R. Bird, quoted by C.G. Burge, *The Annals of 100 Squadron* (London: Herbert Reiach Ltd, 1919), p.17.

4. L.G. Taylor, quoted by C.G. Burge, *The Annals of 100 Squadron* (London: Herbert Reiach Ltd, 1919), p.139.

5. L.G. Taylor, quoted by C.G. Burge, *The Annals of 100 Squadron* (London: Herbert Reiach Ltd, 1919), pp.139–40.

6. L.G. Taylor, quoted by C.G. Burge, *The Annals of 100 Squadron* (London: Herbert Reiach Ltd, 1919), p.140.

7. L.G. Taylor, quoted by C.G. Burge, *The Annals of 100 Squadron* (London: Herbert Reiach Ltd, 1919), pp.140–41.

8. L.G. Taylor, quoted by C.G. Burge, *The Annals of 100 Squadron* (London: Herbert Reiach Ltd, 1919), p.141.

9. A.R. Kingsford, *Night Raiders of the Air* (London: Greenhill Books Limited, 1988), p.102.

10. A.R. Kingsford, *Night Raiders of the Air* (London: Greenhill Books Limited, 1988), pp.102–03.

11. A.R. Kingsford, *Night Raiders of the Air* (London: Greenhill Books Limited, 1988), pp.116–17.

12. A.R. Kingsford, *Night Raiders of the Air* (London: Greenhill Books Limited, 1988), pp.104–05.

13. A.R. Kingsford, *Night Raiders of the Air* (London: Greenhill Books Limited, 1988), pp.105–06.

14. O.B. Swart, quoted by C.G. Burge, *The Annals of 100 Squadron* (London: Herbert Reiach Ltd, 1919), p.160.

15. O.B. Swart, quoted by C.G. Burge, *The Annals of 100 Squadron* (London: Herbert Reiach Ltd, 1919), pp.160–61.

16. O.B. Swart, quoted by C.G. Burge, *The Annals of 100 Squadron* (London: Herbert Reiach Ltd, 1919), p.161.

17. O.B. Swart, quoted by C.G. Burge, *The Annals of 100 Squadron* (London: Herbert Reiach Ltd, 1919), p.161.
18. A.R. Kingsford, *Night Raiders of the Air* (London: Greenhill Books Limited, 1988), p.109.
19. A.R. Kingsford, *Night Raiders of the Air* (London: Greenhill Books Limited, 1988), pp.116–17.
20. IWM DOCS: A.S. Keep, Manuscript account.
21. IWM DOCS: A.S. Keep, Manuscript account.
22. IWM DOCS: A.S. Keep, Manuscript account.
23. IWM DOCS: A.S. Keep, Manuscript account.
24. IWM DOCS: A.S. Keep, Manuscript account.
25. IWM DOCS: A.S. Keep, Manuscript account.
26. IWM DOCS: A.S. Keep, Manuscript account.
27. IWM DOCS: A.S. Keep, Manuscript account.
28. IWM DOCS: A.S. Keep, Manuscript account.
29. IWM DOCS: A.S. Keep, Manuscript account.
30. H. Trenchard, quoted by H.A. Jones, *The War in the Air: being the story of the part played in the Great War by the Royal Air Force* (Vol. VI), p.136.
31. IWM DOCS: A.S. Keep, Manuscript account.
32. IWM DOCS: A.S. Keep, Manuscript account.
33. A.R. Kingsford, *Night Raiders of the Air* (London: Greenhill Books Limited, 1988), pp.140–41.
34. IWM DOCS: E. Garland, Typescript Diary, 31/8/1918.
35. IWM DOCS: E. Garland, Typescript Diary, 4/9/1918.
36. IWM DOCS: E. Garland, Typescript Diary, 7/9/1918.
37. W.E. Johns, quoted by Peter Berresford Ellis & Jennifer Schofield, *Biggles! The Life Story of W.E. Johns* (Godmanstone, Dorset: Veloce, 1993), p.58.
38. W.E. Johns, 'My most thrilling flight', *Popular Flying* (6/1932), pp.142–43.
39. W.E. Johns, 'My most thrilling flight', *Popular Flying* (6/1932), pp.142–43.
40. W.E. Johns, 'My most thrilling flight', *Popular Flying* (6/1932), pp.142–43.
41. W.E. Johns, 'My most thrilling flight', *Popular Flying* (6/1932), pp.142–43.
42. W.E. Johns, 'My most thrilling flight', *Popular Flying* (6/1932), pp.142–43.
43. P. Berresford Ellis & J. Schofield, *Biggles! The Life Story of Capt. W.E. Johns* (Dorset: Veloce Publishing PLC, 1993), pp.91–92.
44. IWM SOUND: R. Shillinglaw, SR 4224, Reel 1.
45. H. Trenchard, quoted by H.A. Jones, *The War in the Air: being the story of the part played in the Great War by the Royal Air Force* (Vol. VI), p.136.

Chapter 10
1. W. Lambert, *Combat Report* (London: William Kimber, 1973), p.221.
2. IWM DOCS: W. Grossart, Typescript letter, 9/10/1936.
3. IWM DOCS: W. Grossart, Typescript letter, 9/10/1936.
4. IWM DOCS: W. Grossart, Typescript letter, 29/9/1936.
5. IWM DOCS: G.T. Coles, Manuscript diary, 9/8/1918.
6. IWM DOCS: W. Grossart, Typescript letter, 9/10/1936.
7. IWM DOCS: W. Grossart, Typescript letter, 9/10/1936.
8. IWM DOCS: L.G. Semple, Typescript diary, 2/9/1918.
9. IWM SOUND: F. Roberts, AC 9466, Reel 1.
10. L.T.E. Taplin, quoted by F.M Cutlack, *The Australian Flying Corps in the Western and Eastern Theatres of War, 1914–1918* (Sydney: Angus & Robertson Ltd, 1935), pp.357–58.

11. Y. Kirkpatrick, quoted by L.H. Rochford, *I Chose the Sky* (London: William Kimber, 1977), pp.190–91.
12. RAF Museum: J. Middleton, Typescript diary, 27/8/1918.
13. IWM SOUND: R. Sykes, AC 301, Reel 5.
14. IWM DOCS: Y. Kirkpatrick, Typescript copy of letters, 28/9/1918.
15. IWM SOUND: J. Gascoyne, AC 00016, Reel 3.
16. IWM DOCS: G.L. Pargeter, Typescript account, pp.4–5.
17. S. Douglas, *Years of Combat* (London: Collins, 1963), p.334.
18. L. Strange, *Recollections of an Airman* (London: The Aviation Book Club, 1940), p.199.
19. IWM DOCS: Y. Kirkpatrick, Typescript copy of letters, 3/11/1918.
20. G.H. Cunningham, *Mac's Memoirs, The Flying Life of Squadron-Leader McGregor* (Wellington: A.H. & A.W. Reed, 1937), pp.68–69.
21. D. Grinnell-Milne, *Wind in the Wires* (London: Grub Street, 2014), pp.229–30.
22. D. Grinnell-Milne, *Wind in the Wires* (London: Grub Street, 2014), pp.226–27.
23. IWM DOCS: L.G. Semple, Typescript diary, 10/11/1918–11/11/1918.
24. IWM DOCS: C. Dixon, Microfilm typescript diary, 10/11/1918.

Chapter 11
1. IWM SOUND: T.F. Rogers, 00171, Reel 1.
2. S. Douglas, *Years of Combat* (London: Collins, 1963), pp.252–53.
3. IWM SOUND: T.E. Rogers, AC 171, Reel 7.
4. IWM DOCS: Y. Kirkpatrick, Typescript copy of letters, 13/12/1918.
5. L.W. Sutherland, *Aces and Kings* (London: John Hamilton, 1937), p.27.
6. IWM DOCS: J.S. Blanford, Typescript manuscript, *Sans Escort*, Appendix D, pp.40A–40B.
7. IWM DOCS: Y. Kirkpatrick, Typescript copy of letters, 23/11/1918.
8. IWM DOCS: E. Garland, Typescript diary and subsequent note, 15/6/1918.
9. IWM SOUND: P. Townsend, AC 14910, Reel 1.
10. IWM SOUND: P. Townsend, AC 14910, Reel 1.
11. W.E. Johns, first printed as 'The Airman's Philosophy' in *The Modern Boy's Book of Aircraft* (1931) and as 'Biggles' Philosophy' in *Spitfire Parade* (1941).

Index